A HISTORY OF THE UNIVERSITY CLUB OF NEW YORK

1865–1915

The University Club
From a charcoal drawing made and presented to the Club by F. Hopkinson Smith

A HISTORY OF THE UNIVERSITY CLUB OF NEW YORK

1865-1915

BY

JAMES W. ALEXANDER
PRESIDENT OF THE CLUB, 1891-1899

PRINTED FOR THE UNIVERSITY CLUB BY
CHARLES SCRIBNER'S SONS
NEW YORK, MCMXV

University Club
Fifth Avenue & 54th Street

New York, October 12, 1914.

To Mr. Alexander, for the making of this History, to which he has given so much time and toil, so much thought and judgment, and so much skill and ability, the University Club and its members are deeply indebted. That it has been a labor of love, enjoyed by him, only increases our appreciation of what he has done for us, since it reminds us of his cordial interest in the Club during more than thirty-five years, of his important contributions to its success while in its management, and of the place which he has held, and still holds, in its membership. We note here and there an incompleteness of statement due to his modesty. He was a member of the Council from 1879 to 1908, and President from 1891 to 1899; and more of the credit for the Club's success belongs to him than appears from what he has written. But the members—the older ones at least—will have no difficulty in recalling his exceptional services, especially in connection with the building of the Club-house and in the making and development of the library. We would record here our thanks to Mr. Alexander and our hope that his membership with us will long continue.

By direction of the Council.

THOMAS THACHER,
President.

NAUMKEAG, STOCKBRIDGE, MASS.,
July 22, 1914.

DEAR MR. ALEXANDER:

I am greatly obliged to you for giving me the opportunity to go over the proof of the first part of your "History of the University Club of New York," and am very glad to comply with your request to supply a couple of pages about it, which you are at liberty to use in any way by way of preface or introduction; but I beg you not to call it a foreword, as that word is not of my invention or to my special taste.

In the history of the City of New York, and still more of the University Club, it is a far cry from 1865 to 1915,—fifty years of most hustling and exciting history, and I think that both the City and the Club are greatly indebted to you for the infinite pains you have taken in studying and narrating the story of the University Club from the beginning until now.

It is true that Dr. Chandler, Mr. Wetmore and myself are the sole survivors of the Charter members, the more is the pity of it, for what a noble set of men the others were. It is difficult to recall the meetings and memories of those early days, and I congratulate you very much on the wonderful success you have had in gathering them up from all possible sources. As I was a member and an habitual attendant of the Century Club at that time, I fear that I was a very negligent and infrequent attendant at the University's meetings of those days, but your pages recall with very great clearness the struggles and infinite difficulties of starting and keeping the Club on foot at that time.

The War was just over when our Charter was obtained on the 28th of April, 1865, the very month in which Lee surrendered to Grant at Appomattox, and the tragical death of President Lincoln occurred. The City and its citizens were very poor. The university men in the City were comparatively very few, and wholly unable to keep on foot a club suited to their character and needs, so that it is not to be taken as indicating a lack of interest, but only of ability, that the Club went into a state of absolute suspension for the twelve years from 1867 to 1879.

But though dormant through that long period, thanks to Professor Dwight and George Baldwin, Theodore Bronson and the Kernochans, although dormant, its life did not wholly go out. It has had, since its resurrection in 1879 until the present day, a noble and ever growing career. Its Presidents, one after the other, have been true representatives of the university men of the City. Its membership has consisted of the cream of the graduates of all the colleges, and I do not hesitate to say that it stands foremost to-day among all the clubs of the City for its character and its light and leading.

The administration of its affairs through the Council has been simply perfect. It has kept the Club, not only out of politics, so far as those concerned public affairs, but out of internal politics, so that I hardly recall any disturbing controversy within it in its entire history.

Its high standard of admission to membership has been steadily and scrupulously maintained, and its Library is not only choice in the character of the books it contains, but is a most peaceful and refreshing place of retreat for all who wish to read or to study.

You have set forth with delightful interest its various places of abode, from the red room in Mr. Kernochan's house, where it was born, to its present magnificent and costly building at the corner of Fifty-fourth Street and Fifth Avenue, one of the great triumphs of the architectural skill of our fellow-member, Charles F. McKim, which I hope it will continue to occupy a half century to come.

Its surviving founders will soon disappear, and at the end of the half century almost every one of its present members will be gone to his last sleep, but the noble institution, which has been built up, will survive, and as I believe, will in the future, as in the past, add much lustre and glory to the character of our great metropolitan City.

It is pleasant to learn from your pages that many great and flourishing clubs throughout the land have been its natural offspring and imitators, and that so it has had a very considerable national as well as municipal influence.

I believe that the lofty character which it has cherished until now will be steadily maintained, and that scholars and authors and all other choice university men will always seek admission to it as their natural and proper home.

Thanking you again for the immense labor and trouble which the production of your book, so worthy of its great subject, has involved, I am, my dear Mr. Alexander,

Most truly yours,

JOSEPH H. CHOATE.

JAMES W. ALEXANDER, ESQ.

CONTENTS

APPENDICES

ILLUSTRATIONS

A HISTORY OF
THE UNIVERSITY CLUB
OF NEW YORK

1865–1915

CHAPTER I

THE GENESIS OF UNIVERSITY CLUBS

THE existence of the University Club in the city of New York is due to the proclivity of birds of a feather to flock together. An English writer has laid down the principle that the primary motive of all clubs is eating and drinking, and John Aubrey, the antiquary, says, about the middle of the seventeenth century: "We now use the word *Clubbe* for a sodality in a tavern."

Indeed, even as far back as 200 B. C., Cicero, in his treatise "On Old Age," represents Cato as saying:

> To begin with, I have always remained a member of a "Club." Clubs, you know, were established in my quæstorship on the reception of the Magna Mater from Ida. So *I used to dine at their feast* with the members of my club—on the whole with moderation. [In this respect unlike the frequenters of the London taverns in Doctor Johnson's day.] It was a good idea of our ancestors to style the presence of guests at a dinner table—seeing that it implied a community of enjoyment—*a convivium*—"a living together." It is a better term than the Greek words which mean "a drinking together," or "an eating together." For they would seem to give the preference to what is really the least important part of it.*

There is no doubt that the oldest English clubs were an evolution from the coffee-house, but the names of many of those who made those early clubs famous are the great ones of England. The club which met at the Mermaid Tavern in Bread Street, at the close of the sixteenth century, had

* Harvard Classics, vol. IX, p. 62.

among its members Shakespeare, Beaumont, Fletcher, and Raleigh. And such was its fame that it was repeatedly made the subject of verse by poets of renown. Beaumont sings of it in his rhymed "Letter to Ben Jonson," and the following lines were written of it by Keats:

"Souls of poets dead and gone,
What Elysium have ye known,
Happy field or mossy cavern,
Choicer than the *Mermaid Tavern?*
Have ye tippled drink more fine
Than mine host's Canary Wine?
Or are fruits of Paradise
Sweeter than those dainty pies
Of Venison?"

Froude has also paid his tribute to this mother of clubs, for it was the circle at the Tavern which developed into the organized club.

Ben Jonson was the founder of a club at The Devil Tavern, between Middle Temple Gate and Temple Bar. Milton was a frequenter of the Rota Club, which was founded in 1659. This was a political club, taking its name from the annual change by *rotation* of a certain number of members of Parliament. The place of meeting was crowded every night. Here Milton, Marvell, Cyriac Skinner, Harrington, and others debated, and of it Butler wrote:

"But Sidrophel, as full of tricks
As *Rota*—men of Politics."

Swift and Pope were members of the Scriblerus Club in 1714. Besides those named Bolingbroke, Gay, Oxford, St. John, and Arbuthnot were members. The dissolution of this club, devoted as it was to the satirization of the abuse of learning, was declared by Warburton to be the greatest possible loss to polite letters.

WHITE'S AND THE FAMOUS BOW WINDOW, LONDON.

Many noble dukes and earls met with Sir Robert Walpole, Addison, and other illustrious men at the Kit-Kat Club, which was formed as a Whig society in 1700. Gibbon, Pitt, Fox, and other famous Englishmen were in the circle at Almack's between 1764 and 1780, while Brooks's, originally a gaming-club, included among its membership such celebrities as Burke, Sir Joshua Reynolds, Garrick, Hume, Horace Walpole, Gibbon, Sheridan, and Wilberforce. Lord Holland, in his tales, describes the bacchanalian evenings at Brooks's, and the potations which rewarded the statesman's toils and shortened his days.

White's was a Tory club as Brooks's was Whig, and its gatherings were graced by the Duke of Devonshire and numerous noble lords in and after 1736. Heavy gambling and suppers after the play were its earlier features. Pope wrote of this club:

> "Or chair'd at White's amidst the doctors sit,
> Teach oaths to gamesters, and to nobles wit."

On the books of the club at Tom's Coffee House, in the eighteenth century, were David Garrick, the great Lord Clive, Doctor Samuel Johnson, the father of Lord Brougham, and many others known to fame. Canning shone in the brilliant assemblage of the Clifford-Street Club, a society for debating. Sir Joshua Reynolds, Doctor Samuel Johnson, David Garrick, and Oliver Goldsmith were lights of the Literary Club, founded in 1764.

Out of the two thousand "coffee-houses" which flourished in London in the beginning of the eighteenth century, the "Cheshire Cheese," in Fleet Street, is perhaps the only one still existing. The seat in which Doctor Johnson was accustomed to sit in the "Cheshire Cheese" is preserved as a relic in the dining-room, and a part of the inscription above it is the following quotation from the lexicographer, which indicates his opinion of what was in that day the club *in embryo:*

"No, sir! there is nothing which has yet been contrived by man by which so much happiness has been produced as by a good tavern."

Lord Byron once said of a certain club: "A pleasant club —a little too sober and literary, perhaps, but on the whole a decent resource on a rainy day."

Among those who founded the Athenæum Club, in 1824, now comprising so many famous scholars, were Sir Humphry Davy and Sir Walter Scott.

These familiar names are only a few selected from the multitude of scholars, statesmen, and peers who have by their lives illustrated the craving of humankind for comradeship, and, much as they may in some cases have enjoyed the cakes and ale, have demonstrated that the gregarious instinct was not solely based on eating and drinking.

And so we find that in the course of years, namely, in the early part of the nineteenth century, university men began to associate themselves together in clubs, in London, to the exclusion of the non-educated.

The Athenæum Club, whose fine building, with its valuable library, is a familiar object in Pall Mall, may well be considered the precursor of the purely university club. It was and is essentially an association of scholarly men, including authors, littérateurs, members of Parliament, and promoters of the fine arts.

It was founded by such men as Sir Humphry Davy, Sir Thomas Lawrence, Sir Walter Scott, and Thomas Moore. Perhaps the most popular of its members, in the past, on account of his witty conversation, was Theodore Hook, who was the author of the following rhyme:

"There's first the Athenæum Club, so wise there's not a man of it
That has not sense enough for six (in fact, that is the plan of it);
The very waiters answer you with eloquence Socratical,
And always place the knives and forks in order mathematical."

THE ATHENÆUM CLUB, LONDON.

But, however satisfying the Athenæum may have been on the intellectual side, there were those among its early members who refused to approve its "cuisine." Sir Edwin Landseer, for example, who knew something about live animals, and presumably about cooked ones, in speaking of the food at the Athenæum, said: "They say there is nothing like leather; this beefsteak is."

Characterized, as the Athenæum has always been, by scholarly men, nevertheless the *New Quarterly Review*, writing on London clubs, has said: "Ninety-nine hundredths of this Club are people who rather seek to obtain a sort of standing by belonging to the Athenæum, than to give it lustre by the talent of its members."

It adds: "Nine-tenths of the intellectual writers of the age would be certainly blackballed by the dunces. Notwithstanding all this, and partly on account of this, the Athenæum is a capital Club."

Emerson says that M. Guizot was blackballed at the Athenæum, because the Englishman had made up his mind to hate and despise him.

At this club the excellent reference library, and the facilities afforded to those wishing to use it, induce authors to do much work within its walls. Any one desiring to study any particular subject has only to notify the officials to that effect, and at an appointed time he will find spread upon a table every book relating to his subject, ready for examination.

In later years a Junior Athenæum has been established.

The original University Club in London was the United University Club, in Suffolk Street, Pall Mall, East. This was instituted in 1824, and the club-house was opened in 1826. The membership is limited to one thousand—five hundred of the University of Oxford, and five hundred of the University of Cambridge. On the roster of this club are members of Parliament, judges, and clergymen.

The Oxford and Cambridge Club was started in 1830 at a

meeting presided over by Lord Palmerston, at the British Coffee House, in Cockspur Street. Its membership is limited to those who have been at one of the two great English universities (with an exception hereafter noted). It is frequented by deans and bishops, as well as other men of university training. All princes of the royal blood, archbishops and bishops, judges of the superior courts of the United Kingdom, the Speaker of the House of Commons, chancellors, high stewards, and members of Parliament for either university, and all persons having held any of the above offices (being otherwise duly qualified) are admitted on application to the committee, as supernumerary members, without being subject to ballot. A similar provision is to be found in the regulations of certain other clubs. Graduates of Trinity College, Dublin, being archbishops, bishops, and certain other dignitaries enumerated, are also admitted under certain rules.

Under the general head of university clubs, the National Club might be included. It was founded sometime before 1845, that being the date when it acquired its club-house from Lord Ailsa, and with it the most valuable artistic possession owned by any London club, namely, a fine set of Flemish tapestries.

This club, while not exclusively a university club, was founded by men of education and scholarly attainments, chiefly those holding evangelical views of religion, the late Lord Shaftesbury having been a prominent member; and although the austere tone has been somewhat modified by the introduction of a number of government officials and purely literary men, the aroma of severe Protestantism has clung to it, as evidenced by the fact that (alone among London clubs) morning and evening prayers are daily read in the club-house.

The New University Club, in St. James's Street, was established in 1864. The qualification for membership is a residence of one year as a student of some college or hall in either

OXFORD AND CAMBRIDGE CLUB, LONDON.
Founded 1830.

university, or the possession of an honorary degree of Master of Arts or of Doctor.

The Eton and Harrow Club, No. 3 Pall Mall, East, was founded in 1873, and is limited to those who have been educated at one of those famous schools.

The Junior Oxford and Cambridge Club was established in 1878, and admits graduates of Dublin University, as well as those who have studied at the two English universities. Its aims are similar to those of the original club bearing its name.

The University and Public Schools Club was formed in 1878, for the association of gentlemen who have been educated at the universities and public schools.

The University Club of Edinburgh was instituted in 1864 for the benefit of those connected with the universities of the United Kingdom or with foreign universities.

The University Club of Dublin, 17 Stephen's Green, Dublin, admits those who have taken a degree or diploma in arts or any faculty in the University of Dublin, or any other university whose degrees are recognized by the University of Dublin.

There is also a University Club in Victoria, Australia.

This mere sketch of the evolution of clubs for university men and scholars, necessarily brief and not exhaustive, is introduced here for the purpose of showing that the University Club of the city of New York had honorable precedents in the mother country, and it will be seen hereafter that it in turn became the parent of or example for numerous other clubs of similar character in the cities of our own country, furnishing directly and through its followers a conspicuous and stimulating proclamation to the young men of America of the value of a college training. (See Appendix XV.)

CHAPTER II

EARLY DAYS, 1865–67

ALTHOUGH the University Club of the city of New York did not, like its English predecessor, have its origin in a tavern, it was evolved out of the comradeship of a dinner-table. The distinction of having conceived the idea of a university club in New York, and having brought it into being, must be accorded to a little group of choice spirits who had been intimate friends at Yale College. Without any such deliberate purpose, but solely to cultivate their mutual friendship, these men—most of whom have passed away—formed a sodality for social enjoyment around the table.

The germ of the Club was planted in the fall of 1861 at the residence of Mr. Joseph Kernochan, at 145 Second Avenue, corner of 9th Street, by his son, Francis Edward, dear to many as Frank, who had been graduated at Yale in the preceding summer.

At the right of the entrance on Second Avenue was a little reception room, papered in red, and there at "Frank's" invitation, on Saturday nights during that season and several subsequent ones, assembled sundry members of Mr. Kernochan's class and classes near it. This embryo organization took, from the place of its meetings, the name of the Red Room Club, and from first to last included Francis Edward Kernochan (Yale '61), his brother J. Frederic Kernochan (Yale '63), William H. Fuller (Yale '61), George C. Ripley (Yale '62), Franklin MacVeagh (Yale '62), Walter L. McClintock (Yale '62), Buchanan Winthrop (Yale '62), Luther Manard Jones (Yale '60), Eugene Schuyler (Yale '59), Alfred

J. Taylor (Yale '59), William C. Whitney (Yale '63), Robert Kelley Weeks (Yale '62), Henry F. Dimock (Yale '63), Horace W. Fowler (Yale '63), and Henry Holt (Yale '62).

The only survivors of this pioneer band are Franklin MacVeagh, J. Frederic Kernochan, and Henry Holt, to the last two of whom the compiler of this history is indebted for the particulars here given.

Mr. Holt, in a memorandum furnished by him, says:

> After two or three years, Mr. Kernochan's illness interfered with his sons receiving the Red Room Club, and in the early part of 1864 the Club met with me at 7 West Thirtieth Street. One evening toward the close of that season, when my wife and I contemplated leaving town for an indefinite period, the recent and impending changes in the quarters of the Club were the subject of some rather gloomy conversation, and somebody, I think it was Winthrop, Fuller, or Ripley, said: "We must found a University Club," and the idea was hailed with enthusiasm.
>
> In the Winter of '64-5 Mr. Kernochan's death led to the breaking up of the home, and the sons who had created the Club took rooms in West Twelfth Street, where they resumed their hospitality, and it was there that the first meeting to consider the feasibility of a University Club was held, in the Winter of '64-5.
>
> The meeting for formal organization was held in the first rooms of the Columbia Law School in University Place. Most of the members of the Red Room Club were or had been students under Professor Theodore W. Dwight. He readily fell into the scheme, and was the unanimous choice for President.

In this choice that circle of Yale men showed that admirable taste and good judgment which has characterized the action of Yale members of the Club ever since. Instead of selecting for the head of the new Club a graduate of their own college, they chose an alumnus of Hamilton College, Clinton, N. Y. ('40), and at the time of his election, a professor of law in Columbia College. Here was inaugurated a wise course of procedure which has never been relaxed, a determination to suppress in the University Club all college rivalries and to foster only a catholic spirit among the sons of all reputable educational schools. Great credit is therefore due to the Yale men of that period and since, inasmuch as they have outnumbered at all times the membership from any other one college or university.

No better selection could have been made than that of Professor Dwight. He was a gentleman and lawyer who commanded the respect of the whole community, and became so thoroughly identified with the school of law over which he presided, that his name and memory were and are revered by the many lawyers who have profited by his instruction. So decided has been the regard for him and his talents that after his resignation from the Columbia professorship, his former pupils organized themselves as the "Dwight Alumni Association," to perpetuate the sentiment of esteem and affection which he had inspired.

Professor Dwight was a man of commanding appearance and kindly manner. He had taught in Hamilton College in his early days. He made the reputation of being one of the most successful living teachers of the law, and gave lectures at other colleges besides Columbia. He held many positions of honor and public use; was an author on legal subjects; and acted as counsel in numerous cases, a notable one being the trial of five professors of Andover for "heterodoxy," in 1886, in which he appeared as advocate for the accused.

Mr. Holt's memorandum continues:

In the Spring of 1865 the University Club was launched in a house in Tenth Street between Broadway and University Place. Most of its members were young men without Club experience—a commodity of which there was not much anywhere in New York at that time—and without social influence. Naturally the financial management—a difficult matter even in the hands of experience, was not good, and the Club came to grief within two or three years.

The charter was kept alive, however, by the University (dining)

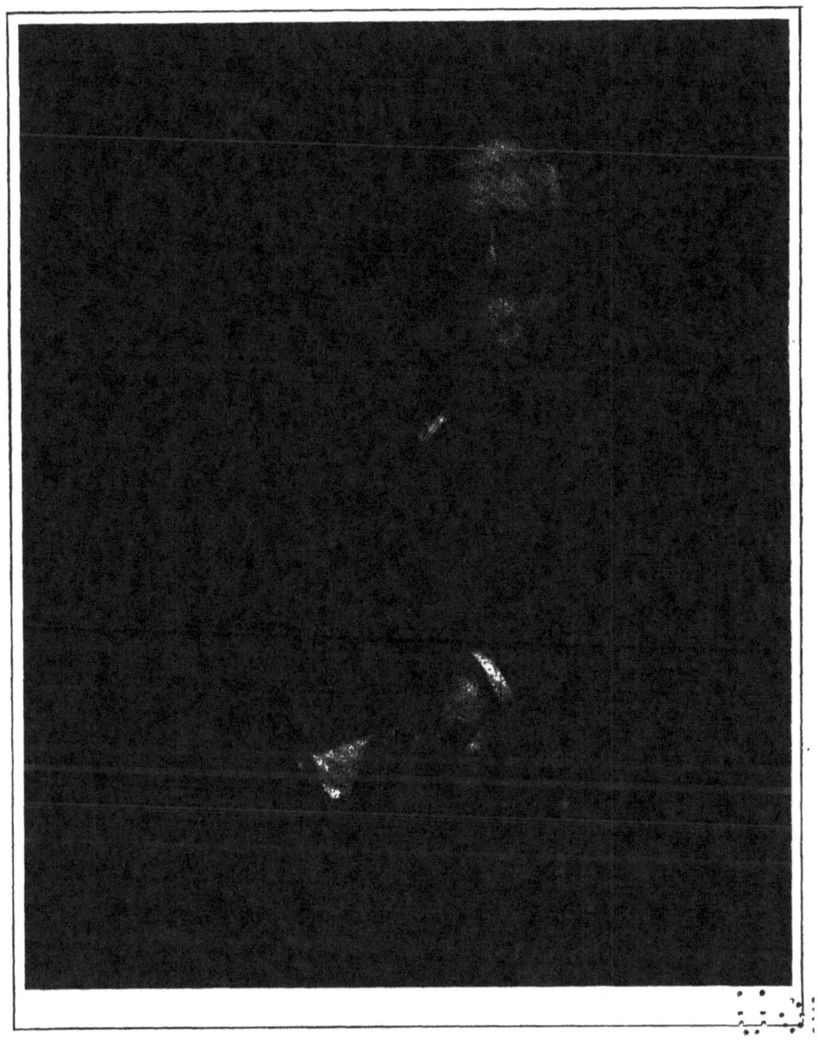

THEODORE WILLIAM DWIGHT (Hamilton '40).
First President, 1865–1867. From a painting by Daniel Huntington, 1891.

Club, which met regularly and elected officers, and in 1879 revived the University Club, on the Southwest corner of Fifth Avenue and Thirty-fifth Street.

By that time many of the young men of the Club of 1865 had attained wealth and position, Club life had made wonderful progress in New York, and the revived Club advanced steadily to its present magnificent success.

Three members of the old Red Room Club were on the management of the revived University Club, Fred Kernochan being chairman of the Committee of Admissions, and Whitney and Holt on the Council.

The great Club has no reason to be ashamed of its young founders. Three of them became trustees of Yale; two, members of the National Cabinet; one, a foreign minister; and others have attained prominence in various pursuits.

Of the fifteen whose names I have given, Fred Kernochan, MacVeagh and I are the only ones now living; but nearly all lived long enough to feel the satisfaction that we veteran survivors still feel in the splendid, famous and useful institution that has grown out of Frank Kernochan's little Red Room Club, and that has been the parent of thriving University Clubs in virtually all the important American cities.

Mr. Holt's narrative takes us a little ahead of our historic account, and it may be interesting to the later generation to have some further details of the infancy of the Club.

The charter of the Club, which is the same under which, as subsequently amended, the organization now exists, and which will be found in full in Appendix I, was granted by the legislature April 28, 1865, with the following incorporators, graduates of various colleges:

Theodore Woolsey Dwight (Hamilton, '40), George T. Strong (Columbia '38), John Taylor Johnston (N. Y. Univ.' 39), Charles Astor Bristed (Yale '39), Henry R. Winthrop (Yale '30), Charles F. Chandler (Göttingen '56), Joseph H. Choate (Harvard '52), Edmund Wetmore (Harvard '60), Francis E. Kernochan (Yale '61), Eugene Schuyler (Yale '59), Edward Mitchell (Columbia '61), Luther M. Jones (Yale '60), and

Russell Sturgis, Jr. (C. C. N. Y. '56), names familiar to all old New Yorkers, and thoroughly representative of the best class of educated citizens.

Of these, Doctor Chandler and Messrs. Choate and Wetmore alone survive.

The original officers were: Doctor Dwight, President; George V. N. Baldwin (Rutgers '56), Vice-President; Theodore B. Bronson (Columbia '48), Treasurer; Edward Mitchell (Columbia '61), Secretary; and the "Council," which was the name then adopted and ever since adhered to for the governing body, was composed of gentlemen who have already been referred to, with the addition of J. P. Kimball (Göttingen and Berlin '55) and W. P. Prentice (Williams '55). The roll of members as published in the first year-book numbered one hundred and twelve, and contained many prominent names, as, for example: President F. A. P. Barnard (Yale '28) of Columbia College, Edward Cooper (Columbia '45), Chauncey M. Depew (Yale '56), Frederic Gallatin (N. Y. Univ. '61), Abram S. Hewitt (Columbia '42), Samuel Huntington (Yale '63), Charlton T. Lewis (Yale '53), Fred. W. Stevens (Yale '58), Henry A. C. Taylor (Columbia '61), and Mason Young (Yale '60). The complete list, with the original constitution, will be found in Appendices VI and II.

The early records of the Club are somewhat confused, and the very first minutes are missing. There is enough, however, to show that the youthful enterprise had a precarious history. Trouble began at the outset, when an adequate home for the Club was sought, and before committing themselves to a contract of lease measures were necessary in order to "collect arrears in dues," the condition being made by resolution that *a house* should only be procured in case there was $4,500 in the treasury. Provisions were made for refunding, if the total was not reached.

So straitened did those fathers of our present prosperous

From a photograph, copyright by the Bradley Studios.

HONORABLE JOSEPH H. CHOATE (Harvard '52).

Mr. Choate was one of the incorporators of the original University Club, 1865.

Club appear, even as to the instrumentalities to be employed in gathering what was actually due to the Club, that they looked outside the existing membership for a treasurer who would be able to give the necessary time and take the requisite trouble. It seemed to be pathetically assumed that nobody could be elected by the Admission Committee, for the Council, without warrant of authority, proceeded at the meeting of November 10, 1865, to elect Mr. Charles W. Woolsey (N. Y. Free Acad.). But, on Mr. Mitchell moving to elect Mr. Woolsey treasurer, he was declared to be out of order, as Mr. Woolsey had not yet accepted membership.

The frail condition of the Club at this early period may be inferred from the following notice sent by President Dwight to the members, in November, 1865:

UNIVERSITY CLUB

New York, November 6th, 1865.

Dear Sir,

Less than half the members of the University Club have paid their initiation fees and dues; it is therefore thought advisable to call a meeting of the Club, in order that its present condition may be made known to its members, and its future action considered and determined upon by them.

The Acting Treasurer will, on Friday evening next, be ready to receive the dues of those who have not paid; he will also give a statement of the sum in the treasury.

The time has now come when the members of this Club must decide whether its condition is such as will justify the hiring of a dwelling place, or whether the money in the treasury shall be divided among those who have paid their dues, and the Club be allowed to dissolve.

It is to be hoped the latter course will not be adopted.

If it is not, it will be incumbent on the Club to decide the status of those members who have not paid; and finally, to determine whether they will have rooms only, or a house.

For these purposes, a meeting of the Club will be held at No.

37 Lafayette Place, in the Columbia College Law School (first floor), on Friday, the 10th day of November, at 8 o'clock P. M.

By Order,

THEODORE W. DWIGHT,
President.

EDW'D MITCHELL,
Secretary.

The effect of this notice was to galvanize a spark of life into the organization, which, as would appear from Professor Dwight's statement, seems to have been almost moribund.

In the autumn of 1865 the Club took a lease of the furnished house No. 9 Brevoort Place, from December, 1865, to November 1, 1866, at $5,000, and the Club held its first meeting in 1866 on January 13 in that building, with Doctor Dwight in the chair.

Although the minutes of the Club for this time are vague and irregular, many acts of importance and much that is amusing are recorded. One of the earliest procedures in the furtherance of the high aims of the Club, which formed a precedent for many interesting and useful steps thereafter, was the sending of delegates to the "Annual University Convocation" in Albany, at the request of Gulian C. Verplanck (Columbia 1801).

The prevailing note which runs through the proceedings of the Club for a number of years after its birth is the constant need of scratching around to get enough dues paid to settle debts already contracted. Indeed, in the summer of 1866, the struggling Club had to resort to compromise in the payment of rent, and found the landlady so benevolent that she was induced to accept $750 in full payment when $1,250 was due to her by the terms of the lease; and to do this subscriptions were volunteered to be credited on the next year's dues. The contrast between this beggared condition and the different state of the treasury in later years is ludicrous, there having latterly been numerous years when the annual surplus saved from what is called the "business" of the Club has been

THE FIRST HOUSE OF THE UNIVERSITY CLUB, AT NO. 9 BREVOORT PLACE.
Occupied 1865–1867.

over $50,000, and the mortgage debt of the Club has been reduced accordingly, as will later appear.

In that same summer of 1866 President Barnard was appointed to represent the Club at the "Convention of the American Association for the Advancement of Science," this and similar actions giving evidence of the ambition of the Club to become an influence in the domain of learning.

But at the very time that such laudable steps were being taken to dignify the character of the organization desperate measures had to be adopted to make two ends meet. We find the Council making vain efforts to sublet a portion of the building, and repeated discussions as to the wisdom of taking the house for another year, a bold venture which was in the end agreed to, but a part of the premises was sublet ultimately to the Loyal Legion. The Club was staggering along under grave difficulty.

In 1867 the uncertainties as to ways and means continued to prevail, and the meetings were characterized by much discussion, appeals from the chair, renewals of appeals, anxiety about finances, complaints about individual members of committees paying bills, coquetting with the Loyal Legion (the subtenant), instructions to the steward to sell wines, liquors, cigars, and billiard tickets *for cash only;* and they culminated in a resolution ratifying the laudable efforts of certain members to raise subscriptions to liquidate "the debt upon the billiard table." These incidents, apparently so trivial in retrospect, after all teach a lesson—namely, that perseverance in a good undertaking, no matter what the difficulties, has its reward in the end. If those fathers of our Club had allowed misfortune to discourage them, the creditable result at length reached might never have been achieved.

Among the propositions considered at about this time was the leasing of the St. Germain Hotel for a club-house, but, after committees had investigated and reported, this scheme was rejected, and in the autumn of 1867 the Brevoort Place house was given up, and *a note* for $770, balance of rent, given to the landlady, Mrs. Penfold. One of the incidents of this period, evincing the stoutness of the hearts of those poverty-stricken Club officials, was their refusal of an offer from the Loyal Legion (who seemed also to be beggared) to settle their debt of $250 by paying $125, Mr. Mitchell being instructed by the Council to notify the Loyal Legion that one hundred cents on the dollar was the least that would be accepted. The keen business sense of our predecessors recognized that a principle of great value in the *payment* of debts became altogether repugnant when applied to the *collection* of debts.

On abandoning the building no other accommodations were at once secured, and a committee was appointed to realize on the assets of the Club, and to levy an assessment to pay the outstanding obligations, annual dues to be remitted on payment of the assessment.

Thus the original University Club became homeless, deserted by the majority of its members, and thenceforth, until 1879, existing as the mere shell of an organization—not dead, as the event demonstrated, but sleeping.

What were the controlling causes which hampered the success of so promising an enterprise it is not easy, after this length of time, to determine with accuracy. One of them undoubtedly was that the time was not ripe. The avidity with which the same proposition was later supported showed that in the increase of the number of university men in and about the city of New York, the need of an institution which would unite them in both usefulness and comradeship was at length beyond question.

CHAPTER III

INTERREGNUM, 1868–79

WITH 1868 began the period of eleven barren years in the life of the Club—barren, however, only in the sense that it was bereft of a rendezvous and almost stripped of membership. For there were enough loyal and hopeful men who adhered to the organization to keep it from expiring and save it intact for its subsequent greatness. The Council, in which body the governing powers of the Club had been centred, ceased to hold meetings, but the Club itself continued to convene annually, in order both to perpetuate the charter and to bind together the faithful remnant of members.

The first of these meetings was held at Mr. Luther M. Jones's rooms, No. 32 Waverly Place, and Mr. George Van Nest Baldwin was elected President, and so continued until the reorganization of the Club in 1879, when he gave place to Mr. Henry H. Anderson, and himself became Vice-President of the enlarged and revivified Club.

Mr. Baldwin was a graduate of Rutgers College, and a member of the New York bar. He was widely acquainted and esteemed, and was, during his connection with the Club, one of its most ardent and industrious supporters. He was active in the movement which resulted in the new birth of the Club in 1879, and continued to give it his valuable services until his death, which occurred February 24, 1908, and was lamented by his associates and by the extensive circle of his friends in the city of New York.

In 1870 the office of Mr. F. E. Kernochan, 23 Broadway, was adopted as the domicile of the Club and for meetings, and in 1871 it was definitely decided that no new quarters be sought, and that no new members be elected.

We find the Club, in the autumn of 1871, meeting at 81 Fifth Avenue, at which time the financial prosperity of the concern (now that it was without expenses) was shown to be enhanced by the authorization of the Treasurer to deposit in some trust company "the funds of the Club."

The Club meetings were held, in December, 1871, at the residence of Mr. F. E. Kernochan, 18 West 33d Street, and at the residence of Mr. George St. J. Sheffield (Yale '63), 11 East 42d Street.

The meetings sometimes took the form of dinners, and often became more entertaining than serious. The membership in 1872 was reported as twenty-eight, and Mr. Frederick H. Man (C. C. N. Y. '61), who had become the Secretary, introduced a facetious strain into the minutes, which were written out at even greater length than when the importance of the proceedings required careful recording.

For example, in the minutes of the meeting last referred to the following paragraphs appear:

> Mr. Winthrop moved that the meeting adjourn, which motion having been seconded, was put and lost.
>
> Mr. F. E. Kernochan moved that a Committee of which he declined to be a member be appointed to go after Mr. Hoffman. Motion not seconded.
>
> Mr. Winthrop moved that at some future day the Club have a dinner and that the last semi-annual dues now in the Treasurer's hands be appropriated for that purpose. . . .
>
> Mr. Kernochan spoke in opposition to the motion, to which speech Mr. Winthrop replied. Mr. Kernochan having again spoken, Mr. Winthrop asked some questions which Mr. Fuller answered. Mr. Whitney moved an amendment. . . .
>
> Mr. Mitchell spoke to the original motion and Mr. Winthrop stated some objections which Mr. Kernochan followed up by asking some questions and stating generally some of the labours and responsibilities attending the office of Treasurer.
>
> Mr. Winthrop replied, speaking of the equities of the question.

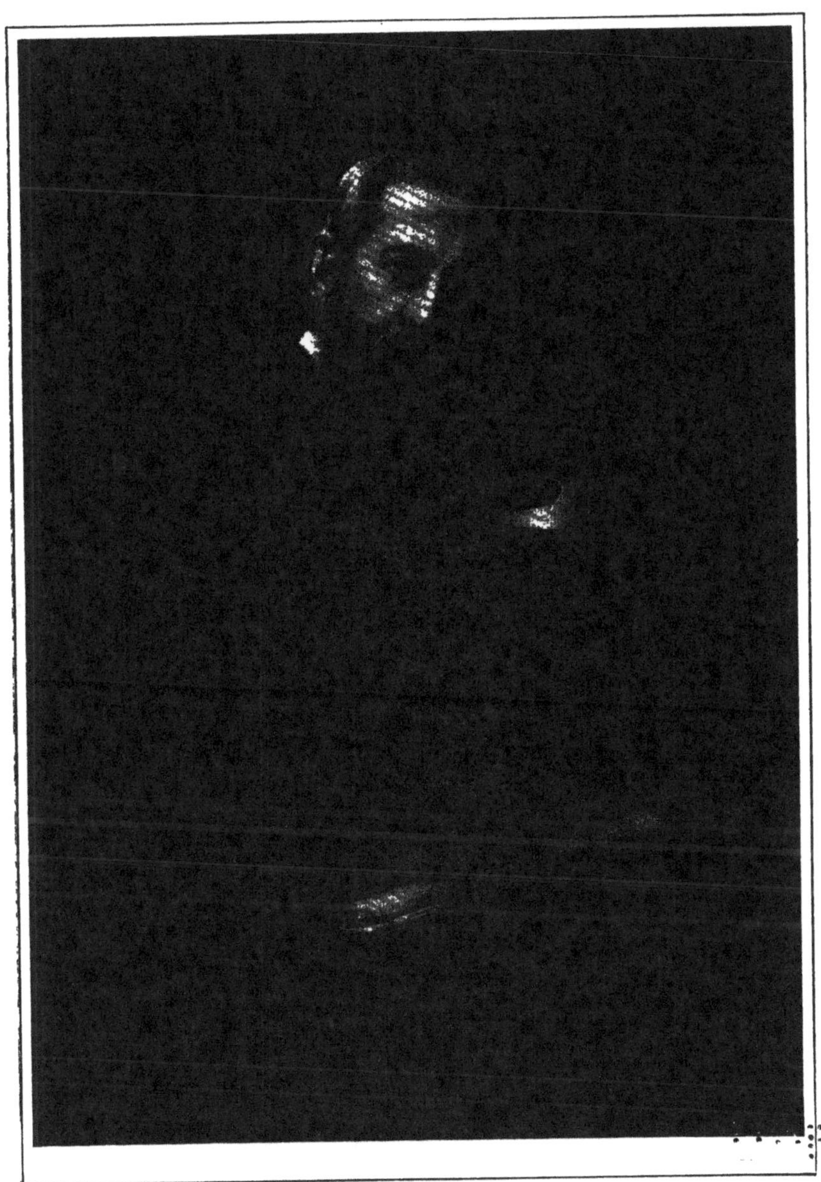

From a photograph, copyright by the Otto Sarony Co., New York.

GEORGE VAN NEST BALDWIN (Rutgers '56).

Second President, 1867–1879.

. . . The President then questioned Mr. Winthrop, who replied, as also Mr. Kernochan, who also explained as to the powers of the Club and spoke as to the possibilities of the future, especially a suppositious billiard-table.

After further similar discussion:

The Chair appointed as the Committee [for a dinner] Messrs. Kernochan, Whitney and Brooks.

Mr. Kernochan requested leave to withdraw from the Committee. Mr. Whitney resigned, and Mr. Brooks asked to do the same. . . .

Mr. John E. Brooks (Yale '65) moved that Mr. Winthrop be appointed a Committee of One. . . . Mr. Winthrop spoke in opposition. . . . Mr. Brooks rose to a personal explanation and explained.

From the minutes of the Club meeting of February 10, 1872:

Mr. Winthrop (*the* Dinner Committee) presented his report (the dinner), which had been laid on the table before all the members, by all of whom it was simultaneously and satisfactorily discussed, and having been, by unanimous action of all the members present, taken from the table, was metaphorically presented to them by said Dinner Committee. . . . Mr. F. E. Kernochan moved that miscellaneous business be taken up.

Mr. Tracy moved as an amendment that after the feast of reason and the flow of soul be finished, the meeting adjourn. Which amendment being accepted, the motion was seconded.

Mr. Taylor moved as an amendment that in the meanwhile Mr. Winthrop be excused from singing his favourite song. The motion was put and carried. Mr. Kernochan being called upon to express his sentiments said that it seemed to him amongst other things, that it was seven or eight years since anything had been done. . . . Mr. Winthrop then moved that the Club startle the people in the next room, and no objection being made, it was accomplished by singing "Lauriger," after which Mr. George Hoffman (Yale '63) being called on to respond to three cheers for the Author of said song, speaks a speech and sings a song, in which all the members, as their abilities enable them, join.

Mr. Winthrop suggests that Mr. Man sing, but the President

calls him to order and a spirited and lively discussion ensues between Mr. Man and the President. Mr. Winthrop . . . sings it (air from Don Giovanni) solo.

Mr. Taylor is called upon to sing a worse song, but declines to attempt it on the score of impossibility.

The minutes continue to record pleasantries and to omit serious business, at the meeting of March 9, 1872.

The minutes of subsequent meetings are formal, until that of January 28, 1875, when it was resolved "that the President appoint a committee to take measures to put the Club on a permanent basis."

And so the Club haltingly but persistently endured. So great, however, was the disorganized state of affairs that on the passage of a resolution early in 1879 that the rooms of the Club be at 120 Broadway, at the office of the Treasurer, any possible neglect during previous years was rectified by a formal declaration that "for the last six years the rooms of the Club have been at the office of the Treasurer for the time being." Whatever of laxity there may have been in the formal transaction of business during the interval of inaction, the officers of the Club were careful at least to preserve the entity of the institution.

And now came the revival of interest and the burst of enthusiasm which resulted in the reorganization and the real genesis of the remarkable career of the University Club.

It was not alone the little band of old members who entered with spirit into the new enterprise. Fresh influences made themselves felt. Among those coming into the circle of reorganizers from without was Mr. Mason Young, a graduate of Yale '60, and a most ardent and diligent supporter of the movement. Mr. Young died March 29, 1906. Others active at this period were Messrs. Henry H. Anderson (Williams '48), Franklin Bartlett (Harvard '69), Henry E. Howland (Yale '54), William C. Whitney (Yale '63), and Doctor Woolsey Johnson (Princeton '60).

The method adopted was for the old Club to elect a body of new members, and afterward call the whole number into convention for reorganization. In pursuance of this plan, at the meeting of January 18, 1879 (at Pinard's Restaurant, and inferentially at a dinner), it was resolved "that the Committee on Admissions be instructed to proceed to elect new members when two hundred names are proposed and seconded by members of the Club, and that until two hundred names shall be thus proposed it is the sense of the Club that no new members be elected."

Here is the actual beginning of the movement for the establishment of the Club on a substantial basis.

Amendments to the constitution were discussed at the meeting of March 8, 1879, in anticipation of the influx of a large number of new members, and a resuscitation of the Club on a working scale. On Mr. Whitney's motion, it was "resolved that the various amendments proposed by the Committee on Constitution, be reported to the whole Club as amendments recommended for consideration, with the suggestion that a sufficient number of the present members to prevent the adoption of said amendments object to amending the constitution in such important respects just prior to the great increase of membership, preferring to submit all such questions to the judgment of the new members."

The first printed list of newly elected members, who were, with additions, to convene for the purpose of putting the Club on a permanent basis, comprised nearly three hundred names, which were soon increased to five hundred and two. These names will be found in Appendix VI.

The preparations were now complete for the organization of the Club as reconstructed.

CHAPTER IV

REORGANIZATION, 1879—THE THIRTY-FIFTH STREET CLUB-HOUSE—GENERAL POLICIES

The little band of college men, who, disappointed in the hope of maintaining a flourishing club during the first fifteen years of its corporate existence, faithfully kept the organization alive, at length found that a genuine desire prevailed among university men in New York to come together and establish an association on the very basis originally adopted. A number of college graduates, not members of the Club, made known their desire to those in control of the corporation, and the time being obviously ripe for a fresh attempt, consultations were had in the latter part of the year 1878, which resulted in the vigorous and hearty movement culminating in the reorganization of the Club in 1879.

It is interesting, after the lapse of more than thirty years of successful growth, to note the names of some of those who were prominent at the new birth of the enterprise.

Naturally, the remnant of the old Club—many having died or resigned—were active in the promotion of a scheme which, somewhat tardily it is true, but with emphasis, confirmed the judgment of the pioneers as to the need in the city of New York of a social institution dedicated to the cause of education.

Among these old-timers were George V. N. Baldwin (Rutgers '56), who had for many years been Vice-President of the Club and was, at the time of the reorganization, its President; Buchanan Winthrop (Yale '62), Edward Mitchell (Columbia '61), Philip S. Miller (Trinity '64), Edward Cooper (Columbia

'45), William C. Whitney (Yale '63), J. F. Kernochan (Yale '63), John E. Brooks (Yale '65), C. D. Ingersoll (Yale '64), Francis E. Kernochan (Yale '61), Edmund Wetmore (Harvard '60), William H. Fuller (Yale '61), Frederick W. Stevens (Yale '58), George Hoffman (Yale '63), Henry Holt (Yale '62), George St. J. Sheffield (Yale '63), George Van Slyck (Williams '63), William G. Lathrop, Jr. (Columbia '62), B. F. Lee (Williams '58), F. H. Man (C. C. N. Y. '61), Charles F. Chandler (Göttingen '56), Theodore W. Dwight (Hamilton '40), George T. Strong (Columbia '38), John Taylor Johnston (N. Y. Univ. '39), Charles Astor Bristed (Yale '39), Joseph H. Choate (Harvard '52), Buchanan Winthrop (Yale '62), Eugene Schuyler (Yale '59), Luther M. Jones (Yale '60), Russell Sturgis, Jr. (C. C. N. Y. '56).

The number of new men co-operating in the revival was much greater than that of the old members, immediately running up into the hundreds, a fact conclusively showing the avidity with which the college men seized upon the opportunity to combine, and furnishing a remarkable contrast to the apathy which very nearly strangled the enterprise of fifteen years before.

Among the men who enthusiastically supported the new movement were Henry H. Anderson (Williams '48), who was to be the first President; John J. Astor (Columbia '39), George A. Adee (Yale '67), Franklin Bartlett (Harvard '69), Charles T. Barney (Columbia '74), Frederick H. Betts (Yale '64), Hugh L. Cole (Princeton '59), Frederick R. Coudert (Columbia '50), Robert C. Cornell (Columbia '74), Robert W. De Forest (Yale '70), Austen G. Fox (Harvard '69), William C. Gulliver (Yale '70), Parke Godwin (Princeton '34), Henry E. Howland (Yale '54), Joseph W. Harper, Jr. (Columbia '48), William B. Hornblower (Princeton '71), Woolsey Johnson (Princeton '60), Frank P. Kinnicutt (Harvard '68), Charles F. McKim (Harvard '70), Charles McBurney (Harvard '66), Howard Mansfield (Yale '71), Sidney E. Morse (Yale '56), DeLancey Nicoll

(Princeton '74), John McLean Nash (Columbia '68), George A. Peters (Yale '42), Henry E. Pellew (Trin. Col., Cambr. '50), Thomas Thacher (Yale '71), Alexander T. Van Nest (Princeton '64), F. W. Whitridge (Amherst '74), Mason Young (Yale '60), and the compiler of this history.

The new membership included graduates of all the leading American universities, and some of those in England and on the Continent. The spirit was catholic from the first, and at the very outset care was taken to avoid college rivalries, the continued success of this laudable effort being due to the unanimous opinion that, in the affairs of the Club, the college or university from which a member came should never be a consideration for his eligibility to office or otherwise. In making up tickets for election to the Council and the Committee on Admissions, all Nominating Committees have endeavored to give as wide a representation to the various colleges as was practicable under existing circumstances.

The reorganization took shape at a meeting of the Club held at Delmonico's, then at the corner of Fifth Avenue and 26th Street, on March 20, 1879, President Baldwin in the chair.

A number of meetings of the original Club had been held before this date, at the Union Club, Pinard's (a fashionable restaurant of that time), and the Manhattan Club, at which preparations for the influx of new members had been made.

At the meeting of the Club on March 20, on motion of Henry H. Anderson, a committee of five was appointed to ascertain what house suitable for the Club could be obtained, to report to the Council or governing body, who were requested to act on such report without delay. This committee consisted of Messrs. H. H. Anderson (Williams '48), F. W. Stevens (Yale '58), Brayton Ives (Yale '61), Charles F. McKim (Harvard '70), and James W. Alexander (Princeton '60).

A committee was also appointed to examine the proper

methods of conducting a restaurant, consisting of Messrs. Frederick R. Halsey (Harvard '68), Henry E. Pellew (Cambridge '50), Francis M. Weld (Harvard '35), Morris J. Asch (Univ. of Pa. '52), and William C. Gulliver (Yale '70).

So it will be seen that here the new undertaking was definitely launched, and the propriety of establishing a completely organized club, with modern conveniences, recognized.

Meetings of the Club were held at Delmonico's on April 12 and May 10, 1879, at which the constitution was duly amended so as to conform to the changed conditions, the Club having been reorganized under its original charter of 1865.

The membership at this date (March 20, 1879) was reported as 415 resident and 87 non-resident—total, 502.

All the executive powers of the Club were vested in the Council, a body of twenty members, elected five in every year by the Club, to serve for four years; and to the Committee on Admissions, a body of twenty-one members, elected seven in every year by the Club, to serve three years, was confided the duty of passing upon the eligibility of candidates proposed for membership. This dual authority has been maintained with no material change through the history of the Club.

The following men were elected on May 10, to serve on the Council and Committee on Admissions, respectively:

COUNCIL

F. W. Stevens (Yale '58).
G. V. N. Baldwin (Rutgers '56).
George Hoffman (Yale '63).
Brayton Ives (Yale '61).
H. H. Anderson (Williams '48).
Woolsey Johnson (Princeton '60).
J. J. Astor (Columbia '39).
William C. Whitney (Yale '63).
Henry Holt (Yale '62).

Alexander S. Webb (U. S. M. A. '55).
George A. Peters (Yale '42).
Henry E. Howland (Yale '54).
Benjamin K. Phelps (Yale '53).
Charles F. Chandler (Göttingen '56).
Henry E. Pellew (Trin. Col., Cambr. '50).
John O. Sargent (Harvard '30).
Charles F. McKim (Harvard '70).
Joseph W. Harper, Jr. (Columbia '48).
Franklin Bartlett (Harvard '69).
James W. Alexander (Princeton '60).

COMMITTEE ON ADMISSIONS

J. Fred. Kernochan (Yale '63).
Jonathan Edgar (Princeton '43).
W. Bayard Cutting (Columbia '69).
Mason Young (Yale '60).
George W. Van Slyck (Williams '63).
Philip S. Miller (Trinity '64).
Francis M. Weld (Harvard '35).
William T. Bull (Harvard '69).
C. B. Mitchell (Columbia '62).
Edmund Wetmore (Harvard '60).
Fred. R. Coudert (Columbia '50).
J. Coleman Drayton (Princeton '70).
George L. Peabody (Columbia '70).
James T. Soutter (Oxford '72).
Austen G. Fox (Harvard '69).
Robert C. Cornell (Columbia '74).
Charles K. Gracie (Columbia '65).
Hamilton Cole (Yale '66).
Nathaniel S. Smith (Harvard '69).
Buchanan Winthrop (Yale '62).
T. Frank Brownell (Harvard '65).

At a meeting of the Council held May 14, 1879, the Council and Committee on Admissions were classified by lot as to length of service, and officers of the Club were elected as follows:

HENRY HILL ANDERSON (Williams '48).
Third President, 1879–1888. From a painting by George B. Butler, 1890.

President............H. H. Anderson (Williams '48).
Vice-President.......Geo. V. N. Baldwin (Rutgers '56).
Secretary............Woolsey Johnson (Princeton '60).
Treasurer............George Hoffman (Yale '63).

House Committee:

Henry E. Pellew, Chairman (Trin. Col., Cambr. '50).
Doctor George A. Peters (Yale '42).
James W. Alexander (Princeton '60).

Other committees were appointed, including special committees on rules for the government of the Council and for the admission of strangers, these rules being reported later and adopted.

At this point it seems fitting that a word should be said in regard to the invaluable services of the late Henry H. Anderson as President of the Club from the time of its reorganization until 1888, when he positively refused re-election.

Mr. Anderson was, in temperament, in address, in intellectual force, and in diplomacy particularly fitted for the headship of the new undertaking in its formative period. Through his wisdom and watchfulness the Club passed successfully through its years of infancy, and many a peril was avoided by its President's calm and keen management. At all times courteous and considerate, he was, nevertheless, firm and decided, and the verdict of those who were his associates in those early days upon his administration has been that to it the Club owes, in no small degree, the flourishing career so ably pioneered from 1879 to 1888.

Mr. Anderson was a lawyer of eminence, having held a number of responsible offices and represented the interest of many corporations and men of wealth in the community. He was born in Boston, Mass., November 9, 1827, and died at York Harbor, September 19, 1896.

Mr. Henry E. Pellew, the chairman of the first House Committee, is an Englishman, and was educated at Cambridge.

He was the son-in-law of John Jay, of New York. Probably no House Committee chairman since his day has voluntarily taken upon himself the detail with which Mr. Pellew considered it his duty to manage the housekeeping of the Club.

Remarkable as has been the history of the Club since those early days, and brilliant as has been its success in every way, no sumptuous halls or accumulated conveniences could dim in memory the comfort enjoyed by its members in the house at the corner of Fifth Avenue and 35th Street. This building belonged to the estate of John Caswell, and was let to the Club at an average annual rental of $9,000, for five years. Under the direction of Robert H. Robertson (Rutgers '69), a member of the Club, as architect, the structure was so altered and improved as to adapt it admirably to the requirements of the organization at that day—requirements later so increased as to render the house altogether inadequate.

In the front part of the building on the 35th Street side was the lounging-room—a most attractive and homelike apartment. In the rear of this was the dining-room, sufficiently large for its needs, but of a size which could be included (with much spare space) in the one large private dining-room of the present Club, known as the "Council Room" on account of its being the place of meeting of the governing body.

An ample piazza on the west, approached by windows in the dining-room, reaching to the floor, provided space for tables, where in warm weather members enjoyed the opportunity of taking their meals in the open air, with a fair-sized garden below them. The incipient library and the billiard-room were on the second floor.

At a meeting of the Council held September 17, 1879, Charles F. McKim (Harvard '70), who had been asked to submit a design and description of a Club flag, presented his report, which was adopted, and the flag ever since and at present in use, flying on great occasions at the masthead and

THE THIRTY-FIFTH STREET CLUB HOUSE.

Occupied by the University Club from 1879 to 1884. This house, at the corner of 35th Street and Fifth Avenue, was afterward occupied by the New York Club, by whose courtesy this photograph is reproduced.

standing at half-mast on the death of a member, is the one thus adopted.

A search has been made for Mr. McKim's report, with the accompanying design, as everything from his master hand is prized by the Club members, but unfortunately they have been mislaid or lost.

The greatest pains were taken in starting the administration of the new Club House to organize a service and cuisine which should be inferior to none and far better than most. Even in the selection of a man to officiate at the front door particular care was taken, and the older members will remember the imposing presence of the incumbent of that office. A head waiter and a chef were secured, also, who were fully up to the high standard set by those in charge. Mr. Pellew gave much of his time to the supervision of the house and the providing. It would, of course, be impossible, even if desirable, for a House Committee chairman of the Club in the present day personally to examine the butchers' and grocers' books, and habitually to keep the larder under his eye; but that was precisely what Mr. Pellew made it his custom to do, and he even called into requisition the experienced services of the gentler sex to aid him in his economies.

Those were happy days, and the foundation was laid through careful and sensible management for the prosperity which has ever since been enjoyed.

Two controlling principles were the bed-rock upon which the superstructure was built, namely: That all the executive powers of the Club should rest in the body known as the Council, elected by the Club itself, one-fourth at each annual meeting, and that the decision as to the admission of candidates to membership in the Club should rest absolutely and without other or further authority in the Committee on Admissions, elected by the Club itself, one-third at each annual meeting.

In the constitution, as adopted at the time of reorganization, it was provided that "members to replace the outgoing class [of the Admission Committee] shall be elected in each year by the members of the committee other than those belonging to such outgoing class."

In 1882 this article was amended so as to provide that such members to replace the outgoing class should "be elected in each year by the Club, by ballot, at its annual meeting."

These two principles have at no time since been altered or questioned, and their operation has been satisfactory. Indeed, the smooth running of the whole machine has been in no small degree attributable to them.

Instead of the election of the President and other officers by the Club at large, that function has always belonged to and been exercised by the Council, the Club in choosing members of the Council naturally taking care to include candidates qualified by position and capacity to hold those offices. The President, Vice-President, Secretary, Treasurer, and the various committees are elected annually by the Council in being.

In this way the wrangles incident to heated campaigns have been reduced to a minimum. On few occasions has an "opposition" ticket been submitted to the Club for its votes, and in only one instance has an opposition ticket been wholly successful.

It is interesting to observe that in the original constitution of the Club its objects are definitely stated to be: "The advancement of Literature and Art, and the Promotion of Friendly and Social Intercourse between men of education and culture," while in the constitution as adopted on the reorganization, and now in force, no reference whatever to these objects is made, the statement in the charter being obviously regarded as sufficient, namely: "The promotion of Literature and Art, by establishing and maintaining a library, reading-room and gallery of art, and by such other means as shall be expedient and proper for such purposes."

The Council at the outset consisted of the President, Vice-President, Secretary, Treasurer, and five "Trustees," whereas, under the reorganization and now, it consists of twenty members, but the same absolute powers were given to the original Council as are confided to them to-day.

The annual dues under the first constitution were $30. A diligent search through such early records as have been procured fails to discover any provision for initiation fees, although references are made in some of the minutes to such a charge. If an entrance fee was originally provided for, it does not appear in the constitution of May 12, 1865. *No* non-resident or army and navy membership seems to have been recognized at the outset as a distinct class, as is the case at present.

The provision against gambling was the same in the original constitution as it is in the existing one, namely: "No betting or card-playing for stakes shall be allowed in the Club-Rooms."

This principle has undoubtedly commended itself to a large majority of the members.

In the earlier years of the Club, even after reorganization, graduates of less than five years' standing were made ineligible for membership. This period of ineligibility was later on reduced to three years. This wise limitation, which has been incorporated into the constitution in force since 1879 and which enables the Committee on Admissions to ascertain the character and habits of candidates during three years succeeding their graduation, was not required at first in the original Club. This is shown by the fact that a special reduction in dues was in 1866 authorized to graduates of less than three years' standing.

No ladies have been admitted to the Club excepting on a few special occasions, such as the days set apart for an inspection of the new Club House at Fifth Avenue and 54th Street, immediately after its first occupancy. The wisdom of providing an annex with restaurant, for the wives and other ladies of members' families, was discussed when the new Fifth Avenue Club House was contemplated, but the question was decided in the negative.

It has been a standing rule of the Club that its privileges should not be extended to minors.

Persons not members of the Club and not residing within thirty miles of the City Hall of New York and not having a place of business in said city, have since 1886 been eligible to introduction as visitors for a week at a time, under the sponsorship of members, but up to 1886 the privilege was given only to a "person eligible to membership" and so residing. It has been the invariable rule not to admit residents of New York City as guests. This exclusion does not apply to dinners given in private rooms. There is no limitation in respect to these.

The practice of London clubs is quite different from ours, and many Englishmen who have enjoyed the hospitalities of New York clubs during sojourns of one or more weeks, have expressed their regret that under the rules governing London clubs it was impossible for them to reciprocate in kind.

This exclusiveness as to strangers has always existed in the English clubs, and so deep-seated was this feeling in the olden time that Nevill, in his book on London clubs, quotes some one as saying that, if a non-member should fall down in a fit at the door of one or two of the more exclusive clubs, he would be denied even a glass of water. This may or may not be a fair criticism, for it is a fact that in many of the London clubs a stranger may be introduced for a meal, but he is oftentimes obliged to take it in a room set apart for the purpose and not in the room where the members eat.

Presidents and professors in colleges and universities not in the city of New York are entitled to the privileges of the Club for limited periods, on the invitation of members of the House Committee.

Strangers of distinction and distinguished Americans residing abroad are admitted to the privileges of the Club House for thirty days on the invitation of the House Committee.

It will thus be seen that a governing principle of the management has been to secure to actual members the greatest possible exclusiveness in the enjoyment of the conveniences of the Club House.

The club houses occupied in the past and at the present receive more particular attention elsewhere, but it may be stated in this connection that the ambitions of the originators of the Club were so modest that they incorporated into the first charter the provision that the Club should not hold any real estate the value of which should exceed the sum of $100,000.

In 1883 the charter was amended so as to authorize the holding of real estate to the extent of $500,000.

Even this last limit proved to be too narrow, when the new Fifth Avenue property was secured and built upon, and a general law was enacted in 1894 authorizing all clubs to hold real property of the value of $3,000,000, exclusive of improvements. This limit has since been raised to $6,000,000, and it may be added here that the present Club House, with the ground on which it is built and its contents, is worth upward of $2,500,000—the ground (exclusive of improvements) being worth over $1,625,000 (assessed value). The appraised value of furnishings is $289,485.79, exclusive of library.

As to the qualifications of members, the usage and rules of the Club have been rigid, and have been strenuously observed. There have been certain changes which will be referred to, but these have arisen from experience in the conduct of the Club, and in pursuance of its original purposes, and the general course of the Club's practice in this regard has been consistent.

Those eligible to membership are persons who have received

from a university or college a degree, to obtain which, in regular course, at least three years' residence and study are required, or who shall have received an honorary degree from such university or college, or who shall have been graduated at the United States Military Academy or at the United States Naval Academy, provided that, in the case of the holder of an honorary degree, the candidate shall be distinguished in literature, art, science, or for public services.

The limitation in regard to the holders of honorary degrees did not exist until 1882, when the constitution was amended in this respect. Before that time a number of candidates were admitted without necessary inquiry as to their "distinction." Among the holders of honorary degrees who have been admitted under the more stringent rule, and have therefore had the Club's stamp as being "distinguished" men, may be mentioned:

HENRY S. PRITCHETT.—Administrator in educational affairs; President of the Carnegie Foundation for the Advancement of Teaching.

MORGAN G. BULKELEY.—Ex-Governor of Connecticut and Ex-United States Senator from Connecticut.

JAMES FORD RHODES.—Historian; President of the American Historical Association; author of numerous works of high merit; recipient of many honorary degrees in the United States and Europe.

EDWIN WILBUR RICE.—The electrical engineer; prominent in the Thompson-Houston Electric Co. and the General Electric Co., and otherwise; chevalier of the Legion of Honor of France.

F. HOPKINSON SMITH.—The versatile engineer, artist-painter, author, and lecturer, who built the Race-Rock Light House, Block Island Breakwater, and foundation of the Statue of Liberty, New York harbor, etc. He has been decorated and honored by many artistic and educational institutions for engineering, art, and literature. Author of numerous works of high merit.

J. PIERPONT MORGAN.—The banker, of world-wide fame, and liberal patron of art, literature, and science.

ENDICOTT PEABODY.—The famous head of the celebrated Groton School.

JOHN H. JOWETT.—The pastor of the Fifth Avenue Presbyterian Church, at the corner of 55th Street; called to that charge from England on account of his fame as a preacher and his character as a man and clergyman.

A. BARTON HEPBURN.—The eminent banker. He has been president of banks, President of the New York Clearing House, President of the New York Chamber of Commerce, and other institutions of importance, and has been a recognized factor in the civic and financial affairs of the city, State, and nation.

The following were elected, on the strength of honorary degrees, as eminent men, before the rules of the Committee on Admission were amended so as to permit preference to be given to such candidates in the order of election:

NIKOLA TESLA.—The gifted electrician and inventor. Born in Servia. Performed distinguished services in Paris. Since 1882 one of the most prominent in his profession, having co-operated with Edison, and made important researches individually.

SIR WILLIAM OSLER.—The eminent physician, professor, scientific investigator, and author. Has held high positions in Johns Hopkins, Oxford (Eng.), and other universities. Recipient of numerous degrees in the United States and Europe. His works are regarded as authorities.

AUGUSTUS SAINT-GAUDENS.—The famous sculptor. Born in Ireland of French extraction, he made his brilliant reputation in the United States. His equestrian statue of

General Sherman in the Central Park Plaza, and his statue of Admiral Farragut, are among his many successful works.

CLARENCE CARY.—Littérateur and lawyer.

The privileges of the Club have been open to the following public men during their terms of official service: The President of the United States, the Vice-President of the United States, the Chief Justice of the Supreme Court, the Associate Justices of the Supreme Court, the General-in-Chief Commanding the Army, the Admiral of the Navy, the Rear-Admiral Commanding the North Atlantic Squadron, the General Commanding the Department of the East, and the Commandant of the Brooklyn Navy Yard.

Up to the year 1901 the Committee on Admissions determined what degrees from universities and colleges, and from what universities and colleges, should qualify the holders for membership, but this function was transferred to the Council in that year. This important subject receives greater attention in another place.

Members whose names shall have been on the roll of the Club for ten consecutive years are entitled to become life members on the payment of $1,000 (formerly $750), and the number of life members is limited to 100. At the present writing there are 59 life members. A list of their names will be found in Appendix VII.

In the constitution of 1865 no limitation of the number of members is made. The constitution, as amended May 10, 1879, the time of the reorganization, provides that "the number of members of the Club shall not exceeed 750," without any reference whatsoever to apportionment between resident and non-resident members.

The limitation of the number of members has been extended from time to time, as appears elsewhere in this history, until at the present time the number of resident members, exclusive of life-members, is limited to 2,000, and of non-resident and army and navy members to 1,500.

The Club is now full, and vacancies occur only by death and resignation. Such vacancies average about 90 to 100 per annum. There were on March 10, 1914, 1,289 names of candidates, duly proposed and seconded, on the list of those awaiting election.

Candidates now elected from the general list have been about seven years posted, as duly proposed. It is further found that each year the period of waiting is increased by about six months.

In the constitution of May 10, 1879, it was provided that the entrance fee should be $50 for all members proposed on or before the 10th day of May, 1879, and for all members proposed after that date, $100, and no modification appears to have been made in favor of non-residents. The annual dues of resident members were made $50, and of non-resident members $25. Graduates of the Military or Naval Academy, if elected while on duty in the service of the United States, were to pay $50 in lieu of all fees and dues thereafter, "so long as they remain in the service."

At a meeting of the Club, held April 16, 1880, the initiation fee of resident members was continued as theretofore, at $100; but a fee of $50 was established for non-residents, who up to that time had been exempt.

Various other changes have from time to time since been made. At present the entrance fee for resident members is $200, and for non-resident and army and navy members $100, while the dues for residents are $90, for non-residents $45, and for army and navy members $35 (1914).

It was found desirable in the early days of the Club to inflict a penalty on members of the Council who failed to attend meetings. The usage among financial corporations of rewarding attendance on the meetings of directors with a gold piece varying in amount from $5 to $20 not being feasible, the method was reversed, and a fine of $1 was imposed upon each absent member. In later years the infliction of this penalty was discontinued, and one more effective put into operation. It has been the custom of the Council, from the time of the reorganization, and still is kept up, to meet at dinner before each meeting. This dinner has invariably been paid for *pro rata* by the members themselves, and never made a charge upon the Club. For a number of years the cost of the dinner was assessed upon those present and partaking of it. This usage was afterward changed, and the cost was assessed on all the members, whether present or not. This operated as a penalty upon absentees far more potent than a fine, as few people like to pay for a meal that they do not eat. But the original method of assessment on members present has been resumed.

The sound principle has always ruled in the Club that no gratuities of any kind may be made by individual members to the servants of the establishment, complete equality without preference being thus secured to all in the enjoyment of the Club's conveniences. In lieu of particular gifts, a fund is annually raised by subscription among the members, and at Christmas time equitably distributed among the employees. The last annual subscription (1913) amounted to $10,822.45.

It has been the invariable principle of the management of the Club to subject the conduct of its business to the strictest rules of reasonable economy and sound financial usage. An examination of the successive reports of the Council will bear out the statement that this principle has been faithfully upheld.

The business caution and vigilance here referred to are significantly illustrated in the first report of President Anderson, dated April 30, 1880. He there says:

For a Club to begin its existence as a fully organized Club, complete in all its equipments, was almost without precedent, and the expenses at the commencement, of necessity, so greatly exceeded receipts that the Council felt much anxiety lest the expenses of the first year should exceed the income of the year. The Club is under very great obligation to its House Committee, to whose watchful care it is owing, that while every necessary comfort has been provided, no unnecessary expense has been incurred, and that the Council can report that even in this, the first year of its existence, the Club has lived within its income.

The Club has been so conducted that in no year since its reorganization have its disbursements for current business exceeded its income, and during the greater part of its history a surplus has annually been laid aside. This has been more emphatically true since the occupation of the Club's present quarters, as will elsewhere appear, the surplus income over and above expenditures having in a number of years been sufficient to cancel $50,000 of debt on first mortgage, reducing the same to a figure below one-half the fair valuation of the property.

During late years a "budget" has been made an annual requirement, which consists of an estimate and authorization for the expenses of the ensuing year.

Much stress is laid upon the orderly conduct of members in the Club House. As might be expected among university men, necessity has only occasionally arisen for discipline or even reminder. But in a body of 3,500 men, no matter what their antecedents, there will be discovered here and there one who is forgetful of the proprieties. The Council, however, has always been swift to exercise its functions as a court, and, after proper notice and opportunity for defence or excuse, to inflict appropriate penalties in cases of infringement of rules or the canons of good breeding. Such cases, as has been intimated, have been rare, and the members of the Club who unanimously desire its life to be untainted by noise, disorderly behavior, or breach of rules in any respect, have had little occasion to complain. In fact, the atmosphere of the

Club has always been that of a quiet home of educated gentlemen.

At a meeting of the Council, February 18, 1885, the first case of expulsion of a member occurred. The name is purposely omitted, as will be those of the three others thereafter expelled. In every instance the accused member had the opportunity to defend himself, and in no case has this extreme penalty been resorted to except for cause so obvious and so conclusive as to leave no room for doubt.

CHAPTER V

ELIGIBILITY REQUIREMENTS—THE TWENTY-SIXTH STREET CLUB-HOUSE—1880–1884

The Club having been auspiciously launched on a new career in 1879, the former beggarly condition was soon replaced by a budding prosperity.

A novel and interesting event occurred at the Council meeting of November 1, 1880, being the authorization of an investment in interest-paying securities of $10,000, the first act of the kind in the history of the Club, which had now ceased to eke out a miserable existence, living from hand to mouth, and had become a capitalist.

At the same meeting the Treasurer was authorized to employ a clerk at an expense of not more than $250 per annum. The incidents just mentioned present in retrospect a very modest appearance from the standpoint of the present stage of the Club, which has developed into such full-blown success financial and otherwise; but they marked a decided change, at the time, from penury to affluence, and gave heart to the group of enthusiastic college graduates who had staked their faith on the renewal of the enterprise.

The constitution of the Club adopted in 1879 provided as the qualifications for membership, besides character and personal fitness, that the candidate *should have been graduated from or have resided at least three years at some college, university, or school of medicine, law, science, or theology.* The placing of theology at the foot of the list is not to be interpreted as a disparagement. It was more probably intended as a climax.

Provisions followed as to honorary degrees, and degrees from the U. S. Military and Naval Academies. In the Appendix will be found the original constitution, the later amendments made from time to time, and the instrument as it stands at the date of this publication.

The foregoing restriction was thought to be too loose and easy. Consequently, on January 30, 1880, the rule was amended so as to limit eligible candidates to persons *who shall have received from a university or college a degree, to obtain which, in regular course, at least three years' residence or study is required.*

The Club has always been jealous to maintain a rigid but reasonable standard in regard to admissions, and determined to prevent as far as possible the creeping in of those who have not had the advantage and training of a real college life. The late Henry A. Cram (Princeton '37), an eminent member of the New York bar, and a member of this Club, once said to the writer that the University Club had the distinction of being the only club which possessed among its essential principles a "canon of exclusion." That canon, as will appear in the ensuing chapters, it was the never-flagging endeavor of the membership wisely but firmly to preserve in its integrity.

A clause was also introduced into the constitution imposing upon the Council the duty to determine what degrees from foreign universities, and from what universities, should qualify the holder for membership. (March 16, 1901.)

So it will be seen that up to this time the Committee on Admissions was left absolutely to its own views and opinions as to what American colleges and universities were to be recognized as giving degrees qualifying the holders to admission. This important subject was at a later date confided to the direction and decision of a competent special committee, under the responsible care of the Council, as will appear hereafter.

It has been already noted that the first lease of the Caswell property was for a term of five years, at an average annual rental of $9,000.

As the Club grew and prospered it seemed to the Council to be wise and prudent to make more permanent arrangements for its accommodation. The situation at Fifth Avenue and 35th Street was admirably adapted to the needs of the association, being at that time very central, and on the great residence avenue of the city, but the necessity for more ample quarters was a present and growing one. The deliberations and negotiations looking to future improvements began in 1881.

Propositions were made to the owners of the property for extending the term of the lease, and enlarging the area by the addition of vacant land adjacent belonging to the same owners, with a view to building an annex to the house.

The negotiations failed, and the Council subsequently took up the question of buying the property. In the course of the deliberations on the subject of site, it was provided, at the meeting of the Council of May 7, 1883, that if $100,000 could be obtained for the use of the Club upon bonds without interest (to be redeemed thereafter from surplus income) the Committee on Building might treat for the purchase of the Fifth Avenue property on the basis of $500,000, and bonds as aforesaid were authorized to be issued. An offer of $500,000 was made for the house and lot occupied by the Club, together with the adjoining lot, the intention being to pay for the same by a loan on bond and mortgage, and the sale of bonds to members.

This offer was declined and efforts to secure the property were discontinued.

The Club then turned its attention to a purchase or lease in some other locality.

A Committee on Lease had been appointed in the earlier stages of the negotiations just described, and continued their activities. At the meeting of the Council, December 4, 1882, this committee was authorized "to purchase any appropriate corner property on Fifth Avenue at a price not exceeding $300,000," a figure which to-day, after the lapse of over thirty years, and the enormous increase in Fifth Avenue values, looks almost absurd.

A last effort was made, October 15, 1883, when the special committee was authorized to offer the Caswell estate $18,000 per annum, and if not accepted to negotiate a lease of the property of Mr. Leonard Jerome (Princeton '39), at the southeast corner of Madison Avenue and 26th Street.

Having failed to induce the owner of the property at the corner of Fifth Avenue and 35th Street to make a lease or to sell at a price within the means of the Club, the alternative proposition was adopted, and at the meeting of the Council, November 27, 1883, a lease of the Jerome property was authorized and directed, at a rental of $22,500 per annum for five years, with the option of a renewal for five years at $24,000 per annum.

Mr. Anderson, the President, reported at the meeting of December 3, 1883, that the lease had been duly executed, whereupon the following circular was ordered to be sent to the members of the Club, which was accordingly done:

NEW YORK, December 3, 1883.

The Council submit to the members of the University Club the following statement of their action respecting the Club's future quarters, taken in accordance with Article 6, Section 1, of the Constitution:

[This article provided and still provides that "the Council shall have general charge of the affairs, funds and property of the Club. They shall have full power, and it shall be their duty to carry out the purposes of the Club according to its Charter, Constitution and By-Laws."]

The Council were unanimous in the opinion that the premises at the corner of Fifth Avenue and Thirty-fifth Street should be secured, if possible, by purchase or lease.

The result of negotiations was, that the landlord refused to lease on any terms, and placed the price of the property at $600,000 cash. $550,000 was believed to be the lowest sum which would be accepted, and this was more than the Club could afford to pay. The necessary extensions and improvements would have made an aggregate of $600,000 to be raised and carried. Even if a subscription could have been successfully raised for $190,000 (the sum probably necessary in addition to mortgage and cash assets) the annual interest account, with taxes, would have made a liability for rental, without any allowance for repairs, or for a sinking fund against the principal, greater than the Club was warranted in incurring.

The Council have not omitted to investigate other possible sites on Fifth Avenue, and were reluctantly forced to the conclusion that there was no property to be obtained.

The building formerly occupied by the Union League Club, at the corner of Madison Avenue and Twenty-sixth Street, although further down-town than the Council would have preferred, was found to answer all the demands and requirements of the Club, excepting position on Fifth Avenue.

The Council have therefore, by unanimous action, taken a lease of the premises last named, for a term of five years, at an annual rental of $22,500, with the option to the Club of a renewal of five years at an annual rental of $24,000. This includes the theatre and a dozen bed-rooms suitable for renting to members of the Club, and there are no taxes. The Club will take possession of the premises on the 1st of February next, so that sufficient time will be allowed for complete fitting up and removal without incommoding the members. The experience of previous tenants shows that the renting of the theatre and bed-rooms will yield a considerable income, which will materially reduce the net rental of the premises.

The Council regard the step taken as unquestionably the best within their choice, and point out the following among its advantages:

The Club has outgrown its present accommodations, and there is no available building or group of buildings on Manhattan Island as well adapted to the requirements of the Club as the one secured. It comprises more than double the space for convenient uses of the present House. The dining arrangements will be much superior to those in the Club House in Thirty-fifth Street. The library accommodations will be greatly improved. The billiard-rooms are better, and there are excellent bowling-alleys. The theatre will be of peculiar advantage to our Club when a meeting is to be held. And the sleeping accommodations will fill a *much* needed want of non-resident members.

The financial condition of the Club is excellent, and the Council are anxious to continue the policy under which the cash assets of the Club have reached the sum of over $70,000. If the estimates are not incorrect, the expenses of the new Club House will be within the income from annual dues, and the initiation fees and interest on investments will, as heretofore, go to capital account.

If there should be any among the membership who feel disappointed at the result, the Council recommend them to regard the occupancy of the new Club-House, for a period of five or even ten years, as a measure sanctioned by prudent management, in order that the Club may, after husbanding its resources during a reasonable period, establish itself upon a solid and lasting financial basis, and in permanent quarters worthy of the name and future of the University Club.

By Order of the Council,

WOOLSEY JOHNSON,

Secretary.

Here will be observed the cautious and businesslike method which has characterized the conduct of the Club's affairs throughout its history, and which has been a signal factor in its practical success.

It is admitted that if those having the responsibility of the Club's management had possessed the gift of prophetic foresight, and had further been able to command the necessary funds, the purchase of the 35th Street property even at the figure demanded by the owner could have been made a very profitable speculation, for so enormous has been the rise in values on Fifth Avenue, that what could have been bought at $600,000 would to-day sell on the open market at $1,500,000 or upward. But no trustworthy prediction of the future market could have been made at the time, and it would have been an unpardonable risk for the Council to have taken, to overload the Club with an embarrassing commitment, with no guaranty of a rise in values to offset the difficulty and danger, even if the necessary funds could have been raised.

THE CLUB HOUSE AT TWENTY-SIXTH STREET AND MADISON AVENUE.
Occupied by the University Club from 1884–1899, now occupied by the Manhattan Club.

Although the prophetic instinct was wanting as regards the subsequent market values of Fifth Avenue property, it was emphatically present in regard to the results expected from the temporary occupation of the Jerome property. The "husbanding" of "its resources during a reasonable period," by "the occupancy of the new Club House for a period of . . . ten years," has as a matter of history established the Club "upon a solid and lasting financial basis, and in permanent quarters worthy of the name and future of the University Club."

The building now to become the home of our Club was erected in or about 1866, by Leonard Jerome (Princeton '39) as a residence, and was in its day one of the finest private establishments in the city. Mr. Jerome was at that period a well-known citizen and clubman. He was the father of Lady Randolph Churchill, and the uncle of William Travers Jerome, at one time district attorney of New York. The house was, until after the marriage of Lady Randolph Churchill, the scene of many notable society functions, and the theatre was utilized as a ballroom, in which danced the belles and beaux of a day when the social circle of New York was more compact than is the case at present.

Upon the abandonment of the premises by Mr. Jerome as a home the building was taken by the Union League Club and adapted to their purposes. That club afterward erected the house now occupied by them, at the northeast corner of Fifth Avenue and 39th Street. The Turf Club, an association devoted, as its name would imply, to the encouragement of sport, succeeded the Union League as tenants, and they in turn were followed by the University Club.

Looking back upon the transactions of that period (1883–93), nothing could have been more fortunate in all respects than the selection of this commodious, convenient, and homelike place. Not only did the Club flourish financially, but its members enjoyed, during the decade of its occupancy, an almost ideal existence. There hung about that old place an aroma of comfort and contentment. And even with all the luxuries of the present permanent quarters, old members remember, with a feeling akin to regret, the good times spent in the Jerome mansion, which lent itself in a peculiar sense to comradeship and social freedom.

On January 7, 1884, the Council appointed a committee "to take charge of the new Club House, and make such arrangements as may be necessary for the present," and report. This committee consisted of Messrs. Frederick W. Stevens (Yale '58), J. Frederic Kernochan (Yale '63), George C. Clark (C. C. N. Y. '63), Henry Holt (Yale '62), and the members of the House Committee; and C. C. Haight (Columbia '61) was retained as architect.

The annual meeting of May 17, 1884, was held in the new Club House, which had been thoroughly altered and equipped. In June, 1886, the kitchen, which had been in the basement, was put on the fourth floor above the "theatre," which was transformed into a capacious dining-room, the stage having been retained for a time, and the hall used for lectures, exhibitions, and plays.

On the ground floor to the east of the entrance hall was an ample café, and immediately adjoining this, and approached through it, a billiard-room with eight tables, and with an annex fitted with two bowling-alleys. In the large front room on the ground floor the newspapers and periodicals were spread upon the tables. In the lounging-room on the second floor, easy chairs and soft carpets furnished comfort to those making use of it. The house was unpretentious and cosey, and made for sociability. The arrangements were well adapted to the purposes of a club with a membership of 1,000, and it was possible for acquaintance to be more general than in a club of 3,500, as at present. One looks back with delightful memories on the informal gatherings now quite impossible in grander if more complete surroundings.

It was no uncommon thing for the graduates of the various colleges to collect in the café after one of the great intercollegiate games and celebrate the victories on one side or the other, and a pleasant feature of such unpremeditated meetings was the good fellowship shown by graduates of a defeated college joining in the jubilations of the victors.

The library, then assuming respectable proportions, was on the mezzanine floor, just above the front reading-room, and its comforts were most satisfying. Nothing could be more conducive to the quiet-loving reader and student than the present stately library, with its impressive fittings, but there are those living who remember with a sigh that modest, book-lined retreat in the old Club House.

Sleeping-rooms for the use of members were now for the first time installed in the Club, and filled a decided want.

Those were happy days, in that old Club House, never to be forgotten, and many were the occasions, both private and general, when through dinners, gatherings for musical and intellectual pleasure, and celebrations, the members had the opportunity of "getting together" and strengthening the bonds of friendship.

At a meeting of the Council held May 5, 1884, the fees of Mr. C. C. Haight, as architect for reconstructing the Club House, were ordered to be paid, and a vote of thanks passed for the admirable manner in which he had performed the service.

CHAPTER VI

PORTRAITS PURCHASED AND PRESENTED—1886-1889

At the meeting of the Council, June 23, 1886, the officers of the Club and the House Committee were authorized to expend $16,000 for altering the theatre in the 26th Street Club House into a dining-room, and installing an elevator, improvements postponed until then for economical reasons. This fact is mentioned as again illustrating the careful and deliberate custom of the Club in its earlier days, no impulsive step being at any time taken, even for ends praiseworthy in themselves. The conservative character of the management is further shown in the hesitation of the Council in regard to the purchase of desirable and historical works of art. They were greatly tempted when Mr. George C. Clark (C. C. N. Y. '63) announced in April, 1887, that at the Stewart sale he and Mr. Willard P. Ward (Columbia '65) had bought the Gilbert Stuart portrait of George Washington at a cost of $3,100, and that they now tendered the same to the Club at that price. The matter was referred to the Committee on Literature and Art, who afterward reported that they could not recommend the expenditure, in view of the scale so far adopted and the pressing needs of the library. So the portrait was not then acquired, but it was not to be permanently lost to the Club, as will hereafter appear.

This incident led to more or less agitation among those prominent in the direction of the Club's affairs, on the general subject of paintings, and on October 3, 1887, Mr. John O. Sargent (Harvard '30) brought to the attention of the Council the wisdom of taking some action looking to the acquisition of portraits of distinguished men.

In 1888 an event occurred of marked importance to the Club. Henry H. Anderson ceased to be its President. No form of words could be too strong adequately to describe the value of Mr. Anderson's services during the formative period of the Club's existence. He had been its only President from 1879 until 1888, and had he chosen to acquiesce, could have continued in that office indefinitely, so great was the confidence reposed in him by the membership and so unanimous was the appreciation of his fitness. At the full tide of his successful administration he absolutely refused a re-election and retired from office to the extreme regret of his associates.

The following minute was ordered to be put on record by the Council, at its meeting of June 4, 1888:

> Henry H. Anderson has been the honoured president of this Club from the time of its reorganization in 1879 until the Annual Meeting in 1888, when, at his own request, he was not renominated for membership in the Council; during all this time by his constant attention and watchful intelligence he has been a great good to the Club and has largely contributed to its present prosperity.

In 1888 the Club availed itself of its option to renew the lease of the house at the corner of Madison Avenue and 26th Street for five years.

At the same meeting George A. Peters (Yale '42) was elected President of the Club, and continued in that office until 1891.

Doctor Peters was not only a prominent and popular member of the Club, but was a fit representative of the medical profession, so numerous in the list of university graduates in our body. He had long been one of the leading physicians of New York, and had before his election as President attained the highest eminence as a surgeon. From the time of the reorganization of the Club, in 1879, until his death, December 6, 1894, Doctor Peters contributed generously and effectively of his time and talents to the development of the Club's prosperity and added greatly by his companionable qualities to the social enjoyment of its members.

At the meeting of the Council June 3, 1889, the first step was taken toward establishing a financial system with a view to the purchase of a building. A resolution was passed instructing the Treasurer to open an account to be called "The Building Fund," and that all securities owned by the Club be transferred to such account (the Club then possessed investments amounting to $137,333.33), and that thereafter all interest on securities and all initiation fees should be credited to that account.

In 1884, the first portrait was presented to the Club, that of the late President Woolsey, of Yale College, by Eastman Johnson, being the gift of the Yale members, who thus had the honor of inaugurating a custom which has since been followed by others.

In 1885, for example, a portrait of President Mark Hopkins, of Williams College, was presented by the Williams members; and in 1886 a fine painting of President M'Cosh, of Princeton, by the celebrated artist M. Munkacsy, was presented by the Princeton members.

A proposition having been made that the graduates of a certain college should subscribe for a portrait of a former president of that institution to be placed in the University Club, and the suggestion made that any surplus over and above actual cost would be returned to the donors pro rata, an alumnus, renowned for his talent, his humor, and his incisive style of expression, wrote as follows when making his contribution:

Do not bother to send me my share of whatever surplus there is. I will subscribe to put a portrait of you or of myself or some other

GEORGE ABSALOM PETERS (Yale '42).
Fourth president, 1888–1891. From a painting by Eastman Johnson, 1891.

distinguished graduate of the college in the University Club, but I did not care much about [the late president referred to] as a person, and I do not believe any living artist can paint a portrait of him which will be decorative. In reply to your request as to the alumni who will be likely to subscribe to the portrait of [the president referred to], I refer you to the list of ministers of the Congregational Churches of New England, most of whom graduated at [the college referred to] and were disciples and admirers of the late [the president referred to]. They ought to be willing to subscribe to perpetuate his memory. In addition to these gentlemen, there is a large number of missionaries in Turkey and other heathen lands, whose addresses can be got from the American Board of Foreign Missions, who would, I suppose, also be glad to subscribe to ——'s portrait.

On April 1, 1889, the Council initiated the usage, ever since observed, of ordering a portrait painted for the Club of the retiring President, Mr. Henry H. Anderson, which was painted by George B. Butler; and on May 5, 1889, the gift of a portrait of the late President Eliphalet Nott, painted by John F. Wier, was made by the Union College members.

In 1887 a movement was initiated for the acquirement of portraits, and a volunteer committee organized for that purpose.

The following circular shows the progress made:

UNIVERSITY CLUB

INDEPENDENCE DAY, 1887.

TO THE MEMBERS OF THE UNIVERSITY CLUB:

Dear Sirs—The Volunteer Committee with whom originated the project of adorning the walls of the University Club with portraits (in oil) of men distinguished in literature, in the professions, and in the public service, are gratified in being able to say that the plan has met with such favour among the members of the Club as in their opinion insures the accomplishment of the object.

The Committee have secured the refusal of original portraits of George Washington, by Gilbert Stuart, and of Chief Justice Marshall, believing that the great leader who made possible the Constitution of the United States, and the great jurist universally recognized as its wisest interpreter, would furnish the most fitting nucleus for such a gallery. This selection seems to meet with general approbation.

The Committee have received contributions from about fifty members (whose names are appended hereto), in amounts ranging from one dollar to five hundred dollars; and they will be as well pleased to receive the smallest sums that express sympathy with their purpose and a desire to assist in executing it, as to receive still larger sums than the present *maximum*, from gentlemen who feel justified by their interest in the object in making such contributions.

The attractions of our Club-house would be greatly enhanced by such a collection of portraits, and every year would add to its value. Original contemporary portraits by eminent artists can be procured only at rare intervals and at considerable expense; but well executed copies by excellent artists of the best-known portraits of eminent men now in private hands may be obtained on comparatively moderate terms.

In some instances, it is hoped, originals will be presented when our gallery shall have attained an extent and reputation worthy of the character and ability of the Club. When we consider the means and the class by which Cathedrals are built, it would be a sad reflection on our fourteen hundred members with University degrees, if we should fail to establish a portrait gallery of inestimable attractiveness and importance.

Subscriptions will be received and acknowledged by George C. Clark, Treasurer, 51 Wall Street, New York.

Yours very truly and respectfully,
JOSEPH W. HARPER, JR. (Columbia '48),
JOHN O. SARGENT (Harvard '30),
GEORGE BLAGDEN (Harvard '56),
J. J. HIGGINSON (Harvard '57),
GEORGE C. CLARK (C. C. N. Y. '63),
Committee.

Later, namely on December 17, 1887, the Volunteer Committee issued another circular, again calling the attention of members to the project. In this it is stated that "the existence of a Committee on Art and Literature in the University

Club from its very inception indicates the intention on the part of its founders to establish something more than a hostelry with modern conveniences." The arguments in favor of the undertaking are rehearsed in this second circular, and in connection with the report of success in procuring the Washington and Marshall portraits the belief is expressed "that when our posterity celebrate the Second Centennial of the Constitution, there will be no two portraits among those of the many illustrious men then adorning our walls that will be regarded with deeper interest, or whose originals will on that day be held in more grateful remembrance." The circular further reports the acquisition of "the likeness of General U. S. Grant, kindly presented to the Club, and the two admirable portraits of the eminent teachers, Hopkins and Woolsey, for which we have been indebted to the loving liberality of their scholars," and appends a list of subscribers to the fund, which had increased to the number of eighty-one.

At the meeting of the Council, April 1, 1889, Mr. George C. Clark (C. C. N. Y. '63) advised the Council on behalf of the Volunteer Art Committee that the portrait of George Washington, by Gilbert Stuart, and a portrait of Chief-Justice Marshall, had been actually secured, and also that Mr. Edward King (Harvard '53) had presented to the Club a portrait of Daniel Webster. These gifts were accepted with thanks.

As to the authenticity of the portrait of Washington, the Club possesses documentary evidence, of which the two following letters are sufficient for the present purpose:

The Portrait of Gen. Geo. Washington purchased by A. T. Stewart of New York was painted by Gilbert Stuart for Wilson Hunt formerly a wine merchant in Philadelphia (who was an intimate friend and contemporary of Stuart) Said picture remained in the possession of Wilson Hunt until his death, when it came into possession of W. P. Hunt, who was his nephew, and who owned it during his life, which ended on the 21st of December, 1866—since then it was owned by his widow by whom it was sold to A. T. Stewart, Esqr., of New York.

St. Paul, May 2, 1867.

ELIZABETH HUNT widow of the late W. P. Hunt
WILLIAM EDGAR HUNT only child " " " " "

WILSON HUNT, Esq.

Sir:

I very readily accord my opinion of the portrait of Washington painted by Stuart which I had the pleasure of inspecting at your residence a few weeks ago.

I consider it the most faithful copy of Stuart's original portrait that I have yet seen executed by his hand. I am very familiar with the original having had it in my painting room when at Boston for some time.

Respectfully your obt svt
THOS. SULLY

Phila., July 14, 1834.

The following letter identifies and authenticates the Marshall portrait:

DEAR MR. SARGENT

You wish to know if I remember anything about the picture of Chief Justice Marshall? I remember it hung in my father's drawing room on one side the fireplace and Mr. Alexander Hamilton's on the other and opposite the fireplace hung a portrait of my grandfather Governor Sullivan. When Lord Stanley was in Boston I remember his showing him these pictures and telling him how much he valued them—and that Chief Justice Marshall's was by Trumbull—and Governor Sullivan's by Gilbert Stuart. It is useless for me to write you what I recall of the conversations.

Wishing you a safe voyage and happy sojourn in a foreign land I am

truly yours
MANANNE SULLIVAN SCHLEY

April 15th Monday (1889)
The Marlborough.

As to the Webster portrait, the evidence of originality is complete. The following letter from the late Reverend Doctor W. R. Huntington to the late Edward King, the donor, is both valuable and interesting:

GRACE CHURCH RECTORY
NEW YORK

Saturday March 23rd, 1889

MY DEAR MR. KING

Lawson was a patient of my father's in Lowell for many years, and as a boy I was constantly in the way of seeing him,—in fact I once sat to him for a picture myself while still in jackets. He was proud of his picture of Webster, and fond of quoting the commendation which the great lawyer bestowed on it when finished,—"That's the face I shave!"

The phrase was such an odd one and so telling that it stuck in my memory. As a tradition, and an authentic one, it certainly adds to the value of the picture as a likeness.

Faithfully yours
W. R. HUNTINGTON.

To
Edward King, Esq.

And the following extract from a letter of the artist, Walter L. Lawson, to use Doctor Huntington's language, "seems to set the question at rest":

My father's original Webster is now hanging in my Boston office No. 40 Water Street and is for sale—one or two committees are already interested and I of course prefer some public place for it.

On October 7, 1889, the Council accepted a portrait of the late Doctor F. A. P. Barnard, President of Columbia College, presented by his widow; and a portrait of Admiral Farragut, presented by naval and ex-naval members.

The portrait of General Grant, mentioned in the foregoing circular, was by William Curtis, and was presented to the Club by Edmund A. Hurry (Columbia '60), now deceased.

Departing for the moment from the chronological narrative, the further addition of portraits and works of art may be mentioned here, in consecutive order.

In 1890 the portrait of President Woods, of Bowdoin, was presented by Bowdoin members.

In 1891 the portrait of President Eliot, of Harvard University, painted by Robert Gordon Hardie, was presented by Harvard members.

The portrait of Doctor George A. Peters, by Eastman Johnson, was purchased by the Club in 1891, on his retirement from the presidency; and that of James W. Alexander, upon the completion of his terms of office, in 1899, painted by John W. Alexander.

The portrait of President Porter, of Yale, painted by Miss Bannister, was the gift in 1902 of Henry Prescott Hatch (Yale '74).

In the same year the Club accepted the portrait of President Wayland, of Brown University, from Brown members. It was copied from the one in Sayles Hall, by Carroll Beckwith.

The portrait of Charles C. Beaman, by John N. Marble, was purchased by the Club, in 1903, on Mr. Beaman's retirement from the presidency.

The portrait of Henry E. Howland, by F. P. Vinton, was purchased in 1905.

The portrait of Edmund Wetmore, by Irving R. Wiles, was purchased in 1910.

The portrait of B. Aymar Sands, by W. T. Smedley, was purchased in 1914.

In addition to portraits the Club possesses the busts of philosophers, presented by John W. Simpson (Amherst '71), which are described in connection with the library.

Doctor David L. Haight (Yale '60), in 1911, presented the Club with a bronze bust of Voltaire. The Club has at different times purchased busts in plaster of Franklin, Milton, and Shakespeare, and statues in plaster of Augustus and Demosthenes.

In this connection, grateful mention is appropriate of the generous act of Mr. John F. Talmage (Yale '95), a life member and a permanent resident in the Club House since its erection, in loaning the following valuable works of great painters, which, until 1913, hung in the large lounging-room on the Fifth Avenue front, and which were so precious as to be (without the kindness of Mr. Talmage) altogether beyond our reach. This evidence of devotion to the Club is warmly appreciated by its members, and was an addition to the attractions of the house so unique and so artistic as to put its decorations in a class by themselves, unattainable by others.

1

Sir Thomas Lawrence, P. R. A. (1769–1830)
Lady Mary Anne Beaumont

2

George Romney (1734–1802)
Lady Twisden

3

George Romney (1734–1802)
A Lady of Quality

4

Sir Joshua Reynolds, P. R. A. (1723–1792)
Portrait of Mrs. Mordaunt

5

John Hoppner, R. A. (1759–1810)
Portrait of Mrs. Jordan

6

Thomas Gainsborough, R. A. (1727–1788)
Portrait of H. R. H. William Henry, Duke of Clarence, afterwards King William IV.

7

JEAN BAPTISTE GREUZE (1725–1805)
PORTRAIT OF A GIRL

8

SIR HENRY RAEBURN, R. A. (1756–1823)
PORTRAIT OF JAMES EDGAR

9

SIR HENRY RAEBURN, R. A. (1756–1823)
PORTRAIT OF A LADY

10

GABRIEL METSU (1630–1667)
LADY PLAYING WITH A DOG

CHAPTER VII

INCREASE OF MEMBERSHIP—DUES AND EXPENSES—1883-1891

THE pains taken to guard the Club against error in the admission of candidates not obviously entitled to be ranked as university men are shown in various ways, and among others in the limitation of honorary degrees.

Up to the year 1882 the constitution had made eligible those "who shall have received an honorary degree," without qualification as to the fitness of the candidate for the degree conferred. Under this provision several gentlemen had been admitted to full fellowship in the Club. Owing to the vigilance and discrimination of the Admission Committee, the members so elected were of a class to which no reasonable objection could be raised. But it was felt that the rule was too broad, and that, considering the facility with which degrees were sometimes secured from some colleges for men of mediocre attainments who had achieved nothing to compensate for the loss of a college career, a more definite and restricted provision should be put into operation. Accordingly, at the annual meeting of the Club of May 20, 1882, the constitution was amended so as to provide that "in the case of the holder of an honorary degree the candidate shall be distinguished in Literature, Art, Science, or the Public Service."

Under this provision a number of thoroughly acceptable members have been elected, while at the same time more than one has been rejected by the Admission Committee as not coming clearly within the category of "distinguished" men. Opinions have differed as to whether the exclusion was or was not too rigidly or harshly exercised in one or more cases, but it is conceded that the committee have acted on the safe side, and that there has never been any tendency to "let the bars down."

Some years later, namely on March 20, 1909, an amendment of the constitution substituted for the words "the Public Service," the phrase "for Public Services," as more exactly expressing the original intention; the term "Public Service" having been interpreted by some as a limitation to the class of office-holders.

As the Club grew in numbers and the membership of thirty-five hundred became full, the "waiting list" of candidates regularly proposed and seconded increased enormously. So much so, indeed, that six or seven years elapsed before an eligible person could even be acted on. Such a delay, while not insufferable to men of the younger ages, was found to be prohibitory to those advanced in life, and the Club was thus deprived of the companionship of some of the most desirable men. The same difficulty presented itself in the case of the holders of honorary degrees who were "distinguished," for it was generally the case that those most decidedly coming within the category were of mature years. A remedy for this was devised which in no material way changed the ordinary procedure. The Committee on Admissions, in March, 1909, enacted a rule providing that "At each meeting the Committee shall take up for election the names of candidates who have been duly posted beginning at the top of the list. Preference, however, may be given to a candidate of special distinction, or, for special reasons, to a candidate who has held the degree which renders him eligible for election for at least twenty-five years, provided that such preference shall have been granted at a previous regular meeting of the Committee by the unanimous vote of the members present. The name of a candidate to whom such preference is granted shall forthwith be specially posted, and may be voted upon at any subsequent meeting."

Under the twenty-five-year rule the following gentlemen have been elected:

George L. Rives (Columbia '68).
Henry Buist (Yale '84).
Edward Robinson (Harvard '79).
Fanning C. T. Beck (Columbia '63).
Wilbur F. Corliss (Williams '63).
Calvin Tomkins (Cornell '79).
Henry S. Howe (Harvard '69).
George V. Leverett (Harvard '67).
Richard H. Dana (Harvard '74).
Frederick B. Hawley (Williams '64).
Samuel A. Lynde (Harvard '77).
William C. Demarest (Columbia '81).
Francis S. Phraner (Princeton '79).
William O. Wiley (Columbia '82).
Albert E. Lamb (Yale '67).
Richard Aldrich (Harvard '85).
Sidney J. Jennings (Harvard '85).
Alfred Von der Ropp (Freiberg '82).
Edwin W. Smith (Bowdoin '56).
Dwight A. Jones (Yale '75).
Louis D. Ricketts (Princeton '81).
Nathaniel T. Guernsey (Yale '81).
Ralph S. Rounds (Amherst '87).
Louis L. Seaman (Cornell '73).
Charles C. Burlingham (Harvard '79).
John A. Staunton (Hobart '58).
John R. McArthur (Harvard '85).
John R. Hardin (Princeton '80).
Theodore N. Vail (Dartmouth (Hon.) 1911).
Henry P. Davison (Univ. of Pa. (Hon.) 1913).
James C. McReynolds (Vanderbilt '82).
Thomas C. Hall (Princeton '79).
Frederick H. Gillett (Amherst '74)
Charles Francis Adams (Harvard '56).
Peter D. Vroom (Rens. Pol. Inst. '62).
Sir William Mulock (Univ. of Toronto '63).
Joseph P. Blair (Univ. of Va. '81).

It will thus be seen that the amended rule has worked well, and has enriched the Club membership by the admission of a few eminently desirable men of whose society, on account of their age, the members might otherwise have been altogether deprived. This movement, inaugurated in recent years, has here been noticed out of chronological order and the narrative returns to the incidents of earlier days.

The popularity of the Club was so manifest after the first few years of its new life, and the advantage of increasing its funds for present and future purposes so obvious, that at the meeting of May 19, 1883, the entrance fee for resident members was increased to $200, while the entrance fee of $50 for non-residents was not changed. The annual dues of resident members were increased to $60 and of non-residents to $25.

These radical alterations were discussed in full meeting, and met with some opposition. The overwhelming sentiment, however, was in favor of the movement, and the result has proved its wisdom, for in no other way would the Club have been prepared for the important developments which have since that time enhanced the reputation and sealed the lasting usefulness of the organization.

An attempt was made at this meeting to reduce the number of years necessary to elapse after graduation in order to qualify candidates for election from five to three, but was defeated. At the meeting of February 9, 1884, however, an amendment to the constitution was adopted, effecting this change.

As usual, the Club was slow to alter its constitution in the direction of greater leniency, but not averse to approving reasonable measures after study and deliberation.

The question was raised during the first five years of the Club's reorganized existence, why army and navy officers should be exempt from dues. They were and are recognized as constituting a most desirable part of the membership. In fact, their presence in the Club had and has at all times greatly enhanced the pleasant companionship so essential to Club life. But those belonging to other classes, as for example the ministry, were, in the opinion of some, equally entitled to exemption. So at the meeting of February 9, 1884, army and navy members, who had up to that time been a class by themselves, were put on the same basis with non-resident members, both as to initiation fee and annual dues, with the proviso that "when ordered on service outside the limits of the United States, or when stationed at a post distant more than two hundred and fifty miles from New York City, for a period longer than one year, shall be exempt from the payment of dues during the period of such service."

In December, 1885, a committee composed of Messrs. Horace White (Beloit '53), Walter Howe (Columbia '70), James

B. Fry (U. S. M. A. '47), P. T. Barlow (Harvard '79), Morris K. Jesup (Williams, Hon. '81), Benjamin H. Bristow (Wash. and Jeff. '51), Sherburne B. Eaton (Yale '62), George Haven Putnam (Göttingen), and Theodore Roosevelt (Harvard '80) was instrumental in linking the Club's name with those of other organizations and prominent citizens in doing honor to the memory of the late Lieutenant-Commander Henry H. Gorringe, of the United States Navy, and an esteemed member of the University Club, by the erection of a monument over his grave.

Commander Gorringe had made his name renowned throughout the world by the signal feat of transporting the obelisk which stands in Central Park, New York, from Egypt to the United States, an unprecedented and difficult undertaking, successfully accomplished. The Club members above named in a circular note expressed the belief "that the members of the Club generally will be glad to contribute something as a testimonial of their affection for one of the most eminent and beloved of their number, who passed away under circumstances of peculiar sadness."

The incident is recorded because it not only relates to a distinguished member of the Club, but illustrates one of its commendable usages, namely the recognition of conspicuous careers among its members.

As the years rolled on, the list of candidates waiting for admission grew steadily, and it became apparent that the limitations as to numbers might well be extended, so that in 1886 it was enacted that the number of resident members be increased from 750 to 850, and in 1887, to 1,000, and a limitation to 650 non-resident members was for the first time made a constitutional rule. This was enlarged to 750 in 1890. And in the case of candidates both for resident and non-resident membership the rule was established that not more than ten of each of those classes should be elected in any one month, in addition to the members required to fill vacancies, the object being to protect the Committee on Admissions from the pressure natural at a time when many candidates were impatient to be acted on, and consequently from the danger of haste and perfunctoriness in examining the qualifications of those proposed. Here again, as always, the Club manifested its determination in every way to guard against laxity and by salutary rules to maintain a high standard in selection.

Up to the year 1890, there had been no provision in the constitution for the nomination of candidates for the Council and Committee on Admissions at the annual meeting. The tickets were unofficially prepared. At the meeting of May 17, 1890, an amendment was adopted, which is still in force, requiring the Council "to appoint at their stated meeting in February of each year a Nominating Committee of five whose names shall be posted immediately. Such Committee shall nominate and post a ticket of candidates for the Council and Committee on Admissions at least ten days before the annual meeting."

This course has been pursued ever since, and the Nominating Committee being naturally composed of impartial men selected for their fitness, their tickets have generally been elected with little or no opposition. From time to time, nevertheless, owing to one circumstance or another, independent tickets have been posted and submitted to vote, containing one or more substituted names, as at the election referred to in the next chapter.

It now becomes necessary, in recording all the essential proceedings of the Club, to refer to the first serious break in the harmony of its conduct. In doing so, the compiler will endeavor to avoid all expression of opinion as to the merits of one side or the other in a controversy which at the time aroused feeling and divided the Club temporarily into hostile camps. The heat engendered at that time has happily long since given way to contentment and cordiality, and the statement of the facts as they occurred, without coloring of prejudice or sympathy either one way or the other, will answer the purposes of this history.

In the annual report of the Council dated March 9, 1891, the following appeared:

> In submitting its report the Council desires to recommend the adoption at the Annual Meeting of the amendment to the Constitution proposed and approved by it raising the amount of the annual dues of resident members to seventy-five dollars and that of non-resident members to thirty dollars, which if adopted will go into effect necessarily only on the first of September next. The experience of the management of the Club during the past two years has shown that the Club cannot be run with the income derived from the annual dues of the members upon the present basis, upon the somewhat more liberal scale with respect to the expenditure of money, particularly in the department of the kitchen and restaurant, which was heretofore adopted with, it is believed, the full approval of the frequenters of the Club-house. It is natural that the members should expect and require the same provision for their comfort and convenience as is afforded by the other important social Clubs of the City, and the Council has thought it proper to endeavor to approach this standard so far as the means at its disposal would permit. The dues of the only Clubs with which ours is or ought to be compared are seventy-five or one hundred dollars a year, and it is quite apparent to the Council that the University Club must advance the amount of its dues to the sums proposed if it is desired to maintain its present character with respect to accommodations afforded to its members and to continue the plan of adding its initiation fees and income from investments to a permanent fund. It has been from the beginning the policy of the Club to lay aside some money each year to form a permanent fund that might be useful when the time should come for the Club to build its own house, and the Council has thought proper in carrying out this policy to provide that all initiation fees and income from invested funds should form a part of such permanent fund. It is believed that no member of the Club wishes it to be conducted on a less liberal scale of expenditure or that the plan of the building fund should be given up, but it has been suggested that a revenue from dues, sufficiently larger than the present one,

could be derived from an increased membership. The Council is satisfied that this would not be found to be the case. The determination of what is a desirable limit of membership in a Club is a matter of individual opinion and there are many successful Clubs of various sizes, but the Council is advised by the House Committee and is of the opinion that an increased resident membership could not be satisfactorily accommodated in the present Club-House and it has no doubt but that a larger membership, so far from obviating the necessity of an increase in the amount of dues, would make such increase absolutely necessary.

This report having been, according to usage, circulated among the members, an opposition to the proposition to increase the dues at once developed and organized.

The following anonymous circular thereupon made its appearance and was placed in the hands of members:

For Consideration

An amendment to the Constitution of the Club, increasing the Annual dues, is proposed, by the House Management, for the reason "that the Club cannot be run with the income derived from the annual dues of members upon the present basis." And your attention is called to the following facts, appearing from the annual reports of the Council for the several years:—

In the first ten years, from May, 1879, to May, 1889, in which the membership increased from about 200 to 1,642, the Club accumulated and invested cash surplus of $148,670.83. This surplus grew steadily during those ten years,—even in the years 1884–5 and 1886–7, when $31,000 and $38,785, respectively, were expended for furniture and extraordinary repairs.

In the twenty-two months since May, 1889, while the membership has increased from 1,642 to 1,710, and with no other apparent changes of condition, there is an apparent deficit of over $10,000, that is to say the cash assets (funds, credits, and stock on hand) of the Club are about $10,000 less today than on May 1st, 1889.

The present report of the Council shows that the invested funds today represent only $141,240.83, a decrease of $7,340 in principal since May, 1889.

A careful examination of the financial reports since 1884 shows that this result cannot be explained by any decrease in receipts from entrance fees, but is due to a change in business methods or management of the House, a change certainly NOT in the direction of economy.

Thus, the net annual Club expenses in excess of all receipts outside of dues and entrance fees, in other words, ***the gross amount used annually from the dues***, has been as follows: (not including the annual expenditures for furniture and extraordinary repairs, which are so much larger some years than others, that, to make this comparison of any value, they must be omitted from it).

USED FROM DUES FOR EXPENSES.

For year ending	
May, 1885	$36,700
" 1886	33,900
" 1887	41,600
" 1888	52,800
" 1889	50,100
" **1890**	**68,900**
" **1891** On basis of 10 Mos. reported	**70,700**

MEMBERSHIP HAS BEEN AS FOLLOWS

	Resident	Non-resident	Total
May 1st, 1886	750	509	1,259
" 1887	823	572	1,395
" 1888	903	640	1,543
" 1889	995	647	1,642
" 1890	995 (5 Elect)	650	1,650
March 1st, 1891	994 (6 Elect)	710	1,710

A portion of this large increase results from the management of the restaurant. Thus the annual PAYMENTS, RECEIPTS AND LOSS on the restaurant, since itemized reports have been rendered, have been as follows:

GROSS PAYMENTS, RECEIPTS, AND LOSS OF RESTAURANT, 1885 TO 1891

Year Ending	Payments.		Total.	Gross Receipts.	Loss For Years.
	Supplies.	Wages, Fuel, Ice, Laundry, &c.			
1886.....	$34,725.17	$11,202.92	$45,928.09	$41,893.82	$4,000
1887.....	38,681.89	11,538.56	50,220.45	41,357.84	8,900
1888.....	43,232.27	12,670.59	55,902.86	49,068.63	6,800
1889.....	50,489.80	14,102.13	64,591.93	52,186.35	12,400
1890.....	55,744.29	18,128.87	**73,873.16**	**54,499.01**	**19,400**
1891..... On basis of 10 mos.	55,848.17	18,951.61	**74,799.78**	**55,652.22**	**19,101**

The increase in loss on the restaurant in each of the last two years, exceeding $9,000 per annum over the average for all the previous years, is especially striking in view of the fact, that there has been no apparent increase or improvement in food or service, and, DURING EACH OF THE LAST TWO YEARS, THE TOTAL GROSS RECEIPTS FROM THE RESTAURANT HAVE BEEN SMALLER THAN THE COST OF THE RESTAURANT SUPPLIES, NOT INCLUDING FUEL, LIGHT, WAGES, ICE AND LAUNDRY; in other words, THE GROSS RECEIPTS HAVE BEEN SMALLER THAN THE MERE COST OF THE RAW MATERIALS OF THE FOOD SERVED, WHILE THE PRICES IN THE SAME PERIOD HAVE BEEN ADVANCED.

Stockholders of any business enterprise, who have seen a surplus accumulated each year for ten years, and who, within twenty months thereafter are notified of a deficit, and called upon for an assessment to pay current expenses, would naturally question the changed methods of management which have turned a yearly surplus into a deficit.

Is not this a pertinent question now for the members of the Club? And should not an impartial representative committee of at least seven, be specially appointed at the Annual Meeting, with full authority to make a detailed examination with the Council into the House Management, employing expert accountants and clerical assistance, if necessary, and report in thirty days?

It is not intended to reflect on the management of the Club; on the contrary, great confidence in the ability of the Council is felt. It is believed, however, that a new system, or improved methods could be inaugurated; and that this committee of seven of which the house committee should be part, should be appointed to confer with the Council and report to the Club the facts, with their views and recommendations; and that, as at present advised, it is inexpedient to increase the dues.

Printed privately, by subscription of a large number of members.

New York, March, 1891.

The customary antipathy to being taxed beyond the necessary requirements, together with the suggestions in the anonymous circular looking to greater economy in management, naturally rallied a large number of the members to the support of a movement thoroughly organized for the purpose of defeating the Council's recommendation to increase the dues.

When the Club met on March 21, 1891, there was an unusually large attendance, and the champions of the two sides of the controversy were on hand prepared to uphold their respective positions. In no instance, so far as the writer can recollect, have such marked differences of opinion been so vigorously insisted upon in the history of the Club. Whether there was reason for criticism or whether "reform" was then as today a popular cry, may be left to the judgment of those who were witnesses of the struggle, but as a matter of history the demand for improvement in method of management before an increase in the annual dues was agreed to prevailed, as will appear.

The proposed amendment to the constitution was duly submitted for consideration, and at once the leaders in what was interpreted as an opposition to the management were disclosed.

The late Albert Stickney (Harvard '59), a prominent member of the New York bar, and a man of great force and decision, opened the discussion by offering the following resolution, which he supported by argument:

Resolved, That the further consideration of the amendment to increase the annual dues proposed by the Council, be postponed until the coming in of the report of the Committee herein provided;

Resolved further, That a Committee of seven be appointed by the Chair, of which the House Committee shall be three, with full authority to make detailed examination into the system of house management of the University Club and with power to employ such assistants as they may deem necessary and to report their views and recommendations at an adjourned meeting of the Club;

Resolved further, That when the meeting adjourn, it adjourn to meet again at the call of the Council.

The members of the Council regarded this proceeding as an attack upon the management, and vigorously opposed it. Some of the foremost university men in the community took part in the discussion on both sides. The late Charles C. Beaman (Harvard '61), afterward to become the President of the Club, defended the Council and opposed the resolution in an eloquent and emotional speech. On the same side William B. Hornblower (Princeton '71) and others addressed the Club. Mr. Stickney was ably seconded by Edward King (Harvard '53), Alfred Ely (Amherst '74), and others.

Notwithstanding the weight of the Council's influence, usually sufficient to control a vote, the resolutions were adopted, and later the Chair announced his appointment of the following named to act as the Committee:

Albert Stickney (Harvard '59)
Edward King (Harvard '53).
Alfred Ely (Amherst '74).
William H. Fuller (Yale '61).
Willard P. Ward (Columbia '65)
William H. L. Lee (Yale ' 69)
Wendell Goodwin (Harvard '74)
} Members of the House Committee.

The sentiment of the Club in regard to the controversy thus provoked manifested itself in the election of five members of the Council to replace the outgoing class.

A "regular" ticket had been duly posted as well as an "opposition" ticket. Two names, those of Hugh D. Auchincloss (Yale '79) and James W. Alexander (Princeton '60), were on both tickets. Three others not on the regular ticket were elected, namely, Doctor David L. Haight (Yale '60), George Sherman (Columbia '75), and Henry S. Van Duzer (Harvard '75).

The Committee appointed, as stated, entered upon their work with promptness and diligence, and in May, 1891, a majority report was submitted, signed by Messrs. King, Fuller, Stickney, and Ely, and a minority report signed by Messrs. Lee, Ward, and Goodwin. These reports were very voluminous, and as the details of management were treated therein with great minuteness, it seems unnecessary at this late date to reproduce them in full. It will be sufficient for historical purposes to give a brief account of their contents.

The majority report set forth that the committee had made "a detailed examination into the system and methods of house management of the Club, particularly as affecting the restaurant." The books were stated to be "accurate and complete," and "the general system of conducting the business" to have "always been administered with fidelity."

Stress was laid on "the increase in all the expenses of running the Club during each of the last two years," and an analysis of the increase given. Reference was made to the "more liberal policy of expenditure, based upon the wishes of the Club, as they (the House Committee) understood them," and the contention of the House Committee that "this whole increase" was "the result of such policy."

The majority report declared, however, that "while recognizing that this change of policy may have had considerable effect in increasing the expenditures," they "are not satisfied that the adoption of a closer system of checks upon the disbursements and a more frequent comparison of results so as to enable the House Committee to gauge the actual outgo more closely, and at shorter intervals than at present, would not have produced results equally satisfactory to the Club with considerably less expenditure."

After describing the particulars in which changes might be made, the majority submitted specific modifications in the methods, and expressed the hope that "the expenses of the Club House may thereby be brought within the limit of the current receipts and annual dues without trenching upon the entrance fees and interest on invested funds. If this should result, the necessity for an increase in the annual dues would be avoided. The majority of your committee therefore recommend that the value of the change suggested should be tested, and that the consideration of the question of increasing the dues be postponed."

The majority further submitted for consideration the question whether the administration should not be placed in the hands of a general manager of ability and experience.

Appended to this report was a "Summary of Club House Receipts, payments, profits and losses" for the years 1888, 1889, 1890, and 1891.

The minority report concurred in the report of the majority "so far as it deals with facts, with the exceptions" thereafter stated. It proceeded to describe the "fundamental purpose for which clubs are formed"; the prevailing views as to the conduct of clubs; the allowances which should be made in comparing the results of different years, on account of changes in bookkeeping; and quoted the opinion of restaurateurs of established reputation that "a very satisfactory condition of affairs exists." The more liberal policy pursued in 1890 and 1891 "in accordance with what was deemed the wishes of the Club" was defended and the "full responsibility" for the same "assumed." The opinion was stated that "the changes in the detail of methods of receiving and paying for supplies, recommended by the majority, will furnish no important additional security against carelessness or dishonesty," but no objection was offered "to trying the new methods long enough to give them a fair test."

The minority dissented from the view that the employment of a general manager would save even the amount of his salary, but agreed that the "experiment" would be "worth trying," if it would increase "the comfort and luxury of the Club, and if the Club could afford such an expense."

The minority disclaimed responsibility for the "expense of many hundred dollars" for the employment of an accountant who "had had no previous experience in Club accounts" and whose "results, to say the least," were "of a value not at all commensurate with their large cost."

They contended that "no new fact of any general importance has been developed (though of course an infinity of detail)," and reaffirmed their opinion that "the raising of the dues to $75" is "a necessity, if this Club is to afford its members the varied comforts and conveniences of a first-class Club."

Arguments followed, and the statement was made that "all that is necessary to effect a return to the old methods" (involving the deprivation to members of "many little luxuries and comforts which they now enjoy") "is that the management should be instructed to run the Club on that basis."

To this report was appended a "Comparison of Annual Statements of Several Clubs for 1891." In this comparison figures were given in considerable detail, and in the opinion of those who sustained the Council and House Committee, they were of equal importance with those introduced into the "Anonymous Circular" which charged extravagance, and confirmed the view that the University Club showed better results than the other Clubs on equal terms.

The House Committee, consisting of the same members who

constituted the minority of the Committee of Seven, at the close of their term of office in the spring of 1891, made a long and detailed report to the Council, containing information as to the condition and suggestions as to the management of the Club, which they, "in a spirit of loyalty to the Club, hope may be of value."

It reflects great credit upon the moderation of the members that, in a controversy involving decided differences of opinion on a very important question, the amenities of conduct were preserved throughout and the conclusion reached by all that the increase of dues should be postponed until some tests could be made of the soundness of the views expressed by the majority of the Committee of Seven. The Club thereupon adopted the following resolution:

Resolved, That the thanks of the Club be given to the Committee appointed at the last Annual Meeting for the careful and exhaustive examination that they have made of the financial management of the Club and for the statements and suggestions contained in their several reports and that both the majority and minority reports of the Committee be accepted and referred to the Council to take such action upon them as they may deem most advisable for the interests of the Club.

CHAPTER VIII

CLUB MANAGEMENT—COLLEGE MEMORABILIA—1891-1894

At the meeting of the Council held June 1, 1891, James W. Alexander was elected President of the Club, to which office he was re-elected in each year until 1899.

A new House Committee was appointed consisting of Doctor David L. Haight (Yale '60), Chairman; Henry S. Van Duzer (Harvard '75), and Hugh D. Auchincloss (Yale '79).

The Committee of Seven having recommended that the value of certain changes suggested by the majority of that committee be tested, the suggestions were referred to the new House Committee.

The Council in their annual report of March 10, 1892, informed the Club that "they have inaugurated changes in the keeping of the books and accounts of the Club which they consider advantageous." They state that "notwithstanding the labors of the House Committee to retrench the Club's expenses, . . . the annual dues have not been sufficient to meet the current expenses of the Club," and they further admit that "they are not satisfied that the present annual dues will prove sufficient to meet the Club's expenses without using the interest on investments."

It might appear, without careful scrutiny of the processes pursued, that the agitation of the subject of economy had been of no practical benefit, for after making such of the tests as had been recommended, the Council concluded that the proposition to increase the dues must soon be adopted. But the records show improvements made and instrumentalities contrived which were of decided use, and the revived vigilance consequent upon a general overhauling was not without its advantage.

At the annual meeting of the Club on March 19, 1892, the amendment of the constitution to increase the annual dues of resident members to $75, and of non-residents to $30, was again submitted, and lost.

After a year's consideration of the subject the House Committee came to the conclusion that it would be for the best interests of the Club to retain the services of an experienced manager, and the Council authorized the employment of such an officer at a liberal salary together with board and lodging.

Under this authority, on the first day of October, 1892, Mr. Edward Gleason, a man of experience in Club management, was appointed Superintendent of the Club (under the direction of the House Committee), and continued in faithful and efficient service until July, 1914, when he resigned.

In 1893 the Club House had become too small comfortably to accommodate the increasing membership, which had reached the number of 1,884 (of all classes), and the President was authorized by the Council to take a lease of the house adjoining the Club House on Madison Avenue, belonging to the Stokes family, for a term of six years, with right of renewal. This, however, was never put into effect.

The amendment increasing the resident membership to 1,100 and the non-resident to 850 was adopted. On March 18, 1893, the resident membership was increased to 1,200, and on March 17, 1894, the non-resident membership was increased to 900.

On October 9, 1893, the officers were authorized by the Council to renew the lease of the Jerome House at the corner of Madison Avenue and 26th Street for five years from May 1, 1894, which was accordingly done.

The Honorable John Jay was a distinguished member of the Club. Born in New York City, June 23, 1817, and grad-

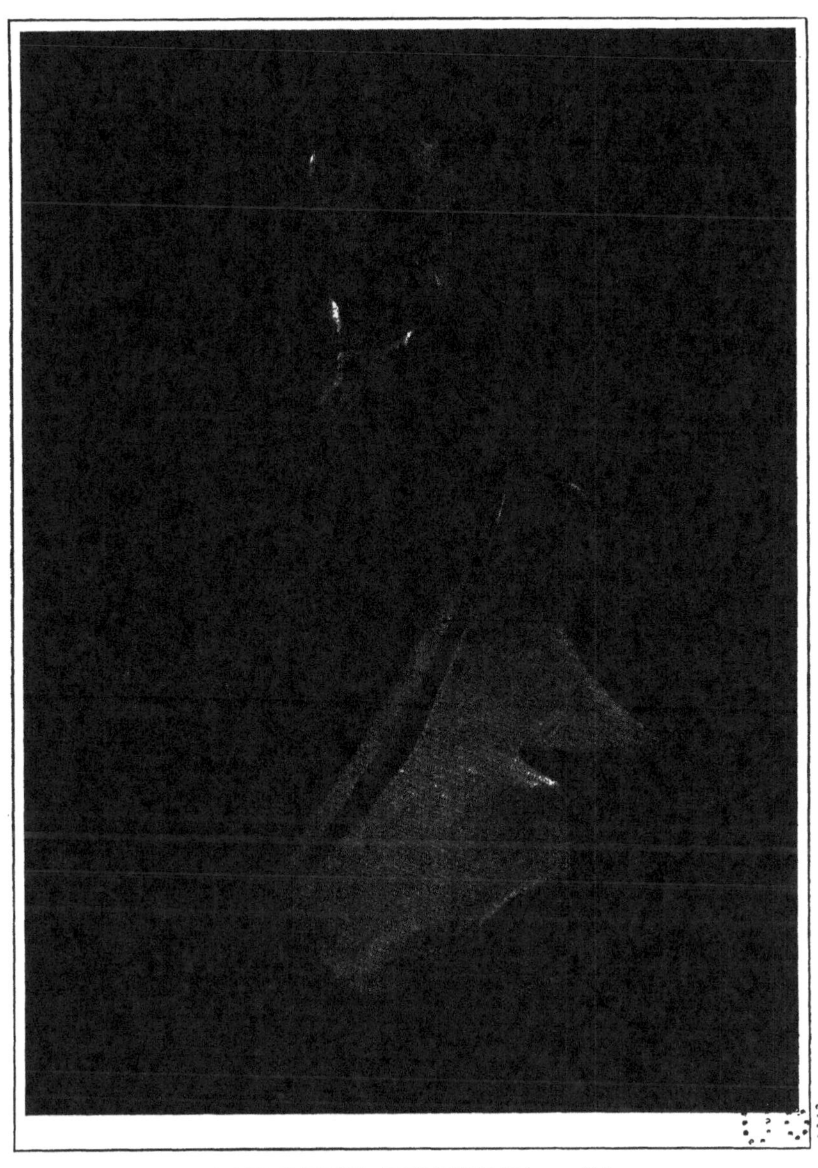

JAMES WADDELL ALEXANDER (Princeton '60).
Fifth President, 1891–1899. From a painting by John W. Alexander, 1899.

uated at Columbia College in 1836, he became a diplomat; a prominent antislavery advocate; an influential factor in the dissolution of the Whig and the formation of the Republican party; manager of the New York Historical Society; president of the Union League Club; American minister to Austria; and one of New York's foremost scholars and citizens. In November, 1893, Mr. Jay resigned from the Club, but in doing so wrote the following cordial letter:

My impaired health induces me respectfully to submit to the Club my resignation. I greatly regret to lose the advantages it affords; and I may add that I anticipate for its future an increasing degree of usefulness, not simply for the City, but for the Country at large.

Such a body of scholarly men has an important part to play in elevating our politics—maintaining the objects of our institutions, and exercising a judicious influence on the Domestic and Foreign policy of the Nation.

With all good wishes for the Club and kind regards to my friends and associates.

At the annual meeting, March 16, 1895, an amendment of the constitution was adopted providing that "any member whose name shall have been upon the roll of the Club for fifteen years may become a life-member on payment of $750. The number of life-members was limited to 100, and they were exempted from dues thereafter. The fee, as has been noted, was later increased to $1,000 and those having been regular members for ten years made eligible.

Joseph F. Loubat (Univ. of France '47) was the first life-member of the Club. The number has increased to 70, a list of whom will be found in Appendix VII.

In the year 1880, the Committee on Literature and Art issued the following notice:

There having been some inconvenience in consequence of the absence from the Library of Catalogues, and other records of Colleges; the Committee beg to refer members for information regarding College records of any kind not found in the Library, to the gentlemen named below. They have agreed to endeavor to collect for the Club Library the Memorabilia of their respective Colleges, and will be glad to receive contributions, which should in all cases be sent to them, and not to the Committee.

Amherst '74........................Mr. F. W. Whitridge.
Brown '69..........................Dr. C. Hitchcock.
Columbia '69......................Mr. R. L. Belknap.
Dartmouth '62.....................Mr. G. S. Hubbard.
Hamilton '65......................Mr. H. B. Tompkins.
Harvard '65.......................Mr. T. Frank Brownell.
Bellevue Hosp. Med. Col. '66........Dr. F. A. Castle.
New York University '65...........Mr. W. F. Morgan.
Princeton '75......................Mr. C. Scribner.
Rutgers '56........................Mr. G. V. N. Baldwin.
Trinity '75........................Mr. W. E. Curtis, Jr.
Williams '74.......................Mr. W. D. Edmunds.
Yale '75...........................Mr. S. R. Betts.
U. S. M. A. '68...................Mr. L. Farragut.

In the same year, the committee called for "Volunteers to perform the same service regarding the colleges not yet represented."

At the meeting of the Council, June 11, 1894, a letter was read from the Princeton members tendering to the Club the Library of Princeton Memorabilia, which was accepted with thanks.

This seems to be the first record of a formal presentation of such a collection, and it naturally introduces the general subject. Princeton was not the first in the field, that honor belonging, as has been already stated, to Harvard, whose interest in this regard had been and continued to be looked after in a masterly way by T. Frank Brownell of the class of '65. His thorough work stimulated imitation by the graduates of Yale and other colleges and universities, but in few if any cases were the efforts of these others as complete and methodical as Mr. Brownell's.

The Yale and Princeton collections were nearest in their approach.

In the early years of the Club, much stress was laid by the Council on the importance of these collections, and the compiler of this history, having had the chief charge of the Princetoniana, has recognized the value of the system. Success in organizing and maintaining a library of College Memorabilia depends on the devotion and persistent painstaking of the person in charge, year in and year out, and the character of the labor is such that collections easily lose their completeness, and consequently their usefulness, if the requisite diligence and unflagging attention is wanting. For this reason, the collections are by no means as full or as comprehensive as they should be.

Some activity followed the appeals made at that time, but it is to be feared that in more than one case the undertaking has languished, and it is submitted that either some thorough system should be adopted, looking to permanence and completeness, or the collections turned over to the Clubs and associations of the respective colleges for such attention as they may naturally be expected to give. For in future years, these college libraries will prove of great use to compilers of history and to those searching for the early incidents in lives which will have become famous.

The Harvard collection, at the time of this publication, consists of about 750 volumes and 200 pamphlets: that of Yale, of about 450 volumes and 50 pamphlets; that of Princeton, of about 600 volumes and 40 pamphlets; Brown, about 150 volumes; and those of the other universities and colleges of smaller numbers. Too much emphasis cannot be put upon the importance of restoring and maintaining all these collections, and the alumni of the respective institutions may well address themselves with zeal and vigor to the work.

CHAPTER IX

FESTIVITIES, 1893–1895

THE University Club in its character of a national institution, and comprising within its membership a large number of officers of the army and navy of the United States, connected itself on the first of May, 1893, in a notable way with the celebration of the quadricentennial anniversary of the discovery of America by Christopher Columbus.

In the month of May in that year there were gathered in the harbor of New York twenty-seven foreign ships of war from Great Britain, Russia, France, Italy, Holland, Spain, Germany, Brazil, and Argentina, to honor the Columbian celebration. Besides these were twelve vessels of America's navy as escorts.

Recognizing the opportunity and participating in the spirit which was general throughout the country, the University Club, contrary to its previous usage, threw open its doors in hospitality to the officers of the visiting fleets as well as to those of our own navy, and tendered them a reception which proved to be one of the conspicuously interesting events of those days, so full of enthusiastic demonstration.

On April 18, 1893, a special meeting of the Council was called, at which Mr. Henry S. Van Duzer (Harvard '75) moved that the Club tender to Admiral Bancroft Gherardi (U. S. N. A. '52), the officers of his squadron, and the officers of foreign ships visiting the port at the time of the Columbian celebration, a reception at the Club House on such evening as Admiral Gherardi might name.

The motion was carried and the following members were

requested to act with the House Committee in arranging the reception and inviting the guests: Commodore Henry Erben (U. S. N. A. '54); Brigadier-General Louis Fitzgerald (Hon. Princeton '75); Captain Frederick Rodgers (U. S. N. A. '61); Colonel Francis Vinton Greene (U. S. M. A. '70); Commander Morris R. S. Mackenzie (U. S. N. A. '66); Commander Jacob W. Miller (U. S. N. A. '67); Captain Charles F. Roe (U. S. M. A. '68); Loyall Farragut (U. S. M. A. '68); Captain George S. Anderson (U. S. M. A. '71); and Hugh D. Auchincloss (Yale '79), Secretary of the Club.

It was also resolved that the privileges of the Club be extended to all officers on foreign war-ships.

Rear-Admiral Bancroft Gherardi, an honored member of the Club, was then the senior officer of the United States Navy, and as commander-in-chief of the fleet of reception, flew at his masthead the blue flag of seniority. At the age of fourteen, he had received from his uncle, then secretary of the navy, his warrant as midshipman. His first service was on the *Ohio*, and his total service had in 1893 extended over forty-seven years. He lived for ten years after the celebration, and died December 10, 1903.

Henry Erben, then commodore, and promoted to be rear-admiral in 1894, was a familiar figure in the Club House during later years. He was a typical example of the old-time fighting sailor, and his famous remark in praise of "the man behind the gun" has become a proverb. Admiral Erben died October 23, 1909.

Louis Fitzgerald was a fine type of the citizen soldier. Although all his life engaged in financial business in New York, his tastes led him to devote much time to military pursuits. He marched with the crack Seventh Regiment of New York to the defence of Washington during the Civil War, through which he served; was later lieutenant-colonel of that regiment, and later still brigadier-general of the New York National Guard. He died October 6, 1908.

Frederick Rodgers is the direct descendant of Commodore Matthew Galbraith Perry, who, in 1854, opened the Japanese ports to America and inaugurated a new era in the history of Japan. Captain Rodgers is now rear-admiral, and one of the strongest naval officers in the United States service.

Francis Vinton Greene was the son of General George Sears Greene, who lived to be ninety-seven years of age. He was graduated from West Point and served in various capacities in the army, being major-general of Volunteers in command of the United States forces at the capture of Manila, in the war with Spain. General Greene is now often seen in the Club.

Morris R. S. Mackenzie (Annapolis '66) served on the various stations and duties and commanded vessels and the Portsmouth Navy Yard, and became rear-admiral in 1896; retired in 1906, and is still one of our members.

Jacob W. Miller, a graduate of Annapolis of 1867, although in the naval service until 1884, engaged in the commercial steamship business. His retirement from the navy, however, did not prevent him from devoting his talents with remarkable diligence and efficiency to the organization and perfection of the New York Naval Militia, a work of great value to the State and public. Commander Miller is an active member of the Club.

Charles Francis Roe was for many years major-general of the New York National Guard and served as brigadier-general of the United States Volunteers. He was graduated at West Point in 1868, and continued in the United States Army until 1886.

Loyall Farragut, although a West Point man, is the son of the renowned Admiral David Glasgow Farragut, the first admiral of the United States Navy. Mr. Farragut has followed civil pursuits, but no member of the Club is better known among both army and navy men. He is also the author of a biography of his father.

George S. Anderson, who was a captain at the time of which this narrative speaks, was graduated at West Point in 1871, and has served in the cavalry ever since, in many parts of the world, including Texas, Arizona, New Mexico, Colorado, Virginia, the Yellowstone Park, the Philippines, and Governor's Island. He is now brigadier-general, retired.

Hugh D. Auchincloss (Yale '79), the Secretary of the Club for the time being, belonged to one of the best and longest-known mercantile families of New York. He was of Scotch descent, his grandfather, whose name he bore, having been born in Scotland. Mr. Auchincloss was for many years one of the active and useful members of the Club, and one of the most popular. He died April 22, 1913.

These descriptions are given as furnishing proof to members not familiar with the events of two decades ago, that principally from our army and navy list the Club was able to form a committee of ten most distinguished men to do honor to the foreign guests. Of the ten there are seven still living.

The preparations for the reception were on an elaborate scale appropriate to its importance. The attendance was very large, more than one thousand civilians and naval and military men being present.

The decorating of the Club was placed in the hands of Architect Charles F. McKim (Harvard '70). The Club House generally was ornamented with growing plants and the walls of the dining-room, from ceiling to floor, covered with alternate strips of red and yellow. A balcony was erected over the entrance to the dining-room, whereon an orchestra played, the balcony being covered with vines and flowers. A buffet supper-table was arranged on the entire south and east sides, small tables being placed in the double private dining-room, which accommodated the senior officers of each of the nations represented by their navy, and accompanying the senior officers were officers and other members of the

Club who were the escort of the naval officers and were seated with them at supper.

Special committees of from five to seven members were appointed to receive the officers of each nation. The special committees were assembled near the door, and as the guests arrived they were first received by a committee consisting of Captain B. H. Buckingham, of the navy, Captain Frederick Rodgers, and Colonel Francis Vinton Greene. This special committee received the guests and introduced the committee that was assigned to each nation. The guests were then escorted to the library and presented to the President of the Club, who was assisted in receiving them by Admiral Erben, who stood at the President's right, and General Louis Fitzgerald.

In addition to the orchestra in the balcony of the dining-room there was an orchestra on the first floor.

Conveyances were sent to meet the guests on the landing-stage at Riverside Drive, and to return them later.

Mrs. Forbes Leith gave a ball the same evening to which the officers of the Club and their guests were invited, and most of the naval officers attended.

An amusing incident happened in the early hours of the next morning. It seemed that during the night one of the foreign ships received orders to leave port; several officers had not returned, and an officer was sent with a guard to find them in the city. They appeared at the University Club to inquire if any of the officers were there. Previous to the reception three bedrooms had been reserved for officers who wished to remain during the night, and the guard from the ship was permitted to visit one of the bedrooms, where they found five officers asleep. Three of them turned out to be the missing ones, and were escorted back to the ship by the guard.

The night had been one of unusual jollification, and the hospitalities of the Club, so cordially offered, had been accepted and enjoyed with gusto. The incident of the missing sailors only goes to show that our foreign guests fully appreciated the merits of the entertainment and to the very extent of their powers gave proof of it, as well as evidence that the sailor on shore is universally the same jolly tar.

At this point it becomes fitting to dwell for a moment on the advantage the Club has enjoyed on its social side by the large membership of army and navy men. It may safely be declared, without invidious comparison, that there is no single class of members who have more thoroughly contributed to the agreeable companionship of our circle, or added to the reputation of the Club for distinction in a greater degree, than our sailors and soldiers.

At the time of this publication (1914) the Club has 172 army and navy members. Many famous men of this body have passed away leaving fragrant memories behind, and the list of those who are still living is rich with the names of men who have honored this country and this Club by their achievements on land and sea.

Mention has already been made of dinners and other entertainments, but it is probable that no occasion has ever been celebrated with more enthusiasm and jollification than the complimentary dinner given to Doctor David L. Haight, then Chairman of the House Committee, on December 20, 1895, by his associates in the Council of the University Club.

The services of Doctor Haight were so highly appreciated that the Council with unanimity through Messrs. Arthur M. Dodge (Yale '74) and Charles L. Atterbury (Yale '64) as a Committee expressed to him their desire to have him as their guest at a banquet, and especially requested him to indicate such friends outside of the Council as he would be pleased to have present. From this beginning the list grew until the number who joined in the festivity approximated one hundred.

The members of the Council at that time were: Otto T. Bannard (Yale '76); Horace J. Hayden (Harvard '60); William W. Hoppin (Brown '61); Henry E. Howland (Yale '54); Charles Scribner (Princeton '75); Charles C. Beaman (Harvard '61); Cornelius C. Cuyler (Princeton '79); Arthur M. Dodge (Yale '74); Loyall Farragut (U. S. M. A. '68); H. Walter Webb (Columbia '73); Charles L. Atterbury (Yale '64); Charles T. Barney (Williams '70); William L. Bull (C. C. N. Y. '64); George L. Peabody (Columbia '70); Charles H. Russell (Harvard '72); Hugh D. Auchincloss (Yale '79); George Blagden (Harvard '56); David L. Haight (Yale '60); George Sherman (Columbia '75); and James W. Alexander (Princeton '60).

The occasion was made one of special importance. The menu was composed of dishes which were veritable works of art on the part of the chef, who at the time was distinguished in his profession. After the "sorbet," which was then a regularly accepted pause in every stately dinner, the head steward, the second steward, and the corps of waiters entered the large front room on the first or drawing-room floor (set apart as an exceptional honor for the purposes of the occasion), divided into two files, and marched around the ends of the crescent-shaped table to the President's seat, bearing aloft huge dishes surmounted by magnificent boars' heads, or, as the menu had it—"Hures de Sangliers à la Shakespeare."

Toward the close of the banquet, two immense bowls of punch were borne in, the liquid on fire, and here an amusing incident occurred. The flames mounted so high and the heat was so great that the bowls began to melt. Now, it so happened that one of the guests present was James R. Sheffield (Yale '87), a former member of the Council and, at the time of which this is written, commissioner of the Fire Department of New York. Whether he felt the official responsibility of preventing a disaster, or whether he, like some others, was suddenly aroused to action by the threatening flames, the fact is that he rushed to the punch-bowl which blazed the highest and covered it with his napkin. As soon as he released his hold, the current created by the fire carried the napkin up to the ceiling, whereupon the whole company, who at this stage of the dinner were in no wise disposed to be serious, united in a shout of applause. The flames burnt out innocently and no harm was done.

One of the features of the dinner was a dozen bottles of old Scotch whiskey of a priceless brand, sent to the Council by William Black, the famous author, through Joseph W. Harper, Jr. The latter gentleman had been one of the most loyal and efficient members of the Council, and, although almost incapacitated by an attack of gout, could not be kept away from the dinner, but hobbled in on two canes, with bandaged hands, and participated in the jovial proceedings to the very end, permitting no rival to outstrip him in lending vim to the enjoyment.

Speeches were made; stories were told; healths were drunk; the rafters rang with laughter. A silver-mounted box for cigars was presented to Doctor Haight, with the following inscription:

Presented to
Doctor David L. Haight
by the
Council of the University Club
of New York City
Dec. 20, 1895

During the after-dinner diversions, the following original lines, composed by a member of the Club, were read:

A Dream of Pythagoras

On the dark shores where Acheron
Holds back its bitter tide, which none
Of men may see and live, the crowd

Of shades assembled, and the proud
Dark Pluto sat in awful state.
This was the day some fortunate
Dead shade should be set free from Orcus,
To live once more in human carcass.
And as this happened once a year,
The rivalry was most severe;
            And ghostly prayer
            From each one there
Was wafted to the monarch's ear.

This one declared his claim to rest
On rotatory precedent;
That introduced a mild request
As being most benevolent.
And so the wraiths did mow and gabble,
While the great king inscrutable
Furrowed his brows in solitude
Over the seething multitude.
"Galen, stand forth!" the sable king
Stretched out his sceptre o'er the ring
Of shuddering souls; then forth there came
A spirit meagre, wizened, lame,
His forehead rippled o'er with thought.
In one hand mighty books he brought,
Pills in the other; he could cure
Sarcoma, phthisis, all the ur-
inary troubles, Bright's disease,
Synovial swellings of the knees,
Pyrosis was to him as plain
As sunlight on a counterpane.

"Galen," said Pluto, "I declare
Because of your surpassing worth
You shall return to upper air
And walk once more a man on earth."

The dignified physician bowed.
            Then from the crowd
A spirit rushed with passionate

Appeal, right to the throne of state.
"I was at dinner," he declared,
"And have just now your mandate heard.
I am Lucullus. I can do
More good on earth than forty surgeons.
I am a master of ragouts,
And can prepare a dish of sturgeons
Or potted pigeons such as oughter
Make the three mouths of Cerberus water.
Let me be born, and pain and grief
Shall have in me a sweet relief."
The bulky suppliant fast perspired,
Release from hell he so desired.
The monarch mused: "The Book of Fate
Supreme, declares that on this date
But one shall be released." Awhile
He pondered. A majestic smile
Spread over Pluto's august head
Like warm molasses; then he said:
"I must obey the law notorious,
But since your claim is meritorious,
I will exert my might and make
Two souls a single form to take.

The man shall heal with wondrous skill,
And, foe to ill,
Shall to a favored few impart
Results of culinary art.
In medicine incomparable
And Grand Past Master of the table."
He swayed his sceptre o'er the pair;
From the embodiment of air
They fused into a single form,
With vital force and heart-beats warm.
The eager mortals stand without
Expectant by the narrow gate,
What form translate shall issue out.
The gate swings back. From out the strait
A form emerges, and the shout
Of glad acclaim rings bravely out,
"He comes, a Haight, a Haight!"

O glorious wisdom that can so combine
A skill in physic and a taste for wine!
O happy mortals who can thus secure
At once a doctor and an epicure!
On Haight bestow your laurels and your bays;
Exult in him, glad Bacchus; in him praise
Apollo, who bestoweth length of days.

CHAPTER X

THE UNIVERSITY ATHLETIC CLUB—NEW CLUB HOUSE PROPOSED—HISTORY OF THE FIFTY-FOURTH STREET SITE—1894-1896

THE success and popularity of the Club were so marked that the number of university graduates desiring to enjoy its privileges grew to proportions greater than the facilities of the Club House could accommodate.

The difficulty and delay in obtaining admission to membership naturally led to discussion about a Junior University Club. Although London had furnished more than one precedent for the formation of clubs to admit those unable to secure election to the parent organizations, there was decided aversion among the members of the University Club to anything in the nature of a split among college graduates. Various schemes were proposed and some tried to meet the exigency thus developed. As previously stated, at the Council meeting of March 12, 1894, a special committee was authorized to make a suitable offer for the Stokes residence, on Madison Avenue, next door to the Jerome house then occupied by the Club, either to lease or purchase. The motive here was such an enlargement of the premises as would justify an increase of membership, and thereby provide for the admission of the large number of eligible university men who were knocking at our door.

This committee conducted negotiations and had elaborate plans prepared by Mr. Charles F. McKim (Harvard '70) showing how the added property could be utilized. The whole plan, however, fell through, and the army of aspirants to membership grew in numbers with rapidity.

In the year 1891 the University Athletic Club was organized. This club, while composed exclusively of university men, was not in the strictest sense a "junior" club. It was by no means intended as an overflow. Its founders were in nearly every case already members of the University Club, and its objects were specifically different from those of that institution. In its certificate of incorporation these objects were stated as follows:

> The particular business and object of said Society or Club shall be the furnishing of proper apparatus and facilities for athletic and social enjoyment and recreation to the members thereof, and for the encouragement of amateur sport.

The first body of trustees and council of the University Athletic Club was composed as follows:

George A. Adee (Yale '67).
Edward D. Appleton (Trinity '80).
Collin Armstrong (Amherst '77).
Wendell Baker (Harvard '86).
Henry W. Banks, Jr. (Williams '85).
Henry Stanford Brooks (Yale '86).
Robert C. Cornell (Columbia '74).
Cornelius C. Cuyler (Princeton '79).
George Walton Green (Harvard '76).
Tracy H. Harris (Princeton '86).
Oliver G. Jennings (Yale '87).
William H. L. Lee (Yale '69).
Charles F. Mathewson (Dartmouth '82).
Edward S. Rapallo (Columbia '74).
William W. Skiddy (Yale '65).
William Stewart Tod (Princeton '84).
Richard Trimble (Harvard '80).
Henry S. Van Duzer (Harvard '75).
Evert Jansen Wendell (Harvard '82).

The club took a lease of part of the old Racquet and Tennis Club building, at 55 West 26th Street, and on May 1, 1892, took possession of these premises. The opening was largely attended, and the club entered upon what appeared to be a prosperous career.

In 1897, it moved to 19 West 34th Street. Its membership was composed, as was natural from the very character of its constitution, of men who were younger on the average than those in the University Club. It became a rendezvous for that large class of college men who took special interest in intercollegiate athletic competitions, and wielded a tremendous influence in raising the standard of those contests. One of the college periodicals stated that "a few years ago there was undoubtedly a large amount of professionalism in the athletics of the larger colleges. The University Athletic Club, recognizing the seriousness of this evil, took the matter in hand and the effect of its crusade was soon felt."

The various prominent universities gladly committed to the University Athletic Club the supervision and management of the football and baseball games played in New York. A marked reformation in the methods and customs of the teams and players followed. It was largely through the influence of the University Athletic Club that the college games were mainly confined to college grounds. Under that club's auspices the rules of the Rugby game of football were revised and adjusted.

In the spring of 1894, at the instigation of the club, League umpires were appointed to officiate at the baseball games between Yale and Princeton. This action gave rise to the custom which now prevails of having all the important baseball games umpired by officials selected by the president of the National League. Its Athletic Committee was most useful as an arbitrator of disputes between college organizations, as well as acting as a tribunal of appeal, both in intercollegiate and interscholastic controversies. It not only performed valuable services in the direction named and others, but substantially provided the needed facilities for those who had advocated a Junior University Club, while not making necessary the divisions which many feared would be occasioned by the foundation of a second club precisely similar to ours.

The University Athletic Club had a brief existence. In the year 1899 it gave up its club-house and practically disbanded, although its charter may be kept alive. The reason for its discontinuance is not to be found within its constitution, or its conduct, but rather in the organization of the various college clubs which, in the period of which we are speaking, became suddenly popular. The formation of clubs for graduates, respectively, of Harvard, Yale, Princeton, and other universities created centres for the younger alumni, and offered peculiar inducements to many who found it inconvenient to belong to two or more clubs. It was no uncommon thing, either, that the very men who had kept the University Athletic Club alive by their interest and energy were leaders in the various new college clubs. There was not room for the two classes, and as college allegiance drew the men irresistibly into the club composed of their fellow alumni, the more general organization necessarily drooped and lost its constituency. The club, however, did good work while it lasted, and its social advantages and pleasures were particularly fine and are looked back upon with delightful memories by those who enjoyed them.

This is the only successful attempt that has ever been made at a university club secondary to our own. Before the days of the University Club, as reorganized, a body of New York gentlemen, either college graduates or men having literary and scholarly tastes, organized the Athenæum Club, whose purposes were similar to those of the London Athenæum. Its membership was drawn from the best of New York's intelligent young men, and for a while it showed signs of prosperity. But it was short-lived and perished from non-support.

In the year 1896, then, we find the University Club in exclusive possession of the field, but threatened with rivalry, by reason of its strained quarters and the multitude of desirable college graduates waiting to be admitted. At this time the constitution limited the resident membership to 1,200 and the non-resident to 900. There were posted more than 500 candidates, regularly nominated, a list increasing in volume from month to month, and the Club was full. It was known that numbers who desired to enter the Club refrained from making application on account of the obvious difficulty in getting in.

The question was therefore sharply presented to the management of the Club as to what steps in the way of relief to the situation could be taken. Matters might be left as they were, and the moderate number of existing members could go on enjoying the comforts of that most fascinating Club House, to the exclusion of hosts of friends and good fellows, or they could look for more ample and permanent quarters elsewhere which would justify the introduction of a great number of new members. Opinions were divided in the Club, some preferring to take the risk of the organization of a rival concern rather than to surrender the cosiness and close companionship of a Club of moderate size; others being averse to a division of college men into two camps, each threatening the welfare of the other, and inclining toward the policy of enlargement and permanence. As will appear later, the great preponderance of opinion was in favor of the latter plan.

The Council, having the responsibility of framing a policy, and composed of men who contributed their time, thought, and talents to the conduct of the Club, by the choice of its members at large, felt bound to take the matter up, examine and discuss it, and decide upon a course.

This they did by appointing a committee of five, at their meeting of February 10, 1896, to consider and report upon a site for a new Club House other than the then present site.

This committee consisted of Messrs. H. Walter Webb (Columbia '73), Charles T. Barney (Williams '70), Otto T. Bannard (Yale '76), Charles L. Atterbury (Yale '64), and James W. Alexander (Princeton '60).

As the considerations which weighed with this committee will be set forth at length in connection with the reports of the Council to the Club, they are omitted here.

The committee reported on May 4, 1896, that they had investigated all desirable sites and recommended the consideration only of the following, namely:

The northwest corner of 54th Street and Fifth Avenue, consisting of five lots 100 x 25 feet each, being a part of the property theretofore occupied by the St. Luke's Hospital, which had removed to Morningside Heights. An option on these five lots had been obtained at $675,000, to remain good for forty-eight hours.

Six lots at the southeast corner of Fifth Avenue and 37th Street.

Six lots at the southeast corner of 44th Street and Fifth Avenue.

(Both the last two properties belong to the Stevens Estate, and each was offered on a ground lease of $35,000 per annum, and taxes for twenty years with two renewals.)

The Council were averse to building upon leasehold property, and at the meeting of May 5, 1896, adopted the following resolutions:

Resolved, That it is the opinion of the Council that the Club should move to some up-town site; that the Club should increase its membership and provide a larger Club house. Also that such a move should be made in the course of the next two years.

Unanimously resolved, That the property on the N. W. corner of 54th St. and 5th Ave. consisting of 5 lots is the most desirable site and that the same should be acquired at not more than $675,000.

Resolved, That a meeting of the Club be called for May 14, to obtain an expression of opinion as to the advisability of this purchase.

The Council, by the constitution, had full power to act, but preferred to take the advice of the Club at large.

A committee was then appointed to prepare a report and necessary resolutions for presentation at the next meeting of the Council. This committee was composed of Messrs. Haight, Auchincloss, Atterbury, Barney, and Alexander.

On May 11, 1896, that committee made its report and submitted the forms, which were amended, adopted, and ordered printed and distributed. The report was as follows:

May 12, 1896.

To the Members of the University Club:

In the unanimous opinion of your Council, the opportunity, as well as the time, has come when the Club, in recognition of its position and proper regard for its future, should contemplate an enlargement of its membership and the erection of a permanent house suited in character and location for the home of an Association which claims to represent the intellectual force of liberal education in this country.

Two courses are open to us: One, an active, progressive policy looking to the enlargement of our present membership and the provision of an attractive club-house in a desirable portion of the city, with ample accommodations for such increased membership, thereby making the University Club in fact as in name the representative of the universities and colleges throughout the country; the other, a policy of restriction of the Club to its present limited membership and continuance in its present quarters, trusting to some good fortune of the future in avoiding what appears to us an inevitable result—namely, the gradual loss of our prestige and position. We can hardly doubt that our members will concur with us in the unanimous adoption of the former policy.

Our resident membership has now reached the constitutional limit of 1,200, and our non-resident membership the constitutional limit of 900; meanwhile, our waiting list has grown to 560, and in our opinion it is distinctly a detriment to the growth and best interests of the Club.

During the past two years comparatively few members have been added to our rolls, and the vacancies caused by death and resignation do not exceed sixty a year, or barely three per cent. of our entire membership; and while, in reaching the limit of our membership, we have also attained a high degree of financial prosperity, it must not be forgotten that this smaller percentage of new members does not furnish that constant addition to the Club of younger members which is essential to its prosperity. In the career of our Club, progress and development are vital to its permanency and its success.

As the standard bearer of college graduates, we also owe a duty which we can fulfill only by opening our doors to those whom we have taught to look forward to association with us.

In recognition of this duty and with an earnest desire for the permanent prosperity of the Club, your Council has, for some time past, been engaged in the consideration of these questions, and has unanimously agreed upon a plan for which we ask your consideration and co-operation.

This plan contemplates, first, an enlarged membership; second, the acquisition of a desirable site of suitable size and the erection thereon of a club-house sufficient to accommodate the proposed increase of members, which, in addition to the usual rooms, shall contain a fireproof library to accommodate our rapidly-increasing collection of books, now exceeding thirteen thousand in number, with convenient niches or apartments for quiet study; sleeping rooms with baths attached; a dining and smoking room for guests; a swimming tank and Turkish and other baths and a roof garden, together with billiard room and bowling alleys and a storage place for bicycles.

In considering the question of site, your Council has given careful consideration to our present location. This is admittedly inadequate, and we have been unable to make any satisfactory arrangement for the acquisition of adjoining property sufficient to satisfy our needs. Even could this be done, your Council regard such an arrangement at the best as temporary and in the nature of a makeshift. A Special Committee of your Council has spent some months in examining the most available sites on the different avenues and cross-streets, and, by a process of elimination, your Council have arrived unanimously at the conclusion that the most available property for the purposes of the Club is the plot of land on the northwest corner of 54th Street and Fifth Avenue, consisting of five lots of 125 x 100 feet, known as the St. Luke's Hospital property. In reaching this conclusion, your Council have taken into careful consideration the convenience of the large majority of the members of the Club, not only for the present, but for the next twenty-five years.

A careful study has been made of the financial part of the plan, and we estimate that with the addition of the new members the necessary funds can be provided to acquire the property and maintain the same and meet our annual expenses without increasing the present dues of $60 a year. As the proposed new club-house will hardly be ready for occupancy in less than two years, ample time will be given toward the election of new members.

Your Council makes this report after earnest and careful investigation and study. Its members are unanimous in recommending the plan for adoption, and trust that it will receive the full support and co-operation of the members of the Club. Personal preferences and individual opinions have been laid aside for what have come to be regarded as the common and best interests of the Club, and in the expectation that the members of the Club will co-operate with the Council in the adoption of a liberal and progressive policy in its future development.

The Council regrets the short notice given to the Club on this subject; but, under the circumstances, this was unavoidable.

By order of the Council.

JAMES W. ALEXANDER,
President.

HUGH D. AUCHINCLOSS,
Secretary.

The Council thereupon by an "aye and no" vote unanimously resolved to recommend to the Club the purchase of the Fifth Avenue and 54th Street property, and the President and Treasurer were authorized to take the necessary steps to provide funds for binding the purchase in case the Club approved the same. It was also resolved: "that it is the sense of the Council that the President should submit the report to the Club with such explanation and recommendation as he may deem desirable."

At this meeting of the Council, it was decided that, inasmuch as Doctor David L. Haight (Yale '60) had been giving for several years and was still continuing to give his entire time and remarkable talents to the management of the Club House and its cuisine and conveniences, and inasmuch as he could not be compensated for his services in a pecuniary way, the obligation of the Club to him should be met in another manner. The following resolution was therefore unanimously adopted:

The Council of the University Club, sensible of the services rendered by Dr. DAVID L. HAIGHT at great sacrifice to himself, as Chairman of the House Committee during the past five years, throughout which the prosperity of the Club has been without precedent, and desiring to recognize his devotion and success by some appropriate tribute and to give to him some pledge of confidence and grateful obligation,

Hereby Resolve, That the free hospitalities of the Club be tendered to Dr. Haight, and that he be regarded, henceforth, as the Club's guest.

On May 14, 1896, the Club met. The pros and cons in regard to the building project had during the days previous been actively canvassed among the members, and it was known that an opposition had been organized, and speakers appointed to represent it in debate.

The President presented to the Club the report of the Council recommending the purchase of the St. Luke's Hospital property as a site for the new Club House and explained fully to the Club the causes and reasons which had led the Council to make this unanimous recommendation to the Club.

Mr. Austen G. Fox (Harvard '69) offered the following resolution:

Resolved, That this Club hereby approves the recommendations of the Council.

SAINT LUKE'S HOSPITAL.

Which occupied the site of the present Club House at Fifth Avenue and Fifty-fourth Street.

This motion was seconded by Mr. James R. Sheffield (Yale '87).

After discussion and inquiries, the question was put, the chair having appointed Messrs. J. W. Curtis (Yale '79) and G. W. Van Nest (Harvard '74) tellers, who duly reported the votes cast: Total, 430; ayes, 298; nays, 132; whereupon the chair declared the motion carried.

At the meeting of the Council May 20, 1896, the President and Treasurer reported that the contract of purchase of the property at $675,000 had been signed and that $67,000 had been paid to bind the same, which action was approved.

The Council then appointed, as the Committee on Plans and Building, Messrs. Barney (Chairman), Haight, Auchincloss, Atterbury, Dodge, and Alexander (ex officio); and as the Committee on Special Finance, Messrs. Blagden (Chairman), Bannard, Cuyler, Webb, Bull, and Alexander (ex officio).

The Honorable Henry E. Howland was appointed as the Law Committee.

At the Council meeting of June 8, 1896, the Special Committee on Finance was empowered to procure loans up to $1,100,000 on bond and mortgage, the rate of interest not to be more than 4½ per cent.

On June 25, 1896, the Council appointed Charles F. McKim (Harvard '70) as architect.

The officers were authorized, in order to enlarge the property and more satisfactorily carry out the plans for a suitable Club House, to buy from William Rockefeller two lots, one on 54th Street immediately in the rear of the property already bought, measuring 100 feet x 25 feet, and one on 55th Street being the extension of the last-named, also 100 feet x 25 feet, at not more than $130,000.

There is so much of historic interest in the tract of land a part of which thus came into the possession of the University Club, that a brief reference to the chain of title will not be deemed inappropriate. The premises acquired by the Club are a part of the common lands which formerly belonged to the mayor, aldermen, and commonalty of the city of New York, which were granted to them by Thomas Dongan, lieutenant-governor and vice-admiral of New York, by his charter dated April 27, 1686. As will appear, there have been but two actual changes of ownership from that time to the date when the Club came into possession.

The odor of sanctity was instilled into the early proceedings touching the property which has since become the home of the Club, inasmuch as the first conveyance by the corporation of the city of New York, on May 10, 1848, was to the "Rector, Church Wardens and Vestrymen of the Anglo-American Free Church of St. George the Martyr in said City" for a hospital and chapel for the accommodation of British emigrants; and it was stipulated in the deed that the conditions of the transfer should not at any time be released, modified or discharged, without the consent of Trinity Church in the city of New York. So it is a matter of record that the early history of our property is entwined with the life and purposes of two prominent ecclesiastical institutions—an augury for that pure and virtuous character which afterward revealed itself in the subsequent possessor of a portion of the property—namely, the University Club.

As it turned out, the Anglo-American Free Church of St. George did not avail itself of the right to build a hospital on the land conveyed, but with the consent of Trinity Church and the corporation of the city of New York transferred that right to St. Luke's Hospital in the City of New York, with the understanding that the advantages of the hospital should be open to the indigent poor of all nations and not confined exclusively to British emigrants.

In order, nevertheless, that the beneficiaries as originally intended should not lose the privileges theretofore provided for them, certain conditions and stipulations were imposed and entered into for their protection. For example, it was provided that St. Luke's Hospital should set apart one portion, ward, or wing of the building to be erected by them for a hospital capable of containing twenty beds for the use of British emigrants, and which should always be called the Ward of St. George the Martyr; that fifteen of such emigrants should be admitted on the certificate of the British consul or the Anglo-American Free Church of St. George the Martyr; that the British consul and one of the wardens or vestrymen of the said church should be ex-officio members of the board of managers of St. Luke's Hospital; and that, under circumstances set forth, the Ward of St. George the Martyr should be extended.

Later on—namely, in 1895—the St. George's Society of New York was substituted for the Church of St. George the Martyr in respect to the agreements and conditions made with St. Luke's Hospital, and instead of a separate ward for British emigrants, which had proved incompatible with proper hospital service, the British emigrants were by agreement distributed and treated in accordance with the ordinary requirements. But it was stipulated that there should always be a ward called "The Ward of St. George the Martyr," and so designated by a tablet.

When St. Luke's Hospital moved to Morningside Heights, it sold the property under consideration to various purchasers, the bulk of the present University Club site being conveyed directly and a small portion in the rear coming to it through William Rockefeller.

Surely the sentiment naturally aroused by the inheritance of piety and beneficence through the title to its home, is one not to be carelessly smothered or ridiculed by those who cherish something like affection for the University Club.

CHAPTER XI

DEATH OF PRESIDENT ANDERSON—PRINCETON SESQUICENTENNIAL, 1896

ON the seventeenth day of September, 1896, Henry H. Anderson (Williams '48), the first President of the reorganized Club, who by his wise counsels and rare executive capacity had been so important a factor in the development and success of the undertaking during its formative period, departed this life.

The sentiment of the Club regarding the value of Mr. Anderson's services was unanimous and strong, and his personal friends and admirers among the membership were many. The death of one who had devoted his great talents to the successful upbuilding of the Club naturally called forth much demonstration of regret.

A meeting of the Council was summoned to take appropriate action regarding the event, and at this meeting the following minute was adopted:

The Council of the University Club of the City of New York having met for the purpose of taking appropriate action upon the death of their former President, Henry H. Anderson, desire to place upon the records of the Club, some expression of the sentiment universally felt among the membership touching the solemn event which has brought them together.

Mr. Anderson, after many years of usefulness and deserved prominence at the bar and before the public, was the unanimous choice of the University Club for its Presidency at the time of its reorganization in 1879. He filled this position with honour and with the cordial approbation and support of the whole membership during nine full terms, and was permitted to resign in 1888 only out of deference to his own decided wish.

The unprecedented prosperity of the Club was largely due to his wise guidance. His upright character and unblemished life were an example not only within this circle, but throughout the community. Both during the incumbency of his office, and afterwards, his presence and his counsels were sought and valued.

He was not simply a respected and trusted leader, but a welcome friend whose absence will be keenly felt by all.

No form of words can adequately express the grief which the death of such a man brings to those who have had the privilege of enjoying his companionship and profiting by his co-operation, but those who have been his associates in the maintenance and development of a representative Club of educated men, wish by the adoption of this minute, to recognize the debt which they owe to the friend now departed, and to pay to his memory the sincere and emphatic tribute of their respect and affection.

At the meeting of the Club held June 16, 1896, the constitution was amended by increasing the resident membership to 1,700 and the non-resident membership to 1,300.

In September, 1896, a question of principle in the conduct of the Club's affairs was raised and decided. This decision was of the utmost importance. A letter was presented to the Council from Mr. James J. Higginson (Harvard '57) requesting that a special meeting of the Club be called to obtain an expression of the sentiment of the Club regarding pending political questions. It was regarded by some as a fair subject for debate whether an association of University men formed "for the purpose of the promotion of literature and art" should be made the arena for political discussion. But the views of those on the Council were unanimous and exceedingly strong. It was their conviction that here was one place where the animosities of party strife should not be allowed to enter, and where men of many and diverse opinions on national and municipal questions could meet in friendly intercourse without the danger of discord arising from political differences. The Council, by the constitution having "full power," and being expressly charged by that instrument with the "duty to carry out the purposes of the Club according to its Charter, Constitution, and By-Laws," considered it unnecessary to submit the question propounded to the Club at large, and took immediate and decisive action, thereby fixing the policy of the Club and in the judgment of a vast majority of those whose opinions found expression protecting the Club from a positive danger.

The Council unanimously requested the President to advise the writer of the letter "that they do not deem it advisable for the Club to enter into political discussions, as a Club."

The celebration of the Sesquicentennial Anniversary of the founding of Princeton University took place in the year 1896, and was attended by such a large number of distinguished scholars and teachers from foreign countries that the Club made a departure from general usage and determined to take notice of the presence of these notables. At the meeting of the Council held October 1, 1896, Mr. C. C. Beaman (Harvard '61) asked consideration of the question of "a reception to the distinguished delegates from foreign Universities visiting America to attend the Sesquicentennial Celebration of the College of New Jersey and inauguration of Princeton University."

It was thereupon decided to put this proposal into operation and it was

Resolved, That a "Committee on Invitations" be appointed by the Chair with full power to issue invitations and arrange in conjunction with the House Committee for the entertainment of the delegates from Foreign Universities, attending the Sesquicentennial exercises of Princeton University, at a dinner and reception to be given at the Club House on the evening of Oct. 23rd.

The President appointed as such committee: Messrs. C. C. Beaman (Harvard '61), Henry E. Howland (Yale '54), and T. Frank Brownell (Harvard '65).

The arrangements for this complimentary demonstration in honor of the guests of a particular university were thus placed in the hands of a committee consisting altogether of graduates of the older sister universities and the incident is only one among many manifestations of that catholic spirit which has during the whole life of the University Club animated its members. Never in the faintest degree have college rivalries crept into the conduct of its affairs. On the contrary, there has always been evinced by the sons of each Alma Mater a fraternal disposition to be regardful of the interests and tastes of those holding degrees from other schools of learning.

This committee proceeded with diligence to prepare lists of the representative men in academic life throughout the country. The names included the presidents and many from the faculties of all the colleges and seminaries of the United States, including those of divinity, law, and medicine, the secretary of the Smithsonian Institution, the presidents of University Clubs, as well as of the social clubs of New York; eminent men in the judiciary and other walks of life; the president of Robert College, Constantinople; the heads of museums of art and science; editors; governors and mayors; Grover Cleveland, President of the United States; and Theodore Roosevelt.

The dinner was accordingly given at the Club House on the evening of October 23, 1896, to which the following delegates were invited to meet the officers and members of the Council:

Chancellor Sandford Fleming, of Queens College, Kingston, Ont.
Reverend John Forrest, president of Dalhousie University, Halifax, N. S.
President James London, University of Toronto, Canada.
Professor Friedrich Karl Brugmann, of Leipzig.
Professor Johannes Conrad, of Halle.
Reverend Doctor William Caven, of Toronto.
Sir J. William Dawson, of Montreal.

Professor Wilhelm Dörpfeld, of Athens.
Professor Edward Dowden, of Dublin.
Professor A. A. W. Hubrecht, of Utrecht.
Professor Felix Klein, of Göttingen.
Professor Henri Moissan, of Paris.
Professor William Peterson, of Montreal.
Professor Edward Baynall Poulton, of Oxford.
Professor Andrew Seth, of Edinburgh.
Professor Goldwin Smith, of Toronto.
Professor Joseph John Tomson, of Cambridge.
Also President Patton and Dean West, of Princeton.

All but six were present at the dinner.

After dinner a reception was given in the Club House which was largely attended by members of the Club and many invited guests, among whom were:

President Seth Low, of Columbia University; President Alexander S. Webb, of the City College; President Potter, of Hobart College; President Austin Scott, of Rutgers College; Professor W. H. Chandler, of Lehigh University; ten professors from the Princeton faculty, fifteen from the Columbia faculty, seven from the Yale faculty; and representative professors from Harvard, Barnard, the Normal College, Stevens Institute, Amherst, Lehigh, Roanoke, New York University, Muhlenburg, University of Pennsylvania, Dartmouth, Brown, and others. The army and navy were also represented, as well as the clergy and judiciary. Among these were the Reverend Doctors Huntington and Greer, Reverends Percy S. Grant, Lyman Abbott, Robert Collyer, R. S. McArthur, Edward Judson, John Hall, George Alexander, Joseph H. Mitchell; Doctors J. D. Bryant, Francis Delafield, W. T. Lark, T. Addis Emmet, Lewis A. Stimson; Rear-Admirals Erben and Bunce, General Ruger, Colonel William C. Church, Commodore Sicard, Captain A. T. Mahan; Judges Gildersleeve, Patterson, Haight, Rumsey, Williams, Bookstaver, Barrett, Ingraham, Wallace, MacKean, Bischoff, and Lawrence, and many others.

There were no speeches made either at the dinner or the reception which followed. The affair was dignified but informal. The weather was inclement, but the Club House was crowded with guests.

This account is given for the reason that the occasion was unique in the history of the Club, being the only one on which a body of distinguished representatives of foreign universities were entertained by the Club as such.

CHAPTER XII

FINANCING THE FIFTY-FOURTH STREET CLUB-HOUSE—1897-1898

Mr. Charles F. McKim (Harvard '70), of the firm of McKim, Mead & White, having been, as already stated, appointed architect of the proposed building, prepared plans and specifications and procured estimates of the cost of its erection. These were submitted, February 8, 1897, to the Council by the Chairman of the Building Committee with recommendation that the Club be asked at a special meeting, to be called for the purpose, to approve the same, and to authorize the issue of $350,000 second mortgage bonds.

The Council was clothed by the constitution with absolute power to proceed in this and all other situations without any action whatever by the Club at large; such, however, was the desire of those in authority to carry with them the approval of the membership, that, as in the case of the purchase of the property at Fifth Avenue and 54th Street, they refrained from taking action in this important matter until the wishes of the Club had been ascertained.

The Council, while approving in general the plans submitted, requested the architect to elaborate them, and to prepare detailed drawings, the further consideration of the report of the Building Committee being deferred until the next meeting. The Finance Committee was requested to report at that time upon a plan for the raising of funds, and the House Committee upon the probable receipts and expenditures of the Club when installed in the new house.

From a photograph, copyright by Frances Benjamin Johnston and Mattie Edwards Hewitt.

CHARLES F. McKIM (Harvard '70).

Member of the firm of McKim, Mead & White, architects of the Fifth Avenue Club House.

These particulars are given to show the care taken in developing a progressive movement involving a certain amount of risk. This risk, however, was reduced to such a minimum, by the cautious and businesslike calculations based on actual facts and experience, as to make the undertaking as commercially certain as any movement of the kind could be, and the result, as will be fully set forth, more than confirmed the judgments formed in advance and upon the strength of which the Club was committed to the scheme.

The original charter of the Club having limited its right to hold real estate, and an amendment adopted enlarging its powers in this respect being still inadequate, a committee was appointed to report upon the matter. All doubt was, however, removed by the discovery that the laws of New York (1894, chapter 9) authorized corporations of the category in which the University Club belonged to hold real estate of the value of $6,000,000 exclusive of improvements, anything in their respective charters to the contrary notwithstanding.

Inasmuch as the question as to the Club's rights in this respect often recurs, it seems proper at this point to insert a legal opinion obtained at a later date to satisfy inquiries made at the time.

Office of the President
No. 31 Nassau Street

UNIVERSITY CLUB

NEW YORK CITY

June 10, 1911.

MY DEAR MR. OAKMAN:

One of the members of the Council having raised the question as to the right of the University Club to hold its real property, which now far exceeds $500,000, the limitation placed upon the amount of real property to be held by the University Club by an amendment to the Charter, I have made an investigation, and find as follows:

The University Club was incorporated under a special Act of the Legislature of the State of New York, known as Chapter No. 594 of the Laws of 1865. Section 3 of that Act is as follows:

"The said corporation may lease, purchase, or take, by deed, devise, or bequest, any real or personal estate, and hold or lease the same; *provided that they shall not hold any real estate the value of which shall exceed the sum of one hundred thousand dollars.*"

By Chapter 139 of the Laws of 1883, Section 3, supra, was amended, so as to read as follows:

"The said corporation may lease, purchase or take by deed, devise or bequest any real or personal estate, and hold or lease the same; *provided, that they shall not hold any real estate the value of which shall exceed the sum of five hundred thousand dollars.*"

There has been no further amendment to the Charter, so that as the matter now stands, if there were no further provisions of law to be considered, the University Club could not hold real property the value of which exceeded the sum of $500,000; but section 12 of the General Corporation Law, which was originally enacted in 1890, and amended and added to by the Laws of 1892 and 1894, and finally amended by the Laws of 1909, Chapter 276, taking effect May 3, 1909, is as follows:

"Sec. 12. Enlargement of Limitations upon the Amount of the Property of Non-stock Corporation.—If any general or special law heretofore passed, or any certificate of incorporation, shall limit the amount of property a corporation other than a stock corporation may take or hold, such corporation *may take and hold property of the value of six million dollars or less*, or the yearly income derived from which shall be six hundred thousand dollars or less, *notwithstanding any such limitations.* In computing the value of such property, no increase in value arising otherwise than from improvements made thereon shall be taken in account."

The University Club, having been incorporated by a special law, and being a non-stock corporation, comes directly within the section last above quoted, and, therefore, the limitation contained in Section 3 of the Charter, while having full force and effect at the time of its passage by the Legislature, has since been abrogated, and the University Club, notwithstanding the limitations in the Charter and its amendment, to use the words of the statute, "may take and hold property of the value of six million dollars or less."

I suggest that this letter be placed on file among the records of the Club, so that, if at any time the question should arise, there will be a ready answer.

Yours very truly,

(Signed) B. Aymar Sands.

Walter G. Oakman, Esq., *Treas.*

The report of the Special Committee on Finance was made to the Council on March 8, 1897, as was the report of the House Committee on probable receipts and expenditures. Both reports were adopted unanimously. A copy of the essential part of the former is here appended:

Report of Special Finance Committee

On the plans submitted by the Building Committee the cost of the new Club House to completion, including cost of site, building, interest, taxes, furniture, etc., and an allowance of $100,000 for extras and sundries, is estimated at			$2,020,000
Deducting from this amount the sum already paid, and interest for three years at 4½% which is included in the above estimate		$306,000	
Deduct also entrance fees of new members for three years,			
Say 500 Resident at $200		$100,000	
Say 300 Non-Resident at $100		$30,000	
Dues of same, one-half estimated for three years,			
250 at $60	15,000		
150 at $25	3,750		
	$18,750	$56,250	
Estimated annual Surplus Three Years		$75,000	$557,250
Leaving			$1,462,750

To provide for this amount it is proposed: 1st. To borrow on mortgage at 4½% of the Equitable Life Assurance Society two-thirds of the cost of the land and building, including in the latter interest and taxes. The total loan on land and building not to exceed One million two hundred thousand Dollars ($1,200,000).

The said loan is to be made in instalments according to the progress of the work, on the schedule of payments to be arranged with the consent of the loaning corporation, after the plans and specifications, survey and diagram have been submitted in accordance with the rules of the Society, annexed, and in each case after the report of the Society's Inspector is made, in accordance with those rules. All the other conditions as shown in the annexed rules are to be complied with.

The Bond and Mortgage are to contain an agreement on the part of the University Club, to begin at the expiration of five years from the completion of the total loan, to reduce the principal of the loan by annual payments of not less than $25,000 per annum until the total outstanding loan shall be reduced to 50% of the valuation then placed on the property by the appraisers of the Equitable Life Assurance Society, unless the said Society shall waive this option.

2nd. That the Club shall issue $350,000 Second Mortgage Bonds at par, bearing interest at 5% of the denominations of $500 and $1,000, the coupons of which shall be received in payment of yearly dues to the Club. Said bonds to run for the period of twenty years; the Club reserving the right to pay off twenty (20) of said bonds at par and interest each year, after the expiration of five years from the date of issue; The numbers of the bonds drawn to be determined by lot at the April meeting of the Council in each year practically at par.

These two mortgages will amount to................	$1,550,000
Amount to be provided for.........................	1,462,750
which will leave an unappropriated surplus of...... which it is believed will be sufficient to cover any deficiency which may occur from loss of income during the first two or three years of the occupancy of the new Club House.	$87,250

The estimates of probable receipts and expenditures have been mislaid, but as the result hereinafter to be more particularly set forth shows, these estimates were proved to have been conservatively based on trustworthy data.

At this stage of the proceedings, a very important consideration was the feasibility of admitting a large number of the candidates on the waiting list, in time to make their initiation fees and annual dues operative as a part of the resources of the Club, without such haste as to involve the slightest modification of the care bestowed on the selection of members by the Committee on Admissions.

A special committee, therefore, was appointed by the Council at its meeting in March, 1897, to wait on the Committee on Admissions and confer with them on this subject. This committee consisted of Messrs. Barney, Blagden, and Alexander.

The Committee on Admissions heartily entered into the spirit of the undertaking, and for several years devoted themselves with assiduity to the work. Although they multiplied their meetings at great personal sacrifice, they did not in the slightest degree modify the care with which they had been accustomed to investigate the fitness of every candidate. The effect of this praiseworthy thoroughness was that it was impossible to admit members from the waiting list as rapidly as the advance estimates of probable new members had predicted, and in this respect alone the prognostications of the Club authorities were disappointed. This partial failure, however, was a distinct advantage, inasmuch as the temptation to overhaste in selection was resisted, and in the end the financial scheme in no way suffered, for, as will be seen later, the remarkable prosperity of the Club in its new quarters was such as to enable the Council year after year to reduce the mortgage indebtedness out of surplus earned.

The Report of the Building Committee was adopted by the Council March 8, 1897, and the plans approved.

At the annual meeting of the Club in March, 1897, the President made an extended and particular statement of the steps taken by the Council to carry out the wishes of the Club in regard to the purchase of the land and the erection of the building, including the approximate ultimate cost, the methods of raising the money, and the possibility of an increase in annual dues after the completion of the building. The President also called the attention of the Club to the plans of the proposed Club House which were exhibited on the walls of the café. No formal action was requisite, but the assent of the Club was indicated by the fact that no objection or criticism was made.

The Building Committee, being authorized thereto by the Council, passed the following resolution, March 18, 1897.

Resolved, That the Chairman of this Committee be, and he hereby is, empowered to close the contract with Mr. Charles T. Wills, of New York, to build the new building, as per plans and specifications, including the cellar and basement of annex, for an upset price of $760,000, said sum to include Wills' compensation of $25,000. Said Wills also agrees to give to the Club the benefit of any reductions or savings he may be able to make in placing the subcontracts, and also to submit all the contracts to the Architects and this Building Committee for approval.

On the 31st of March, 1897, the Council authorized a mortgage of the Club property to the Equitable Life Assurance Society of the United States, for $1,250,000 at 4½ per cent interest, and coupon bonds of the Club for $350,000 at 5 per cent interest secured by a second mortgage.

One of the conditions of the first mortgage was that after a certain date, $50,000 was to be paid each year until the principal was reduced to a sum equal to one-half the value of the property. The success of the Club was such that three annual payments on account of principal of $50,000 each were made, reducing the amount of the mortgage in 1905 to $1,100,000, at which figure it now stands. In December, 1905, a communication was received by the Council from the Equitable Life Assurance Society of the United States, the mortgagee, stating that the Club property was then worth more than double the amount of the first mortgage, and that therefore further payment on account of principal would not be required. As a matter of fact its value is still greater than the mortgagee conceded in 1905.

The authorities of the Club having authorized an issue of $350,000 bonds to be secured by a second mortgage on the ground and building at the corner of Fifth Avenue and 54th Street, an invitation to the members was extended by the Building Committee on April 2, 1897, as follows:

To the Members of the University Club in the City of New York:

Gentlemen:—

As indicated at the Annual Meeting of the Club on March 20th, you are now invited, under the authority of the Council of the Club, to subscribe to the issue of Three Hundred and Fifty Thousand Dollars Bonds of the Club, to be secured by a Second Mortgage on the land and building of the Club, at the north-west corner of Fifth Avenue and Fifty-fourth Street.

The total value of the property, when completed, will be approximately Two Million Dollars. The only lien prior to the Second Mortgage will be the First Mortgage, which will not exceed two-thirds of the value of the property and will bear four and one-half per cent interest. The Second Mortgage Bonds will bear five per cent interest, payable semiannually.

These bonds will mature at the end of twenty years, with the privilege to the Council to pay the same before maturity, in instalments, as follows: At the expiration of five years from the date fixed for the final payments of subscriptions to these bonds, there shall be a drawing of bonds, under the direction of the Council of the Club, of not less than fifteen thousand dollars in amount, and the principal with accrued interest on such drawn bonds shall be paid to the holders thereof under conditions and in a manner to be prescribed by the Council. Similar drawings shall follow annually until all of the bonds are paid off.

The mortgage to secure these bonds will be made to the Central Trust Company of New York, which will act as Trustee for the same.

The bonds are to be issued in denominations of $1,000 and $500, and the coupons upon the same will be receivable by the Club for dues.

Subscriptions for these bonds will be payable to the Club in two instalments of fifty per cent each. The first instalment will be payable on or after the first day of August, 1897, notice thereof in writing to be given to the subscribers. The remaining fifty per cent of principal will become payable on or after January 1st, 1898, notice of the same to be given to subscribers in writing. Interest on first instalments of $500 bonds will be adjusted when the final payments are made.

In cases of subscriptions for one $500 bond a certificate will be issued for the first instalment of fifty per cent, and the bond will be delivered on the completion of the payment of principal. In cases of subscriptions for $1000 or multiples thereof, complete bonds for one-half of the amount subscribed will be delivered on the making of the first payment.

In case the bonds are over-subscribed the Council reserves the right to apportion the bonds, and the method of dealing with subscriptions which may not be paid within the time required will be prescribed by the Council.

The books for subscription to these bonds will be kept open until April 20th, 1897, when they will be closed unless, by special order of the building Committee, more time shall be given.

It is suggested that the subscription for these bonds be made very general, as an indication of the interest of the members in the success of the movement. Prompt replies to this circular are requested in order that the financial scheme of the Club may be closed without unnecessary delay.

Enclosed herewith is a blank form for subscription which the members of the Club are requested to use, forwarding the same to Charles T. Barney, Chairman of the Building Committee, at the Club House, Madison Avenue and Twenty-sixth Street. Members who have heretofore expressed their willingness to subscribe to bonds are requested to confirm such agreements formally on the enclosed blank.

Respectfully yours,

CHAS. T. BARNEY, *Chairman*,
DAVID L. HAIGHT,
HUGH D. AUCHINCLOSS,
CHARLES L. ATTERBURY,
JAMES W. ALEXANDER,
Building Committee.

UNIVERSITY CLUB,
New York, April 2d, 1897.

The good will of the Club membership was evinced at the time the financial arrangements were in progress looking to the building of the house, by the fact that $400,000 was promptly subscribed to the proposed issue of second-mortgage bonds. The Council, however, limited the amount to $350,000, and as a matter of fact the Club found it necessary to sell these bonds only to the amount of $261,500, and as early as 1906 a call was authorized by the Council for $30,000 of the same, to be drawn by lot in accordance with the terms of the loan. In March 1914 there were still, outstanding of this debt, bonds to the amount of $131,500.

In 1906 an agreement was made with the Equitable Life Assurance Society of the United States extending the first mortgage, at 4½ per cent interest, with the privilege of paying instalments of not more than $50,000 each on interest days.

It was a part of the scheme of the new Club House that the dues of resident members should later on be increased to $75, and of non-resident members to $35. With the tremendously enlarged conveniences to be afforded to members, it was confidently believed that this slight increase would be heartily approved by those who were to enjoy them; and such proved to be the case. At the annual meeting in February, 1899, the constitution was amended so as to accomplish this change by a vote of 123 to 12, a decided evidence of satisfaction with the management, when compared with the overwhelming majority by which the same proposition was voted down some years before.

The University Club certainly has just ground for congratulation, in that its business management has been such that comparison with any other known club in this respect can only emphasize its success.

Its comforts and conveniences are not excelled in any other quarter. No social club possesses such a library or has such a comprehensive list of periodicals both domestic and foreign.

It is the only first-class club in the city of New York whose annual dues are under $100; others of like character being $125 or more.

The Club's income in 1880, the first year of its occupancy of the Caswell house at Fifth Avenue and 35th Street, was $102,904.30, including entrance fees of $39,600, while its outgo was $77,519.62. In the year 1913–14 its receipts were $519,579.24 and its expenditures $499,545.42.

These remarks are made in no boastful spirit, but in a compilation intended chiefly to supply information to the members of the Club it seems proper that the prosperity enjoyed by them should be clearly indicated.

CHAPTER XIII

THE FIFTH AVENUE CLUB-HOUSE—1899

THE beautiful and commodious building of the University Club was, in the manner heretofore described, thus conceived and perfected. It was first occupied in the year 1899, the formal opening taking place on the seventeenth day of May in that year. The newspapers of New York spread upon their columns conspicuous notices of the event, with descriptions of the house and its contents together with pictorial views. Terms such as "splendor" and "gorgeous" abounded in the public accounts, and the approval of the result both as to equipment and architectural taste was general.

Of the many fine examples of the architectural skill and taste of that charming and gifted member of the Club, Charles F. McKim, the University Club is certainly one of the most successful. His partner Stanford White had given a distinguished proof of his ability in the design and interior construction and embellishment of the Metropolitan Club Building, at the corner of Fifth Avenue and 60th Street. A more beautiful edifice of its character does not exist among modern buildings. It was for Mr. McKim to produce a structure totally different in conception and style, and yet of equal excellence in every respect. The problem was a more difficult one than White's, for the reason that a house really consisting of nine stories—a height made necessary by the requirements of the Club—was to be so constructed as to conceal this fact, and to present a graceful façade with proportions to satisfy the fastidious eye. The testimony to the success of the undertaking was almost if not quite universal.

In one of a series of articles in *Harper's Magazine*, by Arnold Bennett, entitled "Your United States," occurs the following paragraph:

> One afternoon I was driving up Fifth Avenue in the company of an architectural expert, who, with the incredible elastic good nature of American business men, had abandoned his affairs for half a day in order to go with me on a voyage of discovery, and he asked me, so as to get some basis of understanding or disagreement, what building in New York had pleased me most. I at once said the University Club—to my mind a masterpiece. He approved, and a great peace filled our automobile, in which peace we expanded. He asked me which building in the world made the strongest appeal to me, and I at once said the Strozzi Palace at Florence.

There are many who consider the University Club the best of Mr. McKim's marvellous creations, and in giving him the credit it must not be forgotten that he had the aid, advice, and support of his accomplished partners, Stanford White (N. Y. Univ. '81)—himself without a superior; William R. Mead (Amherst '67), now the sole survivor of the trio and the present head of the firm of McKim, Mead & White; and William M. Kendall (Harvard '76). To both of these last named the compiler of this volume owes much for valuable information. McKim also had the backing of Charles T. Barney (Williams '70), Chairman of the Building Committee, whose cultivated taste, experience in construction and interior furnishing, coupled with a warm enthusiasm for the particular work, made him pre-eminently the man for the hour, and the practical assistance of Doctor David L. Haight (Yale '60), then Chairman of the House Committee.

No wonder, then, that the appreciation of the Club for the satisfactory result led the members after the completion of the building to pass the following resolution, in which they courteously coupled the name of a former officer of the Club who could and would not claim to be deserving of it:

THE STROZZI PALACE, FLORENCE.

Resolved, That the Club having received and accepted the report of the Building Committee, desires by resolution to express on its records that it congratulates the Building Committee and its Chairman, Mr. Barney, and the Chairman of the House Committee Dr. Haight, and our former President Mr. Alexander, that under very difficult situations, they have completed and furnished this Club House substantially within the limits of original estimates and with the general approval and to the great satisfaction of the members of the Club; and the Club knows that this result can only have been attained with the wise expenditure of much time and labour by them, for all of which it gives them its appreciative thanks.

The financial result, reported by the Building Committee, in 1899, was as follows:

Original estimate	$2,019,000.00
Reductions and economies	19,246.72
	1,999,753.28
Additional expenditures [details given]	44,003.50
Making total cost	2,043,756.78

being $24,756.78 in excess of the original estimate. The excess was much more than covered by items deliberately added to the original conception, and which might have been omitted without essential detriment to the plan as laid out. They were in the nature of luxuries, and should not be considered in comparing the result with the estimated cost.

The Council in 1902 directed "that a tablet be placed in the Club House in honour of the Building Committee" and further ordered that "some suitable memorial" be presented "to Mr. Charles T. Barney, the Chairman of the Building Committee, and to the other members . . . as a tribute to the value of their services in the construction of the Club House."

At a later date, as recorded in the minutes of the Council, "the President then made an address of presentation, and presented a memorial to Mr. Charles T. Barney, . . . which was duly acknowledged by him. The President made a further presentation to . . . the other members of the Building Committee."

These memorials consisted of bronze medals, facsimiles of which are shown in the illustrations.

Those who were not intimately concerned with the execution of the project can hardly realize the extent of the obligation of the Club to the three men whose names formed the familiar firm title of "McKim, Mead & White." They were all members of the Club, and the compiler remembers distinctly seeing these three men at the old house on 26th Street enjoying together the relaxation of a game of pool. This friendly intimacy on their part was only an indication of the harmony with which they pulled together. With their partner—also a member of the Club—Mr. William Mitchell Kendall, and others of their extensive office organization; with Barney, the ideal Chairman of the Building Committee; with Doctor David L. Haight, acknowledged in his day to be *facile princeps*, as an expert in the conduct of the Club; with Charles T. Wills as the builder, the Club was fortunate enough to have a combination of talent unsurpassed, and the loyal pride of the members named in the achievement of brilliant results had much to do with the ultimate success of the undertaking, distinguished as it was among all similar attempts.

In a work intended to be a record, it is fitting that a complete description of a creation which is a monument not only to the skill and devotion of the members who conceived and executed it but of the noble purposes of the chief representative social organization of scholarly men, should be included and preserved.

The compiler is indebted for the following particulars to the kindness of Mr. William Mitchell Kendall, who took an active part in the construction.

MEDAL PRESENTED TO THE BUILDING COMMITTEE IN CHARGE OF THE ERECTION OF THE CLUB HOUSE, 1896–1900.

The University Club is a rectangular building 100 feet wide, 140 feet long, and 122 feet from the ground to the top of the cornice. The material of the building is Milford granite, a stone admirably adapted to the character of the architecture. The main façade, upon which is the entrance, is situated on 54th Street, the other façade on Fifth Avenue.

Within, the arrangement in general consists of alternate high and low stories, there being three high stories, two mezzanines, and a low story at the top. The motive of the façade is based upon this division of stories within. The entrance floor, containing the central hall and lounging-rooms of the Club, is lighted by a row of lofty arched windows. Then, succeeding a mezzanine story, comes another row of round arched windows lighting the third story, mainly devoted to the library. Above that occurs again a row of small windows lighting another mezzanine floor, devoted also to bedrooms, and then the third row of large windows lighting the floor devoted to dining-rooms. Above that, the small windows in the frieze light a row of small private dining-rooms on the Fifth Avenue side of the building. The division of the façade is accordingly in three great divisions, each containing a row of large windows surmounted by a row of small.

The general style of architecture used is that of Florence, of the fifteenth century. The whole building is rusticated, the rustication decreasing in relief at each main division. The arches of the large windows have keystones, decorated with heads, classic in character, the work of Niehaus, and consisting of satyrs, nymphs, and the like.

Between the small windows of the two mezzanine floors, are sculptured in Knoxville marble the shields of the various colleges represented in the Club, carved in high relief, and flanked with ornamental borders. Beneath each shield is an inscription recording in Latin the college of which the shield is the emblem. These forms of shields with inscriptions beneath were common in the decorative details of the Italian

Renaissance, and are to be seen frequently in Italy, notably in the court of the Bargello in Florence.

The central arch on the street side, which forms the main entrance to the building, is enclosed in a frame formed by a highly decorated Doric order. The arch over the entrance has a coffered vault ornamented with rosettes, and the keystone is decorated with the head of Minerva, the work of Niehaus. The columns are divided into drums, alternately of decorated flutes and bands ornamented with foliage, in which occur the monogram of the Club, and the initial letters of the various universities and colleges. The entablature is adorned with the usual triglyphs, metopes, and mutules, modified and enriched to harmonize with the ornamented columns.

At the level of the first ornamented string-course above the first mezzanine story, four granite balconies occur, one long one on Fifth Avenue and three short ones on the street. These balconies have railings of bronze, the motive consisting of panels enclosing pierced acanthus scrolls.

At the level of the second string-course, two other smaller balconies occur, opening from the dining-room floor, one on each façade, of a similar design to those below.

The corners of the building are strengthened by rusticated piers reaching from the bottom to the top of the building, and the crowning cornice is ornamented with dentils, eggs and darts, brackets and lions' heads, a type of cornice used during the Italian Renaissance, and based remotely upon the cornice of the temple of Mars Ultor, at Rome. Beneath the cornice is the narrow ornamented frieze referred to above, in which occur the small windows lighting the private dining-rooms.

In addition to the shields of the universities and colleges, a larger shield, placed above the central window of the library, and over the main entrance, bears the arms of the Club, the motive being a representation of two young men grasping one another by the hand in token of their friendship, and in the presence of a figure of Minerva standing on a pedestal in the background. The shield is surmounted by the motto of the Club. The sculpture on the shield in low relief is the work of Kenyon Cox.

Interior

The first floor of the Club is occupied by the central hall, the lounging-room occupying the whole of the Fifth Avenue front on one side and the office and café on the other side. The hall is the central point of the Club, and the same arrangement of hall and surrounding rooms recurs on the next full story, that is, the library story. The hall is square in plan, and has a vaulted ceiling, supported by Connemara marble columns and piers, the latter forming a sort of peristyle. Around the peristyle runs an aisle with a somewhat lower vaulted ceiling, and from this aisle the doors open into the surrounding apartments. The material used in this hall is entirely marble and mosaic. The columns of the peristyle are echoed on the walls of the aisle by pilasters of the same Connemara marble, and the architraves of the doors are of white marble. Between the pilasters are introduced panels of mosaic of several different colors, harmonizing with the green of the Connemara and the white of the cornice and door architraves. The floor is laid out in panels of Italian and Vermont marbles, with insertions of foreign marbles. Immediately opposite the entrance is a fireplace, of which the main architrave around the opening is an antique. The sculptured panel above is by the well-known sculptor, Charles E. Keck, who has taken his idea from the Club shield, before mentioned, but has presented it in an entirely original way.

The figure of Athene in the centre and slightly in the rear is altogether different from the statuette on the shield, but expresses the same idea. The two men with clasped hands, symbolizing friendship, and the torch of learning are introduced in this panel, as they are in the shield, and while the treatment is different the artistic result is admirable and the freedom from mere repetition commendable.

Over the doors to the east and west, leading respectively into the lounging-room and the office, are placed reproductions of the well-known wreath and eagle, a Roman fragment from Trajan's Forum which is now in the portico of the Church of SS. Apostoli, in Rome. Worthy of note in the hall are the candelabra designed after an antique pattern by Edward F. Caldwell. From the hall we pass through three portals into the main lounging-room on Fifth Avenue. This room occupies the full length of the Fifth Avenue façade. The room is treated in a style based upon that of the large state apartments in the Roman Renaissance palaces. The architectural scheme consists of walls decorated with pilasters reaching from the floor to the entablature, with the arched windows in between on the avenue and street sides, and on the hall side three round arched doorways to the hall, elaborately carved, with marble door architraves. The pilasters and woodwork are of Italian walnut, the wall space being covered with a deep-toned red velvet. The architraves of the doors and of the two mantelpieces are of Numidian marble. The pilasters bear a richly decorated entablature and panelled ceiling heavily gilded, and with marble panels introduced into the frieze. Spaces are left for future decorative paintings. On the opposite side of the hall, at the southwest corner of the building, is situated the café, treated in wood and leather.

At the northwest corner of the building are the main staircase and the elevator. The main staircase is in no sense a grand staircase, the elevator being the chief means of access to the succeeding stories. The omission of the usual grand staircase, treated in a monumental way, facilitated greatly the planning of the building, and is a recognition of modern conditions and the introduction of the elevator. Above this

From a photograph, by Tebbs, New York.

THE MAIN HALLWAY LOOKING NORTH.

principal floor occurs the first mezzanine, containing bedrooms and bathrooms, and above that comes the second full floor, occupied by the library, reading and writing rooms, and card-room. The central space of this floor is occupied by the hall, mentioned above, of the same dimensions as on the first floor, but treated in a Pompeian manner, with highly colored columns and walls, the main vertebræ of the architecture being ivory-toned, with a background of panels in rich reds and russets, enlivened with little figure subjects. The same disposition of central space, peristyle, and aisle occurs as on the first floor. Two niches contain statues, reproductions of the antique. The central door on the south leads into the main library, which will be described in the later chapter on the library.

The central door on the eastern side of the hall leads into the magazine-room, situated on the centre of the façade on the Fifth Avenue side. This room has a richly decorated ceiling, consisting of a segmental vault with penetrations. The ceiling, pending its final decoration, is left of a warm ivory tone, and the walls are of buckram, divided into panels, painted and decorated. The color systems of the hall and the magazine-room were done with the collaboration of Elmer E. Garnsey. From the magazine-room and the hall one enters into the northerly room on the Fifth Avenue side, a large room covered with a groined vault.

The second mezzanine floor, immediately succeeding the library floor, contains a small room in the northwest corner of the Club, called the "pipe-room," which has a beamed ceiling and wainscoting, and a mantelpiece in the Dutch style. It also contains a room partly used at present to house the College Memorabilia collections. Above that floor comes the third main story, namely, the dining-room floor. Here, too, a central hall of panelled oak, with a flat ceiling with panels in low relief, gives access by three portals to the main dining-room, occupying the entire length of the 54th Street façade.

This room, which is 33 feet high and 136 feet long, is entirely of English oak. The room is divided into three compartments, the long central division of the full height, and the two end ones, with a lower ceiling, occupying the end bays of the façade, and separated from the main division by a screen of two columns. The walls are treated with pilasters and columns of oak, with panels and the arches of the windows in between. On the long side, opposite the windows, the window arches are repeated with circular lunettes containing round panels with elaborately carved ornamentation around them, designed for and partly occupied with paintings. The columns and pilasters support the main entablature and deep attic, which in turn supports a richly ornamented and gilt ceiling based on Venetian precedent. Here the panels are also left for future paintings. The engaged columns at the entrance support a balcony for musicians. The attic is treated with decorative pilasters and panels, with here and there unusually fine specimens of animals' heads. The two mantelpieces at either end of the dining-room are antiques. The floor of the apartment is made of Istrian stone.

Worthy of note also are the lighting brackets on the engaged columns of the entrance, and also the two great chandeliers, all of which were designed after old models by Edward F. Caldwell. The northwest corner of this floor is occupied by the Council-room, often used also for private dinners (in which the portrait of Henry H. Anderson (Williams '48), the first President, was in 1913 inset as a part of the mantel design), and an adjoining anteroom (in which hang the portraits of ex-presidents of the Club). The Council-room is finished in Italian walnut, with a coved decorated ceiling. The treatment of the walls consists of Doric pilasters with intervening panels of wood and mirrors, the chimney breast being carried to the ceiling, and surmounted by elaborate wood-carving. The cove of the ceiling is divided into lozenge-shaped panels, containing figures reproduced from the antique, on a blue

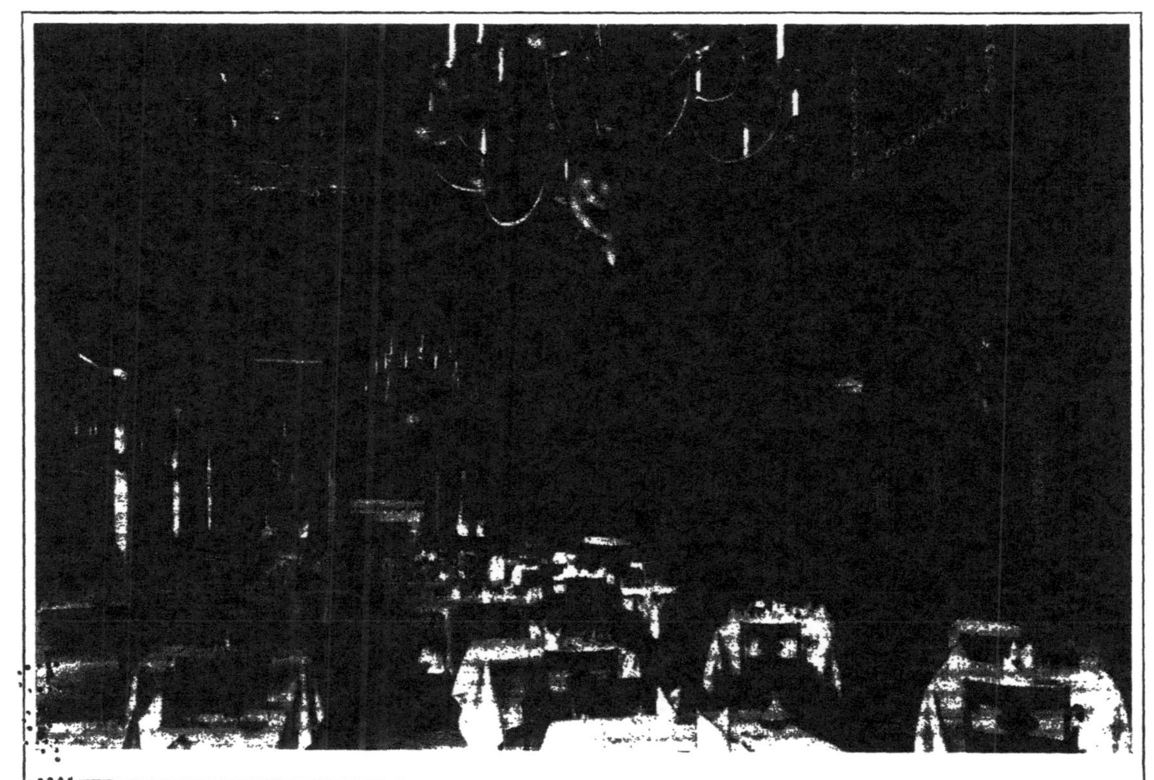

From a photograph, copyright by Sidman, New York.

THE MAIN DINING-ROOM, PANELLED THROUGHOUT IN ENGLISH OAK.

Length, 135 feet. Height, 37 feet. Width, 33 feet.

ground, the ribs and other architectural members of the ceiling being picked out in gold and color. The color system here was made in collaboration with H. Siddons Mowbray. He also executed the paintings for the large oval-shaped panel occupying the main field of the ceiling, and the smaller panel over the fireplace. These panels are surrounded with heavily moulded and decorated frames.

The northwest portion of the building throughout is occupied by the service portion of the Club, the kitchen being in the upper story, and is so located as to be equally accessible to the main dining-room and the private dining-rooms above. The portion of the upper story, lighted by the windows in the frieze on the Fifth Avenue end, is occupied by a suite of these private dining-rooms, designed by William Francklyn Paris. The elevator and staircase continue from this floor to the roof-garden, where a loggia of latticework in the centre of the roof space allows of the partaking of refreshments.

Returning to the first floor of the building, we descend by a staircase to the basement, which is occupied by the heating and lighting plant on the street side, and on the Fifth Avenue side by a swimming-pool, and all of the accessories of a full Turkish bath. The swimming-pool itself is forty-eight feet long and seventeen feet wide, and is built of white marble. The sides are of white glazed brick.

CHAPTER XIV

OPENING OF THE NEW CLUB-HOUSE—THE COLLEGE SEALS ON THE EXTERIOR OF THE CLUB-HOUSE

INASMUCH as the premises occupied by the Club at the corner of Madison Avenue and 26th Street were to be vacated before the first day of May, 1899, and some time was required for the removal to and installation of the Club in its new building at Fifth Avenue and 54th Street, the Council gave notice to the members that the old Club House would be closed on April 26, and that on the last night of occupancy —the 25th—a "club night" would be held. This plan was carried out, and the evening was characterized by good companionship and orderly jollification.

During the necessary hiatus the members were tendered and enjoyed the hospitalities of the following New York clubs: Metropolitan, Union League, Century, Calumet, Lotus, New York, Riding, Racquet and Tennis, Hamilton, Players', Harvard, Transportation, Aldine, Engineers', Democratic, and Manhattan.

The new Club House was opened for the use of members on Wednesday evening, May 17, at nine o'clock. Supper was served, and there was a large attendance.

Before opening the Club, the Council considered the question as to whether the bedrooms should be in any cases let to members for continuous use, and after coming to a conclusion instructed the Secretary to assign by lot four living-apartments in the new Club, to be rented permanently, and expressed the opinion to the House Committee that so far as

VIEW OF THE MAIN DINING-ROOM, LOOKING EAST.

practicable rooms should be primarily for the use of transient members. The four suites were thus assigned.

One was and still is occupied by the Honorable William Williams (Yale '84), former United States Commissioner of Emigration and now Commissioner of Waterworks of New York City, and another by Mr. John F. Talmage (Yale '95). A third was occupied but afterward vacated and never re-assigned. The fourth was and is occupied by Doctor David L. Haight (Yale '60).

With these exceptions the living-rooms are let exclusively to transient members, the rule being that no member shall occupy any room more than twenty days in any calendar month, or more than fourteen days consecutively at any time.

This rule has worked well, and the demand is at times greater than the supply, notwithstanding the number of rooms available.

George Augustus Sala made the cynical observation that "a club is a weapon used by savages to keep the white woman at a distance." However apt this thrust may have been at the time when it was made, it would not stand criticism at the present day when women's clubs abound, and when more than one men's club has a department for the accommodation of the ladies of members' families.

Nevertheless, after careful consideration, the authorities of the University Club had come to the conclusion that a "ladies' annex," such as is in successful operation at the Metropolitan Club, would be an experiment of doubtful wisdom, and refrained from introducing this feature. It was, however, the desire of most of the members that ladies should have the opportunity to see the place where their fathers, husbands, brothers, and sons were to enjoy the privileges of this Club of college men. Accordingly, the new Club House was thrown open for inspection on Thursday afternoons in January, 1900, from 1.30 to 6 o'clock, for ladies and gentlemen; and on Thursday evenings in January, after 9 o'clock, for gentlemen only, on presentation of cards of invitation which, to the number of five for each occasion, were furnished to the members of the Club.

These afternoons and evenings were attended by crowds, among whom were literally thousands of women. Refreshments were served upon the order of members, and for once, at least, the fair sex held sway within the walls of this bachelor house of refuge.

At the time of the opening of the Club, of the "ladies' days," and for a considerable period thereafter, the dining-room and other parts of the house were superbly decorated by the hanging of rare and beautiful tapestries and draperies loaned by Mr. Stanford White from his remarkable collections. The walls of the large lounging-room at the front of the first floor were embellished by a collection of fine examples of paintings by old masters, generously loaned to the Club by Benjamin T. Cable (Univ. of Michigan '76). The necessary removal of most of these decorations created a void which in some measure was for a time filled by the increase in the number of portraits and the valuable paintings already mentioned as loaned by Mr. Talmage.

A most novel and interesting feature of the exterior ornamentation of the Club building was the carved "seals" or "coats of arms" of the universities and colleges introduced into the treatment of the stone façades. The idea having been suggested by Mr. McKim, and adopted by the Council, a committee was appointed consisting of Messrs. H. J. Hayden (Harvard '60), Chairman, Charles T. Barney (Williams '70), Henry E. Howland (Yale '54), Charles H. Russell (Harvard '72), and C. C. Cuyler (Princeton '79), "to consider and report to the Council the eighteen colleges selected as representative American colleges, whose seals shall be placed upon the new building, and also to report as to the order of their placement, after consultation with the architects and Building Committee."

From a photograph, by Tebbs, New York.

THE FIFTH AVENUE CLUB HOUSE, SHOWING THE EAST FRONT.

It was a delicate task which this Committee undertook, involving the selection of eighteen colleges out of the many which were represented in the membership of the Club. The duty imposed upon them was performed with the utmost care and with the wisest discrimination. Their report was made January 10, 1898. This report raised and discussed the question as to whether the numerical representation of the respective colleges in the membership of the Club should be the criterion for selection, or whether the age of the institutions should govern, or yet again whether discretion should be used as to importance. The Committee recommended the order in which the seals should be placed on the building, and advised that the lower row of four seals on the 54th Street front should be considered the principal row; the lower row of four on the Fifth Avenue front the second in importance; the upper row of six on 54th Street the third; and the upper row of four on Fifth Avenue the fourth.

This report and its conclusions were thoroughly discussed at the meeting of the Council of January 10, 1898, and the opinion prevailed that it would not be advisable to run the risk of offending the susceptibilities of the graduates of any college by the use of discretion in selection, which course might lay the Council open to the charge of unwise discrimination, and that the only proper course to be pursued was to adopt a category and take the colleges falling within it, without regard to other considerations, no matter how strongly they might appeal to some. They therefore passed the following resolution:

Resolved, that precedence should be given to those colleges having the largest numerical representation in the Club.

This rule was carried out and resulted in the selection of the following colleges:

Yale, Harvard, Princeton, Columbia, Williams, Amherst,

Cornell, Pennsylvania, Dartmouth, Union, Brown, Rutgers, Hamilton, College of the City of New York, New York University, Trinity, United States Military Academy, United States Naval Academy.

The question then arose as to how the carving of the seals was to be paid for, and the subject was referred to the Building Committee. On their recommendation it was determined that the membership from each college be called on to defray the expense of designing and cutting its seal, which it was estimated would average $900 in each case, and the artistic work involved in the preparation of designs for carving was assigned to the distinguished sculptor Daniel C. French.

The representatives of the various colleges who then undertook the collection of the necessary money from their fellow alumni were as follows:

	Representative of College
Princeton '79	Mr. C. C. Cuyler.
Yale '64	Mr. C. L. Atterbury.
Harvard '56	Mr. G. Blagden.
Columbia '81	Mr. H. Van Sinderen.
Columbia '75	Mr. G. Sherman.
Williams '76	Mr. A. H. Masten.
Amherst '67	Mr. W. R. Mead.
Cornell '75	Mr. Henry W. Sackett.
Pennsylvania '64	Mr. R. S. Hayes.
Dartmouth '79	Mr. C. M. Hough.
Union '52	Mr. S. B. Brownell.
Brown '70	Mr. A. Lincoln.
Rutgers '69	Mr. R. H. Robertson.
Hamilton '64	Mr. E. Root.
College of the City of New York '64	Mr. W. L. Bull.
New York University '75	Mr. J. S. Auerbach.
Trinity '85	Mr. Robert Thorne.
U. S. Military Academy '68	Mr. L. Farragut.
U. S. Naval Academy '67	Mr. J. W. Miller.

In the case of colleges having a large representation in the Club, the work of collecting was not onerous, but in those having a small representation it was naturally difficult, and sometimes impossible. After the lapse of time, during which the efforts made were exhaustive, the Club resolved in the general interest to assume the payment of the moderate amount uncollected, which was done.

The cost of the seals, which varied in the extent of detail, ran from a maximum of $1,157.17 to a minimum of $800. It is generally admitted that the unique addition of these academic insignia to the architecture of the Club's building not only gives dignity to the work and enhances the admirable effect, but contributes a scholarly flavor decidedly appropriate to the purposes of the structure.

It would seem quite a simple matter to procure from the various universities their respective shields (or coats of arms) with the appropriate mottoes. As a matter of fact, the task proved quite a complicated one, and the Building Committee, the architects, the sculptors, and the artist-designers were all put to infinite trouble, involving interviews and correspondence, to attain results satisfactory to all. As an illustration, a letter was written by a distinguished graduate of the United States Naval Academy to Mr. C. F. McKim on the question as to whether the words "Annapolis" and "West Point" should be placed underneath the seals of those institutions respectively, or whether Latin inscriptions should be preferred. The gentleman referred to expressed the opinion that the familiar English designations would be simpler and better. "They are schools of and for the people," he wrote, "and every one knows them as West Point and Annapolis, and the passer-by will immediately understand what is meant. Is it not more or less essential that the ordinary citizen who pays for West Point and Annapolis should not be struck dumb with too much dead language which he cannot understand? Otherwise, I am a trifle fearful that the Club may be put to the expense of keeping a Latin tutor permanently chained inside the railing on the Fifth Avenue side. But this, of course, is only the view of a rough sailor.

"However, I presume that there are architectural reasons why you wish the long and the Latin inscriptions, and therefore leave the whole matter in your hands."

As will be seen by the "ordinary passer-by," the "long and Latin" won out.

A Harvard graduate writes to Mr. McKim: "Has anybody told you that at the University Club—in the inscription on the Harvard seal, one word, viz. 'in,' has been omitted? Was this done purposely?"

A representative of Pennsylvania writes: "There is undoubtedly an error in placing an 'owl' in the Seal of the University of Pennsylvania, as it apparently existed in the imagination of the artist who brought out 'some of the arms of the Universities and Colleges 1897.' While it may be decorative, as you suggest in one of your letters, yet I do not believe that we have any right to change the seal which has existed since 1740, and after advising with other members of the University of Pennsylvania Committee, who furnished the money for the carving, I beg that you will alter the seal to correspond identically with that in use by the college."

Correspondence was had with an eminent member of the New York bar, an alumnus of Union University, as to the seal of that institution, the question having been raised as to whether the word "Sigillum" should be placed under the seal, in order to secure uniformity, the view of the alumnus evidently being that a legend (probably invented for the purpose) in the words "Universitas Concordiæ" would be more satisfactory.

A graduate acting for Princeton wrote: "First, the cutting should be made so much deeper as to emphasize the shield. Second, the shield is not of the shape which Princeton men regard as an essential characteristic. It has been rounded so as to follow the line of exterior ornamentation, whereas our shield is a pointed shield."

And later another graduate of prominence in Princeton af-

From a photograph by Alinari.

PALAZZO SPADA, ROME.

Used by Mr. McKim to reinforce his argument for the appropriateness of lettering with heraldic designs on the exterior of a building.

fairs wrote: "I am glad to hear that the Building Committee have decided to use the arms of Princeton University on the Club House and not to substitute therefor something different as was done last week."

There was hardly an instance in which points were not raised and in many cases there were actual differences of opinion to be adjusted, requiring the attention of the Building Committee, the architects, the sculptor, and the members of the various universities.

In one case, that of Annapolis, it was discovered that no seal or coat of arms existed, and the requirements of the University Club actually brought about the adoption for the first time of a suitable emblem.

There was more or less competition between naval men and architects as to the nature of this shield, one of the Annapolis graduates of high standing writing that "the so-called shield of the Navy Department" was probably handicapping the designers, which shield he describes as "an extremely ugly thing. It represents nothing, symbolizes nothing, and is trite and stupid like other Government things. Can we not have something original, even if we decide to keep the anchor and the stripes and stars? Making our shield in form of a Norseman's war shield? Put around it the emblems of the Anglo-Saxon's domination of the sea—the crest perhaps to be the iron beak of a Norseman's war galley. Such a Shield would if properly worked out be something with snap and character in it."

After protracted consultations, the Navy Department at Washington officially reported to Commander J. W. Miller (U. S. N. A. '67), of New York, representing the Annapolis members of the Club, the final adoption of the seal, and submitted the design which is now carved upon the walls of the Club. The following description of it was furnished by Commander Miller:

"The idea is to assert the equality of the Naval Academy

with any of the great colleges; and to distinguish it as an educational institution rather than as a mere part of the war material of the nation. One-third of its living graduates are in civil life; and membership in the Club which for the first time displays its seal beside those of the chief institutions of learning in the country on its building depends upon graduation from the Naval Academy as a college, and not in any wise upon the service of the graduate in the navy.

"The aim has therefore been to reach a design which will correspond in character to the seals of the colleges—that is, in which the form shall be classic and the nautical emblems of that type—rather than a grouping of patriotic features and the naval symbol in every-day use on buttons, buckles, and official badges generally. Eagles, anchors, guns, flags, rope, etc., have therefore been avoided. The trident, the ancient symbol of the sea power, is made prominent in the crest. The scholastic idea is indicated by the books. The motto 'Ex scientia tridens' ('Out of knowledge the sea power') is thought to indicate the specific characteristic of the Naval Academy which exists in order to educate the men by whom that power may be directly wielded. It is not merely the 'man behind the gun,' but the *educated* man behind the gun, who wins battles. This is what we should emphasize; not his patriotism or his weapons.

"The shield exhibits a Roman or Greek war galley, provided with the beak or ram bow, and the usual single low sail. The waves are conventionalized."

Confusion sometimes arose from the working of the various persons concerned at cross-purposes, and once the drawing of the cartouche for the University Club seal itself was lost, and the artist-designer, Kenyon Cox, was found disclaiming the possession of it, stating that he had had the cartmen of the Architectural League take it away and had "never heard of it since."

So it will be seen from these few examples out of many

how much labor had to be expended and how much time lost in what might appear to be one of the simpler departments of the important work of creating a structural monument to the achievements of the University Club, and the enormous detail involved in the whole undertaking may accordingly be inferred.

The greatest care was taken by those in charge to secure accuracy in the Greek and Latin inscriptions.

The difficulties concerning the seals did not end with the selection of the colleges and the determination as to their respective form and character. The members of the Council discovered on a certain day that a few of the shields had been embellished on the face of the building by lettering beneath them. On convening at their next meeting, the opinion was found to be quite unanimous that this feature was objectionable, whereupon the following resolution was passed November 14, 1898:

Resolved, that in the opinion of the Council the inscriptions which have been placed upon the façades of the new Club House, under the seals of Williams, Hamilton and Union, should be removed.

This was communicated to the architects, and Mr. McKim, meeting one of the Building Committee, expressed decided regret that such action had been taken; declared that the inscriptions were a material feature in his architectural scheme; and requested to be heard on the question.

Mr. McKim appeared personally before the Council February 13, 1899, and in his charming and persuasive way presented his views on the question. In support of his contention that lettering in carved stone on the exterior of famous ancient buildings was recognized as a material and appropriate architectural feature, he produced and exhibited photographs of many celebrated fronts, including the Palazzo Spada in Rome, a Roman structure in Taormina, the Porta del Popolo in Rome, the Fontana dell' Acqua Paola in Rome, and the Porta Maggiore in Rome. The following is a condensed account of his argument:

From the time of the earliest Egyptians, inscriptions, expressed in hieroglyphics, and, later, by lettering, in the time of the Greeks and Romans, and during the Italian Renaissance, were used, setting forth the meaning of whole buildings or their details, for the purpose of enhancing, explaining, enriching and adding dignity. The use of external inscriptions of this sort is constantly seen, not only in the needles and obelisks, but in the case of many monuments in Greece, in Athens, at Epidaurus and Olympia. The Romans everywhere depended upon the use of external inscriptions, as explanatory, either of the intention of the monument, or as recording events. The Triumphal Arches of Titus, Severus and Constantine, together with the theatres, temples and baths, abound in examples of great buildings adorned with inscriptions. In the time of the Renaissance, in Florence and Rome, there was hardly a building of consequence, whether public or private, in which large surfaces were not covered in this way. The Cancelleria, the Farnese, the Spada, the Massimi, the Giraud, attest the use of inscriptions of explanatory character, which the world today recognizes as scholarly attributes, adding dignity to their façades. Amongst such examples, the carved shields of the Palace of the Podesti in Florence is an example particularly in point, the legends being written beneath the shields, identical in treatment with those shown on the prospective drawing, accepted by the University Club, and would lose incalculably without their explanatory sentences.

In the use of shields, as architectural elements in the design of the University Club, and upon which it chiefly depends for its enrichment, we submit that the design, without the support of the lettering indicated, would deprive the building of an essential feature, upon which we have relied from the beginning, and upon which the building largely depends for any scholarly character which it may possess.

Convinced by Mr. McKim's argument, the Council forthwith conceded the point, and passed a resolution reversing their previous action, and authorizing the lettering, which

From a photograph by Alinari.

ANOTHER ANCIENT BUILDING SHOWING SEALS.

This also was used by Mr. McKim in reinforcing his argument for lettering with the seals on the Club House.

consisted of the names of the colleges and universities in Latin, under their respective shields, and which now appear, carved in the stone, on the Fifth Avenue and 54th Street façades of the building.

CHAPTER XV

THE UNIVERSITY CLUB SEAL—DEDICATION OF THE GRANT TOMB—ADMIRAL DEWEY—1897–1898

THE University Club had no official seal until the year 1883. At the meeting of February 5, in that year, the Secretary was "directed to procure a seal with the name of the Club in a circle with the date of incorporation in the centre." This modest seal was in use until the Club entered into the occupation of its new building, when the Council felt that it was due to the dignity of the organization that it should adopt one more distinguished in character and design and that it should bear a legend appropriate to its nature and purposes.

In 1898, therefore, the Committee on Literature and Art was requested to consider the subject and report. This committee was at the time composed of men well equipped for the duty, namely: T. Frank Brownell (Harvard '65), Charles H. Russell (Harvard '72), Henry Holt (Yale '62), Henry E. Howland (Yale '54), and Charles Scribner (Princeton '75). These gentlemen regarded the matter as of sufficient importance to justify great care and study, and the services of eminent experts in designing and carving were sought and obtained.

The first sketch submitted to the committee included among other things the figures of two young men in a rather nondescript—more or less barbaric—dress, of an ancient period, one or both of them holding spoon-oars. The motive was obviously to combine the ideas of friendship and athletics, as representative of college life. But the mingling of the modern with the antique was not satisfactory, and fresh drawings with different representations were obtained.

The design finally selected and approved by the Council was made by the well-known artist Kenyon Cox, and the scutcheon was modelled by George Brewster in strict accord with the original drawings. The result was highly satisfactory and was due not only to the skill of the artist, but to the advice of the committee and the architects, after much thought and study.

It was the general wish that the friendship which comes from association and a common interest should be represented, as well as the academic basis of the association and the sympathy of the members. Mr. Russell, who was always thorough and painstaking in all the many interests of the Club to which he lent his valuable services, had much to do with the development of the seal, and it is to him that the compiler owes much information in regard thereto. He states that in the consultations of the committee the expressions "friendship and letters" and "friendship and learning" were used as indicating the idea to be embodied in the design, and it will be seen that both in the emblematic figures and in the legend selected, this idea is most successfully set forth.

The design adopted, and which may be seen carved in stone on the 54th Street front of the building high up above the entrance, represents two Greek youths, their hands clasped in friendship. One of them holds a tablet bearing the word "Patria." The other holds a torch representing learning as well as eternity. The simile is derived from the old Greek race, in which the runner carried a torch burning, until he fell exhausted, when he handed it to another who took it from him and ran on, keeping the light burning until he in turn handed it to another, and so on. This is emblematic of the light of learning which each scholar keeps alive in his time and passes on to those who in turn do the same.

Behind the two youths is the Altar of Pallas Athene and upon it a small figure of that goddess, the deity represented in Greek mythology as presiding over Wisdom and Skill, or in other words the liberal arts and sciences; a happy emblem of the pursuits and aspirations of scholars. The particular figure of Pallas Athene was taken from an antique statuette belonging to the late Stanford White, and a photograph or drawing of it was shown to the committee.

The seal itself having been agreed upon, the Council proceeded to search for a suitable quotation from the classics for a motto to be inscribed upon it and be a part of it. Some of the scholars in the Club ransacked their memories and restudied their Latin and Greek. Letters were written to learned professors in various universities. Numbers of suggestions resulted. Among them all, the Council was disposed to select a quotation from the XLVIth Poem of Catullus—*Dulces Comitum Coetus*, meaning "Sweet is the Fellowship of Friends."

A learned member of the Council, however, made the criticism that there was an unfortunate ambiguity in the signification of the word *coetus* which might lead to misapprehension. Although the Latin professor who furnished the quotation proved quite clearly that the point was not well taken, the Council pursued the safe course and looked for another phrase. The one adopted was submitted by Professor Andrew F. West (Princeton '74), now dean of the Graduate School at Princeton, and was:

ἐν κοινωνίᾳ ἡ φιλία

The translation is, "In Fellowship Lies Friendship." The Greek is a quotation of Aristotle's definition of Friendship in the Eighth Book of his "Ethics." Dean West says: "The word *κοινωνία*, which is best translated *fellowship*, means a great deal more. It means the community of interest, the sharing of things with one another, the communion in things

From a photograph, copyright by Sidman, New York.

SEAL OF THE UNIVERSITY CLUB.

From a design by Kenyon Cox. Modelled by George Brewster in strict accord with the original drawing, and reproduced on the south front of the Club House.

intellectual,—and all the traits that peculiarly distinguish *college* friendships. The classics are not dead yet."

Before carving the motto on the Club's coat of arms, instructions were asked of Dean West as to the exact arrangement of letters and accents. He writes: "In small letters it is exactly as you have written it except that there should be an 'iota subscript' under the final vowel (the alpha) of *κοινωνίᾳ*. But the architects and the engravers of the arms and seal will probably insist on capital letters throughout. In this form it would read:

ΕΝ ΚΟΙΝΩΝΙΑΙ Η ΦΙΛΙΑ

"In using capitals the accents and breathings do not appear and iota subscript appears as a regular letter in the line."

As a matter of history the architects had the legend carved in small letters. This incident, at first sight of slight importance, is given to illustrate the care and pains devoted to every detail of the work on the building.

After the seal had been carved and put in place, namely, on April 7, 1900, the Council ordered a large photographic copy of it to be executed and sent to Dean West with the thanks of the Club, and at the May meeting President Beaman reported that he had enjoyed the pleasure of presenting the same to the dean, on the occasion of a dinner given to the Council at Princeton by the Princeton members of that body which was fully attended. While there the non-Princeton members were initiated into one or the other of the two historic literary societies, the "American Whig" and the "Cliosophic."

In order, so far as possible, to avoid disconnecting events coupled with others of earlier dates, the history necessarily makes leaps, leaving the thread of the general narrative to be picked up later. In this way we return to the year 1897.

The tomb of General U. S. Grant, placed on the commanding bluff at the northern extremity of Riverside Drive, in New York, was dedicated on the 27th day of April, 1897. This seventy-fifth anniversary of the birth of the hero of Appomattox was by act of the legislature made a public holiday. The event was celebrated with much ceremony. The Mayor of New York at the head of a committee of two hundred citizens spared no pains in making the day memorable. The United States Army, including the West Point cadets, to the number of five thousand, the National Guard of New York and other States, a vast representation of civic organizations, vessels of the North Atlantic fleet, and foreign men-of-war, took part in the pageant. President McKinley, Ex-President Cleveland, the diplomatic corps, and other dignitaries were present at the exercises. There was a brilliant reception at the Union League Club in the evening, and the celebration ended with a ball given by the city of New York.

The University Club as a national institution comprising in its membership many of the distinguished men who were prominent in signalizing the day, was not slow in performing its share in honoring the occasion.

At a meeting of the Council held April 12, 1897, the subject was considered and the intention unanimously expressed to support the movement in every feasible way. This desire took form at once in the direction to the House Committee to extend the courtesies of the Club to the foreign naval officers and the officers of the United States Army and Navy visiting New York to take part in the Grant Monument Dedication. This order was carried out with particular care.

Besides the naval and military officers, those invited to enjoy the hospitalities of the Club were the President of the United States, Ex-President Cleveland, the Vice-President, the members of the cabinet, the members of the United States Supreme Court, the diplomatic corps, the Speaker of the House of Representatives, the Governor of the State of

New York, the United States senators from New York, the whole of the numerous Grant family, and general officers who commanded armies during the Civil War. Committees were appointed to receive and welcome the foreign visitors, and all possible steps taken to make it evident that the University Club heartily seconded the movement in honor of the memory of the nation's famous dead.

General Horace Porter (U. S. M. A. '60), a member of the University Club, was President of the Monument Association, and delivered the oration of the day, and transmitted the tomb to the custody of the city. General Porter had been on the military staff of General Grant, and was his private secretary during his presidency. Since that time, General Porter has occupied positions of great national distinction, among which was that of United States ambassador to the court of France. General Wesley Merritt (U. S. M. A. '60), by virtue of his command of the Department of the East a member of the Club, was the head of the military contingent. General Frederick D. Grant (U. S. M. A. '71), son of General U. S. Grant, was at the time commissioner of police in the city of New York, and was a special guest of the Club. General Merritt died December 3, 1910. General F. D. Grant died April 11, 1912.

Among the members of the Club who were chief officers of the vessels of the United States Navy participating in the ceremonies were Silas Casey (U. S. N. A. '56), Captain of the flagship, *New York;* Walter Cleveland Cowles (U. S. N. A. '73), Lieutenant-Commander of the *Fern;* Henry C. Taylor (U. S. N. A. '63), Captain of the *Indiana;* John A. Rodgers (U: S. N. A. '68), Lieutenant-Commander of the *Indiana;* and Frederick W. Rodgers (U. S. N. A. '61), Captain of the *Massachusetts.*

In September, 1897, Mr. Charles Stewart Davison (Harvard '75) presented the Club with a fine mounted specimen of a tarpon, which was accepted by the Council with thanks. This great fish weighed one hundred and fifty-eight pounds and measured six feet six inches, and was caught March 21, 1897, on rod and reel, in thirty-five minutes, off Four Mile Island, Caloosahatchie, Port Meyers, Fla.

At a later date, namely in 1907, another excellent specimen was presented to the Club by W. W. Skiddy (Yale '65). This one was caught on the Panuco River, near Tampico River, Mexico, in February of that year.

Both these specimens hang in the anteroom of the dining-hall.

It was in the latter part of 1897 and the early part of 1898 that Mr. Anthony Hope Hawkins, the famous English author, was welcomed to the Club as a special guest. Among the archives is his letter of acknowledgment as follows:

EVERETT HOUSE, NEW YORK.

Mr. Anthony Hope Hawkins, on leaving America, desires to renew his very grateful thanks to the House Committee and the members of the University Club for their kindness in extending to him, so freely and for so long a period, the privileges of the Club, of which he has gladly availed himself.

THE HOUSE COMMITTEE
UNIVERSITY CLUB,
13th January, 1898.

The privileges of the Club were also in the same year extended to Admiral W. T. Sampson for himself and the officers of his fleet, after their signal operations in Cuban waters. The following is a copy of the admiral's acknowledgment:

U. S. F. S. "NEW YORK"
TOMPKINSVILLE, S. I.
August 20, 1898.

MR. JAMES R. SHEFFIELD,
UNIVERSITY CLUB.

Dear Sir:

I have your kind invitation to accept the privileges of your Club during the period of thirty days. I will send the invitation to the officers of the fleet; and I myself feel honored and gratified, and if opportunity permits, I will gladly accept.

Yours very sincerely, W. T. SAMPSON,
Rear Admiral, U. S. Navy.

On the night of the 15th of February, 1898, the battle-ship *Maine* was destroyed in the harbor of Havana. The fire of indignation which swept through the United States culminated in the declaration of war against Spain, on April 24, 1898.

In the conflict which ensued, members of the University Club were so conspicuous as to require a brief account of some of the incidents of that exciting period.

In the lounging-room of the old Club House in 26th Street a familiar figure was that of a naval officer who, when in the vicinity of New York, habitually used the Club for purposes of reading and relaxation. He was well known to many of the members and was a welcome comrade. Well "put up," quiet and courteous, he was highly regarded, but was by no means of the class who claim attention by aggressiveness or self-esteem. This man was Commodore (now Admiral) George Dewey (U. S. N. A. '56).

At the time of the declaration of war, Dewey was at Hong Kong in command of a small fleet consisting of the cruisers *Olympia*, *Baltimore*, *Raleigh*, and *Boston*, the gunboats *Concord* and *Petrel*, and the despatch-boat *McCulloch*. The British Government ordered this fleet to depart from the neutral port, which order was complied with. The last of the fleet left Hong Kong on April 26, 1898. Dewey, in pursuance of the command from Washington to attack the Spanish fleet at Manila, Philippine Islands, and "capture or destroy it," proceeded at once to carry out his instructions and on May 1 destroyed the entire Spanish fleet at Manila without the loss of a single life.

The despatch announcing this victory by one of our valued members is worthy of a place in a record of the Club's history. It was as follows:

MANILA, May 1—Squadron arrived at Manila at daybreak this morning. Immediately engaged the enemy and destroyed the following Spanish vessels: *Reina Christina*, *Castilla*, *Don Antonio de Ulloa*, *Isla de Luzon*, *Isla de Cuba*, *General Lezo*, *Marquis de Duero*, *Cano*, *Velasco*, *Isla de Mindanao*, a transport, and water battery at Cavite. The squadron is uninjured and only a few men are slightly wounded. Only means of telegraphing is to American Consul at Hong Kong. I shall communicate with him.

DEWEY.

This remarkably complete annihilation of the Spanish defences made the proclamation of the Governor-General of Manila, issued only a week earlier, appear in a ludicrous light. In this bombastic document the "North American people," as Governor-General Basilio Augustin Davila described the United States, were declared to be "constituted of all the social excrescences," and to have "exhausted our patience and provoked war with their perfidious machinations, with their acts of treachery, with their outrages against the law of nations and international conventions." "The struggle will be short and decisive!" exclaimed the governor-general in his pronunciamento. *And it was*, thanks to George Dewey of the University Club.

It is probable that the first message of congratulation sent from this country to Commodore Dewey and received by him was from his friends in the University Club. It was wired on the second day of May, 1898, and was as follows:

DEWEY, Manila (via London).

Hearty congratulations your splendid victory. Country admires your pluck entering harbor. All proud of you and your fleet.

UNIVERSITY CLUB.

As soon as the exigencies of the exciting situation permitted, Dewey sent the following autograph letter of acknowledgment to the Club:

FLAGSHIP "OLYMPIA,"
CAVITE, PHILIPPINES,
May 26, 1898.

DEAR SIR:

I heartily appreciate the telegram of congratulation which the University Club of New York did me the honor to send after the complete victory of May 1.

This telegram was read on the quarter-deck of all vessels of the squadron, with all hands at muster.

Again thanking the members of the Club for their kindly appreciation of our efforts,

I am

Very sincerely,

GEORGE DEWEY.

SECRETARY UNIVERSITY CLUB, New York.

CHAPTER XVI

SPANISH WAR AND CLUB MEMORIALS—ARMY AND NAVY MEMBERS—1898

On May 7, 1898, Secretary of the Navy Long cabled to Dewey thanking him in the name of the American people and appointing him acting admiral.

On May 9, Congress, by a rising vote in both houses, passed a resolution of thanks to Dewey and his officers and men, and appropriated $10,000 to present him with a sword, and medals to all under his command.

On the 11th he was nominated and confirmed rear-admiral.

On the 7th of March, 1899, he was created admiral of the United States Navy, which position he still holds.

In May, 1899, the Council by special resolution appointed Admiral Dewey to honorary membership in the Club during his active service.

The University Club having requested Admiral Dewey to accept a reception in his honor, he wrote the following reply:

FLAGSHIP "OLYMPIA"
At Sea,
July 3, 1899.

CHARLES C. BEAMAN, ESQ.
President University Club,
New York.

Dear Sir,

I have the pleasure to acknowledge the receipt of your letter of May 10th, enclosing the formal offer by the University Club of a reception at the Club House in my honor at such early date after my return to the United States as may be agreeable to me.

I need hardly tell you that I am much honored by this action of the Council, and appreciate the compliment at its full value. While my health was much impaired by my stay at Manila, and my great desire is to have rest and quiet, and I have therefore not accepted any invitations, rest assured that it would give me much pleasure to meet my friends of my own Club—the University. If I accept any invitations at New York, that of the University Club will be one of the first, if not the first.

Very sincerely,

George Dewey.

The proposed reception was not held, but in September, 1899, President Beaman reported that apartments had been offered to the admiral during his stay in New York.

On Friday, the 10th of June, 1898, under orders from Admiral Sampson, a landing-party occupied the western entrance of the bay at Guantanamo, Cuba. They were attacked, but routed the assailants with but small loss. But among the killed was John Blair Gibbs (Rutgers '78), son of Major Gibbs, one of the victims of the Custer massacre, and a member of the University Club.

On June 13, 1898, the Council adopted a resolution expressing the "profound sorrow" with which they had heard of the death of "our esteemed friend and fellow-member, Doctor John Blair Gibbs, a volunteer surgeon in the United States Navy, who gave up his life at the post of duty in the service of his country, at Guantanamo, Cuba, on the 12th inst., this record being made not only on account of the high regard entertained by all who knew him, but also to note as an important and solemn event in the history of the Club *this first instance during the present war of the death of a member of the Club in the service of his Country.*"

The roll of heroes in the conflict with Spain contained the names of many University Club men. A feeling of pride in their patriotic self-sacrifice and a sense of what was obviously fitting under the circumstances, led the Council at the same meeting of June 13, 1898, to pass a resolution remitting the payment of annual dues by "all resident and non-resident members actually engaged in the military and naval service of the United States, during the present war with Spain."

General Stewart L. Woodford (Columbia '54), a member of the University Club, was at the time of the breaking out of the war, ambassador of the United States to Spain, and it was he who had charge of the negotiations regarding Cuba preceding the rupture of relations, which terminated the efforts of President McKinley and Ambassador Woodford to reach a peaceable adjustment of differences. General Woodford was an eminent member of the New York bar; had been a colonel in the United States Army during the Civil War; was brevetted brigadier-general of volunteers, May 12, 1865, for "zeal, efficient and generally meritorious conduct"; was the first military commander of Charleston and Savannah; was Lieutenant-Governor of New York in 1866–1868; a member of Congress, and United States district attorney. After his ambassadorship he led the life of a retired gentleman, receiving honors on all sides, including the decoration of the Order of the Rising Sun by Japan and the Crown Order of the First Class by the Emperor of Germany.

In commenting on the resistless fury of the American people after the destruction of the *Maine*, which forced Congress to declare war, General Woodford told the compiler of this book that, intimately conversant as he was at the time with all the negotiations between the two governments, and therefore qualified to express an opinion, he felt sure that had the questions in dispute been left to diplomacy instead of being submitted to the arbitrament of war, a thoroughly satisfactory result would have been obtained without the loss of a single life or the sacrifice of a dollar of property.

General Woodford died February 14, 1913.

Among the officers of the United States Army and Volunteers who were engaged in the war in Cuba, who were members of the University Club, were General James H. Wilson

(U. S. M. A. '60) and General Francis Vinton Greene (U. S. M. A. '70), the former commander of the Sixth Army Corps, the latter colonel of the Seventy-first Regiment of New York National Guard. General Greene was later appointed major-general of volunteers and commanded a brigade of United States troops in the Philippines.

The University Club is justly proud of the achievements of its members, and the many who knew Lieutenant Cameron McR. Winslow (U. S. N. A. '75), now rear-admiral, were thrilled by an act of bravery on his part early in the Cuban campaign. Winslow is the son of the Winslow who commanded the *Kearsarge* when she sank the Confederate privateer *Alabama*, and therefore inherits the fighting spirit. It was determined by the United States naval authorities to cut the cables at Cienfuegos, Cuba, which formed the communication between Havana and Spain. On account of the exceptional danger involved, volunteers were called for, on May 11, 1898, to undertake the service. The entire force of all the ships volunteered and crowded one another to be chosen. A suitable number were selected, and Lieutenant Winslow was put in command. For two hours and a half Winslow stuck to his job, while the enemy on shore hailed bullets at them at short range, to such an extent that the water was splashed about the boats as in a thunder-squall. The water was clear and the cables were visible; otherwise the seizing of the wires would have been impossible. As it was, the work was most difficult on account of the heavy swell. One after another of the men engaged fell, struck by the bullets from the shore. It was the first time our men had been under fire that drew blood. Winslow did not leave the spot until he had successfully cut two cables. In reporting the "coolness and intrepidity" of his men, he only reflected his own courage. No single performance in the course of the war exceeded this in respect to persistent service of the highest importance under circumstances of the greatest peril. A section of the cable hangs, framed, in the west room of the Club library. It was presented by Ernest Carter (Yale '79) and bears the following inscription:

> Section of Sub-marine Cable cut (under galling fire) by Volunteer expedition led by Lieut. Cameron McR. Winslow, U. S. N. Cienfuegos, Cuba, May 11, 1898.

Admiral Winslow is (May, 1914) in command of a fleet in Mexican waters.

Two other grim mementos of the war stand in the "Pompeian Hall" on the library floor. They are framed metal plates over a yard square from two of the United States ships engaged in the destruction of Admiral Cervera's Spanish fleet, outside the harbor of Santiago, Cuba. They bear the following inscriptions:

Deck Plate
of
U. S. S. *Indiana*
Penetrated by Spanish shell
8½ inches diameter.
Presented by Officers of the *Indiana*

Coffer-dam Plate
from the
U. S. S. *Iowa*, Capt. R. D. Evans
Perforated by a shell from the Spanish
Fleet in the battle of July 3rd, 1898
off
Santiago de Cuba
Presented by Lieut. Comdr. R. P. Rodgers U. S. N.
to
The University Club.

The holes are jagged and vary from about a foot square to fourteen inches by six inches.

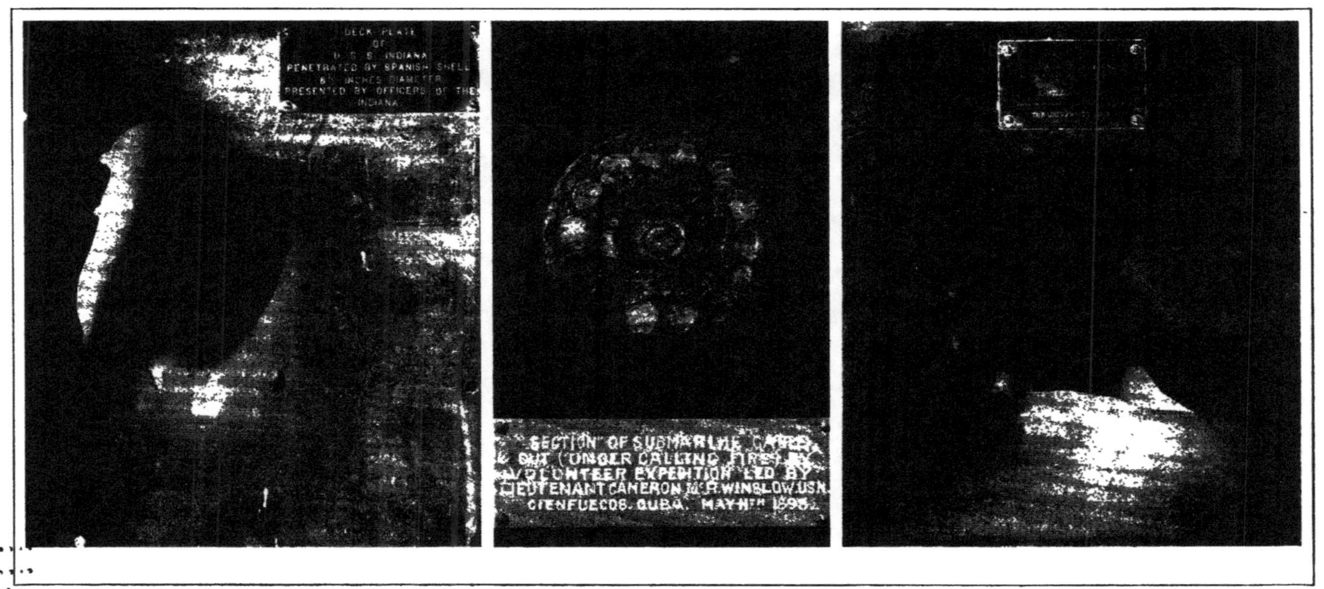

RELICS OF THE SPANISH-AMERICAN WAR.

Deck-plate of the *Indiana* and coffer-dam plate from the *Iowa*, penetrated by Spanish shells, battle off Santiago de Cuba, July 3, 1898. Section of submarine cable cut by an expedition led by Lieutenant (now Rear-Admiral) Cameron McR. Winslow.

Commander (now Admiral) Raymond P. Rodgers (U. S. N. A. '68), who presented the plate of the *Iowa*, was and is a member of the University Club, and was advanced five numbers in rank for "eminent and conspicuous conduct" in the battle which destroyed Cervera's squadron off Santiago.

The part played by members of the University Club in this naval battle, in which there were one killed and one wounded on the American side, and of the original Spanish force of 2,125 men 350 were killed, 160 wounded, and 70 officers and 1,600 men taken prisoners, is certainly worthy of reference in a history of the Club.

Admiral Robley D. Evans (U. S. N. A. '63), then captain of the *Iowa*, and Admiral Henry C. Taylor (U. S. N. A. '63), captain of the *Indiana*, classmates at Annapolis, are no longer alive, but their memory is cherished among their friends in the Club, as well as throughout the nation. Their ships at Santiago were (with the exception of the *Brooklyn*) the only ones of our fleet to be struck by the enemy's projectiles, showing that they were in the thick of the fight. Both were brave and able commanders, but in personality they were quite different. Evans was the personification of the bluff sailor. Taylor, on the other hand, suggested by his mien and carriage the kindly gentleman on shore. No two men were better known and liked in our Club than these.

Evans was born in Virginia in 1847. His mother was a sister of Jackson, who shot Colonel Ellsworth of the famous Zouave regiment for tearing the Confederate flag from the roof of his hotel in Alexandria, early in the Civil War. Known as "Fighting Bob," he was always on the alert in his naval career, but a quiet and inoffensive companion on shore. His readiness at Valparaiso, and his clearing of the Bering Sea of seal pirates, are familiar instances of his force and intelligence. He held many honorable positions and commanded other vessels than the *Iowa*. At one time at Santiago his ship engaged all the Spanish ships single-handed, their fire being concentrated on him as the most formidable antagonist. Later he commanded the great fleet of American war-ships when they started on their memorable trip around the world, during Colonel Roosevelt's administration. It may surprise some to know that the *sobriquet* "Fighting Bob" was not first applied to Admiral Evans. In the life of Commodore Robert F. Stockton, of New Jersey, *published in 1856*, occurs the following paragraph:

> The enjoyment which he seemed to derive from the perils of battle . . . won for him the significant sobriquet of "Fighting Bob."

Admiral Evans died January 3, 1912.

Taylor was not born immediately of fighting stock, but among his ancestors were Revolutionary officers. He was two years the senior of Evans. Once, before the war for Cuba, he had come into opposition with the Spaniards, having been sent to the Caroline Islands to protect American citizens from the oppressions of the soldiery of Spain. He was prominent in the organization of the Naval War College at Newport, R. I. In the fight at Santiago, Taylor's ship, the *Indiana*, was vigorously engaged with every one of the Spanish cruisers in succession. He was afterward in command of the North Atlantic squadron.

But the University Club was not without other distinguished naval members in the active conduct of operations during the Spanish War. Another notable example was Captain (now Admiral) French E. Chadwick (U. S. N. A. '64). Chadwick was captain of the *New York* during the Cuban campaign, besides being chief of staff to Admiral Sampson. Every one is familiar with the incident of the *New York*, with both Sampson and Chadwick, being temporarily absent from the immediate scene of conflict when Cervera's fleet was destroyed, which gave rise to the controversies about Admiral Schley and the extent of his credit for the victory. After the destruction of the *Maine*, Chadwick was a member of the board of inquiry into that disaster, which reported that the explosion which shattered the ship came from the outside. Admiral Chadwick has been an author as well as a sailor. Like the two others mentioned, he has been a welcome habitué of the University Club, when within convenient reach of it.

The limits of this volume preclude the mention of many other military and naval men who have done honorable service for the country and been valued comrades in our Club circle (see Appendix X), but it would clearly be a fault to omit reference to a Club member who has made himself known all over the world as the most authoritative writer on naval subjects living—Admiral Alfred T. Mahan (U. S. N. A. '59). Although he was retired from active service on his own application in 1896, his remarkable talents as a naval expert could not be spared by the government in times of stress. It is an interesting fact that he was born at West Point, his father, who was a West Point graduate, being at that time (1840) a professor in the United States Military Academy. Mahan inherited his gift as a writer, for his father had an international reputation for his text-books on engineering and other subjects. He was president of the Naval War College at Newport, R. I., and during the war with Spain was appointed a member of the naval war board at Washington, which directed the conduct of our campaign. It was in this capacity that he perhaps rendered the most important of his many services to his country. He was a delegate to the Peace Congress in 1899. Honorary degrees were heaped upon him by Oxford and Cambridge, England, Harvard, Yale, and other American universities. His literary works, which have been voluminous, have been almost exclusively on naval subjects, and have been universally recognized as of immense importance. Admiral Mahan is living in New York City, and the University Club Library has been to a considerable extent his workshop. For a time he served on the Library Committee of the Club, and gave it the benefit of his wide knowledge.

Admiral Henry Erben (U. S. N. A. '49) was (especially during the years of his retirement, from 1894 to the time of his death, October 23, 1909) a frequent habitué of the Club. He was a sailor of the old school, bluff and imperious when on duty, but a hearty and enthusiastic companion among his friends. He was with Farragut in the Gulf squadron in 1860, and commanded the *Pensacola* in a cruise around the world.

In 1894 he visited England, in command of the European squadron. His flag-captain was Mahan. The English were then very much taken with Mahan's book on sea power, and gave him a dinner at St. James's Hall, at which, of course, Erben was a guest. It was in the speech that Erben made on this occasion that he used the phrase, now become famous, "the man behind the gun," as being the important factor in naval wars.

Our fellow member, Colonel Robert M. Thompson (U. S. N. A. '68), to whom the compiler is indebted for valuable assistance in gathering the facts here set forth, has, since the time when our two members, Mahan and Erben, were honored guests of our British brethren, been preaching the doctrine that the really important factor is "the man behind the man behind the gun."

Colonel Thompson himself is a member of our Club who has stamped himself as *facile princeps* among enthusiastic and practical supporters of the United States Navy. Although educated at Annapolis and at one time in active naval service, he has long been engaged in successful financial and industrial pursuits, and won his military title by a staff appointment by the governor of one of our States. But retirement from formal naval duties did not in his case involve inactivity in behalf of the service. On the contrary, it is not too much to say that few have been more constant and energetic in its behalf than he. His wealth has been freely used to enhance and promote the welfare of the navy and its officers. His presence among the cadets at Annapolis is the signal for spontaneous cheers. The annual games between the army and navy would be wanting in one of their most characteristic elements, if the large parties of specially invited guests were not brought to them by special trains chartered by Colonel Thompson. The alumni association of Annapolis men in New York owes its success and spirit to his never-failing ardor and devotion. Colonel Thompson is a unique figure among the members of the University Club.

One of our navy members who has been distinguished in the service, as well as a popular frequenter of the Club, is Admiral Willard H. Brownson (U. S. N. A. '65).

At the time of the revolution in Brazil in 1894, Brownson was in command of the little war-ship *Detroit*. The insurgent, Admiral Da Gama, had interfered with American commercial vessels, which were prevented from getting to the docks to unload. Under orders from the admiral of the United States fleet, Brownson warned Da Gama that if another gun was fired, even by accident, he would sink the *Guanabara* and *Trajano*, and advised that they take the men from their guns. As a matter of fact, he put a six-pound shell into the *Guanabara*. The insurgent admiral, who had threatened fire and slaughter if the Americans attempted to land their cargoes, weakened before the determined attitude of Brownson, yielded his point, and allowed the merchant-vessels to be convoyed to the places for discharge of cargo. Although the action of Brownson had no political motive, but only the protection of American ships in the exercise of their rights, the incident had much to do with the collapse of the revolution.

Our late fellow member, Admiral Bancroft Gherardi (U. S. N. A. '52), then commandant of the navy-yard in Brooklyn, was asked by a newspaper reporter: "Who is in command of the *Detroit*, which is reported to have done all the firing?"

"A capable and able officer," replied the admiral. "His name is Captain Willard H. Brownson, appointed from New

York; a man about forty-five years old, and who has a total sea-service of sixteen years to his credit."

Since that time, Brownson has become an admiral, and, among other commands of distinction, was at the head of the Naval Academy at Annapolis. He is now retired.

Although Colonel Theodore Roosevelt (Harvard '80) is not now a member of the University Club, he formerly belonged to it, and, while later President of the United States, was according to the Club rules an honorary member. His remarkable career justifies mention of him among those of our number who have specially distinguished themselves. From the time of his graduation at Harvard he vigorously devoted himself to the public service, besides being a voluminous writer of published books. He has been a politician, a soldier, a hunter, and an author. The compiler of this book remembers his being called out at a Harvard dinner in New York shortly after he left college, and compelled to speak. Even then he displayed that earnestness and confidence which have characterized his subsequent "strenuous" life. He went to the New York legislature when a young man, and made his influence felt immediately. He was police commissioner in New York, and walked the street at night, like Haroun-al-Raschid, to detect for himself the city's needs. He was assistant secretary of the navy when the war with Spain broke out, and immediately resigned to organize the First United States Cavalry Regiment. This celebrated corps, unique in military history, was familiarly called by the public the "Rough Riders," which nickname, at first resented, was finally accepted and adopted by themselves. Roosevelt, at this time an amateur in warfare, yielded the temporary command of the regiment to Leonard Wood (Harvard '99, honorary), then an assistant surgeon in the United States Army, and until recently chief of the general staff. General Wood is a member of the University Club. His rise from army surgeon to colonel of cavalry, and afterward to the chief command of the army, has been unparalleled in the history of our military service. Never before in any country was such a band of daredevils collected together for regular fighting in a war. College athletes, policemen, steer-branders, bear-hunters, fashionable polo-players, firemen, old soldiers, good men, bad men, "dudes," and desperadoes from all parts of the country were organized into a body of aggressive sons of Mars. "Dead-Shot Jim," "Lariat Ned," "Rocky Mountain Bill," "Bronco George," "Fighting Bob Wilson," and their ilk were linked with city men like Woodbury Kane, Willie Tiffany, Hamilton Fish, Jr., Reginald Ronalds, I. Townsend Burden, Waller the high jumper, Dudley Dean and Bob Wrenn the Harvard quarter-backs, and Devereux and Channing, Princeton football men. The Somerset Club, of Boston, and the Knickerbocker Club, of New York, had their representatives in the corps so largely composed of cow-punchers and woodsmen from the Wild West. Some of these Rough Riders are members of the University Club.

Their uniform was picturesque and has become a type—khaki cloth with yellow facings and a rakish sombrero hat. Their arms were carbines, revolvers, and machetes.

San Juan Hill was the scene of their most conspicuous exploits during the war, but they were and still remain a curious and dramatic picture evolved from the active brain of Roosevelt.

Colonel Roosevelt, after being Governor of the State of New York, became President of the United States and was elected to a second term. His defection from the Republican party in 1912, his rally of adherents to the so-called "Progressive" cause, and his defeat for a third presidential term are events fresh in the memory of all.

An indomitable man, he continued his active life as "contributing editor" of *The Outlook Magazine* until July, 1914, as explorer in the Brazilian wilderness, and a factor in the politics of the country.

CHAPTER XVII

DISTINGUISHED GUESTS, 1898–1899

On the 22d of November, 1898, a bronze medal cast in memory of Professor Henry Drisler (Columbia '39), for more than fifty years professor of Greek in Columbia University, was presented to the Council through Mr. John B. Pine (Columbia '77).

On the 13th of March, 1899, a medal example of the seal struck by Princeton University at the time of the Sesquicentennial Celebration, was presented to the Club.

At the March meeting of the Council in 1899 a resolution was adopted prohibiting its members from proposing or seconding candidates for membership, and at the April meeting the injunction was extended to the writing of letters in relation to candidates—steps of importance and wisely conceived. These prohibitions continue to be a rule of the Club.

At the March meeting Judge Howland called the attention of the Council to the fact that this was the last meeting to be presided over by the President, Mr. Alexander, he having positively declined renomination to the Council. A record was thereupon made of congratulation on the success of the Club and assurance of the affection of the members.

The following is an extract from the minutes of the annual meeting of the Club held March 18, 1899, in the 26th Street building:

The President, Mr. Alexander, presented the Annual Report of the Council to the Club, and addressed the Club in relation to his retiring from the office of President and the termination of his services in the Council as follows:

"I ask the indulgence of the Club, while I make a brief personal statement.

"I have been for eight years President of the University Club and while I feel very grateful to the Nominating Committee and to many friends among the membership for asking me to accept a renomination for membership in the Council, I feel that it is altogether for the best interests of the Club that I should retire from its management at this time. I am thoroughly in favour of rotation in office and believe that there could be no more opportune moment for a change in the Presidency than the present time.

"It is a subject of great satisfaction to me that I am able, on vacating the Presidency, to leave the Club in such a prosperous condition. It can safely be said that there is no Club in existence whose management, on what might be called the commercial side, has been more successful than ours, and I know of no Club which has a more homogeneous body of members and whose condition in any respect is better.

"Three years ago you authorized the Council to proceed with the undertaking of purchasing property at the corner of Fifth Avenue and Fifty-fourth Street, and building a Club-house adequate to the requirements of an organization of our importance and character. We afterwards presented to you our general plan of action, which was ratified, and I feel that I am justified in speaking for all those who have been concerned in the direct management of the building project in thanking you most cordially for the confidence and support which you have given to us. Without this, it would have been impossible to achieve the signal success which has crowned our efforts.

"At the very inception of the enterprise, we made estimates as to the cost of the building, as to the numerical membership of the Club, at the time the building should be ready for occupation, as to the receipts from all sources after occupancy of the new building, and as to the expense of running the Club. While those of us who bore the responsibility have had also to bear the natural anxiety which is inseparable from experiments which have not yet been proved to be well-conceived, we have had the great satisfaction of finding the original estimates in every respect below the results, with the one exception of the admission of members. It was originally supposed that the limit of membership, namely three thousand, would be reached by May 1st, 1899. I congratulate the Club on the assiduity and fidelity of the Admission Committee who have permitted no pressure to relax the caution with which they have performed their duties. They have worked with great diligence, but the membership of the Club still lacks 409 of being full. Notwithstanding this fact, the estimates of receipts from all sources have been far exceeded in our actual experience.

"We have laid up about one hundred thousand dollars a year for three years. We have built our building without exceeding the estimates of the cost which were made when the contracts were entered into, the fact being that when the building accounts are closed, and after charging up interest, taxes, and all miscellaneous expenses (including furniture and equipment) against them, we shall not be two thousand dollars under or over the original figure. Such a result I submit is almost unknown—even in individual and purely commercial transactions.

"In regard to the administration of the Club in its new building, the Council came to the unanimous conclusion that it was desirable that the dues should be increased for resident members to seventy-five dollars, and non-resident members to thirty-five dollars, so that every possible comfort and convenience could be given to the members, and a surplus fund laid up for the purpose of ultimately reducing the mortgage debt and the Club has so ordered.

"The prospects are that we shall soon remove to the new building and there is every indication that the attendance and patronage of the Club will be largely increased even over the very satisfactory business which is now done.

"Great praise is due to the Chairman and members of the Building Committee, to the Chairman of the House Committee and to Messrs. McKim, Mead & White, the architects, for the faithful and industrious services they have rendered to the Club.

"I thank you very much for your friendship and support and wish the Club, under its new management, all possible prosperity in the future."

A motion was then made that the Club request the President to continue as a member of the Council for another term. Mr. Alexander declined to put the motion to the Club, and requested that the same be withdrawn as a personal favor to him, which request was complied with. Later he served again from 1900 to 1908.

The courtesies of the Club were extended in October, 1899,

CHARLES COTESWORTH BEAMAN (Harvard '61).
Sixth President, 1899–1901. From a painting by J. N. Marble, 1903.

to Sir Thomas Lipton in recognition of his sportsmanlike conduct in connection with his efforts to "lift" the *America's* cup.

Sir Henry Irving, also, in this same month was invited to enjoy the hospitalities of the Club, the desire of members being general to do honor to this exponent of the drama.

In November, 1899, the courtesies of the Club were extended to the members of the Association of Modern Languages at the request of the late Professor Thomas R. Price (Univ. of Va. '58), of Columbia University.

The practice of doing honor to academic organizations, and men of eminence in literature, art, science, and the public service, has always been fostered by those in authority in the Club. The minutes of the Council repeatedly record their desire to take official notice of events of importance in the world of learning and of the actors in them. Among the numerous occasions when such recognition has taken form may be mentioned the hospitality tendered at the suggestion of the Honorable Seth Low (Columbia '70), President of Columbia University, to Japanese gentlemen visiting the United States to investigate educational institutions; representatives of the Archæological Association, at the request of Professor O. S. Seymour (Yale '94), of Columbia University; distinguished savants from various foreign universities attending the Princeton Sesqui-centennial Celebration; the delegates to the meeting of the Association of American Universities; deputies from the National Academy of Sciences; President Taft; President Lowell of Harvard University; President Garfield of Williams College; President Hibben of Princeton University; Ex-President Eliot of Harvard; President Hadley of Yale; Mr. Long, Secretary of the Navy of the United States; Anthony Hope Hawkins; "Tom" Hughes, the author of "Tom Brown's School Days"; James Bryce, British ambassador to the United States; and Monsieur Jusserand, French ambassador to the United States. Dinners have been given, both by the Council and by bodies of Club members, to many men prominent in the field of letters and affairs; among these were complimentary banquets to Colonel Theodore Roosevelt, and to President Taft while Governor of the Philippines. One of the more recent occasions of the kind referred to was the dinner given February 19, 1909, to the gentlemen elected to membership under the recent rule providing that "preferences, however, may be given to a candidate of special distinction, etc." These gentlemen were J. Pierpont Morgan (Yale '08, honorary), F. Hopkinson Smith (Yale '07, honorary), A. Barton Hepburn (Middlebury '71), and James Ford Rhodes (Harvard '01, honorary).

The membership of the Club is enriched by the admission of men such as these, who but for the wise rule referred to would not be reached for election in the usual order for a period of years, and the Club would thus be deprived of the advantage of their companionship.

The records of the Club have not always been kept—as they were under the careful supervision of our late efficient Secretary, Mr. William Manice (Columbia '86)—with sufficient accuracy to enable the compiler to mention many of the occasions on which eminent men and notable academic bodies and events have been honored.

In December, 1899, a serious question of policy arose and was discussed by the Council, namely: whether it would be wise to yield to the desires of many and agree to an exchange of privileges with other clubs. The necessity for a declaration of policy in this regard was precipitated by a friendly proposition from a sister organization, the University Club of Indianapolis, that there should be an exchange of courtesies between University Clubs of the country. Agreeable as such a plan might be to the members of our own and other clubs, the Council, after mature consideration, came to the unanimous conclusion that our first duty was to our own members and that in view of the already large membership and the lack of facilities for the accommodation of a much greater number, it would be impracticable to adopt the course suggested, and the proposers were so notified with regret.

The same subject was revived in 1903, when kindly overtures were made by the Cocoa-Tree Club of London for an interchange of membership, and in 1907 by the Richmond Club, Surrey, England, with a similar object. The stand already taken by the Council was fortified by the argument that it would be impossible to accede to such amicable propositions in particular cases without being invidious, and it became necessary to withhold the Club's approval. The policy of the Club is therefore well settled, in case of other kindred suggestions being made in the future.

Mr. Bagg, who had served the Club with efficiency as Librarian, resigned that position March 12, 1900, and on May 14, 1900, the Committee on Literature and Art reported the engagement of Mr. William H. Duncan, Jr., as Librarian. They also reported arrangements for a series of lectures during the next winter, and the Council made an appropriation of money for the expenses incidental thereto.

CHAPTER XVIII

DEATH OF MR. BEAMAN—PRINCE HENRY OF PRUSSIA —1900-1902

AT a special meeting of the Council held for the purpose on December 16, 1900, the Chairman, Judge Henry E. Howland, called attention to the sudden and unexpected death of Mr. Charles C. Beaman, the President of the Club; whereupon it was resolved that the Council attend the funeral of Mr. Beaman, that a suitable floral tribute be sent from the Club, and that resolutions expressive of the profound regret of the Club be prepared for submission at a subsequent meeting. All these directions were carried out, and the minute adopted in relation to the death of the President was as follows:

Charles Cotesworth Beaman was born on the 7th day of May, 1840, at Houlton, Maine; was graduated from Harvard College in 1861; admitted to the Bar in 1865; and died at his home in the City of New York on the 15th of December, 1900, after a useful and brilliant career.

Mr. Beaman, at the time of his death, was President of the University Club of the City of New York, and was the first President of the Club to be thus removed during his incumbency.

Taken suddenly from our circle while apparently at the very zenith of his powers, and endeared as he was to every one of us by his companionable qualities, his removal has awakened emotions which we, the surviving members of the Council of the University Club, would wish in some measure to express in a sincere and reverent record upon the minutes of our body.

The relation which Mr. Beaman bore to his fellows on the Council of the Club was not confined to what was merely official. On the contrary, during his many years of service on that body he had so entwined himself into the affections of his associates as to be beloved as a friend. His cordial temperament, genial disposition and spontaneous humour made him universally welcome, and his presence was always a sure stimulus to the enjoyment of any occasion. But the conscientious thoughtfulness, the fearless probity and the strong intellectual force with which he addressed himself to every question constituted a serious undertone to his happy comradeship, so that while his friends—who were legion—loved him for his heart, they honoured him for those sterling qualities, which were at the foundation of his character.

No mere verbal formalities, usual on such occasions, can express the sorrow which we, who were proud to be his friends, experience at the taking away of such a rare companion; and barren though any words we can command may be to convey a sense of the depth and sincerity of our regret, we would nevertheless leave upon our records some attempt to pay a worthy tribute to the memory of a noble life.

Although our friend will no longer sit with us in our gatherings, formal and social, his influence will continue to be felt, and the recollection of happy hours spent in his company will never fade away.

The services of Mr. T. Frank Brownell (Harvard '65) to the Club have already been referred to. This useful member died January 7, 1901. So great was the appreciation of his worth by the Club that, although he was not at the time a member of any of the Standing Committees, the Council placed upon its records the following resolution of respect and regret:

Resolved, That the members of the Council of the University Club have heard with sincere sorrow of the death of their colleague and friend, T. Frank Brownell.

In common with all who knew him, the members of this Board realize that here has passed away an honourable and good man; one who was painstaking and able in the practice of his profession; conscientious, devoted, and thoughtless of self in everything which he undertook; always ready and willing in acts of kindness and service; and one of the most modest and unassuming of men. To all of us who had the pleasure of his acquaintance or the privilege of his friendship, his death has come as a personal loss.

By the members of this Council and the great body of members of the University Club the services which Mr. Brownell rendered to the Club will always be held in grateful remembrance. For fifteen years, during a most important period of the growth and development of the Club, he held the responsible position of Secretary of the Committee on Admissions, the duties of which, involving much labour, he performed with the greatest fidelity and accuracy. His services to the Club in this office were so great that the desire was generally expressed by those most interested in the Club and having the most complete knowledge of the value of his services that he should receive a valuable testimonial of some kind from the members of the Club; but he refused to accept any reward or any public recognition of his services. The collection of Harvard Memorabilia which he made for the Library will be a monument, so long as the Club shall endure, of most intelligent, able, and comprehensive labor, as well as his loyalty to his Alma Mater and to the Club, and it is one of our most valued possessions. His more recent services to the Club as Chairman of the Committee on Literature and Art in the installation of the Library in the new building, and its organization upon an improved and more extensive system, showed the same intelligence and wise judgment and conscientious care which characterized all his acts. The results of his labors, which we now enjoy, and the incentive of his example, live after him.

Resolved, That a copy of this resolution be signed by the President and Secretary and sent to Mrs. Brownell.

On January 14, 1901, Judge Henry E. Howland (Yale '54) was elected President of the Club, and so continued until 1905.

Judge Howland, during all the years of the Club's existence, had been one of its most useful and popular members. Among his fellow graduates of Yale as well as among the students, he was ever an exceptionally marked man. His rich fund of humor and magnetic personal qualities, coupled with a keen intellect and persuasive influence, made him an agreeable addition to every assembly. His taste led him to take an active part in the affairs of his own college and in those of the University Club; he was a congenial friend to men far younger

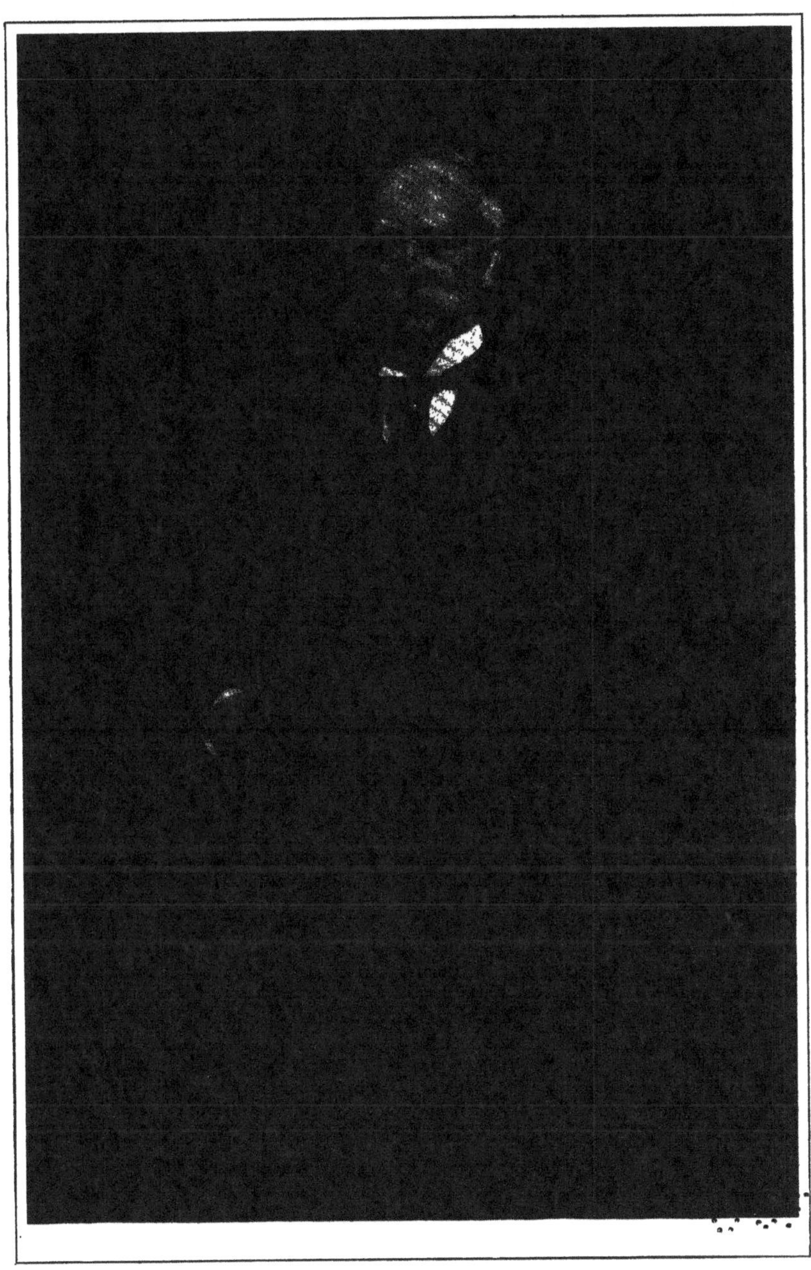

HENRY ELIAS HOWLAND (Yale '54).
Seventh President, 1901–1905. From a painting by F. P. Vinton, 1905.

than himself. No after-dinner speaker excelled him in keeping the table in a roar, and whether as the partner in the law firm of which Mr. Henry H. Anderson, our first President, was the senior, or in the councils of his university, or in the public affairs of New York City, his force was felt and acknowledged. He was continuously a member of the Council of the University Club from the time of its reorganization in 1879 until 1908, when he retired. Judge Howland died November 7, 1913.

Under the direction of the Library Committee, a number of views of the University Club were sent to the Reform Club of London. The following is their acknowledgment:

THE REFORM CLUB

9 November 1901.

DEAR SIR,

I have much pleasure on behalf of the Library Committee, to acknowledge, with hearty thanks, the receipt of your donation of 10 prints representing the University Club of New York.

I knew that Club in its earlier days, having been a temporary member of it at the instance of my friend Mr. Henry Holt; consequently I look with great interest and satisfaction at the prints which show its present imposing and beautiful state.

These prints will be bound and placed on the shelf in the Library here.

Believe me to be

Very faithfully yours,

W. FRASER RAE

Chairman.

In the year 1901 it became evident that an increase in membership was desirable. The ample conveniences of the new Club House, the long "waiting-list," and the advantages of a larger income all combined to justify the expansion. In March of that year there were posted, as candidates for membership, 570 names for resident and 334 for non-resident. The constitution limited the membership to 1,700 resident and 1,300 non-resident, and the Club was full, with no vacancies. An amendment was therefore adopted at the annual meeting of the Club, March 16, 1901, increasing the membership of residents to 2,000, and non-residents (including army and navy members) to 1,500. This limitation continues until the present time.

Mr. Santos-Dumont, the pioneer of aviation, being in New York, the officers of the Club invited him, in the month of April, 1902, to accept the hospitalities of the Club.

His autograph reply is on file and is as follows:

Representation
of an Air Ship
passing the
Tour Eiffel
in Paris

DR. D. L. HAIGHT
of House Committee
of University Club

Je vous remercie ainsi que votre Comité du grand honneur que vous m'avez fait.

Sincèrement à vous
SANTOS-DUMONT.

New York le 12 Avril, 1902.

In the death of William Carey (Notre Dame '87) in 1901, a notable figure passed out of our Club life. Carey was one of the staff of *The Century Magazine*, and by his tastes and the nature of his occupation became intimate with a large number of the most famous literary and artistic men of the period. Not only was Carey a delightful companion, brimming over with humor and charming "camaraderie," but he was in the habit of introducing to the Club, and organizing entertainments for, many of the most interesting celebrities of the day. Through him the members of the Club had the advantage of becoming acquainted with Anthony Hope Hawkins, Rudyard Kipling, and scores of other well-known writers. His hospitalities, in which numerous members of the Club participated, did not end here, but famous musical virtuosos and dramatic personages were among the guests brought into the companionship of the Club.

Our fellow member William H. McElroy (Union '60), himself a literary man of recognized talent and one of the prominent graduates of his university, as well as a learned, witty, and fascinating companion in the charmed circles of lettered men, wrote and published a beautiful tribute to Carey's memory, which is among the archives of the Club. It concludes with these words:

> When such a soul withdraws, the world is impoverished:
>
> "He took our day-light with him,
> The smiles that we love best."
>
> Nevertheless, many a heart which sadly misses William Carey will find a certain serene comfort, a certain pathetic delight and refreshment, in oft recalling and dwelling upon the gracious and sterling qualities which made him so dear to them.
>
> "'Tis better to have loved and lost
> Than never to have loved at all."

It now becomes appropriate to take some notice of an event which, though not directly connected with the University Club, yet as a national affair and one in which many of our members were concerned is entitled to a place in this history.

On the first day of January, 1902, the German Emperor requested of President Roosevelt that the President's daughter Alice, now Mrs. Longworth, should christen the Imperial yacht *Meteor*, then building in the United States. The request was promptly granted, and on February 23 Prince Henry of Prussia, sent as representative of the Emperor at the launching of the boat, landed in New York. Rear-Admiral Robley D. Evans (U. S. N. A. '63), a member of the University Club, was appointed aide-de-camp in the prince's suite, at the Emperor's special request.

The prince was essentially a university man, and, although

the methods of educating royalty differ somewhat from those in democratic America, the discipline through which the brother of the Emperor and second son of the former Emperor, Frederick III, passed, was more severe and thorough than that to which our own university men are subjected. From 1875 to 1877 the prince, at the age of fifteen to seventeen, studied at the Cassel Gymnasium. For two years he acquired the elementary learning afforded by actual service in the navy. In 1880 he entered the naval academy at Kiel, and studied there until 1882, when he returned to the navy and was made admiral in 1901. While in the United States he received the degree of LL.D. from Harvard University.

It is not within the scope of this narrative to follow him through his experiences in America, including his participation in the exercises attending the launching of the *Meteor*, or to dwell for more than a moment upon the effect of his visit to this country and the tactful manner in which he conducted himself. Suffice it to say that much bitterness against Germany as a nation was removed by the fact of his being sent by the Emperor and by the admirable taste and judgment with which he performed the duties of his mission.

Several incidents had occurred to inflame the animosities of the American masses. Just before the destruction of the Spanish fleet at Manila, Prince Henry, as admiral of the German squadron, gave a banquet at Hong Kong to the representatives of all the fleets in port, at which Admiral Dewey was present. In proposing the national toasts, Prince Henry omitted the United States, when in the regulated order of precedence the turn of America came. After the next country was named, the United States was again passed. There had already been rumors of a hostile feeling on the part of Germany against our country. Dewey, regarding the omission as intentional, left the banquet. The next morning the prince sent an aid to make an explanation. Dewey received the envoy courteously, but, always alert on upholding the honor of his country, requested him to inform the prince that the incident was one requiring a written or personal apology. The prince called in person and apologized, declaring that the omission was caused by accidental neglect in the writing of the list. Dewey, not to be outdone by the manly civility of the prince, accepted the assurance with prompt good will.

Later, in Manila Bay, when Dewey was maintaining a watch upon and a blockade of the city, he was much annoyed by what appeared to be the encroachments of the admiral in command of German ships, and was said to have been compelled to send an imperative message to that officer.

These and other occurrences had aroused a feeling among the American people by no means friendly to the Germans, and it was believed by many that in sending his brother to America the Emperor had in his mind the express purpose to allay this feeling by a demonstration which could only be interpreted as indicative of amicable sentiment. Be this as it may, the result of the visit went far toward the modification if not the removal of the bitter feeling which had been smouldering and growing.

One of our members, Joseph B. Bishop (Brown '70), Secretary of the Panama Canal Commission at Ancon until the end of its work, was the author of a wise and sane article on this subject, published in *The International Monthly* of March, 1902.

A newspaper writer, in commenting on the behavior of the prince as well as that of the people, during his procession through our land, says: "Both parties to the incident, so far as it has progressed, have carried themselves well. The prince has shown himself a first-class democrat, and Uncle Sam has managed to hold up his end without tripping upon his sword, or getting his legs inextricably entangled in the folds of his robes."

The University Club, then, in recognition of this ambassadorship of a man of education on a mission of friendship to the United States, believed that it was within the domain of its duty and privilege, as a national institution, to extend to Prince Henry the courtesies of the Club in more than the ordinary manner.

The Council therefore invited the prince to a dinner and reception to be given at the Club House on the evening of March 7, 1902, which invitation was promptly accepted. Inasmuch as the facilities of the Club were not sufficient to accommodate at a dinner all the members who might wish to attend, it became necessary while throwing the Club open to all members at the reception, to confine the dinner to a reasonable number. In order that there should be no just complaint of discrimination, it was resolved that the hosts of the dinner should be the members of the Council, and Standing Committees of the Club, and former members of the Council, and that all expenses, including music, decorations, etc., should be paid for by the hosts as individuals, and only the expense of the reception, open to the Club at large, should be paid for by the Club itself.

A committee was appointed with power to make the necessary arrangements, consisting of Messrs. Barney, Russell, Haight, Bannard, Alexander, and President Howland, and the "hosts" were notified that the expenses to them would not probably exceed $30 each. The courtesies of the Club were extended to the officers of the royal yacht *Hohenzollern* which brought the prince across the ocean. Inasmuch as this was the most notable entertainment ever given by the Club to one outside its membership, a brief account of it may be pertinent:

The banquet took place in the main dining-room of the Club, whose noble proportions and fittings made it most appropriate for the purpose.

The tables, instead of being placed in the conventional position, were on a raised platform running around three sides of the hall—the north, east, and south, leaving the whole space in the middle open, after the manner of a baronial feast in mediæval times. The decorations were of American Beauty roses and growing azaleas. The flags of Germany and the United States were conspicuously displayed. Covers were laid for ninety-four guests, the suite of the prince being large and there being a number of distinguished persons present. On the menu, the only reference which the chef made to the occasion was by the introduction of a dish entitled "Noisette d'Agneau à la *Meteor*." In the central space between the tables, Franko's orchestra and the Mendelssohn Glee Club contributed a dozen artistic numbers, and, in order to give the royal guest some idea of "rag-time" music, several expert banjoists rendered typical American compositions.

Only three toasts were proposed: the President of the United States, the Emperor of Germany, and Prince Henry of Prussia. The prince responded gracefully, assuring his hosts of the special pleasure he enjoyed in meeting so many graduates of American universities.

Prince Henry sat at the right of Judge Howland, the President of the Club, and the German ambassador on his left. Each one of the royal party was escorted to the dinner by a member of the Council who sat next to him. Among these were General von Plessen and Admiral von Tirpitz, and among the invited guests were General Nelson A. Miles, Admiral Robley D. Evans, and other officers eminent in the United States service.

The most unique feature of the dinner was the exhibition of moving pictures taken by the Edison Company of the prince and his suite during their pilgrimage, from the launching up to the very day previous to the Club banquet. These were thrown upon a sheet let down across the room at the end opposite to the prince, and he was immensely amused to see the pantomime of himself and his party flashed on the screen.

After the dinner President Howland conducted the guests of the Club to the large front room on the first floor, where the members of the Club in attendance, numbering over one thousand, were personally introduced to the prince.

On the 9th of March the prince was again a guest at the University Club, the occasion being a luncheon given as a farewell by the President's delegates. These were Doctor David J. Hill (Bucknell '74), assistant secretary of state; Major-General Henry C. Corbin, Adjutant-General of the United States; Rear-Admiral Robley D. Evans (U. S. N. A. '63), honorary aide-de-camp to his Royal Highness; Colonel Theodore A. Bingham (U. S. M. A. '79), military aide to the President; and Commander W. S. Cowles (U. S. N. A. '67), naval aide to the President. Among other members of the University Club present on this occcasion were General William Cary Sanger (Harvard '74), assistant secretary of war; Judge Henry E. Howland (Yale '54), President of the Club; and Lewis Cass Ledyard (Harvard '72), commodore of the New York Yacht Club.

During a tour of the University Club Building made after the luncheon, the prince inspected the engine-room. His eye fell upon the engineer, Paul Nagle, standing erect and coming to "attention" with military precision. "Our engineer was once a soldier of the German army," said Doctor Haight, Chairman of the House Committee, who was escorting the party. Answering the engineer's first salute, the prince had touched his hat, but now stepped forward and extended his right hand. Learning that Nagle had belonged to the Emperor Wilhelm's Regiment, No. 101, grenadiers stationed at Dresden in 1881–1884, Prince Henry introduced him to his Majesty's Adjutant-General, his Excellency General von Plessen.

In 1903, in recognition of the hospitality shown him, Prince Henry presented the Club with a portrait of himself, which now hangs in the writing-room of the library.

CHAPTER XIX

RETIREMENT OF DOCTOR HAIGHT—OTHER OFFICERS OF THE CLUB—1902-1905

THE University Club has had the good fortune to be ably conducted in its house affairs from the time of its reorganization in 1879 to the present. When the Club took possession of the property at the corner of Fifth Avenue and 35th Street, in 1879, Henry E. Pellew (Trin. Col., Cambr. '50) became the Chairman of the House Committee, and reference has already been made to the assiduity with which he performed his duties.

He was succeeded in 1882 by Doctor George A. Peters (Yale '42), who afterward became the President of the Club. Mr. Pellew again held this office for one year, 1884-1885, when he retired in favor of the late Franklin Bartlett (Harvard '69), who presided over the Committee until 1887. In that year Willard P. Ward (Columbia '65) became the Chairman and ably conducted the management of the Club until 1891, when he retired from the office in order to give the Club the opportunity to make the experiments which had been suggested by a special committee. The Club enjoyed marked prosperity and a maximum of comfort and luxury during Mr. Ward's administration, and, as has been set forth in an earlier chapter, the differing opinions of competent men as to the most desirable methods of regulating the economies of the management led to a friendly arrangement by which those opinions could be tested by the members advocating certain policies until then untried.

In 1891 Doctor David L. Haight (Yale '60) accepted the position of Chairman of the House Committee, and continued as such until 1902. At the Council meeting of April in that year Doctor Haight requested that he be permitted to retire both from the chairmanship and the Committee, inasmuch as he believed the time had come for younger men to be trained for those positions. This request was granted, and a resolution was adopted declaring that the existing arrangement by which Doctor Haight was made a guest and resident of the Club should not be discontinued at this time, and a special committee was appointed to prepare a suitable resolution. The minutes of the Council contain the following paragraph:

The President then paid Dr. Haight a glowing tribute and read the following report and request signed by the other members of the House Committee:

NEW YORK, April 11, 1902.

THE COUNCIL OF THE UNIVERSITY CLUB,
Dear Sirs:

At a recent meeting of the House Committee, Dr. Haight announced his intention of declining to be a candidate for reappointment.

The other members of the Committee have not succeeded in dissuading him from this purpose and strongly recommend to the Council that if it consents to relieve him from further service on this Committee, it shall induce him to accept some other official position which will keep him in touch with the Club's affairs and enable the committee to feel at liberty to call upon him in consultation and for advice.

Our experience satisfies us that whoever are to constitute this committee for the coming year will undertake the burden of its duties with greatly increased confidence and prospect of success if they can have the aid of such an arrangement as we have urged.

Respectfully yours,
P. G. BARTLETT [Yale '81],
WILLIAM MANICE [Columbia '86],
EDWARD VAN INGEN [Yale '91].

DAVID L. HAIGHT (Yale '60).

Chairman of the House Committee—1891–1902—and member of the Building Committee that erected the present Club House. From a painting by John W. Alexander.

The President then appointed Doctor Haight Chairman of the "Auditing Committee," which by vote of the Council became a Finance and Ways and Means Committee.

The special committee reported a resolution expressing the views of the Council regarding Doctor Haight, which was unanimously adopted and is as follows:

Resolved, That the Council of the University Club accept the resignation of Dr. David L. Haight as Chairman of the House Committee, with the greatest reluctance, and acquiesce in his determination to retire from that position, only at his earnest request.

The Council desire, in view of this important change in the organization of the University Club, to record its appreciation for the services of Doctor Haight during the last twelve years; services of such value to the institution that it would be impossible to exaggerate their worth. A very large share of the remarkable success of the Club is attributable to the devotion, skill, experience and indefatigable industry of Dr. Haight, and the Council cannot be too emphatic in expressing their sense of obligation.

While the Council agree with Dr. Haight that he is entitled to relief from the exacting responsibilities of the House Committee Chairmanship, they unanimously request him to continue to serve the interests of the Club in the capacity of Chairman of the Auditing Committee, with enlarged powers to that committee, including the functions of a Finance Committee and recognizing the value to the Club of Dr. Haight's presence in the house, where he may be consulted by the House Committee, and give them the benefit of his knowledge and experience, the Council request him to continue to be the guest of the Club, as in late years, and enjoy its full hospitalities.

Doctor Haight continued as Chairman of the Auditing Committee until March, 1907, and as a member of the Committee until March, 1909.

The term for which Doctor Haight was elected to the Council expired March, 1907, and at the annual meeting of the Club, held the 16th day of March, 1907, the Chairman of the Nominating Committee, Mr. Arthur C. James (Amherst '89), when presenting the report of the Nominating Committee of Candidates for the Council and the Committee on Admissions, reported that the Nominating Committee desired to renominate Doctor Haight for member of the Council but that he declined the nomination.

In December, 1903, the Committee on Literature and Art were authorized by the Council to extend to the libraries of Columbia, Harvard, Yale, and Princeton Universities the privileges granted by them as to the interchange of books. By this arrangement, those making use of the Club library obtained the advantages of having to all intents and purposes the great libraries of the universities named added to the collection under the immediate care of the University Club—an arrangement which continues and is of incalculable benefit to those engaged in research.

One of the popular features of the old Club House at the corner of Madison Avenue and 26th Street was the easily accessible billiard-room on the ground floor. Entered through what was known as the "café," that room was a rendezvous for members, who, whether using the tables or not, found it a convenient place for conversation and other social enjoyments. The very fact that it was thus resorted to stimulated the playing of games—not only of billiards and pool, but of tenpins, the alleys being adjacent to and approached from the billiard-room.

In the construction of the new Club House at Fifth Avenue and 54th Street, it was not found feasible at the outset to put the billiard-room on the first floor, and it was placed on the mezzanine floor above the office and café. There were among the members of the Council those who regarded this as a misfortune, and the event has proved correct the fear that both sociability and the use of the tables would lose something by reason of the situation of this department of the Club.

In 1903, therefore, at the request of some of the members, a committee was appointed to consider plans for such an alter-

THE BILLIARD ROOM.

ation of the Club House as would relieve the difficulty referred to, and to report. This committee consulted with the architects, and plans were prepared by which the office would be removed into the 55th Street wing of the house, and the space then occupied by the office and the café turned into a billiard-room, the floor of the present billiard-room to be removed so as to obtain a high ceiling for the room below; and the conveniences of a café to be secured by using the margins of the main room and galleries around it on the mezzanine level for that purpose.

At this period the annual surplus of the Club was so large as to justify the expenditure of the $80,000 which the proposed alteration would entail. The Club was paying off $50,000 a year on its first mortgage in accordance with a clause so providing, but the mortgagee corporation expressly waived the continuation of this payment, being satisfied with the security of the property.

When, however, the Special Committee recommended the change to the Council, the late Edward King (Harvard '53), then one of its members, protested against the outlay until the Club had literally complied with its obligation to reduce the amount of the mortgage to one-half the value of the land and building, and objected to taking advantage of the consent of the mortgagee. Mr. King's views prevailed, and the proposed alteration was abandoned. This episode in the history of the Club is deserving of the notice given to it, as evincing that uniform disposition on the part of those responsible for its management to take the highest possible ground in the determination of all questions arising.

The Club has been fortunate in its Secretaries.

During the period just before the reorganization in 1879, when George V. N. Baldwin (Rutgers '56) was President, Buchanan Winthrop (Yale '62) was Secretary. Mr. Winthrop was one of the original members of the Club, a man well known both in university and social circles, and continued to take a warm interest in the Club's affairs up to the time of his death in 1900.

Doctor Woolsey Johnson (Princeton '60) was the first Secretary of the Club after its reorganization in 1879, and continued in office until his retirement in 1886. It was not long when after a protracted illness he died. He was greatly beloved by his friends, who were many and of the first rank as to social fellowship and standing.

His services to the Club were specially recognized before his death by the Council at the meeting of June 7, 1886, by entering upon the minutes the following resolution, introduced by the Honorable Henry E. Howland:

Resolved, That the Council of the University Club remember with great pleasure the associations they have sustained with Dr. Woolsey Johnson, the Secretary since the foundation of the Club; that as an officer of the Club their relations with him have been harmonious and most agreeable and they desire to express to him their sincere regard both individually and as members of the Council.

He was succeeded by Franklin Bartlett (Harvard '69). In 1889 his place was taken by Allen W. Evarts (Yale '69). Both of these members were active in the early affairs of the Club. In 1891 Stephen H. Olin (Wesleyan '66) took the office and held it for one year. In 1892 Hugh D. Auchincloss (Yale '79) was elected Secretary, and held office for nine years. He resigned in 1902, and Otto T. Bannard (Yale '76) succeeded him, and continued to hold the position until the election of William Manice (Columbia '86) in 1904. Bannard was a man who entered with great assiduity into any work committed to him, and was a particularly valuable officer. Since that time he has been prominent in financial and political circles, and was the Republican candidate for mayor of New York City in 1909.

Mr. Manice died January 19, 1914, and Samuel Sloan

(Columbia '87) was chosen to succeed him. It may be stated without invidious distinction that the records of the Club have never been kept in a more orderly or satisfactory manner, and the repeated choice of Mr. Manice for this office was evidence of the unqualified approval by the Council, with its annual change of personnel, of the manner in which the Secretary's duties were performed.

In this connection reference is due to the valuable services of Walter G. Oakman (Univ. of Pa. '64) as Treasurer of the Club. Mr. Oakman was elected to this important office in 1901, and the organization has been fortunate in having the benefit, during a period of nearly fifteen years, of the experience and skill of one so justly prominent in the financial circles of New York. Mr. Oakman continues to hold the treasurership at the time of this publication and the Club is under more than ordinary obligation to him for his loyal and faithful attention to its interests.

Mr. Oakman was preceded by George Sherman (Columbia '75), one of the highest officers in the Central Trust Company, who filled the position for a period of ten years from 1891 to 1901. These members have been preceded in turn by George C. Clark (C. C. N. Y. '63), Brayton Ives (Yale '61), and George Hoffman, who was the first Treasurer on the reorganization of the Club in 1879.

When the Club was organized, in 1865, Edward Mitchell (Columbia '61) was the Secretary and Theodore B. Bronson (Columbia '48) Treasurer, under the presidency of Professor T. W. Dwight (Hamilton '40), of the Columbia Law School.

In October, 1904, the House Committee was authorized to issue invitations to the press to inspect Mr. Mowbray's Pinturicchio decorations of the library, and in November of the same year two or three days were set aside for the reception of invited guests desiring to see these works of art.

At this same meeting the House Committee and the Committee on Literature and Art were authorized to arrange a reception in honor of Mr. James Bryce, the author of "The American Commonwealth," and more recently his British Majesty's Ambassador to the United States, before his return to England. The invitation was duly sent, but unfortunately reached Mr. Bryce too late, as will be seen by his letter of acknowledgment, which was as follows:

54 PORTLAND PLACE
LONDON
Nov. 29, 1904.

MY DEAR SIR:

Your letter of Nov. 14th conveying to me the kind invitation of the University Club to a reception has only just reached me in England, and I hasten to ask you to convey to the Council of the Club my sincere thanks for the compliment they desired to pay to me, and my great regret that it has been impossible for me to have the opportunity of meeting the members of the Club which they would have given me and which I should have greatly enjoyed.

I left America on Nov. 12th.

Believe me to be

Very faithfully yours,
JAMES BRYCE.

THE SECRETARY
University Club.

The hospitalities of the Club were at the same meeting extended to the members of the National Academy of Sciences, during their sojourn in the city of New York.

On the afternoon of February 14, 1905, Theodore Roosevelt, then President of the United States, was entertained at luncheon at the University Club. The function was a private one, but among the participants were the following members of the Club: Henry W. Taft (Yale '80), Joseph B. Bishop (Brown '70), William H. Taft (Yale '78, later President of the United States), Elihu Root (Hamilton '64), Nicholas Murray Butler (Columbia '82, now President of Columbia Uni-

EDMUND WETMORE (Harvard '60).
Eighth President, 1905–1910. From a painting by Irving R. Wiles, 1911.

versity), Frederick W. Whitridge (Amherst '74), and Chester B. McLaughlin (Univ. of Vt. '79).

At the organizing meeting of the Council in 1905, on the retirement of Judge Henry E. Howland, Edmund Wetmore (Harvard '60) was elected President of the Club, and continued to hold that office until 1910. Mr. Wetmore is living and is a member of the Club at the time of this publication. Distinguished as a member of the New York bar and regarded by the Harvard members as a leader, having served as president of the Harvard Club, he was pre-eminently fitted to hold the highest office in the University Club, and his administration was characterized by continuing prosperity.

When Doctor Haight retired from the Chairmanship of the House Committee in 1902, Edward Van Ingen (Yale '91) was appointed in his place, and proved a most efficient and popular officer. His death, on the 27th of October, 1905, ended a connection with the Club characterized only by what was greatly to his credit and honor. The esteem in which he was held was shown by the memorial placed upon its minutes by the Council November 13, 1905, a copy of which is here given:

The Council of the University Club, as an expression of its sense of the loss sustained by the death of Edward Van Ingen, a member of its body and chairman of the House Committee, has directed the following entry to be made upon its minutes:

The place of Edward Van Ingen is hard to fill and its emptiness brings to each of us a personal sorrow. Not for many years have the interested efforts of a member of the Club in any office or on any Committee been more constant or able in maintaining a high standard of efficiency and economy. His presence on the Council and on the House Committee was the result of interest and activity in all the Club affairs.

His election to any Club office, however, would have imperfectly represented the feeling towards him of all ages and groups in the membership. With those who knew him it was only a question of opportunities for meeting, that acquaintance should pass into friendship, friendship of a kind that craved his company.

His vitality brought men around him and he diffused such a sympathetic atmosphere of the enjoyment of life as to give cheerfulness and spirit to less buoyant natures.

The number of his channels of activity and the remarkable energy and ability he put into them were making his professional career unusual for a man of his age and the promise for his future was increasing with his successes.

Whether in companionship or in outdoor sport, or in the cause of good citizenship, his enthusiasm was always contagious and unflagging. But the best part of it was that with all his interest in politics, in organizations, and in the personality of every man he touched, no one ever found in him a spirit of detraction and not one of us can recall an instance when he failed to show the most cordial feeling, or failed to understand the best part of any man's nature, an understanding which came to him by a kind of genial instinct and made him glow in all social relations.

Great as is the loss to each of us we can partly mitigate it by treasuring the memory of a high-hearted, loyal, generous and affectionate friend.

Ordered,—that a copy of the foregoing suitably engrossed be sent to the family of Mr. Van Ingen.

On September 11, 1905, Courtlandt C. Clarke (Princeton '78) was elected Chairman of the House Committee, and continued in office until 1912, when he ceased to be a member of the Council, and declined a reappointment. Mr. Clarke maintained the traditions of the office in fidelity and devotion to the interests of the Club. Upon the retirement of Mr. Clarke, in 1912, Henry Dodge Cooper (C. C. N. Y. '72), who had been for some years an active member of the House Committee, was persuaded to take the chairmanship, which he held until March, 1914, and in the administration of which office he gave a satisfaction which was evidenced by the universal content of the membership. H. Hobart Porter (Columbia '86) was elected Chairman of the House Committee, and is the present incumbent.

CHAPTER XX

MASON YOUNG—GIFTS TO THE CLUB—CHARLES T. BARNEY—1906-1907

The fact has been stated in an earlier chapter that the time was not ripe for the purpose when the University Club had its beginning in 1865. For lack of hearty support it dwindled, withered, and would have died had not a handful of ardent members preserved its frail life until the desire of university men for an organization became obvious. Such was the case in the year 1878; the tide in the college enthusiasm was at the flood, and it was only necessary for the man to appear who could take the current when it served, for the Club to assume the importance which it deserved.

There were many in the community who were actively interested, and the project of a reorganization of the moribund Club was "in the air," but there was one man, necessary to the hour, to whom the call came and who heard it. It seemed to say to him:

"Why dost thou stay,
And leave undone what should be done today?
Begin—the present minute's in thy power;
But still t' adjourn, and wait a fitter hour,
Is like the clown, who at some river's side
Expecting stands, in hopes the running tide
Will all ere long be past."

That man was Mason Young (Yale '60). His memory should not be forgotten in the whirl of our great present success. It was Mason Young, as much as any other one man, who rallied the scattered army of university men in New York and gathered them under a common standard. This tribute of recognition is made at this stage of our history, because Young departed this life on the 29th day of March, 1906.

The Council was not forgetful of the services contributed by this enthusiastic member, although many years had passed since his activities for the Club were so conspicuous, and at the meeting of May 14, 1906, the following resolutions were adopted and spread upon the minutes:

The Council of the University Club has learned with deep regret of the death of Mason Young, a member of the Club since its organization in 1865, and places upon its minutes this tribute to his memory.

The Club, as is well known, practically went out of existence two years after its organization in 1865. Its Charter was kept alive by a small group of men, some twenty in all, who constituted a dining Club simply, with no Club House and none of the paraphernalia of a club. In 1879, through the initiative of Mr. Young, it was revivified, reorganized, and transformed into a large and prosperous organization which has developed into the Club as it is seen today.

To Mr. Young, as much as to any other man, is due the credit for its existence. Into the work of its re-establishment he entered with his characteristic skill and enthusiasm and with one or two others assisting him he enrolled six hundred members in the spring of 1879, secured the Club House at the corner of Fifth Avenue and Thirty-fifth Street, supervised the election of its officers and as a member of the first Committee on Admissions exercised such sagacity in establishing a high standard in its early membership and management that its success was assured from its foundation.

He was a man of masterful and attractive personality and well equipped for such a service, of great intellectual power, and extensive literary and artistic accomplishments.

He was a natural leader, and though positive in his convictions, which he never failed to assert, he won men to him by the loyalty of his friendships, his open-handed generosity, and his unfailing kindness and sympathy to those in need.

He rendered great service in his time to his Alma Mater, Yale University. All who knew him would bear witness to his marked ability and high principles.

He was a sound and sagacious lawyer and early established an enviable position in his profession which he maintained as long as he continued in it.

Failing health of late years had withdrawn him from the companionship of his friends but they well remember him as one worthy of their high regard, whom to know was to respect and with whom association was a continual pleasure.

Mrs. Abram S. Hewitt in 1904 presented the Club with a valuable collection of war records, which the Council at its meeting of February in that year accepted with thanks.

In 1900 R. D. McGibbon presented to the Club an original pen-and-ink sketch by Thomas Nast, the famous caricaturist of *Harper's Weekly*. This sketch was reproduced in *Harper's Weekly* during the excitement regarding the so-called "Tweed Ring," and represented Tweed with a face disguised as a dollar-mark. This picture has been described in Nast's life as being the most famous of his Tweed caricatures.

In June, 1906, the Council accepted with thanks a present of billiard and pool balls which had belonged to the late Prescott Hall Butler (Harvard '69) and which were the gift of Mrs. Butler. Butler had been for years a prominent member of the Club, and in his hours of recreation enjoyed the relaxation of a game. The present was therefore valued as an appropriate memento of a serious-minded comrade who was not averse to sensible amusement in his idle hours. He had the example of some of the greatest men. It is only when they play too well that suspicion arises. Herbert Spencer, who indulged in the game as a pastime, is reported to have wittily remarked to a successful antagonist: "Though a certain proficiency at the game is to be desired, the skill you have shown seems to argue a misspent youth."

The usage is common in all clubs to surround the infliction of penalties involving disgrace with safeguards against hasty and ill-considered action. Thus, the constitution of the Club in 1905 (Article XII) provided that a vote of three-fourths of the members of the Council was necessary in order to suspend or expel a member, and a notice of a month to the accused member, with a copy of the charges, was required.

It was found, however, as a matter of experience, that the requirement of a three-quarter vote resulted in postponement after postponement, on account of the attendance falling short of the requisite number, and that the swift punishment which is so essential to discipline was from time to time thwarted.

At the annual meeting of the Club in March, 1906, therefore, the constitution was so amended as to cure this defect. The vote of three-fourths of the members of the Council was changed to three-fifths, and the notice to the accused member was made fifteen days instead of a month. It was also provided, as a protection against too harsh a judgment, that "any action under this article may be revoked or modified by subsequent vote of the Council." The twelfth article remains to-day as thus amended.

The minutes of the Council of June 10, 1907, contain an acknowledgment of a fine mounted elk's head presented by Mrs. Lewis, the widow of the late Eugene H. Lewis (Yale '73), a member of the Club, who died March 1, 1907. This head hangs in the dining-room above the inside of the main entrance from the anteroom.

This being the only reference formally recorded in the minutes to a gift of an animal's head, and the Club is so rich in its possession of such specimens, the compiler has been at some pains to trace the history of these valuable ornaments and to identify the donors. The following is the result of this search:

On leaving the elevator, on the dining-room floor one sees just opposite a large head of a musk-ox. This specimen, from the arctic regions, was the gift of Alden Sampson (Harvard '76) in 1901.

Proceeding to the anteroom of the dining-room, two spreading deer horns, without scalps, are to be seen on the two columns nearest the north side of the building. General George S. Anderson, when in command of the Yellowstone Park, brought a number of horns to New York and delivered them to Stanford White, who distributed them among various buildings, some going to the Players' Club, and the two just referred to being hung in the University Club.

Above the left entrance to the dining-room, on the outside, is the head of a mountain sheep, presented by Doctor David L. Haight (Yale '60).

Above the right, or west, entrance to the dining-room on the outside, is another head of a mountain sheep, presented by General George S. Anderson (U. S. M. A. '71).

In the west end of the dining-room, over the mantelpiece, is a magnificent elk's head with twenty-one points. This also was the gift of General George S. Anderson, and is the best specimen in the country.

In the east end of the dining-room, above the portrait of President Woolsey, is a fine elk's head. This is the property of the Club, Mr. Sampson having first loaned it and afterward conveyed it to the Club.

Over the arch which separates the main dining-room from the small enclosure at the eastern end is a moose's head, presented by Henry T. Folsom (Yale '83).

Over the arch which separates the main dining-room from the small enclosure at the western end is a moose's head, presented by Admiral Willard H. Brownson (U. S. N. A. '65).

The buffalo head in the dining-room above the portrait of President Nott was presented by Doctor David L. Haight.

The head of a blacktail deer hung above the portrait of

President Barnard, in the dining-room, was presented by General George S. Anderson.

The head of an elk hung above the portrait of President Barnard, in the dining-room, is a loan from W. C. Camman (Columbia '91).

The buffalo head hung above President Noah Porter's portrait, in the dining-room, was presented by General George S. Anderson.

The collection of "shore birds" in the billiard-room was presented to the Club by Mr. Charles Stewart Davison (Harvard '75).

The following description of these interesting specimens was furnished by Mr. Charles Stewart Davison, at the request of the compiler:

The shore birds in the glass case on the mantelpiece in the billiard-room at the University Club are single specimens of each variety that came to the blind on four mornings (September 8 to 12, 1898) at Chincoteague on the ocean side of and half-way down the exterior peninsula of Virginia. They represent also in a sense the diminution of species. Ten years before that time the varieties would have been considerably more numerous. To-day they would probably be less numerous and—if the question of the protection of migratory birds is not thoroughly taken up—ten years from now some of the varieties will have wholly disappeared. Beginning on the left of the case the varieties are as follows:

1. Ægialites semipalmata (Bonaparte)—Semipalmated Plover or Ringneck.

2. Calidris arenaria—Sanderling.

3. Macrorhamphus griseus (Gmelin)—Dowitcher.

4. Tringa canutus—Robin Snipe or Knot.

5. Totanus flavipes (Gmelin)—Lesser Yellowlegs or Summer Yellowlegs.

6. Totanus melanoleucus (Gmelin)—Greater Yellowlegs, Yelper or Winter Yellowlegs.

7. Symphemia semipalmata—Willet.

8. Charadrius squatarola—Black bellied Plover, or Bull-head Plover (has hind toe).

9. Micropalama himantopus (Bonaparte)—Stilt Sandpiper.

10. Arenaria interpres—Ruddy Turnstone—Calico-back, Brant-bird or Chicken Plover.

11. Tringa maculata—Pectoral Sandpiper, Shortneck or Krieker.

12. Tringa minutilla—Least Sandpiper, or Peep or Oxeye.

In October, 1907, the Council resolved that a reception be given to Ambassador Bryce, of England, and Ambassador Jusserand, of France.

On November 14, 1907, the Club lost one of its most useful members in the death of Charles T. Barney (Williams '70). No better expression of the regard and respect felt for Mr. Barney by the Club at large can be given here than will be found in the following resolutions drawn by Judge Henry E. Howland and passed by the Council at its meeting of January 13, 1908:

Our late associate Charles T. Barney has been so closely identified with the history of the University Club that the members of the Council consider that a special minute is due by it to his memory.

He became a member of the Club upon its reorganization in 1879, and took from the first a deep interest in its welfare. When the change of site and the building of a new Club-house was under consideration he was called to an important position, in its Councils, for which his experience, his judgment and his acknowledged taste pre-eminently fitted him.

As Chairman of the Building Committee he rendered the Club great service. It seemed a colossal undertaking in the condition of the Club finances and membership existing at that time to attempt so large an enterprise, but under the hopeful stimulating enthusiasm of Mr. Barney it was accomplished.

The new Club House was at all times the object of his solicitous care; he urged and made possible by his generous contribution the decoration of the Library which but for him would have been impossible.

He never relaxed his care of the Club and at the time of his death he was engaged in plans for its extension and improvement.

He was a dominant spirit in the civic or philanthropic movements in which he engaged and they were many. His example was inspiring and he spared neither time nor money in promoting them.

He was a member of the first Municipal Art Commission of the City, a leader in promoting the fine portrait exhibitions which have created so much interest here and in Boston; was active in the New York Musical School Settlement; an original member of the Board of Managers of the New York Zoological Society—the Treasurer and Chairman of its Executive Committee, making gifts of money and of animals, and he gave his personal attention to problems of planting and landscape gardening and construction of its buildings.

He was also a trustee of the New York Ophthalmic and Aural Institution and an organizer and principal worker in the organization known as the Anti-Smoke League, which has purified the atmosphere of the Bay and City of New York by abolishing the use of bituminous coal.

His high-strung, impulsive and energetic spirit was manifested in all his undertakings.

Success is often separated from failure by a very narrow margin, and there come times in the life of every man of large affairs when a critical moment brings one or the other.

> "They that stand high have many blasts to shake them
> And if they fall they dash themselves to pieces."

It was the tragic event of Mr. Barney's life that the financial institution which he built up to a high position should have suddenly been subjected to a breaking strain.

The blow was too severe for his proud spirit and he sank beneath it. His sad end only adds to the grief felt by his friends for the loss of his abundant vitality, exuberant spirits, wit and generosity, to which should be added the gratitude of the public for his services to the best interests of art in this City. His record in that service makes his appropriate monument.

The Committee on Literature and Art were authorized to place a tablet in the east end of the library recognizing Mr. Charles T. Barney's contribution to the decoration of the library and stating that the decoration was made by Mr. Mowbray.

CHAPTER XXI

THE HUDSON-FULTON CELEBRATION—EMPLOYEES AND PENSIONS—1908-1909

AT the regular meeting of the Council, in November, 1908, the formal announcement was made of the death of George A. Adee (Yale '67) which occurred August 8, 1908, and the following minute, prepared by Thomas Thacher (Yale '71), was entered upon the records in his memory:

By the death of George A. Adee the aristocracy of University men has lost a gentleman of the finest quality and of the highest character; a man strong in body, mind and soul; a genial companion of peculiar charms; a true sportsman and a staunch friend, respected by all who knew him and beloved by those who had the privilege of knowing him.

An ardent Yale man, especially devoted to the athletic interests of his Alma Mater, he had a host of friends and admirers not only among Yale men but also among the Alumni of other Universities.

His broad sympathy, his thorough manliness, his love of fair dealing and hatred of things mean, and his generosity of mind and soul gave him peculiar influence in furthering that community of interest among University men upon which this Club rests, and it is therefore peculiarly fitting that this Council, of which for years he was a member, should enter this minute upon its records to evidence its sense of the loss which his death has brought to this Club and its members and the whole body of University Alumni.

This "minute" reflects the sentiments universally cherished by university men without reference to their college affiliations. In Adee's death the University Club and the world of American graduates lost one who more than most typified the "all-around" college man. He was respected and esteemed in this Club to a degree which few have attained. His influence in the uplift of intercollegiate ethics, for fair play, and for a catholic spirit which involved no sacrifice of loyalty to Alma Mater was great and its effects are still felt.

From Saturday, September 25, to October 11, 1909, the State of New York commemorated, under the auspices of the Hudson-Fulton Celebration Commission, the three hundredth anniversary of the discovery of the Hudson River by Henry Hudson, in 1609, and the one hundredth anniversary of the first application of steam to navigation, upon that river, by Robert Fulton, in 1807.

Henry Hudson, Englishman, had been sent out from Holland in his little ship, the *Half-Moon*, to find "the strait that leads to the Eastern Sea," and stumbled, by accident as it were, on the noble river which was to bear his name. Robert Fulton, with his steamboat the *Clermont*, built in New York City, demonstrated the feasibility of propelling vessels by steam, and left his name impressed on the city, among other ways, in one of its public streets. Fitting as such a memorial may be, a far more striking tribute is to be found in the modern leviathan transatlantic floating palaces which are the evolution of Fulton's conception.

At the time of the Hudson-Fulton Celebration the Governor of the State of New York was Charles E. Hughes (Brown '81), a member of the University Club and now Justice of the Supreme Court of the United States. The president of the Hudson-Fulton Celebration Commission was also a member of this Club, as was the secretary; the former being General Stewart L. Woodford (Columbia '54) and the latter Henry W. Sackett (Cornell '75). The chairman of the naval-parade committee was our fellow member, Commander Jacob W. Miller (U. S. N. A. '67).

The programme of events was stupendous. Besides the

presence of replicas of both the *Half-Moon* (presented by Hollanders) and the *Clermont*, there were naval parades day and night; military parades; a historical pageant with illustrative floats; a carnival parade at night; exercises by artistic and scientific societies, by libraries, by museums, by universities, and by the Sons of the Revolution; exercises at West Point and numerous towns up and down the Hudson; aquatic sports; religious observances; concerts; exhibitions; aëronautics; music festivals; children's festivals; dedications; banquets; decorations; a reception of official guests at Governor's Island, the headquarters of the Department of the East; and illuminations (some of which were chromatic) of the war-fleet, the monuments, the club houses, private dwellings, and Grant's Tomb.

Among the buildings appropriately decorated was of course the University Club, a representation of which is given among the illustrations, and a commodious stand for spectators among the members built on the Fifth Avenue front. During the period of the celebration the introduction of ordinary visitors to the Club was suspended, and cards of invitation were sent to the officers of the foreign ships taking part in the commemoration, of which there were many, as well as to the distinguished representatives from other lands.

At the meeting of the Council December 13, 1909, the deaths of two honored members of the Club were reported, namely, Charles F. McKim (Harvard '70) and C. C. Cuyler (Princeton '79). These events occurred on the 14th of September, 1909, and the 31st of July, 1909, respectively.

The minutes recorded to express the sentiment of the Club were as follows:

Charles Follen McKim was born in 1847, of Quaker parents, whose great interest and purpose in life was the abolition of slavery. Their love of simplicity and stability, and their passion for freedom, were at work within him from the beginning. He devoted his great powers to destroying those twin tyrants, ugliness and ignorance, which at the close of the Civil War, it has truly been said, "had intrenched themselves in secure possession" of the field of architecture. How well he succeeded is known of all men. The nation has had no more disinterested or public-spirited citizen, and for leadership and enthusiasm, his untiring, unselfish and arduous labor in the cause of art and beauty, his country owes a deep debt of gratitude.

To us of the University Club he was not only the great architect. He was our friend, ever eager to give us the best that was in him; loyalty itself to his friends; full, too, of great-hearted interest in all that concerned the welfare of the University Club, whose honored and much loved architect he was.

"The light he leaves behind him
Lies upon the lives of men."

Cornelius C. Cuyler, a member of this Club since 1884, a member of its Council from 1902 to 1906, and a member of its Auditing and Finance Committee since 1906, was killed in an automobile accident on July 31st, 1909. By the death of Mr. Cuyler, Princeton University has been robbed of one of its most beloved and influential graduates and the whole College world of one of its most widely known and efficient workers.

Mr. Cuyler's interest in and knowledge of matters appertaining to College affairs was one of his strong characteristics. The encouraging support he gave to deserving students was unfailing, and many College men throughout the country gratefully recall the advice and assistance that they received from C. C. Cuyler.

By his sympathetic and lovable nature he endeared himself to all classes and his death is considered a personal bereavement by many members of this Club.

To those who knew him well his memory is ever present.

The members of the Council of the University Club feel his loss most deeply, and they desire to record their love for him by this resolution to be spread upon the Club's minutes and direct a copy be sent to Mrs. Cuyler, to whom they extend their sincere and heartfelt sympathy.

Mr. McKim's services to the University Club have already been referred to in these pages. No faithful historian could fail to emphasize the value of them to the membership. The younger generation who did not know McKim and his works can have but an incomplete idea of his worth. He combined in himself a winning personality, a genius for art in architecture, and a constant devotion to the University Club. The beautiful creation which he evolved from his well-stored mind and cultivated taste—in the building of which we are all so proud—important and satisfying as it is as a monument, is only a small part of what this gifted man contributed to the city of New York and the country. And even if the stately products of his artistic skill did not exist to remind those coming after him of his remarkable talents, those of us who were his comrades would still hold his memory sacred for the high standard of his manliness, public spirit, and loyal friendship.

In a different way, but of no less value, C. C. Cuyler commanded the respect and affection of all college men. While George A. Adee was a representative of Yale spirit, looked up to and confided in by his fellow alumni, C. C. Cuyler occupied a similar attitude toward Princeton, his Alma Mater, and her sons. And both were so catholic in spirit that they successfully co-operated for the good not only of their own universities but of the other institutions, particularly in regard to athletic and social affairs. Many were the times when these two men, by wise and tactful measures, promoted harmony and carved out success under circumstances in which the ordinary play of human nature and the thoughtlessness of youth threatened discord and failure. Cuyler was a figure in the intercollegiate life of his day and Princeton has recognized his services by giving the name of "Cuyler Hall" to one of her newer buildings.

The system of pensions adopted by the Club cannot better be described than by quoting from President Sands's report of March, 1911, as follows:

During the year, the Council has established a permanent Pension Fund for the benefit of the employees of the Club. By the creation of this fund, the policy of the best and most liberally managed corporations has been followed. It was felt that the employees of the Club would perform their work more efficiently, and remain longer in its service, if they knew that, having served the Club faithfully, their declining years would be made comfortable by the pension which they would receive from the Club. The plan adopted provides that all employees who shall have reached the age of sixty-five years, and who shall have rendered continuous service for fifteen years or more immediately preceding the attainment of their sixty-fifth year, shall, at their request, if the Council approve, be retired and pensioned at the rate of two and a half per cent for each year of service, based upon their average rate of pay for ten years immediately preceding such retirement; that no pension shall exceed half the yearly pay of such beneficiary, or the total rate of $100 per month, and that employees who have served the Club continuously for fifteen years and have become physically disqualified may apply for a pension. The Club, however, reserved the right to commute and terminate any pension by the payment of a gross sum, to be fixed by the Council. The employees were notified of the adoption of this plan, and the House Committee reports that they received the announcement with satisfaction, and that it has already produced good results.

The fact that employees continue for a long time in business houses or families is generally accepted as proof that the business or the housekeeping department is wisely and sanely conducted. If this rule be applied to the University Club, it will be seen that its management deserves the same commendation. It is not proposed here to give an exhaustive account of the veterans in the Club's service, but reference may properly be made to those who have continuously been on the pay-roll for more than ten years, one officer of the Club having been with us for over thirty-four years, or almost from the time of the reorganization in 1879.

Hugh J. Ennis, the official last referred to, entered the service of the Club in April, 1881, and on account of his abnormally long tenure deserves especial mention.

Mr. Ennis was a student in the College of the City of New York, and was compelled to suspend his studies on account of ill health. Through the influence of General Alexander S. Webb (U. S. M. A. '55), who was then president of the City College and a member of the Council of the University Club, he was in 1881 employed by Henry E. Pellew (Trin. Col., Cambr. '50), then Chairman of the House Committee, as an assistant in the office. Showing capacity, Mr. Henry Holt, then Chairman of the Committee on Literature and Art, induced Mr. Pellew to let Ennis become Librarian. He continued such for three years, until 1884, and during that period systematized the library and catalogued its books. He afterward assumed the charge of the office and accounts, as Cashier, and continues to act in that capacity to the satisfaction of all, and has been of great service to the compiler in the collection of data. He became acting Superintendent of the Club, July 15, 1914.

Edward Gleason was appointed Superintendent of the Club on October 1, 1892, and resigned July 9, 1914. His services are referred to elsewhere.

Lyman H. Bagg, whose services are elsewhere referred to, entered the service of the Club as Librarian in 1889, and continued in that position until 1900, when he resigned.

Jno. A. Mansfield, an assistant librarian, came to the Club in 1899, and holds that position at the present time.

Otto Schoenborn, assistant librarian, entered upon this work in 1902, and continues it.

John Zimmerman, the bookkeeper, was employed in 1884; continued until 1889; was engaged outside until 1893; returned in that year, and continued to date in the Club.

All the older members of the Club remember Peter Moran, who became head hall captain in 1884 and so remained until May, 1907, when, much to the regret of the management, he resigned and went to the country on a farm. Peter was the ideal Club servant. He knew every member and every member knew him. His manner was always respectful and obliging, and he possessed that kind of memory which made him valuable in the position he held. He is still living.

In the same year, 1884, M. F. Murphy became watchman, and so remained until 1906, when he resigned on account of old age.

The frequenters of the billiard-room would greatly miss the captain in charge of it if anything happened to cause his retirement. His name is Patrick D. King and he has been in the service of the Club since 1886.

William McCallion, the assistant engineer, has been with the Club since 1886.

Washington Dobson, one of the elevator conductors, entered the service of the Club in 1887, and has been going up and down in the elevator ever since. A member, who fancies statistical calculations, has made an estimate that Dobson has travelled more than six thousand miles in the Club elevators during that period.

Paul Nagle, the chief engineer, was formerly in the German Army, and remained in the Club's employ from November 10, 1888, to July 1, 1914, when he was retired on a pension. The incident of his meeting with Prince Henry of Prussia in the Club House is mentioned in another part of this history.

Edward Hooper was employed as a waiter in 1889, and became valet for bedrooms in 1903, in which service he continues.

John O'Reilly became assistant barkeeper in 1891, and in 1904 was promoted to head barkeeper, which position he now holds.

Bruno Daumann, the head barber of the Club, was engaged in April, 1892, and has continued in his position until the present time.

Frank Thomassen was made steward of the Club in 1893, and resigned in 1909. He came to the Club from Delmonico's, where he had for years had the experience which fitted him for his work.

Jean Columbin, who had been second cook at Delmonico's, was secured by the Club in 1893 as *chef*. He was one of the best of his guild. It was he who provided the feast in honor of Doctor David L. Haight in 1895, and won a deserved reputation for *cuisine* while here by his skill, which has been handed down to his successor. Columbin resigned in 1900.

George Getter, the receiving clerk, came to the Club in 1893, and still occupies that position.

S. A. Lee, bookkeeper, was employed in 1893, and continues in the service.

Owen Shanley began his service in 1893. He was hallman until October, 1899, since when and to the present time he has been doorkeeper.

Patrick Malone, porter, commenced service in 1895, and is still here.

A. Bishop was first employed in 1895, as head waiter, which position he held until February, 1910, when he became steward of the Club, and so continues.

John W. Bell entered the service in 1899 as hallman, and so continued until May, 1909, when he was made "inspector of service," a position he now holds.

William Connelly, the head bathman, was employed in 1899, and still acts in that capacity.

Alfred Bascomb, valet, was employed in 1899, and is with the Club still.

On account of the lack of space, the list of employees is not extended to include those employed later than 1902. There are among the men entering the service of the Club at later dates, faithful servants worthy of commendation, and the omission of other names is of no significance except that they have not been as long on the rolls as those mentioned.

Satisfactory as the record is, it may fairly be presumed that had the pension system now in operation been adopted in the earlier stages of the Club's history, the list of deserving employees of long standing would be even of greater length.

The compiler has made inquiry as to the wisdom of this measure, among the veteran experts in the conduct of the Club's affairs. The following opinion of one of them, well qualified to speak, is given as clearly setting forth the merits of the plan:

In my opinion the plan of providing pensions for the employees of the Club is a matter of great importance not only to the employees but also to the welfare of the Club.

Honest, careful, temperate, obedient, and faithful employees are difficult to obtain and more difficult to keep unless they have something to look forward to, as promotion, permanency, increase of wages, etc. Add to these the additional inducement of being taken care of when incapacitated by sickness, accident, or old age and you have employees who are more contented, for they have been relieved of the worry of what is to become of them under any of the foregoing circumstances . . . you will find greater willingness to perform extra services when necessity requires it . . . they will not leave their positions in a fit of temper for any trivial reason as is now the case in clubs and hotels, for they know they can obtain just as good positions, paying just as good wages, in some other club . . . and this provision for their future welfare will be an incentive to think twice before they act. And further they will not be so easily enticed away by offers of small increases in their wages.

Constant changes militate against good service and their effects are felt by the members as well as by the management. Employees who remain say five years or over are well trained and experienced. They make it their business to study the wants and characteristics of the members, and dealing with such employees in the various departments conduces to the comfort and enjoyment of the members . . . and having such employees relieves the management of many cares and worries which it is subject to when employees are continually changing.

CHAPTER XXII

FINANCES—THE BUDGET—FINANCE AND AUDITING COMMITTEES—ART COMMITTEE—COMMITTEE ON PRINTS—1910-1913

At the annual meeting of the Club, March 18, 1911, the following important amendment to the constitution was adopted:

XV.

Executive Committee.

There shall be an Executive Committee which shall consist of the President, Vice-President, Secretary and Treasurer, and the Chairmen of the Several Standing Committees. During the recess of the Council this Committee shall be vested with all the powers of the Council so far as the same can be properly delegated, and it shall be its duty to exercise such powers whenever immediate action is required.

Five members of this Committee shall constitute a quorum.

A further amendment was adopted providing that there should be seven standing committees to be known as the House Committee, the Finance Committee, the Auditing Committee, the Library Committee, the Art Committee, the Committee on Colleges and Degrees, and the Entertainment Committee, and defining their duties and method of appointment.

The following extract from President Sands's report of March, 1911, sets forth the significance of certain of the changes effected by this amendment:

The duties of the Auditing and Finance Committee are separated, and two committees established. The most important duty

BENJAMIN AYMAR SANDS (Columbia '74).
Ninth President, 1910–1913. From a painting by William T. Smedley, 1914.

which will be assigned to the Finance Committee is that of preparing, at the beginning of each fiscal year, a budget setting forth the estimated income and the expenditures of the Club and of its several departments. Appropriations on the recommendation of the committee will be made by the Council, and after the appropriations have been expended, no further outlay can be made without a reference to and a report by the Finance Committee. The expenditures of the Club are now so large and are made by so many different departments that it is important that the income and outgo should be carefully supervised.

It is also proposed to establish an Entertainment Committee, which shall have charge of functions and entertainments given under the auspices of the Club. It is hoped that by putting some of the younger men of the Club on this committee, the character of the entertainments may be made more novel and interesting.

At the meeting of the Council, June 13, 1910, the retirement of $50,000 of the second-mortgage bonds of the Club was ordered and put into execution during the year, and $1,500 and $1,000 were retired November, 1912, and June, 1913, respectively.

These last reductions of the Club's mortgage debt up to the time of publication call for a brief review of the various steps taken in relation to the issue.

In 1897, in contemplation of the erection and furnishing of the new building, and in order to obtain the funds necessary for that purpose in addition to the $1,250,000 borrowed on first mortgage, the following resolution was passed:

At a meeting of the Council of the University Club (said Council being the Trustees and Managers of said Club) duly called and held at 120 Broadway, New York, on the 31st day of March, 1897, at which a quorum was present, the following preamble and resolutions were unanimously adopted:

Whereas, This Club has purchased a tract of land at the northwest corner of Fifty-fourth Street and Fifth Avenue . . .

Whereas, The Club is now engaged in the construction of a large building for the purposes of its organization; and, in order to complete the same, it will be necessary to provide funds by borrowing the same; and

Whereas, The Club is to procure a loan not exceeding $1,250,000 from the Equitable Life Assurance Society of the United States, to be secured by a bond and mortgage of the Club for that amount;

Therefore be it resolved, that, in the judgment of this Council, it is necessary to borrow, for the purpose aforesaid, the further sum of $350,000, to be secured by a second mortgage on the said premises; and,

It is further resolved, That in order to procure a loan of the said sum of $350,000 the President or Vice-President and Secretary of the said Club are hereby authorized in its name, to execute coupon bonds to the aggregate amount of $350,000 in form and denomination as shall be prescribed by the Building Committee of the Club; said bonds to be payable in gold coin of the United States of America, of the present standard of weight and fineness, within twenty years from date, with interest thereon, payable in like gold coin, at the rate of five per centum per annum, payable semi-annually; and in order to secure the payment of the same with interest, the said President or Vice-President and Secretary are hereby authorized and instructed to make and execute in the name and under the corporate seal of this Club, a mortgage to the Central Trust Company of New York, as Trustee, upon the said real property of the Club, with such conditions and provisions as shall be prescribed by the Building Committee of the said Club, and to cause the execution of said mortgage to be duly proved and to deliver the said mortgage to the Central Trust Company of New York, as Trustee, and to deliver the said bonds to the subscribers and purchasers of the same in accordance with the directions of the said Building Committee of the Club.

The following provision for calling these bonds was incorporated in the instrument itself:

The party of the first part reserves the privilege of calling in and paying the said bonds or any of them on the 1st of March or September upon giving notice of its intention so to do by written or printed notice posted in some convenient place in its Club House and by advertisement in at least one of the daily newspapers published in the City of New York at least twice in each week for two successive weeks in which notice shall be designated by their respective numbers the bonds which it shall call in to be paid, and after the time stated in such notice for such payment the interest on the bonds so called shall cease.

The Club, in the proper exercise of economy, found it necessary to issue only $261,500 of these bonds, which were all taken up by the members of the Club.

In March, 1906, the Club under the authority conferred as above, paid off bonds to the amount of	$30,000
In September, 1908, they paid off	40,000
In September, 1910, they paid off	50,000
In December, 1905, they purchased bonds to the amount of	1,000
In November, 1907, they purchased	5,000
In October, 1908, they purchased	1,500
In November, 1912, they purchased	1,500
In June, 1913, they purchased	1,000
	$130,000

Leaving outstanding bonds to the amount of $131,500, the sum of this indebtedness as it now stands.

The question arose at the meeting of the Council of December 12, 1910, as to the expediency of increasing the annual dues, and the consideration of the same was referred to the Finance Committee. This committee reported at the meeting of February 16, 1911, that it was in their judgment inadvisable at present to increase the dues.

At the meeting of the Council of May 8, 1911, the Library Committee was requested to confer with James W. Alexander (Princeton '60) and ascertain whether he was willing to undertake a compilation of the history of the Club during the first half-century of its existence. The Library Committee reported at the June meeting that Mr. Alexander "would gladly compile the history of the University Club," and he was thereupon authorized and requested to proceed with the same.

At the meeting of the Council of May 8, 1911, an appropriation (among others of less amount and importance) was made of about $20,000 for the reconstruction, decoration, and furnishing of the private dining-rooms on the upper floor of the Club, so that they should be in keeping with the general completeness of the Club. The undertaking was referred to the Art Committee, consisting of Samuel R. Bertron (Yale '85), John C. Van Dyke (Rutgers '89), John B. Cauldwell (Columbia '77), William C. Osborn (Princeton '83), and Charles T. Mathews (Yale '86). This committee, composed of one artist, one architect, and three laymen of artistic appreciation, proceeded to carry out the plan of improvement under the direction of William Francklyn Paris, architect, with the result which may be inspected in its completion at the present time.

The University Club having, in accordance with its customary recognition of national and international events, been represented at the service held at Trinity Church in 1911 in honor of the newly crowned King and Queen of England, the following letter was received from the British consul-general:

NEW YORK, July 25, 1911.

Sir!

I have the honour to inform you that a report of the Service at Trinity Church and of the Festivities held at New York to celebrate the Coronation of Their Majesties King George and Queen Mary has been laid before the King.

I am now directed by Secretary Sir Edward Grey to convey to you Their Majesties' sincere thanks for your presence at the Service, and the expression of Their Majesties' high appreciation of the gratifying tribute that was paid to them on that auspicious occasion —a tribute which it has given them much pleasure to receive.

I am,

Sir,

Your Obedient Servant

JOHN J. BRODERICK

Acting Consul General

THE PRESIDENT

University Club

New York City.

From a photograph, by Tebbs, New York.

THE LARGEST PRIVATE DINING-ROOM, LOOKING SOUTH.

Designed and executed by W. Francklyn Paris.

In the year 1912 an incident occurred which was unusual, interesting, and in its results beneficial to the Club members, as clearing up a subject which had given rise to dissatisfaction and misunderstanding in certain circles, and furnishing information to the Club generally regarding the pains taken by the Council and House Committee (1) in providing for the comfort and convenience of members, and (2) in their readiness to pay prompt and thorough attention to the complaints of those who for any reason questioned the conduct of the Club's affairs.

This incident cannot better be described than by reproducing an extract from President Sands's Report of 1912, as follows:

At the November meeting of the Council, there was presented a paper, signed by over fifty members of the Club, containing the following statement and petition:

"We, the undersigned members of the University Club, believe that a considerable portion of the poultry and game served by the Club is cold storage; we therefore, respectfully request the President and the Council of the Club to take such action that the members of the Club may not partake of cold storage food without being duly informed."

The Council appreciated the importance of this petition, and appointed a special committee, consisting of three of its members, James Byrne (Harvard '77), Walter G. Oakman (Univ. of Pa. '64), and William Manice (Columbia '86), to consider the prayer of the petitioners. This committee made a most comprehensive investigation of the subject, and informally reported their conclusions at the February meeting. They stated that, so far as game was concerned, there was very little for the committee to do. The New York Game Law, as amended in 1911, put an end to the sale of fresh native game. The only native game the Club legally could have had after June, 1911, was game that had been in cold storage on that date. Some of this, in response to the request of members, was bought by the Club after October 1, 1911, but purchases ceased November 5th. Imported game is still on the bill of fare, some of it being obtained direct from England, and some from dealers in New York.

As to poultry, the inquiry of the committee extended further than at the outset had been expected. The committee was soon satisfied that the dealers from whom the Club buys its poultry are the best in New York; that the poultry the Club gets is as good as that furnished by any dealer to any club or hotel; that the House Committee makes every effort to get as good poultry (and for that matter game) as can be bought, and that great care is taken by the employees of the Club in the examination of all supplies delivered at the Club to see that they are in proper condition. But the committee was also satisfied that this Club and every other club and restaurant and private house supplied by dealers get cold storage poultry at certain seasons of the year. The Committee thought, therefore, that it ought to find out as well as it could whether the popular prejudice against cold storage poultry is just, and, if it is, to decide whether the Club ought absolutely to refuse to serve any but fresh poultry.

A committee of the United States Senate has been for over a year taking testimony on cold storage of food. This testimony, particularly that of Dr. Wiley and Dr. Pennington, chief of the Food Research Laboratory in Dr. Wiley's Department, the Committee examined. Dr. Pennington testified that she had devoted practically her entire time for five years to the investigation of the storage and handling of poultry, eggs and milk; that the chemical changes in a chicken kept at a temperature of from 65 to 75 degrees for 24 hours were greater than one kept in cold storage for 12 months; and that the acidity of a chicken (which corresponds to rancidity in butter) increases as much when the chicken is kept for five days in a house refrigerator as when it is kept for a year in cold storage; that in her opinion a chicken properly killed and held in cold storage for a year was of a better grade than a chicken killed on an ordinary farm and sold at retail in a city or town; and that if poultry is properly handled before it is put in cold storage, and our entire supply consisted of such poultry, the supply would be better than what we were accustomed to before cold storage became customary and better than most of the poultry sold in the markets at the present time.

Dr. Wiley testified that one of his juries had repeatedly eaten fresh chickens and chickens which had been in cold storage for three months, and had been unable to tell which was which.

The testimony as a whole seemed to show that there was a season for everything when it was at its best and most plentiful; that even if a thing could be produced at all times of the year, when it was scarce it was poor; and that things produced at the proper season and frozen were better several months old than the same things fresh when produced at the wrong season.

After reading this testimony the Committee saw representatives of the firms from whom the Club buys poultry, and was confirmed in its belief that from the latter part of January until May most of the poultry sold by dealers is cold storage poultry, the time in which it has been in storage varying from ten days to three months.

The committee, in the course of its inquiries, examined the places where the dealers from whom the Club buys keep their poultry and also examined the methods of freezing and storage in large warehouses in New York.

The Club has tried to get fresh poultry at all seasons direct from the farm, but has found difficulty in getting a constant supply of a satisfactory kind.

The Committee put the information which it obtained before the signers of the petition, and the House Committee asked for suggestions as to what should be done. Some of those at the conference thought that whoever wanted fresh chickens at all seasons of the year, regardless of whether they were better or worse than cold storage chickens, should have them; and it was agreed, with the concurrence of the House Committee, that that Committee should at all seasons of the year buy fresh chickens direct from farmers, and that such chickens should be described on the bill of fare as "farm chickens," in order to distinguish them from those bought from dealers.

At the meeting of the Council of January, 1912, an innovation was authorized in the conduct of the Club's affairs, which promises to be of great use and to afford much entertainment. The Art Committee was "empowered to appoint a *committee of members* of the Club to obtain by gift, loan, or purchase a collection of engravings and prints to be appropriately hung in the hall leading to the private dining-rooms."

This committee was duly appointed and consists of the following members of the Club:

Committee on Prints

Adrian H. Larkin (Princeton '87), *Chairman.*
Henry H. Benedict (Hamilton '69).
Samuel R. Bertron (Yale '85), (*ex-officio*).
Samuel R. Betts (Yale '75).
John B. Cauldwell (Columbia '77), (*ex-officio*).
Harris D. Colt (Yale '84).
William C. Demorest (Columbia '81).
Loyall Farragut (U. S. M. A. '68).
W. B. Osgood Field (Stevens Inst. '94).
Frederic R. Halsey (Harvard '68).
R. T. H. Halsey (Princeton '86).
Louis C. Hay (Yale '81).
Phœnix Ingraham (Harvard '98).
Arthur Curtiss James (Amherst '89).
Frederick P. Keppel (Columbia '98).
Howard Mansfield (Yale '71).
Bradley Martin, Jr. (Christ Ch., Oxford '94).
Charles T. Mathews (Yale '86), (*ex-officio*).
Charles F. Mathewson (Dartmouth '82).
Russell W. Moore (Princeton '83).
Charles A. Munn (Princeton '81).
John S. Rogers (Yale '98), *Secretary.*
John F. Talmage (Yale '95).
Colonel Robert M. Thompson (U. S. N. A. '68).
Professor John C. Van Dyke (Rutgers '89), (*ex-officio*).
Judge Henry G. Ward (Univ. of Pa. '70).
Evert Jansen Wendell (Harvard '82).

The committee issued the following notice and request to the members of the Club:

Through the action of the Art Committee of the University Club, a Special Committee has been appointed for the purpose of collecting rare, artistic, historic and interesting prints such as portraits of distinguished graduates, views of buildings and localities, and of incidents of the undergraduate life in domestic and foreign colleges and universities.

This letter is being sent to members of the Club with the object of interesting them in the plan, which it is believed can be developed into a very attractive feature of the Club. Any member who may have anything of the kind which he is willing to present to the Club, is invited to forward such material to the Clubhouse, addressed to the Chairman of the Committee on Prints, or to communicate with him in regard thereto. The Committee will be pleased to send for such gifts if it be the preference of the donor.

The Committee desires to make as large a collection as possible, within the scope outlined below; and from the collection so made it will select such prints as it deems most desirable to frame and hang on walls, arranging the balance in portfolios properly classified and indexed. It is hoped that in this manner a very interesting and valuable collection of prints can be formed.

The collection as planned at the present time is limited to prints covering the several varieties of engravings, wood cuts and lithographs, but exclusive of photographic reproductions and photographs: embracing portraits of distinguished graduates published prior to 1850, and prints depicting college views, buildings, incidents, etc., published prior to 1870.

The committee is especially anxious to obtain college prints of the eighteenth century, and any member knowing of such prints, or where they may be obtained, will confer a favor by communicating with the Chairman, Mr. Adrian H. Larkin, at the University Club.

Yours very truly,
JOHN S. ROGERS,
Secretary.

April 10th, 1912.

The work of the committee was subdivided as follows:

SUB-COMMITTEE ON COLLECTING: Charles A. Munn, Chairman; Harris D. Colt, Frederic R. Halsey, Russell W. Moore, Evert J. Wendell.

SUB-COMMITTEE ON CLASSIFICATION, FRAMING AND HANGING: Louis C. Hay, Chairman; Samuel R. Betts, R. T. H. Halsey, F. P. Keppel, John F. Talmage.

SUB-COMMITTEE ON RESEARCH: Charles F. Mathewson, Chairman; William C. Demorest, Bradley Martin, Jr., Colonel R. M. Thompson, Judge Henry G. Ward.

The committee decided that the adoption of a uniform style of framing for the prints was undesirable, as such a plan would do away, in many instances, with the use of old frames of intrinsic artistic value and typical of the period of which the print itself is representative. The committee has acquired a large number of interesting prints, and has framed and hung them. A suitable plate with the name of the donor and any other interesting facts is to be affixed to each framed print. (See Appendix XII.)

The Prints Committee hopes, with the co-operation of the members of the Club, ultimately to make this collection of prints one of the most interesting and important of its kind anywhere.

The question of an increase in the annual dues of the Club having been again made the subject of consideration by a committee, consisting of Robert Thorne (Trinity '85), Walter G. Oakman (Univ. of Pa. '64), and Samuel Sloan (Columbia '87), that committee reported at the meeting of the Council of January, 1912, that it was inadvisable at the present time to increase the dues of members, and on motion the committee was discharged. The Club thus for the second time decided against this measure, notwithstanding that the dues were only $75 per annum for resident members as against $125 in other clubs which furnish accommodations for members on a scale comparable to that maintained in the University Club.

At this meeting the Art Committee reported that Mr. J. F. Talmage (Yale '95) had loaned to the Club a collection of old masters. (A list of these paintings has been given in another chapter.) Whereupon it was

Resolved, That a vote of thanks be tendered to Mr. Talmage for loaning his collection of pictures and that a letter be sent by the Secretary to him.

The Secretary was at the same time directed to write to Mr. H. D. Babcock (Columbia '68) thanking him on behalf of the Council for the loan of three paintings.

It was with extreme regret that the Club were obliged to lose the collection of Mr. Talmage in 1913, it having become necessary for him to remove them for sale. The high prices obtained for them proved the estimate of connoisseurs as to their merit and consequent value.

An acknowledgment should here be made of the valuable services of the Art Committee. Appointed in 1909, they have been most active and efficient and have made many important improvements in the Club's appearance. Among these, besides the private dining rooms mentioned above, were: on the first floor, the redecoration of the reception room, the ceiling of the central hall, the candelabra by the fireplace and the bas relief (by Keck) above it; on the dining-room floor, the completion of the Council Room ceiling (by Mowbray), the redecorating of the anteroom, and the ceiling of the hall (by Garnsey).

At the request of Admiral Alfred T. Mahan (U. S. N. A. '59), the privileges of the Club were extended to the foreign members of the Congress of Navigation during their stay in New York.

At the annual meeting of the Club held March 16, 1912, the following resolution was unanimously adopted:

Whereas, Mr. Courtlandt C. Clarke, whose term as a member of the Council of the University Club has now expired, has been the Chairman of its House Committee for seven years last past, and

Whereas, He has during all that period unselfishly devoted his best energies to the good of the Club and the comfort and convenience of its members,

It is Resolved, By the members of the University Club in their annual meeting assembled, that they hereby express to Mr. Clarke their hearty thanks for his long and successful management and their warm appreciation of his unfailing courtesy and consideration in the discharge of the duties of his office.

That a copy of this resolution be prepared under the direction of the Secretary of the Club and given to Mr. Clarke.

At the June meeting of the Council, the privileges of the Club were extended to the foreign members of the Geographical Congress during their stay in New York.

It would be unpardonable to omit from reference one who has been so remarkably honored by the nation to which he was the American ambassador, as Whitelaw Reid (Miami '56), a member of this Club since its reorganization in 1879.

Mr. Reid during his whole life was a factor in public affairs. Long before the death of his predecessor in the editorship of the New York *Tribune*, he made his influence felt, and his frequent appearance in the caricatures of Thomas Nast was proof positive that he was not a negligible quantity. From editorship he advanced to statesmanship, and he was one of the few men who have been ambassador both to France and England.

The hold upon English respect and esteem won by Mr. Reid was shown by the unprecedented honors bestowed after his death in London, on the 15th of December, 1912. A funeral service was held in Westminster Abbey, attended by the highest in the land, and his body was conveyed to America in the British armed cruiser *Natal*.

The removal of Ambassador Reid naturally draws attention to the mortality among eminent men of New York, both members of the University Club and otherwise, during the years of its existence.

On the 4th of January, 1913, the mortal remains of Whitelaw Reid were borne with a military escort through Fifth Avenue and past the University Club, whose flag was at half-mast. The compiler of this book happened to be one of the spectators of the cortège from the windows of the Club, and by his side stood the Reverend Arthur G. Thompson, D.D. (Yale '82), who recalled the fact that the death of Mr. Reid, then being conveyed to his last home, made him (Doctor Thompson) the only survivor of a notable party of fourteen who met at a dinner in 1883, given by Mr. Hamilton Fish, ex-secretary of state in General Grant's administration, and an officeholder in the church of which Doctor Thompson was the rector. Those present were: Mr. and Mrs. Fish, Ex-Secretary William M. Evarts, Ambassador Whitelaw Reid, Mr. John Jacob Astor (senior), Mr. John Aspinwall, Mr. Cornelius Vanderbilt, Mr. John Jay, Bishop Henry C. Potter, Doctor Morgan Dix, of Trinity Church; Doctor Huntington, of Grace Church; Doctor Morgan, of St. Thomas's Church; and Doctor Samuel Hoffman, Dean of the General Theological Seminary.

All dead!

Some of these distinguished men were members of the University Club, and were the catalogue of the prominent members who have passed away to be continued, it would make a long and impressive procession. These names will be found in the roll of the departed in Appendix VIII of this book. Doctor Thompson, on the occasion mentioned, called attention to the fact that of the 3,476 members of the Club listed in the Club book of 1912, only 154 were among those constituting the membership at the time of the reorganization in 1879. In other words 3,312 members had joined the Club since the election of the two holding the conversation referred to, and only 154 of the original members—veterans—remained.

The London *Punch*, that mirror of British opinion, in its issue of December 25, 1912, contains a serious article in which Whitelaw Reid is spoken of as the most familiar figure in the gallery of the House of Commons on big nights, and a portrait of the ambassador as he appeared on such occasions, leaning on the rail, with the inscription:

He never missed an important debate.

CHAPTER XXIII

PRESIDENT SANDS'S REPORT OF 1913—PROPOSAL TO RAISE THE DUES

ON the night of December 4, 1912, the members of the Council entertained at dinner Professor John Grier Hibben (Princeton '82) in honor of his election to the presidency of Princeton University, and in accordance with usage a reception was tendered to him by the Club on the same night, followed by a supper, at which the guest was toasted by Thomas Thacher (Yale '71). President Hibben was elected a member of the Club in 1912, under the rule providing that distinguished candidates might be acted on immediately without reference to their place on the list.

At the annual meeting of the Club held March 15, 1913, Mr. Benjamin Aymar Sands (Columbia '74), the President of the Club, submitted a report which deserves to be set forth here in full, but the exigencies of space limit the reproduction to several important extracts.

The report goes into detail in regard to the action of the various standing committees, and the status of the Club. In referring to the need of costly repairs and replacements, and the increased expenses in the conduct of affairs, which must almost to a certainty grow larger, the report says:

It would seem that the time must soon arrive for the members to consider a proposition for an increase of the dues. This question has been under discussion for several years by the Council, and has been the subject of a report by a select committee. The Council has been reluctant to recommend such an increase until it became imperatively necessary, but it is now its opinion that at the next annual meeting of the Club it should be asked for. There is, however, much satisfaction in the thought that, notwithstanding the very considerable increase of operating expenses since this Club House was opened, the dues have not been changed.

There is also another financial problem which needs consideration. There are still outstanding $131,500 of the original issue of $261,500 of second mortgage bonds; these bonds will become due on September 1, 1917, and may, upon notice, be paid before maturity, in full or in part. It would seem wise to follow the practice which prevails in most well-managed clubs, and apply the entrance fees, which average about $15,000, to the redemption of these bonds. Such a sinking fund would not retire all of the bonds at maturity, but as their obligation is not likely to be pressing, and as the credit of the Club is good, it could easily be arranged that the bonds remaining unpaid at the time of their maturity should be retired solely through the operation of a sinking fund. The application of the entrance fees to a sinking fund would create a deficiency in the general income of the Club, which would have to be made up from some other source of revenue, and this might best be done by an increase of the dues to an amount sufficient to allow for the application of the entrance fees to this sinking fund.

After giving statistics regarding the admission of members, the report proceeds:

In March, 1912, the waiting list in all classes was 1,216; it is now 1,253. Two years ago the Committee considered names posted six years and eight months before on the resident list; a year ago they had been seven years on the waiting list; while they are now considering names posted seven years and four months ago, showing that the period of waiting for resident applications increases about four months every year. The period of waiting for the non-resident list is the same as it was a year ago, namely five years.

The appreciation of the advantage of membership in this Club, by university graduates, is thus conspicuously demonstrated, and the hardship of a prolonged period of waiting is substantially modified by the rule giving preference, in taking up names by the Admission Committee, to candidates of special distinction and to those who have held the degree which renders them eligible for election for at least twenty-five years.

After referring to the library and its acquisitions, and to sundry improvements in the Club House, the report continues:

The only work of consequence undertaken for the coming year is the completion of the Council Room ceiling, by Mr. H. Siddons Mowbray, who originally decorated this room. This work consists of a painting, in oils, of "Aurora," in the oval centre of the ceiling, and the gilding and tinting of the black panels of the wooden piece high up over the mantel, which, as they are, would detract from the harmonious effect of the painting when finished. This decoration was planned some years ago, but the Art Committee did not deem it justifiable to endorse the estimated expenditure; Mr. Mowbray, however, is anxious that his original plans should be carried out, and his generous offer to complete the ceiling at practically its cost to him, has been accepted by the Committee.

This work of art has since been completed, and the result is a dining-hall of noble proportions, exquisitely ornamented with appropriate decorations, which has no rival, for stateliness and elegance, in the city of New York or probably in the country. The Club is greatly indebted to Mr. Mowbray for putting it within the power of the Club to avail itself of his admirable work. The total cost of Mr. Mowbray's decorations was $9,270.

"The members of the Print Committee," the report proceeds, "after having spent the last year in research and careful examination of many prints and pictures which have been tendered to them, are now exhibiting some of their acquisitions on the walls of the picture gallery. Some of these pictures have been presented to the Club, while others have been purchased by contributions made by members of the Committee. The Committee is critical in its standard, and, while the collection may grow slowly, it will some day become one of great value and interest."

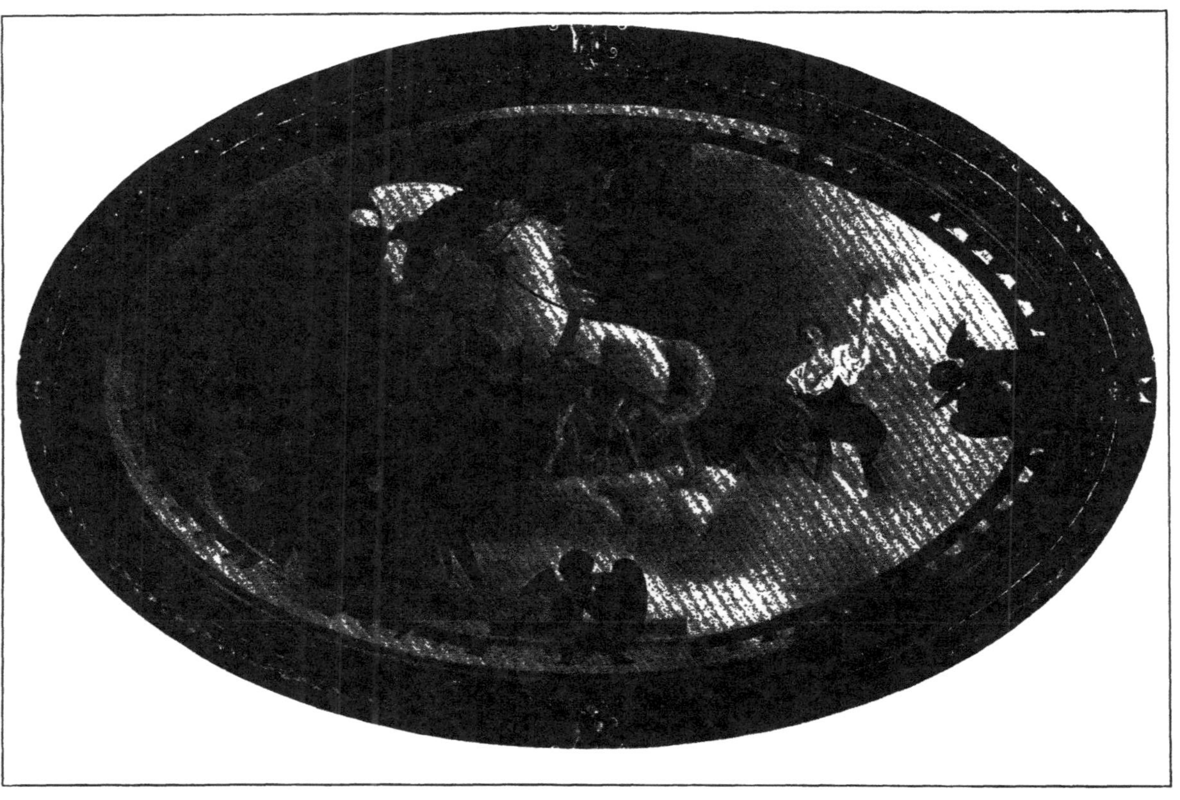

"AURORA"—DECORATION OF THE CEILING OF THE COUNCIL ROOM
Painted by H. Siddons Mowbray, 1913.

A descriptive catalogue of these pictures will be found in Appendix XII, and an examination of the collection, on the top floor of the Club, will repay the time devoted to it.

The report makes extensive reference to the work of the Committee on Colleges and Degrees, calling attention to the fact that while the well-known colleges and universities of the country have already been reported upon, the number of institutions legally authorized to confer degrees is legion. The report makes plain that the rejection of a degree involves no adverse reflection on the candidate, and often involves a distinct loss to the Club by excluding a candidate who may have many friends in the Club and who would personally be most acceptable and desirable as a member, "but it is only by an impartial and rigid adherence to the high standard which has been upheld in the past, that the Club can retain its prestige and character as a University Club."

At the meeting of the Council held April 14, 1913, for organization, Mr. Sands, who had made it known that he would prefer that the highest honors of the Club should now be enjoyed by someone else, nominated Mr. Thomas Thacher (Yale '71) for President of the Club, and that gentleman was thereupon elected. Mr. Henry Dodge Cooper (C. C. N. Y. '72) was elected Vice-President, the other executive officers being re-elected.

In the retirement of Mr. Sands, the Club lost a faithful and painstaking head, whose assiduity and careful supervision of the affairs of the Club had been of incalculable benefit, and it was due alone to his expressed wishes that a rotation in office should prevail that he did not continue his able administration.

Mr. Sands continued to be a member of the Council, and when he completes his term of office as such member in 1915, he will have served the Club for twenty-seven consecutive years, first on the Committee on Admissions, and then on the

Council, which is the longest continuous period of service of any officer of the Club.

Too much praise cannot be given to Mr. Sands for the diligent, intelligent, and conscientious manner in which he has performed the duties of all the positions held by him. During the twelve years during which he served on the Committee on Admissions, he was most active and influential, and the great work of that committee, characterized as it has been by devotion, fair-mindedness, and industry, could only have been accomplished through the endeavors and loyalty of a splendid band of men, among whom Mr. Sands was recognized as a most valued leader.

The services of Mr. Sands on the Committee on Colleges and Degrees were also of a highly important character. He was a member of the original committee, of which Charles H. Russell (Harvard '72) was chairman, and which conferred with a similar committee from the Committee on Admissions, at the time when the function of determining what degrees should qualify applicants for membership was transferred to the Council; and it is fitting in this connection to mention the name of Mr. Samuel H. Ordway (Brown '80), one of the conferees, and later and at present a member of the Committee on Colleges and Degrees. It is no disparagement to others to record the remarkable service which has been rendered by him through a long period of years, in the difficult and responsible duty of sifting and judging the qualifications of the various colleges and degrees requiring examination.

The active part taken by Mr. Sands in what may be called the degree legislation of the Club has been one of the many special contributions made by him to the wise and successful administration of the Club.

The Club was fortunate in having a member ready to assume the responsibilities of the presidency, so admirably fitted for the position as Mr. Thomas Thacher.

Mr. Sands, on retiring, presented to the Council and mem-

From a photograph, by Tebbs, New York.

THE COUNCIL ROOM WITH THE DECORATIONS COMPLETED.

bers of the University Club a silver bowl, with the desire that it be the nucleus to a silver service for the Club, to be added to by gifts of a similar character by each retiring president.

The description of the bowl, furnished by Messrs. Crichton Brothers, of London and New York, is as follows:

> Bowl with inner lining made in London in 1813 by Paul Storr (the best known of all early 19th Century Silversmiths). Weight 163 ozs. (Troy).
>
> The Arms engraved on the Bowl are composed of the Arms of two families: viz, "Ramsden," of Nottingham and "Law" of Cumberland, the portion on the left hand side (showing the fleur-de-lis) being the former and the other side the latter family.
>
> The Heraldic description of both are as follows: Ramsden "Argent, on a chevron between three fleur-de-lis sable as many rams heads erased or."
>
> Law. "Argent, on a bend engrailed between two cocks gules three mullets or."

At the meeting of the Council of May 12, 1913, the Treasurer was authorized to purchase certain second-mortgage bonds of the Club from Messrs. Clark, Dodge & Co. at a price not to exceed par value.

At the same meeting the Art Committee were directed to request Ex-President Sands to allow W. T. Smedley, the artist, to paint his portrait. This has been done, and the portrait now hangs with those of the former Presidents.

On the night of January 19, 1913, a concert was given in the Club House by Nahan Franko and his entire orchestra.

A dinner was given on the evening of February 7, 1913, to Sir Ernest Shackleton, C. V. O., by the Council, and a lecture afterward delivered to the Club members by that distinguished discoverer, on the British South Polar Expedition, which was illustrated by lantern slides and moving pictures.

The night of April 9, 1913, was made the occasion of a "Club Night" in honor of the Honorable William H. Taft, to whom a general reception was given. Before the reception, Mr. Taft was entertained at dinner by the Council, Committee on Admissions, and the Standing Committees, and a supper was participated in by the whole Club, later in the evening.

On April 21, 1913, occurred an event which caused profound regret among the members of the Club, namely, the death of Hugh D. Auchincloss (Yale '79) at the age of fifty-four years.

The class to which he belonged was a notable one at Yale, and the same may be said of '79 at Harvard and Princeton.

Reference to Mr. Auchincloss's family and position in New York has already been made in this history. His connection with the University Club had been a long one, and his services to the Club had been important and various. He was for some years its Secretary, and was an active member of the building committee having charge of the erection of the present Club House. He had a wide acquaintance among our members, and his companionable ways and sterling qualities made him beloved. His loss is a heavy blow to the Club.

On the night of April 28, 1913, the members of the Mendelssohn Glee Club were made the guests of the Club, with a supper. During the evening, the Glee Club gave a choice programme of musical numbers.

The character and services of the Honorable Henry E. Howland (Yale '53) have already been referred to in these pages. On the 7th of November, 1913, this popular member passed away, after a long and trying illness. From the time of the reorganization of the Club in 1879, Judge Howland had been intimately connected with its management down to within a few years before his death. He had served continuously on the Council, and had been its President. He survived many of his contemporaries, but nevertheless left behind him a host of friends. No more genial companion has ever graced the Club's social circle and none has entered with greater zeal into the work of the Club's upbuilding.

At the meeting of the Council held October 20, 1913, it was

Resolved, That from the statements of the Officers of the Club submitted at this meeting the dues of the members should be increased.

It was

Further resolved, That it is the sense of this meeting that the dues of resident members be increased to $100 per year and the dues of non-resident members be increased to $50 per year, and

It was

Further resolved, That a Special Committee of three, of whom the President shall be one, be appointed to prepare a statement of the reasons for the Council's action in recommending an increase of dues and that a Special Meeting of the Club be called in December at such time as the Committee shall determine.

The President appointed Messrs. Thacher, Oakman, and Cooper as such Special Committee.

The Special Committee accordingly prepared the following statement which was printed and sent to all the members:

UNIVERSITY CLUB

NEW YORK, November 11th, 1913.

TO THE MEMBERS:

At the special meeting of the Club to be held December 16, 1913, the Council will recommend the amendment of the Constitution so as to raise the annual dues of resident members to $100 and the annual dues of non-resident members to $50.

It is the opinion of the Council, that all entrance fees and receipts from life memberships should be set aside as a reserve to be used only for extraordinary expenditures, and that the other receipts, including dues, should suffice, with a fair margin for safety, to cover all ordinary expenditures and also to add something each year to such reserve.

The excess of receipts other than entrance fees and receipts from life memberships over ordinary expenses, during the last five years, was as follows:

1908–9	$ 4,143.63
1909–10	11,343.52
1910–11	1,532.08
1911–12	3,479.45
1912–13	661.62
Total	$21,160.30
Average per year	4,232.06

NOTE:—Payments of principal of debt, payment of mortgage interest in excess of one year's interest in 1912–13 made necessary by transfer of mortgage, and one-third of the expenditures for furniture and equipment and extraordinary repairs are treated as extraordinary expenditures. All other expenditures are treated as ordinary, including two-thirds of the expenditures for furniture and equipment and extraordinary repairs, and certain other expenditures which, though unusual, it is thought should not be charged against the reserve, as follows: $2,471.02, Hudson-Fulton Celebration in 1909–10; $3,402, cost of alteration of sidewalk, etc., under City's requirement in 1911–12; $1,500, cost of portrait in 1911–12; and $3,018.25, expense of transfer of mortgage in 1912–13.

How much of the expenditures for furniture and equipment and extraordinary repairs should be treated as extraordinary so as to be chargeable against the reserve, is a matter of opinion; but it is thought that not more than one-third thereof should be so treated.

The expenditures for furniture and equipment and extraordinary repairs were as follows:

1908–9	$12,703.75
1909–10	3,787.15
1910–11	25,372.29
1911–12	23,337.63
1912–13	14,035.28
	$79,236.10

The entrance fees and receipts from life memberships during the five years (to be treated as reserve) were as follows:

	Entrance Fees.	Life Memberships.	Totals.	
1908–09	$16,600	$5,000	$21,600	
1909–10	15,250	12,000	27,250	
1910–11	11,850	4,000	15,850	
1911–12	16,400	3,000	19,400	
1912–13	16,400	3,000	19,400	$103,500.00

And the extraordinary expenditures chargeable against such reserve (as explained above) were as follows:

	1908–09	1909–10	1910–11	1911–12	1912–13	
Principal debt paid or redeemed	$41,500.00	......	$50,000.00	....	$1,350.00	
Less proceeds of investments sold and discount on note purchased	30,177.50	......	....	....	....	
Balance	$11,322.50	......	$50,000.00	....	$1,350.00	
Interest paid on transfer of mortgage in excess of one year's interest	....	......	....	....	$10,394.14	
One-third furniture and equipment and extraordinary repairs	4,234.58	1,262.38	8,457.43	7,779.21	4,678.43	
	$15,557.08	$1,262.38	$58,457.43	$7,779.21	$16,422.57	
Total						$99,478.67
Balance in reserve						4,021.33
Balance in ordinary account, as above						21,160.30
Excess of all receipts over all expenditures for the five years						$25,181.63

According to the estimates of the budget for this year, there is to be expected a deficit of receipts other than entrance fees and receipts from life memberships as compared with ordinary expenses of $2,498.67, and an excess of entrance fees and receipts from life memberships over extraordinary expenditures ($4,833.33) of only $9,166.67, and an excess of all receipts over all expenditures of only $6,668.

These figures seem to the Council to demonstrate the necessity of some increase of dues, especially in view of the fact that the results shown could not have been reached except for the extreme care of the House Committee as to purchases and other expenditures. The amount of increase seems to be the only thing open for reasonable discussion, upon consideration of the probable needs of the future.

Ordinary expenditures may be expected to increase, especially through

(1) Further increase in taxes;

(2) Increase in the cost of food supplies, not only for members but also for employees; and other increase in cost of operation;

(3) A reasonable desire to avoid too strict economy, limiting the House Committee in its efforts for the comfort and convenience of the members and restricting the work of the Entertainment Committee.

Extraordinary expenses in the near future are foreseen for the following purposes:

(1) To pay $131,500 of bonds, due in 1917;

(2) To provide for reduction of First Mortgage of $1,100,000, in case this shall become necessary or desirable;

(3) To replace plumbing and steam fitting, which have nearly reached the age limit, the cost of which, owing to the method of original construction, will be quite heavy, and for other extraordinary repairs and replacements;

(4) To utilize the now unoccupied land of the Club by building an extension to provide further facilities.

In view of the outlook for the future, the Council after consideration extending over many months has decided unanimously to recommend an increase of dues to $100 for residents and $50 for non-residents, leaving the Army and Navy dues as they are. On the basis of present membership, such increase would amount to

$69,890 per year. This is not more of an increase than the Council thinks is reasonable and desirable for the best interests of the Club.

By Order of The Council.
Thomas Thacher,
President.

William Manice,
Secretary.

There being a decided feeling among some of the members of the Club in opposition to the proposed increase in dues, if any other means could be devised for meeting the necessities of the Club, an alternate plan was suggested—namely, an increase in the membership of the Club; and the following notice of an amendment to the constitution was duly posted in accordance with the rules, to be submitted to the special meeting of the Club on December 16, 1913:

Notice is hereby given of a proposed Amendment to the Constitution of the Club as follows:

To amend sections 4 and 5 Article IX of the Constitution so as to read as follows:

"Sec. 4. The number of Resident members of the Club shall not exceed two thousand three hundred."

"Sec. 5. The number of Non-resident and Army and Navy members of the Club shall not exceed seventeen hundred."

Such an increase would enlarge the membership from 3,500 to 4,000, and as there was at the time a waiting list of 1,278 candidates, those in favor of this measure were of the opinion that the amendment would not only furnish the necessary income, but at the same time accommodate a large number of eligible applicants.

On the evening of the 16th of December, 1913, the special meeting of the Club to consider and act upon the proposed amendments was held. The attendance was large and much interest was shown in the matters to be considered. Before and after the proceedings Franko's Orchestra rendered a number of musical selections.

The President of the Club, Thomas Thacher (Yale '71), made a masterly presentation of the views of the Council, as outlined in the circular hereinbefore set forth. He was followed by Henry Dodge Cooper (C. C. N. Y. '72), Chairman of the House Committee, who supplemented the statement of the President with interesting and important data concerning the advance in the price of food, in wages, in taxes, and other necessary expenses, as well as details regarding the requirements of the Club in the way of upkeep of the building, involving, among other things, the repair and renewal of mechanisms.

Amory G. Hodges (Harvard '74) then addressed the Club in behalf of the Council, confining his remarks chiefly to the obligation of the Club to pay off its second-mortgage bonds of $131,500, by the year 1917, and the duty of reducing the first mortgage to $1,000,000, by the payment of $100,000 on account, contending that no other course was consistent with a prudent business management.

Cary T. Hutchinson (Washington '86) then offered the resolution to adopt the amendment proposed by the Council, increasing the dues, and supported the motion in a forcible speech. This resolution was duly seconded. Thereupon, Francis G. Landon (Princeton '81) moved to amend the resolution of Mr. Hutchinson by the substitution of the amendment proposed by himself, and already set forth, increasing the resident and non-resident membership by 500, and addressed the Club urging this measure as calculated to produce the additional income claimed by the Council to be necessary, without subjecting the existing membership to an increase in their annual dues. Mr. Landon's motion was seconded by Walter Graeme Eliot (Columbia '78) in a speech in the course of which a number of suggestions were made of experiments intended to enlarge the opportunities of profitable business for the Club.

Debate became active. A decided impression had been

From a photograph, copyright by Marceau, New York.

THOMAS THACHER (Yale '71).

Tenth President, 1913.

made on the minds of many by the strong presentation of facts by the President and members of the Council. On the other hand, it was evident that a large body of those present were so opposed to the raising of the dues as to be ready to seize upon almost any other reasonable expedient.

Arguments were made on both sides of the question by a number of the members, and while the difference in views was very marked, no word was spoken in criticism of the Council or House Committee. On the contrary, it was a pleasant feature of the debate that the opponents of the Council measure uniformly gave to the management credit for a faithful and skillful administration, and tacitly accepted the declaration of the Council and its officers that a necessity really existed for increasing the revenues.

The question was put upon Mr. Landon's motion, to amend Mr. Hutchinson's resolution, by the substitution of increase of membership for increase of dues. The *viva voce* vote was to the listener almost even, but the chair decided the motion lost. A division being called for, and difficulty being experienced by the tellers, William H. Taylor (Columbia '80) and H. Hobart Porter (Columbia '86), in making the count of the moving assembly, the members were made to pass through one of the doors of the large front lounging-room, the ayes and nays proceeding in turn. The count being made and reported, the President announced that the motion was lost by the vote of 146 ays to 184 nays.

The question then recurred upon Mr. Hutchinson's resolution to adopt the Council's amendment, increasing the dues. After further interesting debate, in which both sides were represented, the same method of counting was employed, and the resolution declared by the President to be lost. The constitution requires a two-thirds vote to amend any of its provisions, and the count showed 242 in favor and 140 against the proposed change.

At this point Mr. Eliot moved that Mr. Landon's amendment be taken up and acted upon as an original proposition, which motion was carried. Adopting the same process as before, the count was made and resulted in 152 votes for and 171 votes against the proposition. The reduced vote is accounted for by the fact that a large number of the members, perceiving that both propositions were defeated, had left the house, or gone to some other part of it.

Thus the Club refused at this time to alter the existing provisions as to dues and limit of membership in any respect.

A supper was served on the dining-room floor, after the adjournment, attended by a large number. During the supper Franko's orchestra furnished music, and the evening closed without the exhibition of any bitterness, and with a prevailing good feeling.

The members of the Council, being unconvinced that the Club could be adequately conducted without an increase in the amount of dues, resolved at its meeting of January 12, 1914, to submit to the Club at its annual meeting to be held March 21, 1914, the following amendment to the constitution, as a modification of the proposal which had failed of adoption, namely:

To amend Section 2 of Article XI of the constitution so as to read as follows:

"The annual dues of resident members shall be ninety dollars; of non-resident members, forty-five dollars; and of army and navy members, except as provided in Sec. 7 of this article, thirty-five dollars; payable semi-annually in advance on the first days of March and September."

At the meeting of February 9, 1914, the resignation of Mr. James Byrne (Harvard '77) as a member of the Council was accepted with regret.

On January 19, 1914, Mr. William Manice (Columbia '86) died, after a long and faithful service as Secretary of the Club. As a special indication of regard and respect, the

Council set aside a page in the records of its proceedings for a memorial of Mr. Manice. The inscription reads as follows:

WILLIAM MANICE.

Elected a member of the Council at the Annual Meeting held March 21, 1903.

He was re-elected in 1907 for a four-year term, and again in 1911 to serve until March, 1915.

Elected Secretary of the Club by the Council, April 11, 1904, and served continuously as Secretary till the date of his death.

Died January 19, 1914, at his residence, 6 W. 53d Street, New York.

At the annual meeting of the Club held March 21, the amendment to the constitution proposed by the Council, increasing the annual dues of resident members to $90 and of non-resident members to $45, was adopted by a two-thirds vote.

At the meeting of the Council, April 13, 1914, the following named gentlemen were elected to fill the offices respectively set opposite their names:

Thomas Thacher (Yale '71), *President.*
Henry Dodge Cooper (C. C. N. Y. '72), *Vice-President.*
Walter G. Oakman (Univ. of Pa. '64), *Treasurer.*
Samuel Sloan (Columbia '87), *Secretary.*

At the same meeting, Mr. H. Hobart Porter (Columbia '86) was appointed a member of the House Committee and designated as its chairman, the remaining members to be selected by the Executive Committee.

At this meeting the resignation of Mr. Edward Gleason, as Superintendent of the Club, was presented, and accepted, and provision made for a suitable pension in consideration of his long and faithful service.

The Art Committee reported at this meeting that Mrs. William Manice had presented to the Club a clock and candelabra, as mementoes of her husband, the late Secretary. The gift was accepted and a resolution of thanks endorsed in the minutes.

CHAPTER XXIV

THE LIBRARY

THE purpose of the University Club as stated in its charter being "the promotion of literature and art, by establishing and maintaining a library, reading-room, and gallery of art," one of the first steps after the reorganization, in 1879, naturally was the creation of a plan for the institution of a suitable library—a plan which from the time of its inauguration has been faithfully and wisely pursued through intervening years until at the present time the Club possesses a conveniently arranged and carefully equipped collection of books, numbering over twenty-eight thousand volumes, and twenty-one thousand pamphlets, and well adapted to the use of members, whether for investigation, study, or entertainment.

At a meeting of the Council held November 3, 1879, a Committee on Literature and Art was appointed, consisting of Henry Holt (Yale '62), the well-known publisher, as Chairman; Doctor Morris J. Asch (Univ. of Pa. '52), a prominent physician; the Reverend Doctor Henry W. Bellows (Harvard '32), famous not only as a preacher, but as a man of great influence in public affairs and for his literary culture; Parke Godwin (Princeton '34), the gifted scholar and publicist, and Horace Walcott Robbins (Newton '58), an educated man of taste and discrimination.

It will be seen at once that the Club was fortunate in having the services of a committee peculiarly fitted to shape the policy of the library, a department designed and destined to become the most important and useful of the Club's conveniences.

It may be noted here that Doctor Bellows resigned from the Committee September 21, 1880, and Doctor Charles Hitchcock (Brown '69), a scholar of renown and admirably equipped for the service required, was appointed to fill the vacancy.

To these gentlemen, and especially to Mr. Holt, the chairman, must be given the credit for taking the steps which were the foundation of and which have since controlled the building of a library of which the members of the Club may well be proud.

The Committee on Literature and Art had been in office during the earlier history of the Club, from 1865 to 1879, but the conditions were not such as to make it possible to accomplish much. The members who at the beginning of this period served in the capacity mentioned, were Doctor Charles F. Chandler (Göttingen '56), Eugene Schuyler (Yale '59), S. Whitney Phoenix (Columbia '59), Russell Sturgis, Jr. (C. C. N. Y. '56), and John C. White.

The Committee at the time this history goes to press (1914) is composed of Messrs. Robert Bridges, Chairman (Princeton '79), Frederick A. Stokes (Yale '79), Frank Moore Colby (Columbia '88), Charles Sheldon (Yale '90), and William M. Grosvenor (Williams '85).

Mr. Holt served as Chairman from 1879 to 1887, and in 1898 re-entered the Committee as a member. He devoted much time and study to his duties, for which his experience made him of great service. The book plate which will be found inside the cover of every volume in the library was devised by him and adopted by the Council.

It was designed by Messrs. Tiffany & Company, and consists of a bust representing Plato, the classic club and university man, underneath which is an owl with outspread wings, both mounted on a pedestal, over which hangs a scroll inscribed "University Club." Across the upper part of the design is a waving ribbon with the library motto of the Club:

Η ΚΑΤ ΟΡΘΟΝ ΧΡΕΙΑ ΤΟΥ ΣΥΜΠΟΣΙΟΥ ΤΕΙΝΕΙ ΕΙΣ ΠΑΙΔΕΙΑΝ

This motto was chosen from the works of Plato, with possibly a very slight modification, by Professor Basil Lanneau Gildersleeve (Princeton '49), of Johns Hopkins University, acknowledged to stand in the first rank of Greek scholars, and freely translated is: "The right use of a Club tends to education."

The first step taken by the Committee was to raise money to buy books, the judgment of its members being adverse to making the library a financial burden on the Club at the outset. At one of the early meetings of the Council in 1879, therefore, a subscription paper for a library fund was passed around, headed by that great friend of the Club, Henry H. Anderson, with a hundred dollars. His lead was well followed, and with this subscription as an example, an appeal was made to the general membership.

This appeal took the form of a circular, dated December 25, 1879, a copy of which follows, and containing in itself a sufficient explanation of the views of the Committee as to what the character of the library should be. Virtually, the whole amount subscribed (about $3,500) was expended for books of reference, and in Greek, Latin, German, and French classics, the reason being that reference-books are needed at all times, and that the members were apt to have the English classics and other important books at home.

As money accumulated year after year, incursions were made into the classics of other languages; English, for the reason just given, with the exception of the leaders constantly needed for reference, being filled out last.

The general idea was, as Henry Adams, on a visit to the

Club, phrased it to the Chairman of the Committee, that the library should be a "big dictionary." This idea probably became traditionary among the Committee, and was pretty well realized before any "frills" were indulged in.

Here follows the circular of December 25, 1879:

To the Members of the University Club:

The Committee on Literature and Art, to which the Council referred the subject of establishing a suitable Library in connection with the Club, are of the opinion that such an object is not only desirable in order to increase the attractions of the Club, present and future, but absolutely indispensable to its complete equipment as a body composed of educated men.

They think it outside of the province of such a Library to provide any strictly professional worker with his professional instruments, and they also think that some preference should be given to books not already in most of the private collections of the members of the Club. Within these limits the Committee hope to be enabled to place in the Club-house a Library, which any member can consult with a reasonable chance of finding any information he may need.

Moreover, they hope that upon one special subject—the subject indicated by the name of the Club—its Library will become the one place where the investigator can go in confidence, that he will find all that is worth finding, and where the author who would write the latest word on that subject *must* go.

The Committee propose, then, to work as systematically as they can, toward the following ends:

1st. *A Reference Library.*—Not only the most valuable books of reference, in the several departments of Literature, Science and Art, such as encyclopaedias, Dictionaries, Gazetteers and Atlases, but also the great standard works of literature, preferably those in the English language, but certainly those in any language which are subjects of such constant allusion as to entitle them to a place in a good reference library.

2d. *A University Library.*—All publications that pertain to the origin, growth and social life of the Universities, Colleges, and other institutions of the higher learning in this country and in Europe. This collection to include college memorabilia—every accessible scrap of printed paper illustrating the colleges as social

From a photograph, copyright by the "New York Times."

GENERAL VIEW OF THE LIBRARY, LOOKING EAST TOWARD MOWBRAY'S FIGURE OF "ROMANCE."

institutions, as well as the vast unexplored mine of biography of men who are and are to become prominent, contained in the reports of their class secretaries.

3d. *A Club Library.*—Books, historical and practical, on the recreations of gentlemen in their social organizations, and in their out-door sports.

In regard to the more transient publications of the day, such as Essays, Travels, Novels, etc., arrangements are already made with established Circulating Libraries, according to the system in use in English and some American Clubs, which will secure an adequate supply of them at a very cheap rate.

As the Council have not felt themselves justified in buying books with the current funds of the Treasury, an appeal is hereby made to the voluntary subscriptions of individual members. The advantages of the scheme are so obvious and so important, that the Committee do not conceive it necessary to waste words in commending it to the intelligence and liberality of the Club.

There is probably no doubt that, to justify the name and objects of the Club, it must have the best Club Library in America. The only question on which opinions can differ is whether it shall be had *now*. Seventeen members of the Club have indicated an answer to that question by subscribing, before subscriptions have been formally solicited, some fifteen hundred dollars. If their spirit is continued in the responses to this appeal, the Club can at once have the Library which is the only thing lacking to its full development, and which, it seems to be agreed, will do more for its reputation and permanence than any other possession could do.

A second circular was issued April 23, 1880, consisting of a report of progress, and an appeal for more subscriptions, a copy of which is here given:

UNIVERSITY CLUB LIBRARY

April 23, 1880.

TO THE MEMBERS OF THE UNIVERSITY CLUB:

At the end of last year, the Committee on Literature and Art caused a prospectus of their plans for a Library to be directed to each member of the Club. The New-Year pressure on the "Special Message Delivery," or some other cause, prevented several copies from reaching their destination; consequently, a copy is printed on the other side of this.

The Committee now wish to state that they have received subscriptions from sixty-two members to the value of about $3,500, and have in the Library, or secured for it, the leading general Cyclopaedias, (including Larousse and Brockhaus,) several special cyclopaedias; the best Dictionaries of English, Greek, Latin, German, French, Italian and Spanish; the best Atlases; a full and most careful selection of Greek and Latin Classics; the English Poets and Dramatists, nearly complete, with the best concordances; a scant collection of good books in Biography, Geography, Travel and Literary History; a moderate number of books on Clubs, Sports and Games; a few valuable books on Colleges and College Life, and some valuable beginnings of a collection of College Memorabilia.

As the Club cannot subscribe for all the College Periodicals, nor discriminate between them, it subscribes for none. Through the liberality of several members, the following are promised, and they will be kept on file in the Reading Room. It hardly need be said that others are desired.

Acta Columbiana.
Amherst Student.
Brunonian.
Columbia Spectator.
Harvard Crimson.
Harvard Advocate.
Harvard Lampoon.
Princetonian.
Yale Courant.
Yale Literary Magazine.
Yale Record.

The gentlemen named below have agreed to endeavor to collect for the Club Library the memorabilia and periodicals of their respective colleges, and will be glad to receive contributions, which should in all cases be sent to them and not to the Committee. Volunteers to perform the same service regarding the colleges not yet represented, will be welcomed by the Chairman of the Committee.

Amherst '74 .... Mr. F. W. Whitridge.
Brown '69 .... Dr. C. Hitchcock.
Columbia '69 .... Mr. R. L. Belknap.
Dartmouth '62 .... Mr. G. S. Hubbard.
Hamilton '65 .... Mr. H. B. Tompkins.
Harvard '68 .... Mr. F. G. Ireland.
Medical Colleges (Bellevue '68) ... Dr. F. A. Castle.
N. Y. University '65 .... Mr. W. F. Morgan.
Princeton '75 .... Mr. C. Scribner.

Rutgers '56....................Mr. G. V. N. Baldwin.
Trinity '75....................Mr. W. E. Curtis, Jr.
Williams '74....................Mr. W. D. Edmonds.
Yale '76....................Mr. H. W. DeForest.

The Committee now appeals to those members who have not yet subscribed, for aid to carry out their work. They especially need money to buy a few more Works of Reference; the Classics of the Modern Languages; translations of all the Classics, Ancient and Modern; and to extend the departments of Science, Travel, Recreation and College Literature.

Subscription lists are in the library and the office, at the Club-house. Ultimately subscriptions will be permanently recorded in a book to be kept in the library. The work of the Committee has reached a point where they will be able to use any money subscribed and not yet paid in, as soon as convenient for the subscribers to send it.

HENRY HOLT,
HENRY W. BELLOWS,
HORACE W. ROBBINS,
PARKE GODWIN,
MORRIS J. ASCH.

As an interesting record of the liberality of members at this early stage, for this commendable purpose, a list of the first subscribers to the Library Fund, without specifying the amounts respectively contributed, will be found in Appendix IX.

The first report on the library was made on May 1, 1881, when 2,006 volumes were stated to be on the shelves, and $5,200 to be the value of the library and unexpended fund.

The names of the earliest donors of books are given in this report, among whom were J. O. Sargent (Harvard '30), Henry E. Pellew (Cambridge '50), Mason Young (Yale '60), DeLancey Nicoll (Princeton '74), Parke Godwin (Princeton '34), J. F. Loubat (Univ. of France '47), and Professor O. C. March (Yale '60).

The Harvard members were the first in the field to install a collection of Harvard memorabilia, and were closely followed by Princeton and Yale; other colleges and universities also took the matter up.

On the fifteenth day of August, 1893, "Library Bulletin No. 1" was issued by the Committee on Literature and Art, then consisting of Henry E. Howland (Yale '54), Chairman, William B. Hornblower (Princeton '71), and Charles Scribner (Princeton '75). The limitations of this book prevent the reproduction *in extenso* of this and subsequent reports, but they evince remarkable care and intelligence, and are well worthy of the perusal of members. They will be found in the successive printed annual reports of the Club in the library.

Great pains were taken by those in whose hands the development of the library was placed to gain all information calculated to perfect our system.

Besides the natural investigation of libraries in the United States, inquiry was made as to the methods of the Athenaeum Club, of London, that nest of literary workers; and the following letter from the Secretary and Librarian of that club is interesting in this connection:

THE ATHENAEUM

PALL MALL
LONDON, S. W.
10 March 1897.

THE LIBRARIAN
University Club
32 East 26th Street
New York City

Dear Sir:

In the first place I must thank you for kindly sending a copy of your interesting *Library Bulletin* as well as your Club Annual for the present year. All the printed matter I can exchange with you is our latest list of Members, which I have the pleasure to send by mail.

The Library of the Athenaeum now contains some 60,000 volumes which have been accumulating from the foundation of the Club. When the house was first built in 1830 the possibility of the Library ever reaching so large a figure was of course never con-

From a photograph, copyright by Tebbs, New York.

"HISTORY"—THE DECORATION BY H. SIDDONS MOWBRAY AT THE WEST END OF THE LIBRARY.

templated, and the books have to be accommodated to the premises. All the rooms on the principal floor are lined with books on the walls with a few in large print tables in the centres of the rooms. The large library, which is about 30 feet high, has two light galleries all round and contains 17,000 volumes, the long Drawing Room contains about 8,000 volumes in cases against the walls without a gallery, and a smaller library with one gallery contains about 12,000 volumes. There are several other smaller rooms containing books. A few years ago I arranged a couple of the attics, formerly used for servants' apartments, so as to form a store library wholly occupied by shelves running across the floor. Room for about 17,000 volumes can be found here and we find it useful to house long sets of little used periodicals and other works seldom referred to. The Library of the Athenaeum is of course only made use of by the Members who are about 1,300 in number and by a simple system of plans and directions members help themselves to the books. All our arrangements therefore are of a kind more suited to a private than a public library. I presume your requirements are the same. In the public rooms referred to above only wall cases are made use of. There are no cases standing out in the rooms, except the print tables. The height of the cases varies in the different rooms, some are 8 or 10 feet high. The galleries are about 6 feet 6 inches high.

I am sorry to say that I cannot send you any photographs which would be of any use, but the Illustrated London News of March 11th, 1893, contains a very good account of the Athenaeum with many illustrations, among them being one of the large library. If you do not possess a set of the Illustrated London News you will very probably be able to consult it in the New York Public Library.

I shall be very happy to give you any further information.

I am, Dear Sir,

Faithfully yours
HENRY R. TEDDER
Secretary and Librarian.

The growth of the Athenaeum Library has been as follows: 4,000 volumes in 1830; 20,300 in 1844; 31,000 in 1852; 48,000 in 1882; 60,000 in 1892; *over 80,000* in 1913.

No account of the library would be complete without special

reference to the services of the late T. Frank Brownell (Harvard '65).

Mr. Brownell, from the time of the Club's reorganization in 1879 until his death, January 7, 1901, devoted himself with an industry almost without equal, not only to the perfecting of the collection of memorabilia of his Alma Mater, but to the general interests of the library. His activity in creating the Harvard collection began as soon as the Club was housed at the corner of Fifth Avenue and 35th Street, and a subscription of money to that end was reported at one of the earliest meetings. He not only purchased and accepted gifts of books for this purpose, but himself contributed to the collection in volumes and funds.

He was for a number of years Chairman of the Committee on Admissions, and later Chairman of the Committee on Literature and Art. In 1895 he made what was described as "the most noteworthy gift" to the Club, being "an index to some of the periodical literature relating to Harvard University contained in the Library of the University Club." "This is a volume of 400 type-written pages, foolscap size, compiled with the most exemplary thoroughness, comprising 'the entry of over 21,000 titles.'"

"It is not a catalogue of the books and pamphlets which make up the collection of Harvard Memorabilia, nor is the indexing limited to periodical publications contained in that collection, but it embraces also those contained in the collections of the Memorabilia of other colleges, as well as all the miscellaneous and general periodical literature which is preserved in our Library."

At a meeting of the Council, April 8, 1895, the donation of the Index was accepted with thanks, and a tribute in the form of a resolution paid to Mr. Brownell in recognition of his various services, in which it was also declared that "the present prosperity of the Club is due in large part to Mr. Brownell's labors as Secretary of the Committee on Admissions," and that

"ROMANCE"—THE DECORATION BY H. SIDDONS MOWBRAY AT THE EAST END OF THE LIBRARY.

his assistance to the Committee in "unremitting work and intelligent scrutiny" has been most important, and that the Club "is under deep and lasting obligations to him."

Much credit is due to the late Lyman H. Bagg (Yale '69), then Librarian, for the completeness of the bulletins. Mr. Bagg died October 23, 1911. The following is the list of successive Librarians of the Club: Hugh J. Ennis, June 1, 1881, to June 30, 1884; Lewis Barney, July 1, 1884, to June 30, 1885; Stuart N. Clarke, July 1, 1885, to September 15, 1886; George A. Baer, September 16, 1886, to July 31, 1887; Harvey C. Williams, August 1, 1887, to March 19, 1889; Lyman H. Bagg, March 20, 1889, to April 30, 1900; William H. Duncan, Jr., July 21, 1900, to July 31, 1906; and Arthur W. Colton (Yale '90), the present incumbent, from October 15, 1906.

The general policy which has been pursued in book purchasing has looked to the upbuilding of a "cultural" library, rather than a "technical" or "specialized" library, on the one hand, or a "popular" library on the other. More than two-thirds of the collection at present fall under the heads of history, biography, description and travel, literature, the fine arts; and in the remaining third there are small groups of works on medicine and law, consisting largely of general treatises and reference-books. In purchasing volumes, the Librarian and the Committee on the Library have not relied solely on their own judgment; the opinion of men eminent in their several domains has been sought and followed. A list of books in the medical section was prepared and submitted to medical members of distinction. Competent authorities were consulted as to fine arts. The Columbia Department of Education (through the courtesy of President Nicholas Murray Butler, himself a member of the Library Committee) furnished the Club with a list of educational works. Purchases in the section of "science" and "useful arts," although of the highest value, have been made subsidiary to those of a more decided cultural character. Dictionaries, encyclopædias, and indexes of all kinds are at members' disposal, making investigation easy and convenient, and the facilities of the library are multiplied many times by the existing arrangements with other large libraries in New York and elsewhere, under which books on all subjects may be called for and used as if they were a part of the Club library itself.

The demand for current novels is supplied by the use of the loan libraries; that for new books other than fiction by the Publishers' Exhibition and the Club's own conservative purchases. Ephemeral literature is avoided except in the way of temporary loans. The degree of conservatism in fiction may be indicated by the fact that it has only been recently that the collection has included the works of Mrs. Harriet Beecher Stowe and F. Marion Crawford. In this respect the University Club has been governed, however, by a caution less extreme than that which exists in the Athenaeum Club of London, which has only within a few years added Robert Louis Stevenson's works to its catalogue, while at latest accounts they were still lacking Thomas Hardy and Rudyard Kipling.

In regard to arrangements for convenience, the objective point has been to make the system so easily understood that any member can find what he wants without assistance, if he wishes to do so, although the Librarian or one of his assistants is always present to direct and explain. Bronze signs, extra shelf guides, and floor plans are provided to help the members in finding books, while the card system of index, duplicated so that a search may be made both of authors and subjects, is made as perfect as the latest methods of cataloguing can provide.

The periodicals of the world, including reviews, magazines, and illustrated papers, are spread upon tables in the subsidiary rooms of the University Club, and are numbered by the hundred.

Since the organization of the Club the accessions to the library by gift and purchase have exceeded 33,343 volumes (June 1, 1914). The constant weeding out which has been judiciously carried on under the direction of the Library Committee had reduced this number to 29,542 volumes, at the date of the report of the Committee for June 1, 1914, and 21,534 pamphlets.

The Librarian, under the direction of the Committee, has agents in various parts of the world, who, under instructions, are on the look-out for books considered desirable.

The gradual increase in the library has so enlarged the collection that there is hardly shelf-room for the books now owned. The rooms on the library floor have become more and more glutted with the overflow, and it has been found necessary to occupy what was formerly the card-room, on a floor higher up, for the interesting collections of university memorabilia and other books not in constant demand.

It would be out of place in a narrative like the present to give a complete list of the works of extraordinary value, especially as the primary object of the collection is not to emphasize rare and curious books. As a mere illustration, however, of the beginnings made in this direction, sometimes through the generosity of members, it may be mentioned that in the department of history, the "Valentine's Manual of New York," possessed by the Club, is probably worth $300 to $500 as it stands. Dugdale's "Monasticon" cost $157.50. Schoolcraft's "Indians" cost $100. Its value is rapidly increasing. Hutchinson and Minot's "Massachusetts" is a set steadily rising in price. Its cost was about $50, but one of the volumes alone is worth that sum. The Massachusetts Historical Society Collection (55 volumes), though incomplete, is valuable, one of the missing volumes having been offered at $30. One of the curiosities of the library is Brent's translation of Sarpi's "History of the Council of Trent." The "Jesuit Relations" (73 volumes); Thwaite's

"Early Western Travels" (32 volumes); "The New England Historical and Genealogical Register" (70 volumes); Blair and Robertson's "Philippines" (55 volumes), and the "New York Historical Society's Collections" (44 volumes) are all valuable. The library contains the facsimiles of the first four folios of Shakespeare; the Publications of the Shakespeare Society, the New Shakespeare Society, and the Shakespeare Society of New York (95 volumes) (there are 233 volumes in the Shakespeare Collection alone); the Camden Society Publications (193 volumes); the Cadell edition of Scott (100 volumes, with Turner plates); Coleridge's works, mainly in Pickering editions; Cooper's works (with Darley plates); and Nichols' "Literary History and Anecdotes."

Among the artistic works are Walter's "Oriental Keramic Gallery" (5 portfolios); Berenson's "Drawings of the Florentine Masters"; Furtwängler's "Antiken Gemmen"; and others.

Among the sets of periodicals, the most notable, perhaps, are the *Edinburgh Review*, complete, and *Notes and Queries*, complete. In archæology the club has the Egyptian Exploration Fund Publications, nearly complete to date (61 volumes); six volumes of Mexican codexes, edited by Seler; the three Mexican codexes reproduced by Loubat; and 15 volumes of the Peabody Museum Publications, some of which are now rare.

In biography, Bayle's Dictionary, revised by Maizeaux (London, 1735. 5 volumes, folio), may be mentioned as of more than ordinary value. Also "Les Bibliothèques françaises de la Croix du Maine et de du Verdier" (1772. 8 volumes). These two works one would hardly expect to find even in a library like that of the Club. They are foundations of Renaissance biography.

In bibliography the library possesses works which will usually be found in few New York collections, as, for example, Brunet's "Manuel du Libraire," with Vicaire's continuation, called "Manuel de l'Amateur," down to 1893; Watts's

From a photograph, copyright by Tebbs, New York.

THE MAGAZINE ROOM, LIBRARY FLOOR.

"Bibliotheca Britannica"; the three Roorbach and Kelly volumes that cover American bibliography from 1821 to 1871, and a large number of the Dibdin books.

These instances will serve to indicate the progress which is being made in the Club library in directions other than the obvious and the essential, and a more thorough examination of its possessions will repay the time devoted to such an investigation.

During the period from 1879 until the present time, the following members have served on the Library Committee:

Doctor Fessenden N. Otis (Union '51), General Alexander S. Webb (U. S. M. A. '55), Doctor Charles F. Chandler (Göttingen '56), George C. Clark (C. C. N. Y. '63), Stephen H. Olin (Wesleyan '66), Judge Henry E. Howland (Yale '54), Austen G. Fox (Harvard '69), William B. Hornblower (Princeton '71), Charles Scribner (Princeton '75), Charles H. Russell (Harvard '72), T. Frank Brownell (Harvard '65), John W. Harper (Columbia '52), Loyall Farragut (U. S. M. A. '68), Professor William M. Sloane (Columbia '68), Horace Russell (Dartmouth '65), Admiral Alfred T. Mahan (U. S. N. A., '59), Thomas Thacher (Yale '71), Edward Van Ingen (Yale '91), Courtlandt C. Clark (Princeton '78), President Nicholas Murray Butler (Columbia '82), Samuel R. Bertron (Yale '85), Robert Bridges (Princeton '79), Frederick A. Stokes (Yale' 79), Walter H. Page (Randolph Macon '76), Frank Moore Colby (Columbia '88), Charles Sheldon (Yale '90), William M. Grosvenor (Williams '85), and James W. Alexander (Princeton '60).

The compiler is greatly indebted to Mr. Arthur W. Colton (Yale '90), the Librarian of the Club, for information here recorded, as well as for much additional assistance.

One of the many indications that the Club library is appreciated by authors of distinction, as a convenient and useful "study" in which to work, is the fact that such men do actually frequent it and avail themselves of its advantages. It has been already stated that many of the admirable works of Admiral Alfred T. Mahan (U. S. N. A. '59) have been written in the University Club, and it is not an unusual thing to find this gifted authority on naval subjects in the library, either writing or consulting the books on the shelves. Admiral Mahan has also given the benefit of his knowledge and experience to the Library Committee, of which he has been a useful member.

Another author renowned in naval circles, who has made use of the Club library in the preparation of his books, is Admiral French E. Chadwick (U. S. N. A. '64), whose prominence in the war with Spain and later is known to all.

Professor William M. Sloane (Columbia '68), the historian of Napoleon; the late Charles Dudley Warner (Hamilton '51); the late Admiral Robley D. Evans (U. S. N. A. '63); Thomas Nelson Page (Univ. of Va. '74), the author of so many charming works; Doctor Henry van Dyke (Princeton '73), the poet; Jesse Lynch Williams (Princeton '92), writer of fiction; Edward S. Martin (Harvard '77), the essayist, and Arthur L. Frothingham, Jr. (Leipzig '83), the archæologist, have been among those seen from time to time at work in the library.

To catalogue the names of others who find the facilities and comforts of this fascinating retreat conducive to quiet study and serene contemplation is unnecessary. It is not infrequently the case that all the tables provided for literary work are occupied at once.

The library is, therefore, fulfilling the expectations and intentions of those who wisely projected and patiently fostered it, and has proved, as was originally hoped, the most important and useful department of the many practical facilities offered to members of the University Club. What it may become, as the process of enrichment goes on through future years, and more space is obtained for its accommodation, is a question which may well excite the imagination of the book-lover and the literary producer.

CHAPTER XXV

THE LIBRARY FLOOR

It would be difficult to imagine a more ideal place for the reader and the author than this noble library. One is struck on entering the centre portal with the beauty of the vaulted arches decorated, as has been described, in rich but subdued colors, and the ample alcoves and galleries lined with books—a furniture ever fascinating to the eye and suggestive of scholarly enjoyment. An atmosphere of quiet dignity pervades the room. Ample provision is made at the numerous tables for research. Easy chairs in every corner afford comfortable accommodation for readers, and it is seldom that they are not occupied. Current literature spread upon tables furnishes the means of keeping *au courant* with the latest publications, while the shelves groan with books of reference and of permanent importance. In the centre of the library stands the large globe of the world, the gift of Samuel Hill (Harvard '79).

By common consent the library floor of the Club House is unsurpassed for beauty, comfort, convenience, and that atmosphere of repose which is conducive to the contentment of the reader and the student.

The second full floor of the Club House (or the one just above the first mezzanine, which is devoted to bedrooms) is occupied by the library, reading and writing rooms, and the cardroom. The last named, being a large apartment on the north half of the Fifth Avenue front, was formerly sacredly preserved as a conversation-room for those using the library, absolute silence being required by members within the walls of the library proper. Both the progressive and aggressive influence of "bridge" at length broke down the prejudice of that portion of the membership who were jealous of encroachments upon the precincts of the library, and card-tables have been substituted for other furniture, and groups of men intent upon games of "auction" have taken the place of readers and the exchange of bookish conversation.

Nevertheless, the orderly and subdued conduct of the card-players, it must be admitted, has not materially marred the scholarly serenity of the neighboring rooms.

The central space of this floor is occupied by a dignified hall, of the same dimensions as the hall on the first floor, treated in a Pompeian manner, with highly colored columns and walls, the main vertebræ of the architecture being ivory-toned, with a background of panels in rich reds and russets, enlivened with little figure subjects. Two niches contain statues, reproductions of the antique. The central door on the south leads into the main library.

The library proper is one of the most beautiful examples of interior architecture in this country. It consists of a gallery something less than one hundred feet in length by sixteen feet wide exclusive of the alcoves, which are nine feet in depth. There are five alcoves on each side, lighted by windows on the south side. A flood of light pours in through the day, and appropriate electric fixtures furnish an adequate substitute by night. The central alcove on the north side communicates by a marble portal with the central hall already mentioned. Access is also given to the library at the two ends. The main ceiling, which is semicircular in section, is a groined vault divided into a number of compartments corresponding to the alcoves. The central compartment is domical, the remaining four are groined, formed by the intersection of the vaults of the alcoves with that of the main portion of the library. The alcoves themselves are vaulted

From a photograph, by Tebbs, New York.

ATRIUM OF THE LIBRARY FLOOR.

with a barrel vault. The bookcases, which are of a rich walnut, reach to the spring of the vault, thus leaving, at the ends of the main apartment and at the ends of the alcoves, lunettes semicircular in form.

In niches above the doors, between the alcoves which lead to stairways of approach to galleries, are bronzed busts, and in the Pompeian Hall marble busts of Æschylus, Sophocles, Euripides, Plato, executed by M. Ezekiel, of Rome, and presented to the Club in the year 1905 by Mr. John W. Simpson (Amherst '71). The Æschylus is after the bust in the Capitoline Museum, Rome, a supposedly true likeness. The Sophocles is a copy of the head in the Lateran, which was found about 1830 at Terracina and which resembles the bust in the Vatican found in 1778; but whether this or any likeness that has come down to us is an actual one or not, there is little evidence to show. The bust of Euripides is a copy of the one in the Naples Museum, and is valued as an authoritative portrait. The bronze head of Voltaire on the centre-table was presented to the Club by Doctor Haight. The head of Socrates in the magazine room is taken from the bust in the Villa Albani, Rome. This latter work was discovered in 1736 in Tusculum, on the grounds of Cicero's estate, and is recognized as a good likeness of the philosopher from his own description of himself and from a reference in Lucian's "Dialogues of the Dead." The bust marked Plato is a copy of the so-called Plato taken from the Villa Ercolanese, Herculaneum, now in the Naples Museum. Archæologists regard this head as an ideal one, representing Dionysus.

The vault of the main library has been elaborately decorated by Mr. H. Siddons Mowbray, the distinguished mural painter. The painted decorations begin at the spring of the vault, except at the two ends of the main room, and in the alcove enclosing the main entrance, where they extend down to the walls on either side of the doorways.

These decorations completed the stately and charming design of Charles F. McKim (Harvard '70), that gifted architect to whose taste and genius the building of the University Club is a signal monument.

The compiler of this history remembers with appreciation a consultation which took place on a certain night in the home of the late Charles T. Barney, on Park Avenue, with reference to this proposed work. Mr. Barney was the efficient Chairman of the Building Committee, and his own house with its contents of rare furniture and decorations, collected from many old countries and comprising exquisite examples of artistic antique and modern beauty, was a convincing proof of his fitness to direct the instalment of a building intended to be a marvel of delightful effects. Besides himself, the President of the Club was present, as well as Mr. McKim and the famous sculptor St. Gaudens. It was at this conference that the decision was made to adopt for the decoration of the library ceiling the mural paintings of Pinturicchio in the Borgia apartments of the Vatican, a work of unsurpassed excellence and grandeur, and singularly appropriate for the object in view. Then, also, it was agreed to recommend to the Council the appointment of Mr. Mowbray to execute the commission.

At a meeting of the Council held May 12, 1902, Mr. McKim appeared and presented this recommendation and outlined the plan for reproducing the Pinturicchio frescoes. He stated that it would be necessary for Mr. Mowbray to visit Rome for the purpose, and that it would require about three years to perform the work, and that the cost would be about $25,000. Mr. Barney, who was most enthusiastically in favor of the undertaking, moved that the Council authorize this expenditure, the same to be at the rate of about $8,000 a year for three years, and upon some doubt being expressed as to the wisdom of the Club's incurring so large an expense for such a purpose, generously offered personally to contribute $10,000 toward the proposed outlay. This characteristic

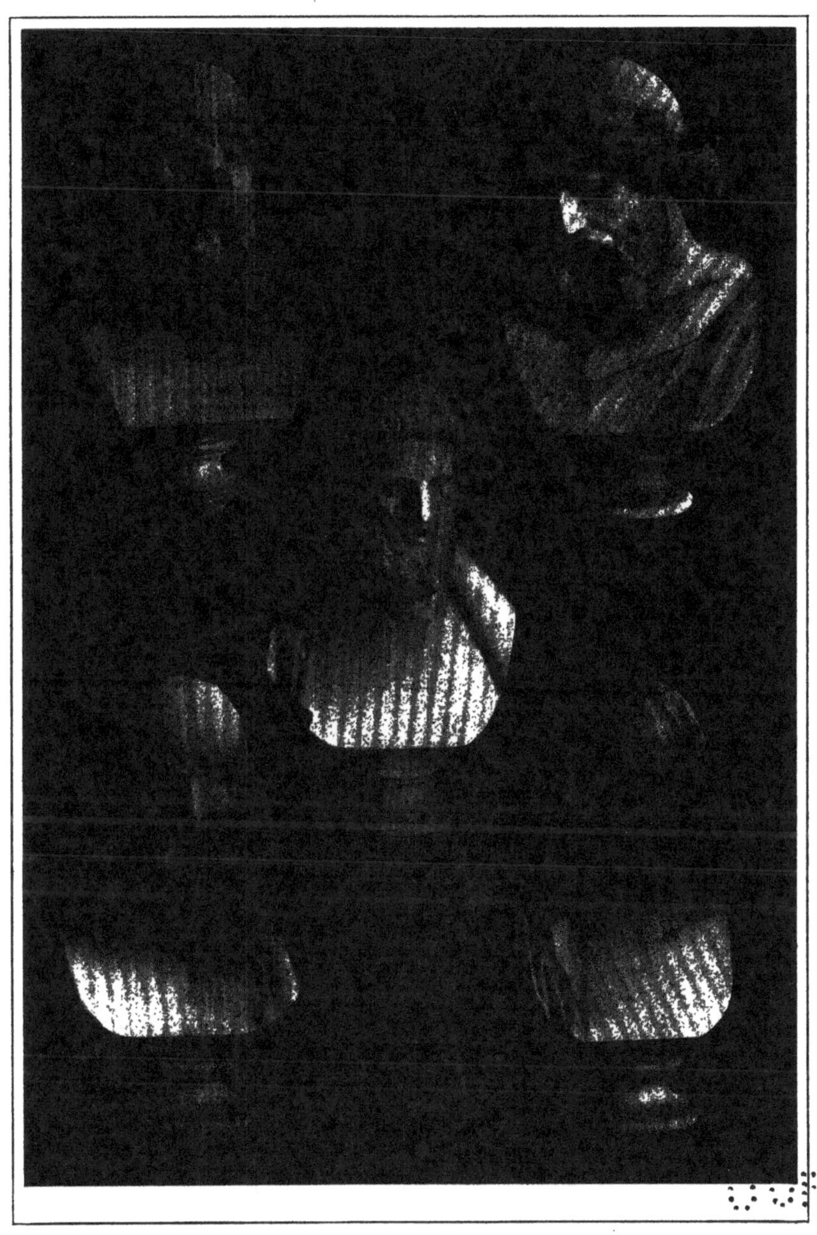

SOCRATES.		PLATO.
ÆSCHYLUS.	SOPHOCLES.	EURIPIDES.

BUSTS IN THE ATRIUM, LIBRARY FLOOR.

By M. Ezekiel. Presented by John W. Simpson (Amherst '71), 1903.

act on his part was made the subject of a vote of thanks to go on the record.

A subscription was thereafter started and a large part of the money necessary was thus secured, the Club paying the balance unsubscribed.

Mr. Mowbray was in Rome, engaged on the decorations, from September, 1902, to May, 1904, and the work in the library itself was commenced June 7, and completed September 15, 1904.

The fresco comprises the entire surface of the walls, ceilings, and arches above the cornice, and is composed of paintings and panels and ornament in relief with the treatment of all in color. Of the paintings, the four lunettes in the first, second, fourth, and fifth alcoves are copies of Pinturicchio, as are several of the smaller pieces in the vaults and arches; the large end lunettes, the entire central bay, the panels in relief, the ornament of the arches, and the other secondary paintings, are by Mr. Mowbray. The original paintings, as well as those adapted, symbolize, among other things, Geometry, Arithmetic, Music, and Rhetoric. History, Romance, Science, Philosophy, Literature, and the Fine Arts are also illustrated. The success of Mr. Mowbray in adopting the style of the great Italian artist has been described by a competent critic as "astonishing," and the verdict generally pronounced has been formulated in the declaration that "Mr. McKim and Mr. Mowbray between them have here created one of those works of art which bear the mark of permanence upon them."

The general effect of this architecture and decoration, with the soft neutral-tinted carpet, the ample tables with writing-materials, the easy chairs for readers, the solid lines of books on all sides of the alcoves, reaching from the floor to the spring of the vault, the central tables supplied with tempting books, the great globe of the world, the busts of philosophers in niches, the heavy-curtained windows, the members scattered through the room at tables for work or engaged in reading, is inexpressibly charming and suggestive of what is high and noble and in severe contrast with the nervous practical activities furiously in operation without the walls of this secluded home.

The following description of the library was furnished by our fellow member, William Mitchell Kendall (Harvard '76), of the firm of McKim, Mead & White:

For the decorative finishing of the library of the University Club it was thought that no other combination of design and color in one architectural decoration would be so appropriate as one founded on the work of Pinturicchio in the library at Siena and in the Borgia rooms in the Vatican, which in splendor of design and color surpasses Raphael's Stanza. Bernardino di Betti, called Il Pinturicchio, was accepted by his contemporaries as "a princely painter," an artist remarkable for delicacy of execution and richness of color. In 1898, before the building of the University Club was entirely completed, Mr. McKim developed his idea and selected his artist, though the shape of the field, the scale and the tone, were quite different from those of the Borgia apartments, taken as the type to follow. These apartments consist of moderate-sized rooms separated by simple doorways, and not to be seen en suite; the walls are of light plaster, toned in patterns to imitate marble and varied stones, while those of the New York club, lined with woodwork, shelves, and books, are of necessity different. But in the question of decoration the Borgia was preferred because of a general similarity of construction of arches and lunettes of ceiling, and because Pinturicchio's decorations with their grave richness were looked upon as peculiarly suited for a library. Another of this painter's characteristics is the expression of humanity in his figures in contrast with the more impersonal and academic forms which came later. The very good tonality which characterized them as a whole was taken for an inspiration for Mr. Mowbray's different scheme, in which every important object in the library—books, woodwork, floor-covering—had to be considered. But even where Pinturicchio is followed most faithfully he had to be translated, so to speak, to meet new conditions of scale and light, and to bring about a harmony with the varied warm tones below.

Very fortunately, these apartments in the Vatican, after having

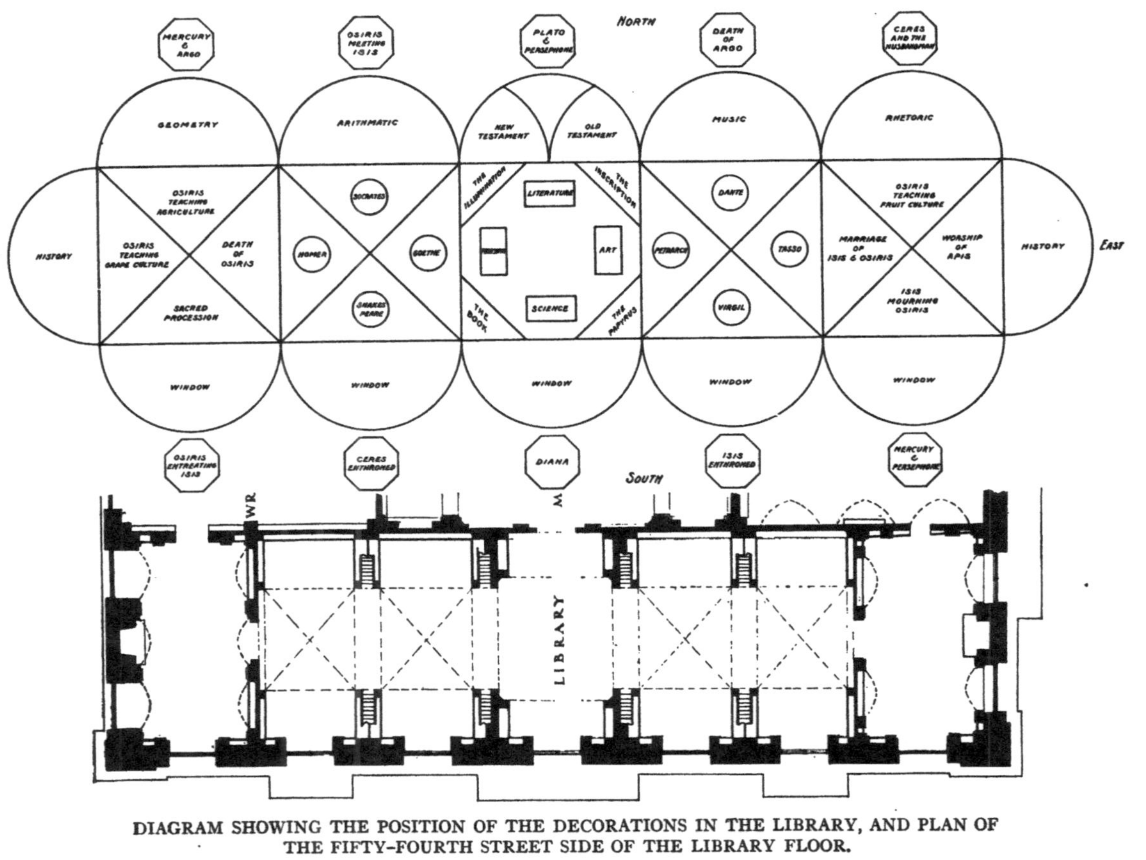

DIAGRAM SHOWING THE POSITION OF THE DECORATIONS IN THE LIBRARY, AND PLAN OF THE FIFTY-FOURTH STREET SIDE OF THE LIBRARY FLOOR.

been long closed to the public, had been solemnly reopened by Pope Leo XIII on March 8, 1897, cleaned and restored, and were not closed again until 1903, on the death of this pontiff, shortly before the end of Mr. Mowbray's sojourn in Rome, when he had practically completed his studies of the decorations. On his return to this country he was enabled to begin his actual work on the club ceiling in June, 1904, it being understood that he was to be in possession only a few months; and by dint of incessant industry on the part of himself and his workmen, shut in between the scaffolding and the ceiling, in comparative darkness and in very positive heat, the work was finished by the first of September following. As it was impossible to get any general view of the result in this construction piece by piece, the artist solaced himself with the consideration that as the scaffolding came down he could make such modifications as would be necessary to insure the general harmony; but when this ceremony took place the timbers fell so rapidly before the blows of the workmen that no amendments were possible. It was found, however, that there was nothing in the completed decoration of the ceiling, the coves, or the walls which required alteration.

The library-room is a long gallery, something less than one hundred feet in length by sixteen feet in width exclusive of the alcoves, which are nine feet in depth, making the total width thirty-four feet. There are five alcoves on each side, and the gallery is lighted by windows in the five on the south side. The central alcove on the north communicates by a white marble portal with the central hall of the club. Access is also given to the library at the two ends. The main ceiling, which is semicircular in section, is a groined vault divided into a number of compartments corresponding to the alcoves. The central compartment is domical, the remaining four are groined, formed by the intersection of the vaults of the alcoves with that of the main portion of the library. The bookcases reach to the spring of the vault, thus leaving at the ends of the main apartment and at the ends of the alcoves, lunettes, semicircular in form. The painted decorations begin at the spring of the vault, except at the two ends of the main room and in the alcove enclosing the main entrance, where they extend down the walls on either side of the doorway.

Not only the paintings, but the small figures in relief in the panels, and the final architectural mouldings were designed by Mr. Mowbray and, with the exception of the last, entirely executed by him. These mouldings were all done by hand (mechanical repetition being thus avoided), having been executed in Rome under his direction by native workmen. The ceiling, with the principal mouldings of the arches, as received from the architects of the building, was finished only in plaster. Both the shape of the fields and the scale, as well as the general tonality, are different from Pinturicchio's. The device of filling the sky in the lunettes with gold bosses instead of a flat sheet of the metal was adopted as breaking the background up into light and shade and preventing any flashes of light from the gold. It may be added that the doubters, of whom there were some, were converted by the sight of the completed library; that Mr. McKim's enthusiasm was in more than proportion to his previous anxiety; and that John La Farge expressed his opinion that the decoration was most scholarly and had been executed with great elegance of design.

In viewing these paintings the visitor will be at a loss to determine which are Pinturicchio's and which are Mr. Mowbray's. On the north side the four large lunettes—Geometry, Arithmetic, Music, and Rhetoric—are copies of Pinturicchio, as are several of the smaller pieces in the vaults and arches. The large lunettes at the ends of the gallery, Romance at the east and History at the west, are Mowbray's, as are also the entire central bay, the panels in gold relief, the ornament of the arches, and most of the secondary paintings. The religious element, an important feature of the Borgia decorations, is introduced in two demi-lunettes over the central white marble portal—the Old and the New Testament. The secondary panels in the arches and the ceiling, carrying out two of Pinturicchio's themes, are devoted to Greek mythology and the myth of Isis and Osiris; the four smaller rectangular panels over the central bay, to Literature, Art, Science, and Philosophy; the four medallion portraits over each of the compartments on either side of the central one are, on the east, of Dante, Tasso, Virgil, and Petrarch, and, on the west, of Homer, Socrates, Goethe, and Shakespeare. The two very narrow panels, heavy in relief and gold, which descend on the wall on either side of the central white portal, represent, like medieval illuminations, the Illumination and the Inscription, and on the opposite wall are the Papyrus and the Book. In all these paintings, so very varied in theme and composition, the painter has never once forgotten his text. Except in general qualities—general artistic taste and intelligence, a discreet and excellent color sense—the visitor would not recognize the author of the portraits and easel pictures—lighter perhaps in conception and touch—by which Mr. Mowbray had previously been known. The observer familiar with his previous mural decorations will feel a new inspiration, a recasting of conception and execution, in this academic and scholarly work, a delight both to the eye and to the intelligence, and fitly completing and crowning the architect's work.

CHAPTER XXVI

RECOGNITION OF DEGREES, OR A HISTORY OF THE ELIGIBILITY REQUIREMENT FROM 1879 TO 1914

We now come to a most important and interesting subject, namely: the degrees, and the colleges and universities conferring them, which are recognized by the Club in passing upon the eligibility of members.

Naturally, this subject received the attention of the Council at the very beginning of its renewed existence in 1879.

At the outset the responsibility for interpreting the intentions of the Club in this respect was placed unreservedly in the Committee on Admissions. In 1880 a clause was introduced into the constitution imposing upon the Council the duty to determine what degrees from foreign universities, and from what foreign universities, should entitle the holder to membership in the Club, and a committee was appointed by the Committee on Admissions to report on the subject to the Council, with recommendations.

This committee consisted of Frederick W. Whitridge (Amherst '74), T. Frank Brownell (Harvard '65), and J. T. Soutter (Oxford '72), men thoroughly fitted for the task.

How laboriously their work was done is evidenced by the bulky report made to the Council, and accepted by them October 4, 1880. It consists of nineteen pages of closely written letter-paper, containing the titles of one hundred and fifty-one universities in thirty-two foreign countries, as well as the particular degrees to be recognized in each case; preceded by a letter from Mr. Whitridge explaining the views of the committee.

The policy adopted at this time was more liberal than was afterward considered to be wise, as will hereafter appear.

The provision of the constitution as it stood in the year 1879, as to the qualification of members, was simply that the candidate should have been graduated from "Some College, University, or School of Medicine, Law, Science, or Theology," etc.

In 1880, this clause of the constitution was expunged and in lieu thereof it was provided "that the candidate must have received from a University or College a degree, to obtain which, in regular course, at least three years' residence or study are required," etc. Then follows the assignment to the Council of the selection of foreign universities and their degrees. As yet the determination as to American universities and their degrees was left with the Committee on Admissions. It was not until 1901 that the sole responsibility was placed in the Council, by the enactment of the following:

> The Council shall determine what degrees from Universities and Colleges, and from what Universities and Colleges, shall qualify the holders for membership; and a list of such degrees and of such Universities and Colleges, as from time to time determined by the Council, shall be posted in the office of the Club.

A communication was received by the Council at their meeting in February, 1897, from Mr. Isaac Iselin (Freiberg '74), suggesting that those holding degrees from the German Polytechnics be made eligible to membership, and that the names of those institutions be added to the list of foreign universities.

This raised a question which the Council did not feel prepared to answer, and the matter was referred to the Committee on Literature and Art for investigation and report.

This committee then consisted of Henry E. Howland (Yale '54), Charles Scribner (Princeton '75), and Charles H. Russell (Harvard '72). Mr. Russell, of the committee, went to Germany and made an exhaustive examination into the character and scope of these technical schools, and made a report October 11, 1897, to the Council, which so admirably shows the pains taken to reach a just and wise conclusion that it is here given in full:

NEW YORK, October 11, 1897.

TO THE COUNCIL OF THE UNIVERSITY CLUB:—

The Committee on Admissions having declined to consider as eligible to membership a candidate who was represented to have received the degree of Mechanical Engineer from the Polytechnic School at Dresden, in Germany, upon the ground that such degree is not one of those which have been recognized by the Council under the Constitution of the Club as qualifying the holders for membership, and his proposer having complained to the Council of this decision, the subject was referred to the Committee on Literature and Art for report.

The Committee report as follows: The Constitution of the Club, Article VIII, defines as eligible to membership any person "who shall have received from a university or college a degree, to obtain which, in regular course, at least three years' residence and study are required," and further, "that the Council shall determine what degrees from foreign universities, and from what foreign universities, shall qualify the holder for membership, and a list of such degrees shall be posted in the office of the Club. The holder of any degree named on such list shall be eligible to membership." The institution referred to in the candidate's application as the Dresden Polytechnic School does not appear upon the list, which, in accordance with the above requirement of the Constitution, has for many years past been posted in the Club-House. Consequently, in the opinion of this Committee, the Committee on Admissions had no power to elect the candidate to membership.

This Committee has understood that the Council desired that they should further report upon the question as to whether the holders of degrees from the so-called polytechnic schools of Germany should be made eligible to membership and the list of foreign degrees amended accordingly. They have therefore given the subject considerable investigation, and the presence of one of the members of the Committee in Germany during the past summer has enabled them to procure accurate information in regard to it.

ENTRANCE TO THE CLUB, ON FIFTY-FOURTH STREET.

While the term polytechnic, as understood in this country, properly describes the character of many schools of a high order in Germany, and is sometimes used even in Germany in connection with them, yet none of the schools of this character which are of sufficiently high rank to justify the consideration of the holders of their degrees for eligibility to membership in the Club, are officially known by that name. The German title of such schools is "Technische Hochschule." There are nine of these technical high schools in Germany, situated at the following places: Aachen, Berlin, and Hanover, in Prussia; Karlsruhe, in Baden; Munich, in Bavaria; Dresden, in Saxony; Stuttgart, in Würtemberg; and the cities of Brunswick and Darmstadt.

These nine schools are technical and scientific schools of a high order. Their range of study is very extensive, rather more so than that of our scientific and technological schools. The number of students is large, and many of the professors are men of distinction. The course of study is not less than three and is usually four years, and residence of not less than three years is required to enable a student to take the final examination. Residence, however, in the German technical high schools (as also in the German universities) has a different meaning from residence in an American university, as generally understood. The student is obliged to register his name with the Professors whose courses he elects to pursue, at the beginning of a term and again at the end of a term, but as a general rule, to which the exceptions seem to be unimportant, no record is made of his attendance at lectures, nor is he obliged to show that he has been present between the beginning and the end of the term. Moreover, the three years' residence need not have been at the particular high school at which the final examination is taken. It is quite common for technical high school students to go from one of these schools to one or more of the others, during their years of study, in order to hear particular lecturers, to have the advantages of special collections or laboratory work, or for any other reasons which may appeal to them. Upon successfully passing the final examination at the particular technical high school which the student elects for that purpose, he receives, if successful, a diploma. "No title or special privilege is conferred by the diploma." The term "degree" is not used in Germany for any academic distinction, except those conferred by the universities. The universities of Germany are still almost exclusively confined in their departments to the faculties of theology, law, medicine and philosophy, and the degrees of those faculties are the only recognized degrees so-called. The universities do not include what in this country are known as scientific or technological schools. In this respect they differ from our principal universities, in which the scientific school is as much a part of the university as the undergraduate department, and which confers the degree of mining or civil engineer in the same manner as it confers the degree of Bachelor of Arts. It seems proper therefore to consider the diploma of one of these German technical high schools as equivalent to a "degree," within the intention of the Constitution of the Club.

It appears to be the fact that only a small proportion of the students at the German technical high schools take the final examination, or ever have any wish or purpose to do so, except those who intend to enter the service of the State. One important object in the establishment of these schools, as appears from their history, was to educate young men for the civil service of the various States of Germany; and the public service in the departments of railways, telegraphs, public works of various kinds, etc., offers a large, and in Germany very attractive official career to young men of technical attainments. In the case of students desiring to enter the service of the State, it is customary for them to pass these examinations. Subsequently, there is also a so-called State examination; and from some of the literature in relation to these high schools, it appears that an effort is being made to combine the two examinations (and in Bavaria, it is understood that this has been done); but, as already stated, it appears to be unusual for students, who contemplate employment other than that of the State, to pass these examinations. Employers throughout Germany in general make no requirement of the diploma of a technical high school in the case of young men coming into their employment; and as a result students usually pursue courses of study, in the one or more departments which they elect, only so long as they consider desirable in order to procure the necessary practical education and training.

The chief departments of study in these schools are classified by them under the heads of civil and mechanical engineering, chemistry, mathematics, natural sciences and architecture. Under these principal divisions is included a great variety of studies, among them: Electrical and factory engineering, metallurgy, textile industry, ship building, machine building, pharmacy, public health, political economy, geology, and languages. In some of the schools instruction in mining is given; but it may be mentioned incidentally that the most esteemed mining schools in Germany are distinct schools, and not the technical high schools.

The courses of study, as will be seen, are almost entirely practical, and are intended to prepare men for immediate work in technical and scientific employment.

It is undersood that few Americans now go to these schools, except in the department of ship-building. The development of the scientific schools in the United States and the inconvenience which has been found to result to Americans on entering into the practice of their professions here from having been trained to work under the metric system in Germany, are said to be the chief reasons why Americans do not now attend these schools to any great extent; although many of them attend the universities.

Your Committee has also endeavored to learn how the requirements for a diploma and the attainments of the recipients of such diplomas in the German technical high schools compare with the requirements and attainments in the case of students who receive degrees from scientific schools in this country. Now and for many years past the graduates of American scientific schools have been considered eligible to membership in the Club, and a considerable number of the graduates of the Harvard and Yale Scientific Schools, the Columbia School of Mines, the Massachusetts Institute of Technology, the Rensselaer Polytechnic Institute and the Stevens Institute are now among our members.

Your Committee are of the opinion that, so far as such requirements and attainments go, the holders of the diplomas of the German technical high schools are to be considered as not less qualified for membership than the holders of the degrees of American scientific schools.

It is well to note in this report that these technical high schools must not be associated in the mind with the many other technical schools which exist in Germany. Throughout the Empire there are many schools such as we should describe as "training schools" or "trade schools," as well as agricultural, forestry, and other schools, which, however, are of inferior rank and are not entitled to consideration in this connection.

The Committee have received assistance in their investigations from Mr. John B. Jackson, Secretary of the American Embassy in Berlin, and from Mr. Augustus Trowbridge, at present resident in

Berlin; also from Professor C. F. Chandler and Mr. Charles Sooysmith of New York. For detailed information in regard to the German technical high-schools, reference may be had to "Die Technischen Hochschulen und Bergakademien," by Dr. Wilhelm Scheffler, Leipzig, 1893–94; "Die Technischen Hochschulen," by Professor R. Baumeister, Berlin, 1886; and the annual numbers of the "Minerva Jahrbuch," published at Strassburg.

In conclusion, the Committee are of opinion that the holders of the diplomas of the nine German technical high schools above mentioned, who have received such diplomas after final examination upon completion of not less than three years of study, should be made eligible to membership in the Club, as having complied with the constitutional requirement that candidates "shall have received from a university or college a degree to obtain which in regular course at least three years residence and study are required."

The Committee recommend that the Council in the exercise of the power given it by Article VIII of the constitution shall determine that the diplomas of the nine technical high schools referred to, conferred as above mentioned, shall qualify the holders for membership; and they further recommend the adoption by the Council of the following resolution, namely:

Resolved, That the list of degrees from foreign Universities qualifying the holders for membership, which has heretofore been adopted by the Council and posted in the office of the Club, shall be amended by adding at the end of the portion entitled "Germany," the following words:

Technical High Schools

A diploma conferred after final examination, upon completion of a course of not less than three years of study, by:

1.—Aachen. Königliche Technische Hochschule.

2.—Berlin. Königliche Technische Hochschule.

3.—Brunswick. Herzogliche Technische Hochschule Carolo-Wilhelmina.

4.—Darmstadt. Grossherzogliche Hessische Technische Hochschule.

5.—Dresden. Königliche Sächsische Technische Hochschule.

6.—Hanover. Königliche Technische Hochschule.

7.—Karlsruhe. Grossherzogliche Badische Technische Hochschule.

From a photograph, copyright by Sidman, New York, 1900.

MAIN HALLWAY ON THE FIRST FLOOR, LOOKING EAST.

8.—Munich. Königliche Bayerische Technische Hochschule.
9.—Stuttgart. Königliche Technische Hochschule.

Respectfully submitted.

C. H. Russell,
Henry E. Howland,
Charles Scribner,
Committee on Literature and Art.

The resolution thus recommended was accordingly adopted.

In order that the subject of degrees may be intelligently considered, the chronological order of events in the general history will not here be strictly observed.

In 1898 a special committee reported in favor of adding A.B. of Dalhousie University and LL.B. of Cambridge University to the list of foreign universities, which recommendations were adopted. At this stage of the Club's history, a strong sentiment manifested itself against the admission of candidates holding degrees in law and medicine who had never had the advantage of a residential college life. The Committee on Admissions were believed to coincide with this sentiment, but inasmuch as the terms of the constitution as it then stood did not exclude professional schools, but merely exacted the three years of resident study, and as the practice had obtained of recognizing these degrees, they were not in a position to use discretion and refuse candidates lacking a college education, without some express or implied authority from the Club.

This delicate question was brought up for the action of the Club at its annual meeting, March 19, 1898, when an amendment to the constitution was proposed by the Honorable E. Henry Lacombe (Columbia '63), of the United States Court, providing that after March 19, 1898, a degree in law or medicine, even when obtained by three years of resident study, should not alone render the holder eligible to membership.

There was a very full discussion, and while it appeared to

be the desire of an overwhelming majority to put Judge Lacombe's proposal into practice, still, out of consideration for the feelings of those of the class under consideration already admitted and the minority who preferred to retain the custom, the amendment was laid on the table; but the known objection of the Committee on Admissions to the recognition of merely professional degrees without a previous college course, was endorsed by the passage of the following resolution:

Resolved, That this Club expresses its confidence in the Committee on Admissions.

Since that time the committee has not recognized degrees from schools of law and medicine, unpreceded by college degrees.

The constitution having been amended, as stated, so as to constitute the Council the final authority on degrees, a special committee was appointed at the meeting of March 11, 1901, on universities and colleges, their degrees and qualifications. This committee reported at the May meeting of the Council upon its preliminary work.

The report, which was unanimously adopted, is now given in full, as expressing the views of the Council at this stage after careful examination:

Report of Special Committee appointed by the Council at its meeting held on March 11, 1901, to prepare a list of degrees which shall qualify the holders for membership in the Club, and to report the same to the Council for its action under Section 3 of Article VIII, of the Constitution which as amended reads as follows, namely:

"The Council shall determine what degrees from Universities and Colleges, and from what Universities and Colleges, shall qualify the holders for membership; and a list of such degrees and of such Universities and Colleges, as from time to time determined by the Council, shall be posted in the office of the Club."

DECORATION ADAPTED FROM THE UNIVERSITY CLUB SEAL BY CHARLES E. KECK.

Over the mantel in the main hallway.

Your Committee requested the Committee on Admissions to furnish it with copies of any written reports which had been made to the latter, or of extracts from its minutes, in relation to the numerous degrees of American Universities and Colleges upon which it had passed, and also to appoint a sub-committee with which your Committee might confer. It subsequently appeared that no formal written reports have ever been made to the Committee on Admissions; but that it has been the practice in each case to refer the question of the eligibility of a degree to one or more members of the Committee on Admissions, whose report has been made orally. The only record therefore in the minutes of the Committee on Admissions is the entry from time to time of the fact that an oral report was made by a member of the Committee as to a certain degree, and that the Committee thereupon voted that the degree was satisfactory or otherwise. The investigations by the Committee on Admissions for many years past have been conducted chiefly by Mr. Ordway, and the Committee appointed him to confer with your Committee. With Mr. Ordway we have gone very carefully and in detail over the entire list of American Universities and Colleges now represented in the Club membership, and have considered also several other American Universities and Colleges not yet represented in our membership; and after careful consideration we have prepared a list which we submit as a part of this report.

In considering the eligibility of degrees, we have sought information chiefly upon three grounds: First, as to the course of study required for the degree; second, as to the period of residence required in regular course to obtain such degree; and third, the character of the life and surroundings of the students while pursuing the studies required for obtaining such degree.

As to the course of study and instruction required, it is impossible to make any general rule, as the requirements and range and importance of the studies differ so greatly among the various Colleges, so much so that in some of the larger Colleges the holders of even the A. B. degree of certain other Colleges are not admitted without examination higher than to the Sophomore or Junior class. Consequently all that seems practical or necessary is to ascertain, taking everything into consideration, that the course of study and the life of the students are really those of a College and not merely those of a school; and this basis of selection has been followed by us.

In regard to residence our understanding of the policy and traditions of the Club is that the three years' residence required is that of *undergraduates*, namely: that character of residence at the University or College which necessarily includes American College life: the life of undergraduates, with all the intimacy, comradeship, societies, sports and interests which are inseparable from that life, which distinguish it from all other experiences, which give to the men who have enjoyed it those advantages and traditions and sympathies which they so greatly value, and which constitute that common possession, which, as we understand it, is the basis of the membership of this Club. In considering degrees therefore we have rejected as insufficient such degrees as do not require this precedent undergraduate life, notwithstanding that in some cases a residence of three years may be required. Residence at a University is usually required for the degrees which are commonly regarded as "graduate degrees," such as M.A., M.S., Ph.D., and others, and those degrees are in many instances open to men who have not previously been graduates. The same is usually true of degrees in medicine, theology and law. Although in many of these cases the conditions of residence as to term of years may be found to comply with the requirements of the Club, yet the character of the residence and of the life of the students in our opinion clearly do not include those elements which make up the undergraduate life. We have therefore not included such degrees.

Were existing conditions as conditions were forty years ago, the principle which we have followed as to degrees probably would have limited us to the degree of Bachelor of Arts alone; but the development of scientific and other special lines of study in our Universities has led to the creation in many of them of what are in reality undergraduate courses for degrees other than that of Bachelor of Arts. Undoubtedly some of these degrees are purely professional degrees, as for instance those of mining and civil engineer. But these courses are followed by young men who are required to reside at the University or College for not less than three or four years, and in many cases are pursued concurrently and to some extent in the same class rooms with the men who are studying for the degree of Bachelor of Arts; and even when they are pursued in separate institutions in the same University, nevertheless the life of the students following those courses complies in all respects with the conditions which constitute the undergraduate life. In addition there are purely technical schools such as the Massachusetts Institute of Technology, the Stevens Institute, the Rensselaer Polytechnic Institute, and others, not connected with any University, but in which we have found not only that the number of years of residence required complies with our provisions, but that the life of the students is substantially the undergraduate life. It may be suggested that no graduate of one of these independent scientific or technical colleges, or even of institutions of the same character which are departments of a great University, really has all the valued associations and traditions of men who have received from their alma maters the degree of Bachelor of Arts. Undoubtedly something might be said on this point, but we have found it impractical to make any such distinction, where the requirements as above outlined are fully satisfied; and we have therefore included many of such degrees in the eligible list.

One other important consideration requires the determination of the Council as a matter of policy, and involves an interpretation of the first section of Article VIII of the Constitution. The first part of that section, omitting immaterial words, provides: "Any person . . . shall be eligible to membership . . . who shall have received . . . a degree to obtain which, in regular course, at least three years' residence and study are required." It has become quite common at Harvard, and it is understood also to a less extent at others of the greater Universities, to admit students to what is called "advanced standing"; that is to say, to permit them to enter classes above the Freshman class in the college and in the scientific school upon examination. In such cases not less than one year's residence, which of course in each case would be at least the senior year, is required. Consequently it is possible at Harvard, for instance, for a student to enter the senior class in either the college or the scientific school, and to receive upon graduation, after one year's residence, the degree of Bachelor of Arts, or the degree of Bachelor of Science. Such cases are no doubt exceptional; but the fact clearly appears that a student after only one year's actual residence may receive a degree "to obtain which (to quote the Constitution) in regular course at least three years' residence and study are required." On this question two courses seem to us open to the Council: One is to make no inquiry as to what was the actual length of residence at his University of the holder of a degree which has been accepted by the Council as satisfactory for the reason, among others, that not less than three years' residence is usually and in "regular course" required for such degree; the other is to require in the case of every candidate for admission, as a condition precedent to the consideration of his name, that his application papers shall specify that the actual residence at his University which preceded his obtaining his degree was not less than three years. So far as we have been able to learn the greater proportion of the men admitted to advanced standing at Harvard (where this privilege seems to be availed of more than elsewhere) appear to be men who already are the holders of the degree of Bachelor of Arts from some other College; and it seems reasonable to conclude that the number of men who have had no previous College life at all who enter classes later than the beginning of the Sophomore year, is small, and therefore that instances of the candidacy of holders of degrees obtained after less than three years' actual residence are likely to be exceptional and rare. We therefore recommend in all cases in which in the usual and regular course at least three years' residence is required for a particular degree, that no special inquiry shall be made in the case of a candidate, who is the holder of such a degree, as to the length of his actual residence at his University.

The list which is presented herewith has been prepared with care, but of course is not a final list. We have prepared and submit a notice to precede it and to be printed with it (should it be approved by the Council), reciting that it is subject to amendment by the withdrawal and addition of degrees as the Council may from time to time determine; and also that members desiring to propose a candidate who is the holder of a degree not included in the list are requested to submit the name of his University and his degree to the Council for its consideration. It will, therefore, be understood by members that the burden of affirmatively proving the eligibility of any degree not upon the list is upon them. In such case it would not be necessary to name a candidate. All that would be necessary is that the simple question of the eligibility of a certain degree of a certain college, conferred at a certain time, or it may be at any time, should be judicially passed upon by the Council. Your Committee believe that only in this way can the eligibility of the degree not included in the present list be satisfactorily investigated and decided.

In regard to degrees of foreign Universities, your Committee recommend that the existing list as heretofore adopted by the Council remain unchanged for the present.

Respectfully submitted,

CHARLES H. RUSSELL, *Chairman*,
B. AYMAR SANDS,
CHARLES STEELE.

List of Degrees of Universities and Colleges situated within the United States qualifying the holders for membership, as determined by the Council. This list is subject to amendment by the withdrawal of the names of any of the Universities or Colleges or degrees contained in it, or by the addition of others, as the Council may from time to time determine. (Article VIII, Section 3, of the Constitution.)

Members desiring to propose a candidate who is the holder of a degree not included in this list are requested to submit the name of the University or College of which the proposed candidate is a graduate and his degree to the Council, with full and detailed information as to the requirements of study and residence for such degree, and particularly as to such requirements at the time the candidate received his degree.

Amherst, A.B., B.S.
Brown, A.B., B.P.
Bowdoin, A.B.
Columbia, A.B., M.E., C.E., E.E., Ph.B., B.S.
Cornell, A.B., M.E., C.E., B.S., B.L., Ph.B.
College of the City of New York, A.B., B.S.
Colgate, A.B.
Colby, A.B.
Columbian University, A.B.
Dartmouth, A.B.
Georgetown, A.B.
Harvard, A.B., B.S.
Hamilton, A.B.
Hobart, A.B.
Haverford, A.B.
Johns Hopkins, A.B.
Kenyon, A.B.
Lafayette, A.B., C.E.
Lehigh, A.B., M.E., C.E.
Massachusetts Institute of Technology, B.S.

Middlebury, A.B.
New York University, A.B., B.S.
Northwestern University, A.B.
Ohio Wesleyan, A.B.
Oberlin, A.B.
Princeton, A.B., B.S., C.E. (E.E. to and inc. 1895).
Rutgers, A.B.
Racine, A.B.
Rensselaer Polytechnic Institute, C.E., M.E., B.S.
Stevens Institute, M.E., B.S.
Swarthmore, A.B., B.S.
Tufts, A.B., B.M.A.
Tulane, A.B.
Trinity, A.B., B.S.
University of Pennsylvania, A.B., B.S.
University of Virginia, A.B.
University of Michigan, A.B., C.E.
University of Chicago, A.B.
University of Illinois, A.B.
University of North Carolina, A.B.
University of Wisconsin, A.B.
University of Georgia, A.B.
University of Nebraska, A.B.
University of Rochester, A.B., B.S.
University of Vermont, A.B., Ph.B.
University of Minnesota, A.B.
Union, A.B.
Williams, A.B.
Wesleyan, A.B.
Western Reserve, A.B.
Western University of Pennsylvania, A.B.
Washington University, A.B.
Yale, A.B., B.S., Ph.B.

The Report thus made and adopted has served as the groundwork for the Committee on Colleges and Degrees ever since it was prepared. Mr. B. Aymar Sands, who was for many years Chairman of that Committee, sent a copy of this report to each new member when added to the Committee, as a guide.

The Special Committee on Colleges and Degrees was continued from time to time, and later made a Standing Committee. It first appears among the published committees in the Club Year Book of 1903, when the membership of it consisted of Messrs. B. Aymar Sands (Columbia '74), Francis R. Appleton (Harvard '75), and Samuel H. Ordway (Brown '80). The only changes in this committee have been the appointment of Mr. Charles O. Brewster (Harvard '79) in the place of Mr. Appleton in 1906; of Mr. Robert Thorne (Trinity '85) in Mr. Brewster's place in 1909; and of Mr. A. Henry Mosle (Yale '89) in 1911 in the place of Mr. Sands, who had become the President of the Club. At the time of the compilation of this history (1914) the committee consists of Messrs. Robert Thorne, Chairman; A. Henry Mosle, and Samuel H. Ordway.

The writer can testify from his own experience, supported by the unanimous opinion of all members of the Council throughout the period beginning in 1901, to the invaluable work of this committee. It has been done with unflagging industry, and a rare sense of just discrimination.

The usage has been, whenever a candidate was proposed for membership, holding a degree not already stamped with the approval of the Club, to refer the matter to the consideration of the Committee on Colleges and Degrees, who after painstaking investigation made a written report giving at length the qualifications of the college in question and stating its conclusions for or against the case in hand, with the reasons.

These reports are all on file among the archives of the Club, and would well repay perusal, evincing as they do a keen insight into the subject and an intelligent array of facts in each case necessary to the formation of a sound judgment. These reports have often covered many typewritten pages of foolscap, and have invariably gone thoroughly into the history, character, and methods of the college concerned.

The very first action of the Special Committee on a particular case was unfavourable to the institution involved. At the meeting of the Council of November 11, 1901, Mr. Russell, Chairman, made a report against recognizing the degrees of an institution which, while doing satisfactory work within its sphere, did not come within the category of colleges in the sense set forth in the declaration of principles adopted by the Council.

Since that time, the committee has been constrained to report adversely on thirty-two so-called colleges and universities (in several cases the rejection being only of certain degrees in approved institutions) and its conclusions have, after deliberation, invariably been unanimously adopted by the Council—the fair inference from which is that the judgments rendered were based on facts and formed with wisdom.

In 1902 the Council was so much impressed by "the thorough and intelligent work performed by that Committee" that a formal vote of thanks was given to its Chairman, Mr. Charles H. Russell (Harvard '72), and reported on the minutes.

The following is an example of an adverse report:

Report of the Special Committee on Degrees in relation to the degrees of Bachelor of Arts and Bachelor of Science of . . . College situated at . . .

The charter of . . . College was granted in . . . and the College was opened in . . . Into it was merged . . . School founded in . . . and opened in . . . From the list of alumni it seems that there were graduates in most of the years up to 1830 (although as the alumni between 1811 and 1822 are, for some unexplained reason, grouped without distinction of years, it is not possible to make this statement definitely); and in each year with few exceptions after 1830 a class was graduated until the outbreak of the Civil War, in 1861, at which time the exercises of the College were suspended. The College was reorganized in 1867 and a class has been graduated in each of the years from 1871, inclusive, to the present time. The classes for the last ten years have numbered generally from 12 to 15 upon graduation. The class of 1900 numbered 19 upon graduation.

The College consists of two parts, namely: The College proper containing 93 undergraduates, and a preparatory school containing 48 boys. "The Collegiate department embraces four years, viz: 1. The Classical and the Latin-Scientific, both of which lead to the degree of Bachelor of Arts. 2. The Scientific and Mechanical Engineering courses which lead to the degree of Bachelor of Science." (Catalogue 1901, page 19). The requirements for admission to the Classical course and the range of study during the four years are about upon the average of the smaller American Colleges, and are satisfactory within the regulations of the Council. There is a fair range of electives in the Junior and Senior years in both of these courses. The so-called Latin-Scientific course is substantially the same as the classical course, except that no Greek is required, and in lieu thereof more time is given to scientific studies. In the Scientific and Mechanical Engineering courses, each of which leads to the degree of Bachelor of Science, neither Latin nor Greek is required, and the four years are given chiefly to scientific studies, English and modern languages. The Mechanical Engineering course includes shopwork. It is impossible to learn from the catalogue and its statements and tables of studies in the Scientific and Mechanical Engineering courses how thorough those courses are and how they compare with like courses in other Colleges which are not strictly scientific schools; and it does not appear exactly what are the facilities for laboratory and other practical work. Only a small proportion of the students take these courses. A recapitulation by courses shows that of the 93 students 6 take the Mechanical Engineering course; 14 the Scientific; 53 the Latin-Scientific; 14 the Classical; and 6 are special students. (The term Latin-Scientific is really a misnomer, as was pointed out by Professor Root in one of his letters quoted in the Committee's report upon the Hamilton College degree of B.S.) The scientific courses are taken by only 20 out of the 93 undergraduate students. An examination of the requirements during the four years of the Scientific and Mechanical Engineering courses gives the impression that those courses would hardly be sufficient to qualify men for entrance upon professional scientific careers. Nevertheless, the range of subjects included in them, under a proper system of instruction, would undoubtedly give at least a very good general education in mathematics, physics, chemistry, history, philosophy and modern languages. So that so far as range of study and period of residence are concerned, the Committee are disposed to regard those courses, as well as the

Classical and Latin-Scientific courses, as satisfactory within our regulations.

The Committee are, however, of opinion that the conditions of undergraduate college life are not such as to make the graduates of this College eligible to membership.

It is not known to the Committee what proportion of the 93 students are the holders of State scholarships. The . . . legislature provided in 1872 and 1879 for furnishing board, fuel, lights, and washing to the holder of one State Scholarship from each Senatorial District in the State, to be chosen by competitive examination. "The law requires that the candidates shall produce before the Board of School Commissioners satisfactory evidence . . . of their inability or the inability of their parents or guardians to pay the regular college charges. . . . These scholarships are tenable for four years and the incumbents are required by law to pledge themselves that they will continue students of the College for the full term of four years, unless prevented by unavoidable necessity, and that they will teach school within the State for not less than two years after leaving college. . . . The incumbents of these scholarships will hereafter be required to provide their own text books." (Catalogue of 1901, page 57.) A later act, 1894, "granting an additional appropriation to the College, provides for the education of 26 State students, in addition to the foregoing, free of expenses for tuition. These scholarships will be distributed among the Counties of . . . in order of priority of application. The holders of these scholarships will be required to provide the cost of their board, and pay incidental fees for Church, gymnasium, heat and hire of furniture." (Id., page 58.)

The catalogue for 1901 shows that of the 93 undergraduate students 87 were residents of . . .

There are two college dormitories, and apparently there is no charge for room rent in them, except in the case of students lodging in the college buildings, but boarding elsewhere, who are charged a small amount for room rent, care of room, light and washing. "All students holding scholarships are required to lodge in the college halls and those holding Senatorial scholarships are provided with room furniture for the care of which they are held strictly accountable. Students not holding Senatorial scholarships are required to provide themselves with furniture. Furniture may, however, be hired from the College authorities at from $3.50 to $5. per term. (Catalogue 1901, page 51.) "A student is

THE TURKISH BATH AND SWIMMING POOL IN THE BASEMENT, ON THE FIFTH AVENUE SIDE.

also expected to provide himself with table napkins, towels, and the requisite bed clothing for a single bed. . . . Funds of students may be deposited with the President of the College or with some other member of the faculty who will disburse the funds thus received in accordance with instructions he may receive from parent or guardian." (Id., page 50).

The undergraduates, together with those pupils of the preparatory department who are big enough to wear long trousers (id., page 48), are organized into a corps of cadets and are drilled daily. A uniform is worn which is said to be a modification of that worn at the United States Military Academy at West Point, and is of gray cloth with dark blue cap. Concerning the uniform the catalogue states "The uniform is required to be worn at all times and all college students are required to provide themselves with it." (Id., page 48).

The Committee are of opinion that, although the requirements as to study and residence appear to be satisfactory, within the rules of the Council, yet evidently the life of the students is that of a military boarding school rather than that of an American College; and they therefore recommend that the degrees of Bachelor of Arts and Bachelor of Science conferred by . . . College shall not be added to the eligible list.

COMMITTEE ON DEGREES,
(Signed) C. H. RUSSELL [Harvard '72],
B. AYMAR SANDS [Columbia '74],
CHARLES STEELE [Univ. of Va. '78].

NEW YORK, Jan. 13, 1902.

The committee from time to time acted favorably upon the merits of a great many institutions, in each case submitting a report with information in detail. It is unnecessary to enumerate the colleges here, inasmuch as the complete list of those approved to date will be found in the Appendix.

For the purpose, however, of enabling the members of the Club to realize the amount of research, study, and care involved in the investigation of these institutions, several reports are here reproduced, as specimens. The fact that many schools claiming to be universities and colleges fail to receive the imprimatur of the Club, and that in the course of examination of those which are finally approved there frequently is correspondence with the authorities of the college under consideration to clear up doubtful points, is calculated to have a stimulating effect upon the administration of all such schools, and the University Club is thereby performing one of its highest functions, namely: to create a standard of excellence which must be reached by all before their graduates can be received on an equal footing with those colleges and universities which are unquestioned.

Report of the Special Committee on Degrees in relation to the degrees of Bachelor of Philosophy and Bachelor of Science of Hamilton College, Clinton, New York.

There are two undergraduate courses at Hamilton College, each requiring four years' residence and study, and called respectively the Classical and the Latin-Scientific course. The former results in the degree of Bachelor of Arts which is already upon our list.

The Latin-Scientific Course leads to the degree of Bachelor of Philosophy, or in case of especial excellence in the physical sciences, implying advanced laboratory courses, to the degree of Bachelor of Science. (Hamilton College Catalogue, October, 1900.)

It appears that the requirements for admission to this course are substantially the same as to the classical course, except that one year of French and one year of German or two years of either is allowed instead of Greek. The course thereafter includes Latin for two years and mathematical and scientific studies and English and modern languages. For the last two years the instruction is substantially identical with that of the classical course, with a liberal range of electives common to both courses. The courses of study appear to be full and comprehensive.

Dr. Oren Root, Professor of Mathematics in Hamilton College, has written to the Committee as follows: "With us, the degrees of Ph.B. and B.S. are rested upon a course as rigorous and exacting, demanding as thorough preparation and as careful study as the degree of B.A. The only difference is in the dropping of Greek and the intaking of more German, French, Italian and Spanish or of the sciences. The question is at the last simply: Can a man be liberally educated without the study of Greek? I was for a long time a most pronounced Grecian. The observation of our work here has, during the last fifteen years, changed my position.

I would give two degrees, B.A. and B.S.; the latter to those who have during the last two years specialized purely in science. I deem our Ph.B. as fully equal to B.A. In three out of four classes recently graduated, the valedictory has gone to B.S. or Ph.B. men. . . . I enclose our catalogue and call your attention to the so-called 'Latin-Scientific Course' (a misnomer) on which our Ph.B. and B.S. are based. The requirements for admission are identical in English, Latin, Mathematics; two years' modern language takes the place of Greek and the history requirement is increased. We allow *no* conditions on the modern languages. Really,—all in all—our work for the B.S. and Ph.B. candidates is a shade harder than for our B.A. candidates."

Dr. Root also mentioned in his letter that there was a time when the degrees of Ph.B. and B.S. were not satisfactory, being "given often after a brief and superficial course." Further inquiry was therefore made of him as to since what date in his opinion those degrees may be considered to be as worthy as they now appear to be, and he replied as follows:

"The sentence in my letter of the 17th June, which you quote, has naturally the application which you give. But my remarks about the B.S. degree based upon superficial courses were based not on anything occurring here; they came from knowledge of other colleges. Some twenty years ago, I strenuously opposed in our faculty a proposition asking our trustees to authorize the B.S. degree. The advocates of the plan urged the example of other colleges—some of them in this State. My attention was then called to the character of the courses on which in many cases this degree was based. I urged that in such cases the degree was an affront to Science, an imposition on the young men, a disgrace to the institutions. Hamilton College was not then prepared to give a course on which the degrees of B.S. and Ph.B. could be properly based and I protested against joining in the conspiracy of sham in higher education. The proposition was defeated and a course was *not* formulated until our appliances and corps of instructors were so increased that the basis for *other* degrees could be made as full, and as thorough as that for B.A. This was done in 1892; really somewhat later than might have been, for the work of our so-called 'Latin-Scientific Course' had been done for some three years though not formulated. There has been, I think, no 'short-cut' and no 'false-front' behind our degrees of B.S. and Ph.B. since they were offered. In the matter of residence, our laws provide for four years in all cases. We have young men, especially from the West, who, spending two or three years in home institutions, enter with us one year later and obtain our degrees after two or three years of residence here. That is, residence with approved work at another college is taken as residence here. We have *no* arrangement by which a student can complete our course and secure a degree in less than four years. As I may have written in my former letter, while I have been a strong Grecian, yet now our work without Greek is so rigorous and its results so satisfactory, that I am in favor of making the Latin-Scientific Course equally with the Greek course, the basis for the Arts degree."

The students for these degrees are classed as undergraduates and appear by the college catalogue to be members of the Psi Upsilon, Delta Kappa Epsilon, and other Greek and Latin societies, and are in some cases registered as living in the fraternity houses.

The Committee recommend to the Council that the Hamilton College degrees of Bachelor of Philosophy and Bachelor of Science be added to the eligible list.

Respectfully submitted,
CHARLES H. RUSSELL,
B. AYMAR SANDS,
CHARLES STEELE.

NEW YORK, Dec. 9, 1901.

Report of the Special Committee on Degrees in relation to the degrees of Bachelor of Philosophy, Bachelor of Science, Engineer of Mines, and Electrical Engineer conferred by Lafayette College.

Lafayette College is situated at Easton, Pennsylvania, and was established in 1826. It provides seven distinct courses of undergraduate instruction, each one requiring in regular course four years of residence and study. The seven courses and the degrees conferred upon the completion of each one respectively are as follows:

The Classical course, Bachelor of Arts.
The Latin-Scientific course, Bachelor of Philosophy.
The General Scientific course, Bachelor of Science.
The Chemical course, Bachelor of Science (in Chemistry).
The Civil Engineer course, Civil Engineer.
The Mining Engineering course, Engineer of Mines.
The Electrical Engineering course, Electrical Engineer.

The degrees of Bachelor of Arts and of Civil Engineer of this College are already upon the eligible list.

The Latin-Scientific course is the same as the Classical course, except that other studies are substituted for Greek. The General Scientific course "consists of a curriculum in which mathematics, the modern languages, and their literatures, especially English, and the natural and physical sciences, receive principal attention. It includes, however, the more general studies of the arts course, such as history, logic and rhetoric, mental and moral philosophy" (extract from catalogue 1900–1901, page 52). The Department of Engineering is sub-divided into the three courses already mentioned, Civil, Mining, and Electrical Engineering, and there is also, as above mentioned, a course in Chemistry. The curriculum in each of these courses appears to be very thorough and comprehensive.

The total number of the undergraduates in the various departments is 360.

The students live partly in the College dormitories and partly outside. All the requirements of undergraduate life appear to be fulfilled.

Lafayette College draws its students mostly from Pennsylvania, and has a good standing and reputation. Its scientific and engineering schools stand high in the estimation of the members of those professions; and the location of the college, in the centre of a great railway, manufacturing and mining region, is especially favourable for engineering study and practical experience. The graduates of the scientific departments stand well in their professions; and the College has been noted in recent years for the distinction of some of its professors.

The Committee are of the opinion that the degrees under consideration should be added to the eligible list.

In this connection the general subject of undergraduate scientific degrees has necessarily required consideration. The degrees of Bachelor of Science and of Civil Engineer and of Engineer of Mines have been conferred by Universities and professional schools for many years past and are familiar to all college men. Such degrees when conferred by Universities or Colleges of the first class carry with them the guaranty that the recipient has completed such a course of residence and study as fulfills the requirements of the Council, but many degrees, such for instance as those of Mechanical Engineer and of Electrical Engineer, are comparatively new degrees; and the question naturally arises as to whether they are to be received with the same respect as the older degrees above mentioned. It is perhaps difficult for Bachelors of Arts of more than twenty years' standing to realize that any undergraduates, other than those who are candidates for the degree of Bachelor of Arts, can have the real American undergraduate college life; just as it may also be difficult to consider men as "college men" who have had no classical course and whose undergraduate study has been directed not so much to obtaining what used to be called a "liberal education" as to obtaining an education leading directly to a professional career. Nevertheless such changes have taken place in the last twenty years as to create entirely new conditions. Even the historic degree of Bachelor of Arts has, with the introduction of the elective system, lost its old and valuable significance, except in some of the smaller colleges; and in many colleges the students for the separate degrees of arts and of science meet daily in the same class rooms, are classmates, belong to the same student societies, and lead an identical undergraduate college life. These existing conditions were recognized by your Committee when they made their preliminary report in May last; and upon the first list of eligible degrees then submitted by them and adopted by the Council are a number of scientific and professional undergraduate degrees conferred either by universities having also an arts course or by some purely scientific institutions such as the Massachusetts Institute of Technology and the Rensselaer Polytechnic Institute.

Mr. Charles Sooysmith, the well-known engineer, has stated to a member of your Committee that the requirements of a thorough course for the degree of Mechanical Engineer or of Electrical Engineer are more severe and require more intellectual effort than the courses for the degrees of Civil or Mining Engineer.

In connection with the subject of undergraduate scientific degrees it is unfortunate that there is no uniformity of practice on the part of American Colleges as to the degree conferred for identical work. For instance, the Rensselaer Polytechnic Institute, which gives instruction in mechanical and electrical engineering, as well as in many other technical courses, confers no specific degrees in any course, except that of Civil Engineer; all other courses of study in that institution result only in the degree of Bachelor of Science.

The Columbia School of Mines on the other hand confers the

undergraduate degrees of Bachelor of Science, of Civil Engineer, of Engineer of Mines, of Electrical Engineer, of Mechanical Engineer and of Engineer of Metallurgy. The Massachusetts Institute of Technology, which gives instruction in many technical branches, including mechanical and electrical engineering, confers only one undergraduate degree, the same for each course of study, namely: Bachelor of Science. The same is true of Harvard, whose scientific school has courses of study in these departments, and yet confers only one undergraduate degree: Bachelor of Science. The same is true of the University of Pennsylvania. The Sheffield Scientific School of Yale University confers only one undergraduate degree, that of Bachelor of Philosophy. It also confers the degrees of Civil Engineer and of Mechanical Engineer, but only as graduate degrees.

The different conditions thus apparent under which, for example, the degrees of Bachelor of Philosophy and of Civil Engineer are given by Yale and by Lafayette College, illustrate the impossibility of ascribing any distinct and uniform meaning to the same degree when conferred by different institutions.

It results therefore that no general rule can be made, except that the real meaning as well as the value of each degree of each college must be considered by itself.

The Committee are of opinion that the Lafayette College degrees of Bachelor of Philosophy (Ph.B.), Bachelor of Science (B.S.), Engineer of Mines (E.M.), and Electrical Engineer (E.E.), should be added to the eligible list and they so recommend to the Council.

Respectfully submitted,

CHARLES H. RUSSELL,
B. AYMAR SANDS,
CHARLES STEELE.

NEW YORK, Dec. 9, 1901.

Report of the Special Committee on Degrees to the Council in relation to the degrees of Bachelor of Science, of Bachelor of Philosophy and of Master of Philosophy conferred by the University of Michigan, situated at Ann Arbor, Michigan.

This University comprises seven departments, namely: The Department of Literature, Science and the Arts (including the graduate school); the Department of Engineering; the Department of Medicine and Surgery; the Department of Law; the School of Pharmacy; the Homeopathic Medical College; and the College of Dental Surgery. The University is co-educational and contains in all of its departments (exclusive of its summer schools) 3,482 students. It stands high in the opportunities which it offers to students, and in the extent and comprehensiveness of the courses of study.

The degrees of Bachelor of Arts and of Civil Engineer conferred by this University are already upon our eligible list. The latter degree (of Civil Engineer) was placed upon the original eligible list of the Council in June last upon the recommendation of the Committee on Admissions. In the course of investigation of the degrees now under consideration, it was learned that the degree of Civil Engineer is now a graduate degree, but that it was an undergraduate degree until and including 1881. The Committee will, therefore, recommend that as a part of this report the present eligible list be amended so that this degree shall read upon the list as follows, viz.: "C. E. prior to 1882."

The degree of Bachelor of Science is now conferred by the University of Michigan in the Department of Engineering, and also in the School of Pharmacy. The degree as conferred in the Department of Engineering will first be considered. That department, quoting from the "Calendar" of the University for 1900–1901 (the last one published), includes "Courses in Civil, Mechanical, Electrical, Chemical, and Marine Engineering and in Naval Architecture. The work extends through four years." (p. 141.) "The amount of credit toward graduation assigned to each course is indicated by the expressions *one hour*, *two hours*, &c, an *hour of credit* being given for the satisfactory completion of work equivalent to one exercise a week during one semester. Lectures and recitations are usually one hour in length, but in laboratory work, drawing and other practical exercises, a longer attendance is required to secure an hour of credit." (p. 159). "To earn the degree of Bachelor of Science in Civil, Mechanical, Electrical or Chemical Engineering, the student must secure *one hundred and thirty hours of credit* in a prescribed course of study, and must present a satisfactory thesis. The diploma given indicates the line of study pursued. A time limit is not fixed, but four years is usually needed for the completion of the 130 hours of work" (p. 172). It is perhaps worth while to make some explanation of this system of "hours of credit." As mentioned in the extract which precedes, an hour of credit is given to an undergraduate student "for the satisfactory completion of work equivalent to one exercise a week during one semester" or term. There are two terms in each year. Each student must take a minimum of 15 hours per week, and may be permitted to take as high as 18 hours a week. Consequently, it will be seen that at 15 hours a week per term, a student must obtain a minimum of 30 hours of credit per year, which would be an aggregate of 120 hours for the four years; or if he takes the maximum of 18 hours per week, he may obtain 36 hours of credit per year, or an aggregate of 144 hours for the four years. As from what has already been quoted, it appears that a student "must secure 130 hours of credit" to earn the degree of Bachelor of Science in this department, it follows that the degree cannot be earned in less than something over 3½ years. As the Committee found it difficult to obtain accurate information in regard to these requirements and other matters, special inquiry was made, and a letter answering a number of categorical questions has been received from Dr. James B. Angell, the President of the University, which is annexed to this report. Upon this particular subject he says: "In the Department of Engineering, the B.S. degree is given for one hundred and thirty hours of work, which means four years of full work running at least fifteen hours a week, and it may carry as high as eighteen hours a week. It can be obtained only in four years of very hard work."

It was evident from the requirements that not less than three years of study would be necessary to earn this degree; and this is confirmed by Dr. Angell's letter. Residence also is required; and the conditions of admission and study are entirely satisfactory within the requirement of the Council. The Committee are of the opinion that this degree should be accepted.

(Incidentally, in connection with the general subject of the completion of a full undergraduate course in less than the usual four years, reference may be made to an article by Professor Hart, in *The Harvard Graduates' Magazine*, for December, 1901, entitled "Actualities of the Three-Year A.B. Degree.")

The degree of Bachelor of Science, as before stated, is also conferred in "The School of Pharmacy," and at the end of a four years' course. This school is thus referred to in the "Calendar" of the University for 1900–1901 (p. 215). "The School of Pharmacy gives training for all branches of pharmacy and for various chemical pursuits. It provides a well grounded preparation for services as a manufacturing chemist or as an analyst. The graduate is assured a thorough qualification for the prescription table and for the most responsible positions in pharmacy. He is fitted to act as the chemist of a medical profession."

The requirements for entrance appear to be substantially the same as those of candidates for the degree of Bachelor of Arts; and the course of study in pharmacy, general and analytical chemistry, etc., seem to be good. In regard to this degree Dr. Angell writes: "The Bachelor of Science, upon completion of the four years' course in pharmacy, is virtually a scientific course equal in its requirements to the regular B.S."

Prior to 1900–1901 the degree of Bachelor of Science was conferred also in the Department of Literature, Science and Arts. At the present time the only degree conferred in that Department is that of Bachelor of Arts. It was conferred upon students who took not the distinctly scientific courses of the Department of Engineering, but who took a general course of scientific and other studies, without the study of the classics required of the candidates in the same Department for the degree of Bachelor of Arts. Dr. Angell writes that at the time it was conferred "it covered work which would now be rewarded by the degree of B.A.," and also that it may still "be conferred upon those who especially desire it, but it is supposed that most of them would prefer to take the degree of B.A. It has always been a four years' course of full work."

At the time when Bachelor of Science was conferred as one of the regular degrees in the Department of Literature, Science and Arts, one hundred and twenty hours of work were required as a minimum (the same requirements which now prevail in that department for the degree of Bachelor of Arts), although "sometimes students were allowed to take as high as eighteen hours a week."

The opinion of the Committee in regard to the degree of Bachelor of Science as separately conferred by these three distinct departments of the University is as follows: 1. That the degree as conferred by the Department of Engineering should be placed upon the eligible list. 2. That that degree as conferred by the College of Pharmacy should not be passed upon at present. It is understood that the candidate who is the holder of the degree of Bachelor of Science, in whose behalf application is now made for the listing of that degree, is not a graduate of the College of Pharmacy; so that the Council is not at present required to pass upon this degree as conferred by the College of Pharmacy. The question of recognizing an undergraduate degree in pharmacy involves important consideration. In the opinion of the Committee, such a degree should hereafter be considered in connection with others of the modern degrees given in purely professional schools, such for instance as the degrees in Dentistry, Forestry, Veterinary, Medicine, etc., as involving distinct principles. Any definite action taken by the Council in regard to any such degree would make a precedent which should not be made without careful consideration. Therefore the Committee have not passed upon this degree of Bachelor of Science as conferred by the College of Pharmacy at the present time, and make no recommendation in regard to it. The statements contained in this report in regard to this degree may, however, be useful hereafter for reference.

The conferring of the well-known degree of Bachelor of Science, having a generally accepted meaning, upon graduates in pharmacy, is another illustration of the unfortunate lack of uniformity among American Universities in the character and significance of their degrees, to which subject the Committee referred more fully in a recent report upon certain degrees conferred by Lafayette College.

3. The degree of Bachelor of Science as regularly conferred heretofore in the Department of Literature, Science and Arts, and as possibly conferred occasionally hereafter in that Department, appears to comply with all the requirements of the Council and the Committee will therefore recommend that it be placed upon the eligible list.

The degree of Bachelor of Philosophy was conferred prior to 1901. The "Calendar" of the University for the year 1899–1900 shows that the requirements for admission, study and residence were substantially the same as those of the course for the degree of Bachelor of Arts, except that no Greek was required. Dr. Angell writes in regard to this degree: "The course leading to the degree of Bachelor of Philosophy was one that could not be obtained in less than four years. A minimum of sixteen hours a week was required. Sometimes we allowed eighteen hours,—120 hours in all." This degree was conferred in the Department of Literature, Science and Arts, and seems to be as fully entitled to be placed upon the eligible list as the degree of Bachelor of Arts, already accepted.

In regard to the remaining degree which received consideration, namely, that of Ph.M., it was not known to the Committee whether Ph.M. meant Master of Philosophy or Master of Pharmacy, both of which degrees it was found have heretofore been conferred by this University; and in reply to inquiry Dr. Angell writes as follows upon that subject:

"The degree of Ph.M. meant Master of Philosophy but it is no longer given. It was a graduate degree following the attainment of Bachelor of Philosophy, and was obtained only on study and examination covering one year, and in some cases two years, after the bachelor's degree was obtained. The degree of Master of Pharmacy was not an undergraduate degree. It was given only to those who had taken the first degree in Pharmacy and is no longer given. The preceding undergraduate degree of Master of Pharmacy was Pharmaceutical Chemist, Ph.C."

The degree of Ph.M. consequently, being purely a graduate degree, cannot within the rules of the Council be placed upon the eligible list.

A graduate of the University has informed a member of the Committee that the undergraduate life of the men students is in all respects the same which prevails in the principal American colleges.

In conclusion, the Committee recommend to the Council that the present list of eligible degrees shall be amended so that under the title *University of Michigan* (C.E.) shall read "(C.E.) prior to 1882"; that the degree of Bachelor of Science conferred in the Department of Literature, Science and Arts, and in the Department of Engineering only, shall be added to the eligible list; that the degree of Bachelor of Philosophy, conferred prior to 1901, also shall be added to the eligible list.

Respectfully submitted,

CHARLES H. RUSSELL,
B. AYMAR SANDS,
CHARLES STEELE.

NEW YORK, Feb. 10, 1902.

At the meeting of the Council of April, 1902, the Committee on Colleges and Degrees reported, as to degrees from German universities, the technical objection that the wording of the constitution of the Club did not seem to permit the certificates issued by the government to be regarded as qualifying candidates for admission.

Thereupon, on motion of Mr. Walter G. Oakman (Univ. of Pa. '64), the following preamble and resolution were unanimously adopted:

Whereas, In certain foreign countries governmental examinations and certificates are substituted for University Degrees,

Resolved, That where, in the judgment of the Committee on Degrees, Certificates of Foreign Governments indicated an education and experience which was equivalent to what is represented by an acceptable degree from American Colleges, upon the favourable report of said Committee, candidates offering such Certificates should be posted by the Committee on Admissions; and that at the next annual meeting of the Club, the Council should prepare an Amendment to the Constitution which might preserve their place upon the list of applicants, and if the Amendment to the Constitution is adopted by the Club, these candidates may then be considered by the Committee on Admissions.

It does not appear from the records that any such action as thus proposed was either taken by or suggested to the Club at its next annual meeting, probably because Article VIII of the constitution confers full authority upon the Council to determine the eligibility both of colleges and degrees. But in February, 1906, the Committee on Colleges and Degrees directed the attention of the Council to the subject of foreign degrees in the following memorial:

To the Council of the University Club:

The Committee on Colleges and Degrees desires to call the attention of the Council to a paper which has been for many years publicly posted in the Club, entitled "List of Foreign Universities and of the Degrees from Them Which Shall Qualify the Holder for Membership in the University Club," as determined by the Council pursuant to Sec. 3, Art. VIII of the Constitution of the Club. This list was prepared about the time of the organization of the Club; it contains the names of the principal colleges and universities of the world, and specifies a large number of degrees of all varieties and kinds which qualify their holders for membership. Among the colleges enumerated are the principal German universities some of whose graduates have in recent years applied for admission to the Club. The Council, however, has invariably refused to report favorably on these applications, as, by examination, this Committee has ascertained that the universities thus under consideration do not confer undergraduate degrees; on this account, for the present at least, the standing of those universities should be considered on their individual merits. The English universities appearing on this list are probably all satisfactory, but even with these it would be best to pursue the practice, already adopted by this Committee in the case of applications from domestic colleges, to inquire into the standing of the colleges as graduates apply for membership. The remaining foreign universities and the value of their degrees have not been investigated, but we are inclined to think that in most cases the degrees conferred are professional, or post-graduate, degrees—not recognised by the Council.

As a matter of interest and curiosity, attention is called to several universities whose graduates are declared to be eligible:

China. University of Pekin. "Kwoh tsz. Kien." Certificate of having passed examination for any rank above the seventh, either as Scholar, or Mandarin in the public service.

Egypt. University of Cairo. Certificate of possession of degrees of Mollah or Ulema.

Spain. Any degree or certificate of the completion by the applicant of a regular course of study as prescribed by the Diplomatic School, Madrid.

It would seem as though this list had simply been compiled from some catalogue of leading colleges and universities of the world, making them all, together with the degrees which they confer, eligible, and that the standing of each college and the value of each degree could not have been critically considered. The illustrations given are sufficient to prove that it is unwise to continue to advertise this list in its present form.

Sec. 3, Art. VIII of the Constitution of the Club provides as follows:

"3. The Council shall determine what degrees from Universities and Colleges, and from what Universities and Colleges, shall qualify the holders for membership; and a list of such degrees and of such Universities and Colleges, as from time to time determined by the Council, shall be posted in the office of the Club."

This section does not discriminate between domestic and foreign colleges, but requires that the standing of both should be determined by the Council. It therefore does not seem proper that graduates of foreign universities should be allowed preference over those of domestic universities—which is the result of the present system, practically effected by admitting graduates of foreign universities without action by the Council, while applicants from domestic universities are subjected to a very critical examination into the standing of their colleges and the value of their degrees.

Graduates from certain of these colleges have been heretofore admitted to the Club, the colleges and degrees under which candidates obtained admission being as follows:

Great Britain and Ireland:

Oxford University, B.A.
Cambridge University, B.A.
London University, B.A.
Edinburgh University, B.A.
St. Andrew's University, B.A.
Aberdeen University, B.A.
Glasgow University, B.A.
Dublin University (Trinity College), B.A.

France:

École des Beaux Arts, Diploma of Grand Prix de Rome.
University of France, any Degree from the Paris Faculty of Letters or Faculty of Science.

Germany:

Berlin University, Ph.D.
Göttingen University, Ph.D.
Freiberg University, Ph.D.
Heidelberg University, Ph.D.
Königsberg University, Ph.D.
Leipzig University, Ph.D.
Dresden Polytechnic High School, Ph.D.

Canada:

McGill College, Montreal, B.A., B.Ap.Sc. (Prior to 1899) and B.S. (after 1898).
University of Toronto, B.A.
Dalhousie College, of New Brunswick.

Switzerland:

University of Geneva.

Belgium:

University of Liège.

Some of the colleges whose graduates have been admitted may, with propriety, be retained on the eligible list, their standing being in all respects satisfactory and conforming to the requirements of the Council.

We therefore recommend that all the universities and colleges enumerated on the list of foreign universities be dropped as ineligible for admission, without prejudice, however, to any application which may hereafter be made on the part of any graduate from any one such institution to have it or any degree therefrom placed on the general, eligible list.

We further recommend that the following universities and colleges and certain degrees conferred thereby be placed on such general list:

Great Britain and Ireland:
- Oxford University, B.A.
- Cambridge University, B.A.
- London University, B.A.
- Edinburgh University, B.A.
- Dublin University (Trinity College), B.A.

France:
- École des Beaux Arts, Diploma or Grand Prix de Rome.
- University of France, any degree from the Paris Faculty of Letters or Faculty of Science.

Canada:
- McGill College, Montreal, B.A., B.Ap.Sc. (Prior to 1899) and B.S. (after 1898).

We also recommend that the explanatory caption of the list of domestic universities and colleges heretofore approved by the Council be amended by adding the words "within the United States," so that it will hereafter in time apply to all universities and colleges, both domestic and foreign.

All of which is respectfully submitted.

COMMITTEE ON COLLEGES AND DEGREES:
B. AYMAR SANDS, *Chairman*,
FRANCIS R. APPLETON,
SAMUEL H. ORDWAY.

Dated New York February 8, 1906.

In March, 1908, the constitution was amended as to Article IX, Section 6, by making members who have belonged to the Club for ten years eligible for life-membership, instead of fifteen years which had heretofore been the limitation.

On January 9, 1911, the Committee on Colleges and Degrees recommended the acceptance and placing on the eligible list of the degrees in engineering conferred by the Royal School of Mines, Freiberg, Saxony, after an exhaustive examination of the conditions there prevailing, which was adopted by the Council.

The only foreign degree added by the Council since that date was Edinburgh, M.A., at a meeting held Nov. 13, 1911.

In the course of the proceedings of the Council in reference to the eligibility of candidates, difficult questions occasionally challenged their judgment. For example, in 1902 a distinguished senator was proposed for membership as belonging to a certain class in a prominent university. It was found that on account of ill health he had not completed his studies, but that after a lapse of years, in recognition of the work he had done while in college, the reason for his failing to finish, and his career afterward, he was given his degree, A.B., "in due course." On the favorable report of the committee, the Council accepted the degree, but expressly declared that it was because the candidate came within the provision of the constitution which made eligible those who were "distinguished in public service." But the report of the committee closed with the following statement, which was approved by the Council:

> We think, however, that the general admission of degrees conferred in course after graduation without the performance of a prescribed course of study and the fulfillment of the requirement of residence, would establish an unconstitutional precedent.

Two other exceptional cases were those of a clergyman of the highest standing, and a Greek scholar of eminence, both nominated as graduates, but neither of them in regular standing as such. They were admitted, but only on the strength of being eminent in their respective spheres.

The subject of colleges and degrees has continued to receive the serious attention of the Council down to the present time, and the following extract from President Sands's report of 1912 indicates the care and attention bestowed upon this important matter:

The important duty and responsibility resting upon the Committee on Colleges and Degrees seems to grow more, rather than less, exacting and onerous as the years roll on.

If the distinctive character of this organization as a University Club is to be preserved, it is essential that every degree which is accepted by the Council as qualifying for membership, should represent an academic training of true collegiate grade and college life in the sense that we understand that term, with its absence of the restraint and close personal supervision of the boarding school, and with its varied interests, influences, and associations, all of which contribute so largely in molding the character of a young man.

There are very few colleges or universities of standing in this country whose degrees have not been passed upon by the Council on the reports of this committee in the past, but the development of modern educational methods not infrequently presents somewhat difficult and embarrassing questions with respect to degrees conferred even by the most important universities. Under the extension of the university idea of higher education, students are required to perform in residence only a comparatively small part of the work for a degree and a student may also spend his academic life at several different institutions, taking his degree finally, after pursuing special courses for a year only, at some university, and thus the old-fashioned idea of the college degree as representing three years' residence and study is becoming more and more difficult of application as an exact and literal measure of the conditions which should make the degree acceptable as qualifying for membership. The committee, however, endeavors to follow the spirit rather than the exact letter of the constitutional provision by accepting degrees which in regular course fairly represent the college life and training which were formerly the necessary precedent conditions to an under-graduate degree.

Candidates are proposed from time to time holding degrees from institutions, particularly in the south and west, which are little known but which claim to have the standing of colleges and even universities. Many of these applications are rejected, but, in fairness to the candidate and his friends, a careful, discriminating, and impartial investigation of the conditions at the particular institution at the time of the candidate's graduation is made by this committee.

It is apparent, therefore, that much of the work of this committee is wholly negative in result, and wisely so, as tending to preserve the distinctive character of our Club as an association of men who have had the full advantages of college life and college training, as measured, broadly speaking, by the courses leading to an under-graduate, as distinguished from a professional degree in our leading colleges and universities.

CHAPTER XXVII

SOCIAL LIFE—CLUB NIGHTS, DINNERS, AND RECEPTIONS

THERE are those in every club, even one ostensibly dedicated to scholarship and learning, who hanker for other entertainment than books provide. It is even believed that most of the very men who delve in musty volumes or produce the literature which supplies us with our education, are not averse to occasional relaxation, in the shape of social enjoyment. One has only to read the accounts of the origin of club life in London, to be convinced that "a little nonsense now and then is relished by the wisest men." The University Club, consisting though it does of a body of college graduates, presumed to place the delights of reading and study among the things most "worth while," has been the scene of many a jovial gathering and a rendezvous for many a social group. The happy abandon of college life, with its comradeship, its gayety, its enthusiasm, happily does not altogether die out as the Tom Browns "harden into the bone of manhood." And there is no cause for shame or regret, and there is no opportunity for the man who has never gone to college reasonably to cavil, because in the University Club serious men, diligent in worthy pursuits, find a place for the lighter enjoyments of life.

The fact has already been referred to that the evolution of the club in England can be traced to the coffee-house, where, as Ralph Nevill, one of the historians of London clubs, says, "a certain number of people met on special evenings, for purposes of social conversation, and incidentally consumed a good deal of liquid refreshment," and at these meetings many of the greatest men of Britain forgot more important things for a time, unbent, and disported themselves like boys.

At the Cheshire Cheese, on a certain night, Ben Jonson and Sylvester competed as to which of them could improvise the better rhyme. Sylvester immediately produced the following:

"I, Sylvester,
Kiss'd your sister."

Whereupon Jonson replied:

"I, Ben Jonson,
Kiss'd your wife."

"But that's not rhyme," objected Sylvester. "No," said Jonson, "but it's true."

Even gambling (which is tabooed by the rules of the University Club) was indulged in by scholars and statesmen. A prime minister of England was referred to in the lines:

"Or chair'd at White's, amidst the doctors sit,
Teach oaths to gamesters, and to nobles wit."

Charles James Fox is reported to have suggested on a certain night to his companions, after a jovial "siderunt" at the club, the formation of a calling, "which was going from horse-race to horse-race, and so by knowing the value and speed of all the horses in England, acquire a certain fortune."

Doctor Johnson was once taken to task for condescending to make merry at clubs, and stoutly defended the institution with its customs, saying: "Sir, the great Chair of a full and pleasant town club is, perhaps, the throne of human felicity."

Not all the old London clubs were the scene of hilarity. Some of them have been described as "gloomy abodes of misanthropic selfishness." But such was not the characteristic of those original clubs which were frequented by Doctor Johnson and Sheridan and Garrick, and Raleigh and Ben Jonson and Shakespeare, and Burke and Sir Joshua Reynolds, and scores of other celebrities whose names are indelibly inscribed on the tablets of fame.

That those early clubmen preferred spirits and beer as a beverage is indicated by a record, the date of which is obscure, that at one time the owner of the Rainbow was indicted for selling "a strong drink called coffee which annoyed the neighbourhood by its evil smell."

The London clubs have not been as liberal as our own in regard to the allowance of smoking in the club-house. In the University Club there is no restriction whatever, except in the dining-room and the limitation of pipe-smoking to the pipe room, billiard room, and café.

At White's, in London, smoking was not allowed at all until 1845, and it was only after a controversy that the Marlborough Club (frequented by King Edward when he was Prince of Wales) was formed, where smoking, for the first time in the history of West End clubs, was everywhere permitted except in the dining-room.

Thackeray, with all his sense of humor, made a fling at the clubs of his day, saying: "All that fuddling and boozing shortened the lives and enlarged the waistcoats of the men of that age." Tom Hood also satirized them. Nevill quotes a wife as saying to her husband: "Abel was killed by a club, and your club will kill me if you continue to go to it every night." She had probably heard the definition of a club by a distinguished bishop—presumably a married man—as a place "where women cease from troubling and the weary are at rest."

The very fact that the Sublime Society of the Beefsteaks had for its emblem "Beef and Liberty" proclaims it as the exponent of good-fellowship, and yet its father was Doctor

From a photograph, copyright by Sidman, New York.

THE PIPE ROOM.

Johnson. Beaumont has recorded in rhyme the spirit that prevailed at the Mermaid:

"What things have we seen
Done at the Mermaid! heard words that have been
So nimble and so full of subtile flame,
As if that every one from whence they came
Had meant to put his whole wit in a jest,
And had resolved to live a fool the rest
Of his dull life; then, when there hath been thrown
Wit able enough to justify the town
For three days past; wit that might warrant be
For the whole city to talk foolishly . . ."

Examples might be multiplied to show that the men who influenced the world in the early days of clubs were not averse to the relaxation of social pleasures and commonplace frolics. Enough, however, has been said to show that we of to-day have high authority for mixing the spice of entertainment with the intellectual food which makes bone and sinew.

Into every club there creep members who do not rise to the quality known as "clubbable." At the governing committee of a prominent club, the name of a member was reported as having laid himself open to being dropped, and it was urged that here was a chance to get rid of a very tiresome man. Mr. Choate, who was a member of the committee, remarked: "If he were the only tiresome member!"

The University Club can claim without inexcusable vanity that the class composed of college graduates who pass the sifting of the Admission Committee is more free from "tiresome" members than most others.

Happily, the excessive drinking habits of our predecessors have yielded to a more wholesome opinion and taste, and drunkenness is so rare as to be almost unknown in the University Club. But those devoted to the prosperity and usefulness of the organization have from the earliest days recognized that the social side of its life should be fostered, while the serious and scholarly side should always be chiefly upheld and protected.

The day has almost passed when club members stand at the windows and ogle the passers-by. There can be no question but that manners have improved in our clubs. One smiles as at an exaggeration when he reads of Beau Brummell taking possession of the famous "Bow Window" at White's, in 1811, and claiming it as his own. When Brummell was dunned for the repayment of a £500 loan, he asserted that he had paid it by saying "How d'you do" from the window as the creditor passed.

It is within the memory of living New Yorkers that clubs were frowned upon by serious people and were generally regarded as evil resorts. To-day our best clubs are supported and frequented by the solid portion of the community, and the University Club stands in the first rank for its wholesome tone and influence.

The first social meeting of the Club with a collation (for the cost of which the modest sum of $125 was formally appropriated by the Council) was held in the Club House, at the corner of Fifth Avenue and 35th Street, on the 21st day of November, 1879, the very year of the reorganization. The members were thus brought together for better acquaintance, and the policy of such gatherings has been continued from year to year, with and without lectures, musical performances, story-telling, and intellectual entertainments, to the great enjoyment and profit of the membership.

One of the earliest occasions when men distinguished in literature and the arts have been entertained by the Club was in October, 1880, when a reception was given to Mr. Thomas Hughes, Q. C., the author of "Tom Brown's School Days." It was largely attended and so much enjoyed that the appetite for similar demonstrations was whetted, and the event frequently repeated in the case of other eminent men.

From a photograph, copyright by Sidman, New York.

THE FIFTH AVENUE ROOM ON THE MAIN FLOOR.

Used as a general meeting and lounging room. It occupies the whole Fifth Avenue front.

Disregarding for the moment chronological order, a brief reference seems appropriate to the many "Club nights" which have been held throughout the Club's history. Beginning with the "social meeting" of November, 1879, these gatherings have repeatedly been arranged and made enjoyable in various agreeable ways, and the fact already demonstrated in other circles has often been confirmed at the University Club, that the provision of a bountiful luncheon or supper invariably draws a large attendance—the scholars of America not differing in this respect from the clergy, who have from time immemorial been skilful with the knife and fork.

On Christmas and New Year's Day, especially, it has always been the custom to provide a delicious luncheon without charge to members, where the traditional egg-nog is consumed in proper quantities, and at which the chef and the pastry-cook exhibit those marvellous "creations" which vie with those of sculptors in the display of artistic genius.

In a notice sent to members, in the early days, of a forthcoming "Smoking Concert," with music by the New York Philharmonic Club, the significant words are introduced: "Cakes and ale will be served at 10.30." At this concert compositions by Chopin, Beethoven, Handel, Zoellner, and Dvořák were rendered, without a note of "rag-time"—a tribute to the taste of our learned membership. And a similar disposition to maintain a high standard in the music presented has characterized the entertainments down to the present time. On many different occasions during the last thirty years, the "Club nights" have been enlivened by the performances (the same musical organizations giving repeated programmes) not only of the one just mentioned, but of the Adamowski Quartette, the Mendelssohn Glee Club, the University Glee Club, the Dannreuther Quartette, the Princeton Banjo Club, Franko's Orchestra, the New York Symphony String Quartette, the Hungarian Orchestra, and others.

On the night of April 13, 1894, Frederic Villiers, an accomplished war correspondent of the order which has well-nigh been exterminated by the telegraph and submarine cable, gave an illustrated lecture on his experiences in the Chinese-Japanese War, an innovation which was so enthusiastically approved that it was followed by other lectures and addresses by famous men.

On May 24, 1895, W. Gordon McCabe, of Richmond, Va. (Univ. of Va. '61), one of the most accomplished littérateurs and raconteurs in the Club's membership, related his "Personal Recollections of Lord Tennyson," with whom he was on intimate terms and whose guest he had been. It was during one of his visits to the great poet that he was called upon to escort two young English women to a social gathering. On this occasion he was surprised by being especially introduced by his hostess with much *empressement* to a lady whom she described with evident satisfaction as being a descendant of Benedict Arnold. McCabe was mystified and asked himself why he, known to be an American, should be in such a pointed way presented to one whose ancestor was execrated by all his compatriots. Musing over the puzzle on the way home, he asked the two young women if they could solve it. There was a hesitation on their part which increased his curiosity, and he pressed his inquiries. At last one of them said: "Mr. McCabe, we know that Benedict Arnold did something nawsty, but what *was* it?" And so it burst on the intelligence of the American that his English friends were oblivious to the fact that Arnold had forfeited his claim to the respect of his countrymen. McCabe is still a frequenter of the University Club, and his familiarity with the literary men both of Europe and America, his store of original anecdotes, and his fascinating conversation always make him the centre of an interested group.

Dwight L. Elmendorf (Princeton '82) has given a number of his admirable lectures, with moving pictures taken by himself, the first being on October 18, 1898, on the war with

From a photograph, by Tebbs, New York.

DETAIL OF THE DOORS AND CEILING OF THE FIFTH AVENUE ROOM, FIRST FLOOR.

Spain. Elmendorf began his career as an amateur photographer, and became so efficient that he easily drifted into a professional. He has travelled in every part of the globe, not confining himself to the civilized, and his illustrated lectures have become so popular that his engagements ahead include almost every night for his annual season. It is believed that he was the originator of this kind of entertainment which has been taken up successfully by others.

On May 2, 1901, the Club was entertained by talks on the Philippines, China, and the Transvaal by Major-General Joseph Wheeler (U. S. M. A. '59), Major-General James H. Wilson (U. S. M. A. '60), and James Barnes, Esq. (Princeton '91).

On March 5, 1904, Commander Robert Peary delivered an address to the Club on the subject of arctic exploration, illustrated with colored views.

Robert L. Dunn, the war correspondent of *Collier's Weekly*, gave a talk on the Russian-Japanese War, illustrated with stereopticon views and moving pictures.

Mr. C. L. Chester delivered a lecture, January 26, 1907, on "The Panama Canal and the Adjacent South American Countries: Ecuador, Peru, and Bolivia," illustrated by stereopticon views.

The taste of the membership was not invariably for history and geography, however, and on December 20, 1907, Doctor Cassius Jackson Keyser (Ohio Normal Univ. '83), professor in Columbia University, entertained the Club with a lecture on mathematics in which he set forth the vast continent of doctrines built up by the agents of the "mathetic spirit" from Pythagoras and Plato to Hilbert and Poincaré, and sketched the evolution of the conception of the science from the notion of counting and measurement up to that of a "universal art apodictic," including non-Euclidian geometrics, hyperspaces, and a summitless hierarchy of genuine infinities. No notice, naturally enough, is found of a supper on this occasion.

On an equally elevated plane, Professor Asa H. Morton (Wabash '82), of Williams College, delivered a lecture on February 7, 1908, on "The Sentimental Psychology of the Renaissance."

The two lectures last mentioned rescue the Club from any flippant charge of unbending too low.

A return was made from these lofty heights to the dead level of the ordinary graduate's intelligence, by a lecture, "The Relief of Peking," February 20, 1908, by Colonel H. O. S. Heistand (U. S. M. A. '78), who was adjutant-general to General Chaffee, commanding the United States column in China, in which he gave a brief description of the advance and siege, with some remarks on China and the Chinese—their government, habits and customs, together with the causes leading to the Boxer Rebellion of 1900, its suppression and results.

On January 22, 1909, Wilfred T. Grenfell, M. D. (Oxon '07 Hon.), gave a lecture on his work among the fishermen of Labrador, illustrated with lantern slides in color; and Colonel Heistand delivered a second address on April 29, 1909, on the United States Army as a career.

Mr. Richard E. Follett, vice-president of the New England Forest, Fish, and Game Association, gave a lecture on May 6, 1909, illustrated by moving pictures, on forest life, moose and caribou hunting, trout and salmon fishing, and log driving.

Mr. A. Radclyffe Dugmore, on February 24, 1910, delivered a lecture on "Snapping Africa's Big Game on the Roosevelt Hunting Trail," with colored photographs of rhinos, lions, and other wild beasts in Africa taken in the very act of charging down upon the observer.

On January 16, 1911, Paul J. Rainey gave his remarkable lecture, "With Gun and Camera in the Arctic Circle," and again on February 21, 1912, he delivered his lecture on the hunting of lions and other wild beasts in Africa with dogs.

Both of these lectures were illustrated by moving pictures, showing with lifelike accuracy the very acts described by him in his addresses.

These lectures, while the list is not exhaustive, show the policy of the Club managers in regard to both enlightening and diverting exercises.

It would be difficult, and is unnecessary, to catalogue all the occasions on which dinners and receptions have been given to distinguished personages.

Among these was a complimentary dinner given by members of the Club to the Honorable Robert T. Lincoln (Harvard '64) on his appointment as Ambassador of the United States near the Court of St. James, at which the Honorable Joseph H. Choate (Harvard '52), afterward himself to be Ambassador to England, presided.

A dinner was given on January 28, 1901, to "his Excellency Wu Ting Fang, his Imperial Majesty's Minister to the United States." This versatile statesman, who has since returned to his native land, and figured prominently and officially in the establishment of the new Chinese republic, was a familiar figure on numerous public and private occasions while he was a temporary resident in America. Perhaps no one thing demonstrated his *savoir faire* more clearly than the fact that all through the exciting times of the Boxer uprising in China, when Americans were threatened with destruction in the legation quarters of Pekin, and the Chinese Government was regarded as culpably negligent in their protection, Wu Ting Fang maintained his good standing with the American people, and apparently lost nothing of their respect and esteem. He was an excellent after-dinner speaker, thoroughly at home in the English language, overflowing with wit and humor, and a welcome guest at hundreds of tables.

On March 31, 1905, a dinner was given by members to Hart Lyman (Yale '73), then editor of the New York *Tribune*, which by the way until 1914 was the only New York daily newspaper which the Club kept on its shelves permanently.

Among the entertainments given from time to time by college men in celebration of athletic prowess, was a dinner given to the "Harvard Eleven" by members of the Harvard Club, December 14, 1901.

In order, it might appear, that the secular should not altogether eclipse the religious, certain members arranged, March 22, 1907, "the Regular Spring Festival of the Pupils of the Children's Hour Sunday School Class" at the Club, and guarded against any suspicion of being too austere by the notification in the call: "If you desire to have a seat reserved for you on the band wagon, sign your name, etc."

A club of the size of the University is quite certain to have within its membership various coteries more or less prominent and distinct. Their existence is perfectly natural, sometimes determined by college associations, sometimes by athletic or other tastes, but they have never been obstructive to the solidarity of the Club at large. The "Sunday School" was one of the conspicuous examples of what is referred to. The late Judge William Rumsey (Williams '61), Joseph B. Bishop (Brown '70), then editor of the *Post*, the late Judge Henry R. Beekman (Columbia '65), Charles Bulkley Hubbell (Williams '74), then President of the Board of Education, Judge E. Henry Lacombe (Columbia '63), F. W. Whitridge (Amherst '74), and DeLancey Nicoll (Princeton '74) were among the first to gather with the company that soon grew to about twenty-five and for several years was known as the "Sunday School Class." It was an interesting crowd and a seat in that circle was greatly esteemed by all who composed it.

The Half-Moon Club holds its annual dinners in the University Club House. This group has within its membership a number of men prominent in letters, public service, art, and discovery.

From a photograph, by Tebbs, October, 1914.

THE DINING-ROOM, LOOKING WEST.

The object of the club is to meet at dinner at the University Club twice every year, and hear addresses from distinguished travellers and investigators. The quaint custom of the association is to regard each meeting as a "Voyage." The presiding officer is called the "Master Mariner," and the principal speaker the "Pilot." The minutes are called the "log," and are always beautifully engrossed and illuminated by Tiffany & Co., at whose warehouse the book is kept. As an illustration of the nature of the eighteen "voyages" thus far made, it may be mentioned that among the "Pilots" have been Amundsen, Shackelton, Peary, and Henry Fairfield Osborn (Princeton '77), and among the subjects of addresses have been: "Search for the North West Passage," "Exploration of Mars," "Explorations at Sardis," "To the Heart of the Antarctic."

These will sufficiently indicate the purpose of the Club. Its membership, which is not large, has included such University Club men as Professor Henry Fairfield Osborn (Princeton '77), Professor William M. Sloane (Columbia '68), Cleveland H. Dodge (Princeton '79), Moses Taylor Pyne (Princeton '77), Joseph H. Choate (Harvard '52), Professor M. I. Pupin (Columbia '83), John W. Alexander (Hon. Princeton), John L. Cadwalader (Princeton '56), and Admiral Willard H. Brownson (U. S. N. A. '65). The character of this unique organization and the fact that a majority of its members are also members of the University Club, and that the "voyages" are always made at this Club, justify this reference.

The Boone and Crockett Club is devoted to the promotion of manly sport with the rifle, the promotion of travel and exploration in wild and unknown portions of the country, the preservation of game, the study of wild animals, the interchange of opinions and ideas on hunting, etc. No one is eligible for membership who shall not have killed at least one individual of "large game." The name of ex-President Theodore Roosevelt (Harvard '80) naturally will be found in the list of members, which includes many other names familiar in public walks.

Another club which holds its annual dinners at the University Club is the African Big Game Club. This association was organized in 1909, and only those are eligible for membership who have killed an elephant, lion, buffalo, rhinoceros, or leopard.

Apart from the mere circumstance that the American Academy in Rome has at times made the University Club the place of meetings and dinners, there are good reasons why in a history of the Club more than passing reference should be made to this institution. Its foundation owes its origin in no inconsiderable way to members of this Club in co-operation with others, and of the American School of Classical Studies in Rome, now incorporated with the academy, the same may be said.

Charles F. McKim (Harvard '70), our lamented fellow member whose skill and genius gave us our beautiful Club House, was the originator of the American Academy in Rome. It was founded in 1894 to promote the study and practice of the fine arts and to aid and stimulate the education and training of architects, painters, sculptors, and other artists.

Among the charter members who are or were also members of the University Club were Elihu Root (Hamilton '64), J. Pierpont Morgan (Yale '08, honorary), Francis D. Millet (Harvard '69), William Rutherford Mead (Amherst '67), Charles F. McKim (Harvard '70), William M. Kendall (Harvard '76), John L. Cadwalader (Princeton '56), Nicholas Murray Butler (Columbia '82), Edward J. Berwind (U. S. N. A. '69), Charles T. Barney (Williams '70), and James W. Alexander (Princeton '60). William Rutherford Mead was the president in 1912, until the union of the Academy with the Classical School, when Jesse Benedict Carter (Princeton '93), of the latter, became president of the combined schools.

The American School of Classical Studies in Rome was

organized in 1895, and the late C. C. Cuyler (Princeton '79), a member of the University Club, became its treasurer. Doctor Allan Marquand (Princeton '74), also of this Club, was professor in the school for a period.

Both these schools, now combined and about to take possession of a thoroughly equipped building in a commanding situation, have been intimately associated with the membership of the University Club, and the reorganized Academy promises to reflect credit and honor, by its usefulness, on the university and artistic men who conceived it and have brought it to its present condition of flourishing success.

The largest of the intramural organizations included in the membership of the University Club is the Farmers Club, now consisting of nearly one hundred members. It was organized in 1904. To be eligible to this agricolous order one must own and operate a hundred acres of land and keep a pig. The dinners of these husbandmen are not the plain repasts of pork and "yarbs" which literary fiction appoints for typical farmers. On the contrary, their annual feasts are quite unique in their bucolic decorations and exquisite menus. On these occasions the walls of the Council room are hung with the implements of the guild, and the table decorated with miniature hay-wagons loaded with fruits and flowers. The first president elected was Charles Bulkley Hubbell, who composed a mock ritual which has since been observed, which includes the presentation of "the golden pitchfork" having three golden (?) tines and an ivory (?) handle of regulation size.

One of the menus, with pictorial cover in color representing cows, pigs, geese, etc., contained characteristic dishes, as for example: Grapefruit à la ferme; celery (Professor Pupin's farm); roast pig (Mr. Cowdin's farm); squab chicken (Mr. Lawrence Hopkins's farm).

The Standing Committee of Arrangement includes Doctor M. Allen Starr (Princeton '76), Professor M. I. Pupin (Columbia '83), James C. Colgate (Colgate '84), Alfred Ely (Amherst '74), Benjamin Barker (Brown '81), Winthrop Cowdin (Harvard '85), and Charles Bulkley Hubbell (Williams '74).

The following is a list of the presidents, poets, and speakers:

PRESIDENT	POET	SPEAKERS
	December 6, 1904	
Chas. B. Hubbell.	Robert Bridges.	Prof. Pupin.
	January 17, 1906	
Chas. B. Hubbell.	E. S. Martin.	Prof. Wyckoff. Geo. F. Moore.
	January 17, 1907	
Alfred Ely.	Thomas Nelson Page.	L. O. Howard. James H. Macdonald (State Highway Com. of Conn.).
	January 6, 1908	
Jas. C. Colgate.	Chas. B. Hubbell.	Dr. S. Crosby. Prof. Wm. Sloane.
	January 7, 1909	
Jas. C. Colgate.	John Kendrick Bangs.	Mr. Law.
	January 6, 1910	
Prof. Pupin.	John Finley.	Julien T. Davies
	January 5, 1911	
Prof. Pupin.	Wallace Irwin.	F. S. Adams. F. Hopkinson Smith.
	January 11, 1912	
Julien T. Davies.	Henry Marquand.	Chas. B. Powell. James H. Hoyt.
	January 23, 1913	
Lorenzo Semple.	Henry van Dyke.	Prof. H. J. Wheeler. James W. Alexander.
	January 15, 1914	
Henry Marquand.	Frederick T. Van Beuren.	Charles H. Mapes.

Although it is not possible to spread all the poems upon these pages, four of them are here given as examples and because in themselves they are worthy of reproduction.

THE CAFÉ, COMMONLY CALLED THE BACKGAMMON ROOM.

First floor, southwest corner.

Verses read before the University Farmers Club by Robert Bridges, 1904:

THE CLUBMAN WITH A HOE

By Robert Bridges

Now from his grinding toil the farmer rests
And celebrates his freedom with his guests;
In high-roofed barns the heaping crops are stored
And cribs are groaning with their golden hoard;
  The year grows old—our labor's in the stack,
  Now is the time for ease, with apple-jack.

The frozen meadow glistens in the sun
And through the clearing frightened rabbits run;
Keen Winter draws her children 'round the fire,—
To social pleasures do our hearts aspire;
  Sweet is past toil, when seasoned with mince-pie,
  Which means: "*Acti labores jucundi.*"

Uncertain Ceres turns the wheel of fate
And pours her bounties on the unjust pate,
While industry and thrift reap scanty crops
And, hungry, watch the gluttons lick their chops.
  Then Farmer Colgate sheds his overalls
  And earns his living out of Puts and Calls.

Sorry our lot—our trials never end—
The patient farmer seldom keeps a friend;
We purchase posts and rails at great expense
And reap a lawsuit from a boundary fence,—
  Then seek relief from all our care and trouble
  And pay a heavy fee to Farmer Hubbell.

The penalty of acrimonious fights
Is many carking days and sleepless nights;
We feel the horrors of impending wrath
And rush in terror to a neuropath;
  Then Farmer Starr, with wise psychiatry,
  Prescribes some phosphates—with sobriety.

If toward the Sunny South we turn our mind,
And hope in fairer climes good crops to find
Where laughing negroes pick the cotton fields
And loamy upland rich tobacco yields,
  There murrain devastates the herds and flocks,
  And Farmer Page reaps only from "Red Rocks."

Freshet or drought, red rust or blighting fly—
Or garners bursting—and no one to buy—
Corn in the husk afflicted with black rot—
These are the sorrows of the farmer's lot;
  But floods and roaring cyclones ain't a marker
  When Farmer Cowdin gammons Farmer Barker.

And still we see some hope for those who dig—
The great Pupin has made a patent pig
And dreams of flying plows to ride the breeze;
While Pinchot plants the plains with waving trees,
  And Stetson whips all Hayseeds into line
  And Syndicates us in one vast Combine!

Verses read by Edward S. Martin, 1906:

THE PRUDENT FARMER

By Edward S. Martin

All farmers who have grown discreet
Have offices on William Street—
    Or Broad will do—
And farms accessible and green,
Where air is pure and water clean,
    And with a view.

This city life's not everything
Of which a poet likes to sing.
    It cramps a man,
And drives him hard and wears his nerves;
He wants no more of it than serves
    To push his plan.

A share of it won't hurt him much.
It profits him to keep in touch
With other guys.
To mark the upshot of their strife
And get some of it for his wife
Is not unwise.

But to be ALWAYS hunting loot—
What sort is he that that can suit?
Out on the cuss!
Ding-dong downtown and rush about,
And ding-dong back. Perpetual rout
And ceaseless fuss!

To such the ticker's baneful click
Sounds sweeter than the rippling creek,
Or eke the birds.
The office buildings' tottering height
Beats hills in his distorted sight.
He passes words!

The disconnected farmer man
Has this defect about his plan,
That average fields
Exact attentions more profuse
Than profitable, to produce
Reluctant yields.

If you would long the country praise
Don't live too much on what you raise.
That way's not best.
But let the city do its share;
The country furnish sun and air;
The town the rest.

Or mix your crops. Like one I knew
Who planted roots that duly grew,
And went to town,
And laid him in a thousand shares
Of Anaconda bought from bears
For salting down.

He phosphatized his roots. They did
Uncommon well. The stocks lay hid
Waiting advance,
Till, roots and stocks becoming dear,
He made a hundred thousand clear
On those two plants.

Farming's a gamble. I don't say
That roots will always act that way,
But when they do,
It's apt to be because combined
With city products of a kind
To pull them through.

So every farmer that's discreet
Hangs out his sign on Nassau Street—
Or Pine or Wall—
And what the farm denies his sweat
He works his wits in town to get,
Nor grieves at all.

Read January, 1912:

A BUCOLIC SYMPHONY

By Henry Marquand

The music that the country yields
Falls sweetly on the ear,
Whether of woods or farm or fields
'Tis goodly for to hear,—
No strain of lyre or stringèd lute
Transcends the creak of farmer's boot.

How proud the cock-a-doodle-do
Bursting at dawn of sun,
Which only breaks our dreams in two
And bids us slumber on,—
You hear the tardy cluck of hen
It's time to doff pyjamas then.

In summer ere the corn is ripe
    The grasshopper lifts his lay,
We listen to his cheery pipe
    Loitering on our way,—
  But science says this tenor sings
  By scratching legs against his wings.

List to the woodpecker's wild tattoo,
    Its cadence and its rhythm,
It must be that his time is true
    For my heart is beating with 'm,—
  Oh, I could stand for hours to heark-
  En to this lively fugue of bark.

The frogs they have their wooing hour,
    He makes his little joke,
She listens in her slimy bower,
    And swallows every croak,
  'Twould melt a heart of stone to pulp
  If man could utter such a gulp.

The humblest creature cannot fail
    To answer Nature's laws,
I've seen the ebon crow turn pale
    When pleading of his cause,—
  And as his heart is in his throat
  When he proposes 'tis by note.

Come where the honey-bee holds sway
    And watch the happy drone,
To love and song he gives his day,
    His night to love alone.
  Nor will he cease his merry bout
  Till union labor throws him out.

Then queen and toilers ply their song
    While fashioning the comb,
They sing together all day long
    To make their Home-Sweet-Home,—
  'Tis christened Charity by some
  For Charity begins to hum.

There's music in the piney swale,
At least it has its pitch,
And each man's orchard has its scale—
Of whom I'm one of which—
The healthy farmer's constant care
Is but to take and keep the air.

The town and country live at strife
With all the usual spats,—
The country has the sharps of life,
The city has the flats.
But, as in business oft 'tis found,
The underlying state is sound.

So Nature hath her symphony,
Though 'tis not played with strings,
To make mankind exult with glee
And angels clap their wings,
And with each various moving thought
Some deep and deadly truth is wrought.

Then to your soul this lesson lay,
Its admonition heed,
Experience hath one thing to say
According to your need,
Though farming casts a potent spell
It never pays to farm too well.

Read January, 1913:

ARS AGRICOLARIS

AN ODE OF MORAL SENTIMENTS
ADDRESSED TO CERTAIN FARMER-GENTS

BY HENRY VAN DYKE

All hail, ye famous Farmers!
Ye vegetable-charmers,
Who know the art of making barren earth
Smile with prolific mirth
And bring forth twins or triplets at a birth!

Ye scientific fertilizers of the soil,
And horny-handed sons of toil!
To-night from all your arduous cares released,
  With manly brows no longer sweat-impearled,
Ye hold your annual feast,
And like the Concord farmers long ago,
Ye meet above the "Bridge" below,
And draw the cork heard round the world!

  What memories are yours! What tales
Of triumph have your tongues rehearsed
Telling how ye have won your first
Potatoes from the stubborn mead
(Almost as many as ye sowed for seed!)
  And how the luscious cabbages and kails
Have bloomed before you in their bed
At seven dollars a head!
And how your onions took a prize
For bringing tears into the eyes
Of a hard-hearted cook! And how ye slew
  The Dragon Cut-worm at a stroke!
  And how ye broke,
Routed, and put to flight the horrid crew
Of vile potato-bugs and Hessian flies!
And how ye did not quail
Before the invading armies of San Jose Scale,
  But met them bravely with your little pail
  Of poison which ye put upon each tail
O' the dreadful beasts and made their courage fail!
  And how ye did acquit yourselves like men
  In fields of agricultural strife, and then,
  Like generous warriors, sat you down at ease
  And gently to your gardener said "Let us have *Pease!*"
But *were* there Pease? Ah, no, dear Farmers, no!
The course of Nature is not ordered so.
  For when we want a vegetable most,
            She holds it back;
            And when in boast
  To our week-endly friends
  Of what we'll give them on our farm, alack,
Those things the old dam, Nature, never sends.

O Pease in bottles, Sparrow-grass in jars,
How often have ye saved from scars
Of shame, and deep embarrassment,
The disingenuous farmer-gent,
  To whom some wondering guest has cried,
  "How *do* you raise such Pease and Sparrow-grass?"
  Whereat the farmer-gent has not denied
  The compliment, but smiling has replied,
  "To raise such things you must have lots of glass."

From wiles like these, true Farmers, hold aloof;
Accept no praise unless you have the proof.
If niggard Nature should withhold the green
And sugary Pea, welcome the humble Bean;
Give it the place of honor at your table.
Even the easy Radish, and the Beet,
If grown by your own toil, are extra sweet!
Let malefactors of great wealth and banker-felons
Rejoice in foreign artichokes, imported melons;
But you, my Farmers, at your frugal board,
Spread forth the fare your Sabine Farms afford.
Say to Mæcenas, when he is your guest,
"No peaches, try this turnip, 'tis my best."
Thus shall ye learn from labors in the field
What honesty a farmer's life may yield,
And like G. Washington in early youth,
Though cherries fail, produce a crop of Truth.

But think me not too strict, O fellows of the plough,
Some place for fiction in your lives I would allow.
In January when the world is drear,
And bills come in, and no results appear,
  And snow-storms veil the skies,
  And ice the streamlet clogs,
Then you may warm your heart with pleasant lies,
And revel in the seedman's catalogues.
What visions and what dreams are there!
  Of cauliflowers obese,—
Of giant celery, taller than a mast,—
  Of strawberries
Like red pincushions, round and vast,—

Of succulent and spicy gumbo,—
Of cantaloupes, as big as jumbo,—
Of high-strung beans without the strings,—
And of a host of other wild romantic things!

Oh, why should Starr declare
That modern habits mental force impair?
And why should H. Marquand complain
That jokes as good as his will ne'er come again?
And why should Bridges wear a gloomy mien
About the lack of fiction for his Magazine?
The seedman's catalogue is all we need
To stir our dull imaginations
To new creations,
And lead us, by the hand
Of Hope, into a fairy-land.

So dream, my friendly Farmer, as you will;
And let your fancy all your gardens fill
With wondrous crops; but always recollect
That Nature gives us less than we expect.
Scorn not the city where you earn the wealth
That, spent upon your farms, renews your health;
And tell your wife, whene'er the bills have shocked her,
"A country place is cheaper than a doctor."
May roses bloom for you and may you find
Your richest harvest in a tranquil mind.

The compiler offers no apology for devoting so much space to a reference to this club. Its membership, its objects, its close connection with the University Club, and the singular completeness with which all its affairs are managed entitle it to a conspicuous and appreciative notice.

The two oldest of the clubs of Princeton University—namely, the Ivy and the Cottage Club—give midwinter dinners every year at the University Club, which are attended principally by the New York members, nearly all of whom are also members of our club. The attendance averages from 50 to 60.

A most interesting group of university men, which formerly held monthly dinners at the University Club, and now has three in the course of the winter, is called the Roman Medical Society, or familiarly among themselves "The Romans." This society had its origin among certain young doctors who happened to be together in Rome, Italy, in 1867, the organization having been formed in April of that year. The object was the discussion of medical topics, and more particularly the promotion of good-fellowship among friends. The founders were Doctors Woolsey Johnson (Princeton '60), George G. Wheelock (Columbia '64), David L. Haight (Yale '60), Thomas T. Sabine (Columbia '61), David Magie (Princeton '59), and Henry C. Eno (Yale '60). Of these, Doctors Johnson, Wheelock, and Sabine are dead.

The Delphic Club, the A. D. Club, and the Fly Club are representative and of high standing at Harvard University. The A. D. probably ranks first among these three. The Fly Club used to be the Alpha Delta Phi, and the Delphic used to be the Delta Phi. They also hold dinners at our Club.

Other clubs and organizations holding dinners at the University Club are: the Board of Governors of the New York Eye and Ear Infirmary; the Alumni of Roosevelt Hospital, of St. Luke's Hospital, and of the Presbyterian Hospital; the Kappa Alpha Fraternity; the Graduates of the Groton School; the Institute of Arts and Letters; the Elihu Club, of Yale, a non-secret Senior Society; the Graduates of the Harvard Medical School; the Older Graduates of Columbia; the Committee on Admissions of the New York Bar Association; the Board of Governors of the Boys Club; the Society of the Cincinnati; the Class of '79, of Princeton (at the dinner of this class held in 1912 in honor of President Woodrow Wilson, a member of the class, there were present eighty members); the Quiz Medical Club; the Graduates of St. Mark's School.

This list is probably incomplete, but it is as nearly perfect as available information will permit.

On December 29, 1909, a reception was given to President Abbott Lawrence Lowell (Harvard '77) in honor of his election to the head of Harvard University.

On December 18, 1908, Harry A. Garfield (Williams '85), a member of this Club, was invited to dine with the Council and to be the guest of the Club at a reception to be given to him in recognition of his election to the presidency of Williams College, and a committee was appointed to invite distinguished Williams College alumni.

These entertainments were held, and, as usual in cases where dinners were given at which the lack of adequate accommodations forbade the presence of the whole Club, the expenses of the banquet were borne individually by the members of the Council.

There have been many such lunches and dinners, in honor of famous men and on great occasions, special reference to which would occupy too much space for the purposes of this history. "Club nights" for social intercourse have been held repeatedly throughout every year.

On January 4, 1912, an illustrated lecture was given by Farnham Bishop, M.A., son of Joseph B. Bishop (Brown '70), secretary of the Isthmian Canal Commission, on the Panama Canal.

Perhaps the most enjoyable of all the entertainments ever provided in the Club were the "Story-telling Nights" in the old Club House at 26th Street and Madison Avenue. One was held on February 28, 1895, and another on April 13, 1895. On these occasions many of the most famous authors and raconteurs followed one after another in five or ten minute talks. The gathering of the galaxies which shone at those memorable "nights" involved great labor and pains, but the result was most successful and repaid all the attention given to them. They might well be revived, if enthusiasts can be found to undertake the difficult work of organizing. The compiler remembers asking Mr. Joseph H. Choate to be one of the story-tellers. His answer was: "I never told a story in my life."

There is no record of the names of those who participated in these unique entertainments, and memory fails to reproduce the list. Among them, however, were such men as Mark Twain, James Whitcomb Riley, F. Hopkinson Smith, and Augustus Thomas. General Horace Porter was then in his prime as a witty and effective speaker and kept the room in a roar with his original anecdotes. E. W. Townsend, the originator of the "Chimmy Fadden" papers, gave readings in the patois of the New York street gamin. Judge Henry E. Howland (Yale '54), who had the reputation of knowing more funny stories than any other living man, and being able to make them fit any situation, presented a few of his best. W. Gordon McCabe (Univ. of Va. '61) was one of the most brilliant of the collection. His stories were generally of a Southern flavor, and in his army anecdotes relating to the events of the great Civil War it was remarked that, though himself an ex-Confederate soldier, he never once told a story that reflected on his Northern brethren. Alexander Wadsworth Longfellow (Harvard '76), of Massachusetts, gave humorous sketches of life among the New England fishermen, in perfectly imitated Down East lingo. Thomas Nelson Page (Univ. of Va. '74), John Fox (Harvard '83), and Sir Gilbert Parker (Trinity, Toronto) read extracts from their own works, and embellished them with anecdotes, and Polk Miller, of Richmond, Va., played the banjo, sang negro songs, and told inimitable stories in the darky dialect.

Besides the various entertainments which have been referred to, there have been from time to time billiard tournaments, pool tournaments, and backgammon tournaments.

The compiler of this history makes no excuse for introducing into the narration these accounts of the lighter proceedings of the Club. The instances given will serve to illustrate to the members of the future the kind of amusement to which even their most eminent predecessors resorted as if to prove that "the true, strong, and sound mind is the mind that can embrace equally great things and small."*

And so ends the History of the University Club of the City of New York.

The compilation of the facts reported has involved more time and labor than would be imagined from the reading of the mere results. The work has been one of intense interest to the compiler, whose connection with the administration of the Club from the time of its reorganization in 1879 to the date of the occupation of the new building at the corner of Fifth Avenue and 54th Street, had been most intimate. Even if he has not succeeded in making the history equally interesting to the members who read it, it is submitted that it constitutes a record to date of important facts and events, including many which, from the lack of an adopted system, might have been wanting in our archives—a record which may now be continued with greater attention to order and details than in the past.

* Doctor Samuel Johnson.

APPENDICES

APPENDIX I

CHARTER

Laws of New York, 1865. Chapter 594

An Act to Incorporate "The University Club," in the City of New York. Passed April 28, 1865

The people of the State of New York, represented in Senate and Assembly, do enact as follows:

Section 1. Theodore Woolsey Dwight, George T. Strong, John Taylor Johnston, Charles Astor Bristed, Henry R. Winthrop, Charles F. Chandler, Joseph H. Choate, Edmund Wetmore, Francis E. Kernochan, Eugene Schuyler, Edward Mitchell, Luther M. Jones and Russell Sturgis, Jr., and such other persons as are now associated, or may hereafter be associated with them, are hereby constituted a body corporate by the name of "The University Club," to be located in the City of New York, for the purpose of the promotion of Literature and Art, by establishing and maintaining a Library, Reading-room and Gallery of Art, and by such other means as shall be expedient and proper for such purposes.

Sec. 2. The said corporation shall have the power to make and adopt a constitution and by-laws, rules and regulations for the admission, suspension and expulsion of its members, and for their government, for the collection of fees and dues, for the election of its officers, and to define their duties, and for the safekeeping and protection of its property and funds, and from time to time to alter or repeal such constitution, by-laws, rules and regulations. The persons named in the first section of this act shall constitute the trustees and managers until others are elected in their places.

Sec. 3. The said corporation may lease, purchase or take by deed, devise or bequest, any real or personal estate, and hold or lease the same; provided that they shall not hold any real estate the value of which shall exceed the sum of one hundred thousand dollars.

Sec. 4. The said corporation shall possess the general powers and be subject to the general restrictions and liabilities prescribed in the third title of the eighteenth chapter of the first part of the Revised Statutes.

Sec. 5. This act shall take effect immediately.

CHARTER

Laws of New York, 1883. Chapter 139

An Act—To amend Chapter five hundred and ninety-four of the laws of eighteen hundred and sixty-five entitled "An act to incorporate the University Club in the City of New York." Passed March 29, 1883, three-fifths being present

The people of the State of New York represented in Senate and Assembly do enact as follows:

Section 1. Section three of Chapter five hundred and ninety-four of the laws of eighteen hundred and sixty-five entitled "An act to incorporate the University Club in the City of New York" is hereby amended so as to read as follows:

§ 3. The said Corporation may lease, purchase, or take by deed, devise or bequest any real or personal estate, and hold or lease the same, provided that they shall not hold any real estate the value of which shall exceed the sum of five hundred thousand dollars.

Section 2. This act shall take effect immediately.

Laws of New York, 1894. Chapter 9

Clubs are authorized to hold property of the value of $3,000,000 exclusive of improvements.

APPENDIX II

THE CONSTITUTION TO 1914 INCLUSIVE

Constitution of the University Club. Adopted, May 12, 1865

I. NAME

The name of this Association is "The University Club." The objects are the advancement of Literature and Art, and the promotion of friendly and social intercourse between men of education and culture.

II. OFFICERS

The Officers of the Club shall be a President, a Vice-President, a Secretary and a Treasurer, who, together with nine other members, shall constitute the Council and Trustees of the Club.

III. PRESIDENT

The President shall preside at the meetings of the Club; and, in his absence, the Vice-President shall preside.

The President shall be Chairman of the Council; he shall, with the Secretary, sign all written contracts and obligations of the Club, and shall perform such other duties as the Council or the Club may assign him.

IV. TREASURER

The Treasurer shall collect all dues. He shall pay all bills, on the certificate of their correctness by any member of the House Committee.

He shall report at every annual meeting, and oftener, if required, on the state of the funds, and his accounts shall be audited by the Auditing Committee once in three months.

V. SECRETARY

It shall be the duty of the Secretary to keep minutes of all meetings of the Club and of the Council; to notify members of their election; to issue notices for all meetings of the Club; to conduct the correspondence, and to keep the records; which minutes, correspondence and records shall be open to the inspection of members at all reasonable times.

VI. COUNCIL

The Council shall have general charge of the affairs, funds, and property of the Club. They shall have full power, and it shall be their duty to carry out the objects and purposes of the Club, according to its Charter, Constitution and By-Laws. They shall submit a general report of the affairs of the Club at each annual meeting, and shall report at other times, if required.

VII. MEETINGS AND ELECTIONS

There shall be an annual meeting of the Club on the second Saturday in May, at which time the officers shall be elected by ballot.

They shall hold office until the next annual meeting, or until their successors are elected.

If any vacancy shall occur in the Council, or if no election shall take place at the annual meeting, the offices may be filled by an election by ballot at any stated meeting of the Club; provided, that at least ten days' notice of such election shall have been posted.

There shall be stated meetings of the Club, for the transaction of business, on the third Saturday of January, and on the second Saturday of other months, at 8 o'clock, P. M., except the months of July, August and September. There shall be social meetings of the Club on Saturday evening of every week. Other meetings may be called by the Council, on the request of any three members of the Club, by posting a notice of the same in the rooms of the Club for one week.

VIII. QUALIFICATIONS OF MEMBERS

Any person shall be eligible as a member of this Club, who has graduated, or resided at least three years at some College, University, or School of Medicine, Law, Science or Theology; or who has received the honorary degree of A.M., LL.D.; or who has graduated at the U. S. Military Academy at West Point, or the U. S. Naval Academy.

IX. COMMITTEE ON ADMISSIONS—ELECTION OF MEMBERS

There shall be a Committee on Admissions, to consist of ten members, to be chosen by ballot at the annual meetings, and to hold office until their successors shall be elected. Vacancies, by death or otherwise, may be filled by the committee for the remainder of the term.

No member of the Council shall be a member of this Committee.

The names of the committee shall be kept posted in a conspicuous place in the Club Rooms.

The name, residence, and college, or place of instruction, of every person proposed for admission, with the names of the members proposing and seconding, shall be posted in a conspicuous place in the rooms for at least two weeks. The matter shall be then referred to the Committee on Admissions, the proceedings of which committee shall be secret and confidential. It shall be the duty of the committee, after careful consideration and examination, to vote upon each name separately and by ballot. No ballot shall be valid unless six members of the committee are present, and one negative shall be a rejection of the candidate.

On the election of each new member, the committee shall forthwith notify the same to the Secretary of the Club.

X. RESIGNATIONS

Resignations of membership shall be made to the Secretary in writing.

XI. DUES

Persons residing at a distance of twenty miles or more from the Club House, and not doing business in New-York, may be elected as Non-Resident Members.

Resident Members intending to be, and actually absent from the city for twelve months or more, or intending to reside, and actually residing at a distance of twenty miles or more from the Club House, and not doing business in New-York, on giving notice thereof to the Treasurer, may become, for such absence and residence, Non-Resident Members.

Non-Resident Members changing their residence to within twenty miles of the Club House, or their place of doing business to the city, shall give notice thereof to the Treasurer, and from such change become Resident Members.

The initiation fee shall be fifty dollars for Resident and for Non-Resident Members.

The annual dues of Resident Members shall be fifty dollars a year, payable semi-annually in advance, on the first day of the months of May and November. Non-Resident Members shall pay no annual dues.

In addition to the initiation fee, members shall pay the dues for the current half year, when admitted. A failure to pay such dues, and the initiation fee within one month after election and notice, forfeits membership.

Graduates of the Military and Naval Academies, if elected while on duty in the service of the United States, shall pay fifty dollars in lieu of all fees and dues thereafter. In case of resignation from service, they shall be placed on the list of regular members.

When the dues of any member shall remain unpaid for the space of three months, the Treasurer shall cause him to be notified that, unless the same are paid within one month thereafter, his membership shall cease; and in case such dues be not paid pursuant to such notice, or such default be not accounted for to the satisfaction of the Council, he shall thereupon cease to be a member.

XII. HONORARY MEMBERS

The President of each College or University, of which any member of the Club is a graduate, shall be an honorary member, and shall be entitled to the privileges of the Club.

Any persons distinguished for literary culture may, by a unanimous vote of the members present at any meeting of the Council, be elected honorary members.

XIII. GUESTS

Strangers temporarily visiting New-York, not exceeding fifty at any one time, may become guests of the Club for terms of four weeks each.

Any member may apply in writing to the Secretary for such guest's ticket, which shall thereupon be issued for the ensuing four weeks, subject to approval or withdrawal by the Council at their next meeting. Such guests shall have all the privileges of the Club, except that of inviting visitors. But no person may be a guest who is not eligible as a member.

XIV. VISITORS

Any member may invite gentlemen to the Club Rooms as visitors for a single day, on registering his own name with that of the visitor in a book kept for the purpose. This privilege may be suspended in regard to any individual member or visitor, at the discretion of the Council.

XV. EXPULSION

Any member may be suspended or expelled for cause by a vote of three-fourths of the members present at any meeting of the Club; one month's previous notice in writing having been given to the member, with a copy of the charge preferred against him. And any officer may be removed for cause at any meeting of the Association, by a like vote, and upon a like notice.

XVI. NO GAMBLING

No betting or card playing for stakes shall be allowed in the Club Rooms.

XVII. RULES

The Council shall prepare Rules, regulating the use of the Club Rooms by the members, which Rules shall be observed by all the members of the Club, but may be changed or amended by the Council at any time.

XVIII. APPOINTMENT OF HOUSE AND AUDITING COMMITTEES

The Council shall appoint, from its own members, a House Committee and an Auditing Committee, each to consist of three members, and to be a standing committee for the current official year.

XIX. HOUSE COMMITTEE

The House Committee shall have charge of the Club Rooms; they shall appoint and remove employees, receive the complaints of the members, and report upon them to the Council; and, from time to time, procure those articles which may be necessary for the use or convenience of members.

XX. AUDITING COMMITTEE

The Auditing Committee shall audit the accounts of the Treasurer quarterly, and report to the Council the accounts audited and allowed since their previous report.

XXI. MEETINGS OF COUNCIL

There shall be stated meetings of the Council once in two weeks from October 1st to May 1st, and once in each month from May 1st to October 1st. Five members present shall constitute a quorum for the transaction of business.

XXII. COMMITTEE ON LITERATURE AND ART

The Council shall appoint from its own members a Committee on Literature and Art.

This committee, under the direction of the Council, shall have charge of the Reading Room and of all books, papers and works of Art belonging to the Club, and shall have power to solicit and receive donations, and select and purchase all books, periodicals and works of Art for the Club.

XXIII. AMENDMENTS

This Constitution may be amended at any annual or monthly meeting of the Club by a vote of two-thirds of the members present, after a notice thereof given at a previous annual or monthly meeting, and posted in the Rooms of the Club, at least twenty days before the vote is taken.

CONSTITUTION AS AMENDED MAY 10, 1879

I. NAME

The name of this association is The University Club.

II. OFFICERS

The officers of the Club shall be a President, a Vice President, a Secretary and a Treasurer.

III. PRESIDENT

The President, and in his absence the Vice-President, shall preside at the meetings of the Club and of the Council. In the event of their absence, a meeting of the Club or of the Council may elect its presiding officers. The President shall, with the Secretary, sign all written contracts and obligations of the Club, and shall perform such other duties as the Council or the Club may assign him.

IV. TREASURER

The Treasurer shall collect all entrance fees and all dues, and shall keep the accounts of the Club, and report thereon at each regular meeting of the Council. His accounts shall be audited by the Auditing Committee semi-annually. He shall pay all bills on the certificate of their correctness by the House Committee. He shall notify persons elected to membership of their election.

V. SECRETARY

The Secretary shall give notice of all meetings of the Club and of the Council, and shall keep minutes of such meetings. He shall conduct the correspondence, and keep the records of the Club. He shall furnish to the Treasurer the names of all persons elected to membership, and shall be the keeper of the seal of the Club.

VI. COUNCIL

1. The Council shall have general charge of the affairs, funds and property of the Club. They shall have full power, and it shall be their duty to carry out the purposes of the Club according to its Charter, Constitution and By-Laws. The members to be elected at the annual meeting in 1879 shall divide themselves into four classes (of five members each), the terms of office of which shall be respectively, one, two, three and four years.

2. The Council shall, as soon as may be after each annual meeting, elect from its own body, a President, Vice-President, Secretary and Treasurer, who shall hold office until the second Saturday of the succeeding May, and until their successors are elected.

3. The Council shall submit at each Annual Meeting a general report of the affairs of the Club, with an estimate for the ensuing year, which shall be printed and distributed to members ten days before the Annual Meeting, and shall report at other times if required.

4. The Council shall meet once a month, except during the months of July and August, and special meetings may be called by order of the President or of the House Committee. A majority of its members shall constitute a quorum of the Council.

5. The Council shall prescribe rules for the admission of strangers to the privileges of the Club.

VII. MEETINGS AND ELECTIONS

1. There shall be an Annual Meeting of the Club on the second Saturday of May in each year. At the Annual Meeting to be held on the second Saturday of May, 1879, twenty members shall be elected by ballot, who shall constitute the Council, and who shall hold office as provided in Article VI of this Constitution, and thereafter at each Annual Meeting five members shall be elected by ballot as members of the Council, (to replace the outgoing class,) whose term of office shall be four years. Vacancies in the other classes shall be also filled at such meeting by ballot, and a majority of the votes cast shall be necessary to elect.

2. Officers and members of the Council shall hold office during the term for which they are elected and until their successors are chosen.

3. If any vacancy shall occur in the Council, such vacancy may be supplied by election by ballot, at a special meeting of the Club to be called by the Council, provided that at least ten days notice of such election shall have been posted.

4. Upon the written request of twenty-five members the Council shall call a special meeting of the Club, which request, as also the notice of any special meeting, shall state the object for which the meeting is called, and at a special meeting no subject not so stated shall be considered. Notices of any meeting, whether annual or special, shall be posted in the rooms of the Club for one week. Fifty members shall constitute a quorum at any meeting of the Club.

VIII. QUALIFICATIONS OF MEMBERS

Any person shall be eligible as a member of this Club who has graduated or resided at least three years at some College, University or School of Medicine, Law, Science or Theology, or who has received the honorary degree of A.M., or that of LL.D., or who has graduated at the United States Military Academy at West Point, or at the United States Naval Academy, provided five years have elapsed since such graduation or residence.

IX. COMMITTEE ON ADMISSIONS—ELECTION OF MEMBERS

1. There shall be a Committee on Admissions to consist of twenty-one members.

2. They shall be chosen by ballot at the annual meeting in May,

1879, and shall divide themselves into three classes of seven members each, the terms of office of which shall be respectively, one, two and three years, and thereafter the term of office of each class elected shall be three years. Members to replace the outgoing class shall be elected in each year by the members of the Committee other than those belonging to such outgoing class, and vacancies in any class shall be filled by the Committee. Eleven members shall constitute a quorum, and two negative votes shall be a rejection of a candidate. No member of the Council shall be a member of this Committee. The names of the Committee shall remain posted in a conspicuous place in the Club rooms. The name, residence and college or place of instruction of every person proposed for admission, with the names of the members proposing and seconding, shall be posted in a conspicuous place in the rooms for at least two weeks. The matter shall then be referred to the Committee on Admissions, the proceedings of which Committee shall be secret and confidential. It shall be the duty of the Committee, after careful consideration and examination, to vote upon each name separately and by ballot.

3. No member of this Committee shall propose any candidate for membership of the Club. On the election of each new member, the Committee shall forthwith notify the same to the Secretary of the Club.

4. The number of members of the Club shall not exceed seven hundred and fifty.

X. RESIGNATIONS

Resignations of membership shall be made to the Secretary in writing.

XI. DUES

1. The entrance fee shall be fifty dollars for all members proposed on or before the tenth day of May, 1879, and for all members proposed after that date it shall be one hundred dollars.

2. The annual dues of Resident members shall be fifty dollars, and of Non-resident members twenty-five dollars, payable semi-annually, in advance, on the first days of May and November.

3. Persons not residing in the City of New York may be elected as Non-resident members, and members who remove their residence from the city, on giving notice to the Treasurer of the change of residence, shall become Non-resident members.

4. Non-resident members who may change their residence to

the City of New York, shall become resident members, and shall notify the Treasurer, in writing, of such change.

5. Candidates elected, on payment of the entrance fee and of the dues for the current half year, shall become members of the Club, and the election of any candidate shall be void if he fail to make such payment within thirty days after notice of his election is mailed, addressed to him at the place given as his residence on the posted list of candidates.

6. Graduates of the Military or Naval Academy, if elected while on duty in the service of the United States, shall pay fifty dollars, in lieu of all fees and dues thereafter, so long as they shall remain in the service.

7. When the dues of any member shall remain unpaid for the space of three months, the Treasurer shall cause him to be notified, that unless the same are paid within one month thereafter, his membership shall cease; and in case such dues be not paid pursuant to such notice, or such default be not accounted for to the satisfaction of the Council, he shall thereupon cease to be a member.

XII. EXPULSION

Any member may be suspended or expelled for cause, by a vote of three-fourths of all the members of the Council; one month's previous notice in writing having been given to the member, with a copy of the charges preferred against him.

XIII. GAMBLING

No betting or card playing for stakes shall be allowed in the Club rooms.

XIV. RULES

The Council shall prepare and enforce Rules, regulating the use of the Club Rooms by the members.

XV. APPOINTMENT OF HOUSE AND AUDITING COMMITTEES

The Council shall appoint, from its own members, a House Committee and an Auditing Committee, each to consist of three members, and to be a Standing Committee for the current official year.

XVI. HOUSE COMMITTEE

The House Committee, subject to the direction and control of the Council, shall have charge of the Club Rooms. They shall appoint and remove employees, receive the complaints of the members, and report upon them to the Council, and from time to time, procure such articles as may be necessary for the use or convenience of members.

XVII. AUDITING COMMITTEE

The Auditing Committee shall audit the accounts of the Treasurer semi-annually, and report to the Council the accounts audited and allowed since their previous report.

XVIII. RULES OF COUNCIL AND COMMITTEE ON ADMISSIONS

The Council and Committee on Admissions shall each have power to make rules for its government, and to prescribe and enforce penalties for the violation of such rules.

XIX. COMMITTEE ON LITERATURE AND ART

The Council shall appoint a Committee on Literature and Art. This Committee, under direction of the Council, shall have charge of the Reading-room, and of all books, papers and works of art belonging to the Club, and shall have power to solicit and receive donations, and to select and purchase all books, periodicals and works of art for the Club.

XX. NOTICE TO MEMBERS

Any member may enter in a book, to be kept at the office, a mail address, to which all notices to be sent to him under the Constitution or rules shall be directed.

In default of such entry, such notices shall be served by depositing them in the Club letter box, addressed to the member, who shall be held to have received them ten days after they shall have been so mailed or deposited.

XXI. AMENDMENTS

The Constitution may be amended at any meeting of the Club, annual or special, by a vote of a majority, until after the Annual Meeting, to be held in 1880, and thereafter by a vote of two-thirds, of the members present. Notices of proposed amendments shall be furnished to the Secretary, and posted in the Club room at least twenty days before the meeting at which it is proposed to consider them, and the Secretary shall cause such notices to be printed, and sent to each member at least ten days before such meeting.

AMENDMENTS TO CONSTITUTION

May 10, 1879, to June 1, 1880

VI, 3. For "ten days" read "five days."

VIII. Amended to read:

1. Any person nominated after February 1, 1880, shall be eligible to membership in this Club who shall have received from a University or College a degree, to obtain which, in regular course, at least three years residence or study are required, or who shall have received an honorary degree from such University or College, or who shall have graduated at the United States Military Academy, or at the United States Naval Academy; provided that, except in the case of the holder of an honorary degree, at least five years shall have elapsed since the conferring of the degree, or since graduation.

2. As to persons nominated before February 1, 1880, the provisions adopted May 10, 1879, shall apply.

3. The Council shall determine what degrees from foreign Universities, and from what foreign Universities shall qualify the holder for membership; and a list of such degrees shall be posted in the office of the Club. The holder of any degrees named on such list shall be eligible to membership.

XI. Amended to read:

1. The Entrance Fee shall be One Hundred dollars for Resident members, and Fifty dollars for Non-resident members; but each Non-resident member, elected as such after April 1, 1880, who shall become a Resident member, shall pay to the Treasurer Fifty dollars in addition to his original entrance fee; and a failure to pay said sum shall be considered a failure to pay dues, and shall subject the member in default to the penalties prescribed in Section 8 of this Article.

2. The annual dues of Resident members shall be Fifty dollars, and of Non-resident members Twenty-five dollars, payable semi-annually, in advance, on the first days of May and November.

3. Persons not residing or having a place of business within twenty miles of the City Hall, in the City of New York, may be elected as Non-resident members; and any member who removes his residence and place of business to a distance of at least twenty miles from said City Hall, on written notice to the Treasurer of such removal, shall become a Non-resident member; but any

Non-resident member elected prior to April 1, 1880, residing or doing business within twenty miles of said City Hall, shall continue to be a Non-resident member, unless he remove his residence to said City.

4. No Non-resident members elected after April 1, 1880, shall be entitled to vote at any meeting of the Club, or to hold office.

5. Non-resident members who may change their residence to the City of New York, shall become Resident members, and shall notify the Treasurer, in writing, of such change.

6. Candidates elected, on payment of the entrance fee and of the dues for the current half year, shall become members of the Club, and the election of any candidate shall be void if he fail to make such payment within thirty days after notice of his election is mailed, addressed to him at the place given as his residence on the posted list of candidates.

7. Officers of the Army and Navy, eligible to membership, if elected while on duty in the service of the United States, shall pay Fifty dollars, in lieu of all fees and dues thereafter, so long as they shall remain on the active list.

8. When the dues of any member shall remain unpaid for the space of three months, the Treasurer shall cause him to be notified, that unless the same are paid within one month thereafter, his membership shall cease; and in case such dues be not paid pursuant to such notice, or such default be not accounted for to the satisfaction of the Council, he shall thereupon cease to be a member.

1882–1883

VIII, 1. Add after the second mentioned "honorary degree": "the candidate shall be distinguished in Literature, Art, Science, or the Public Service; and provided, that except in the case of the holder of an honorary degree, at least five years shall have elapsed since the conferring of the degree, or since graduation."

XVII. Added to close: "They may also act as a Finance Committee, with such duties and powers as the Council may prescribe."

1884–1885

VIII, 1. Next to last line: For "five" read "three."

XI, 1. Amended to read:

The Entrance Fee shall be Two Hundred dollars for Resident members and Fifty dollars for Non-resident members; but each

Non-resident member, elected as such after May, 1883, who shall become a Resident member, shall pay to the Treasurer One Hundred and Fifty dollars in addition to his original entrance fee; and a failure to pay said sum shall be considered a failure to pay dues, and shall subject the member in default to the penalties in Section 8 of this Article.

2. For "Fifty dollars" read "Sixty dollars."

7. Amended to read:

Officers of the Army and Navy eligible to membership who shall be elected after February 9, 1884, shall be considered as Non-resident members, except that, when ordered on service outside the limits of the United States, or when stationed at a post distant more than two hundred and fifty miles from New-York City for a period longer than one year, their dues shall be remitted during the period of such service.

1886 TO MARCH, 1887

VI. New paragraph:

6. The Council may fill any vacancy in its body by election of a member to hold office until the next annual election.

IX, 4. Amended to read:

The number of Resident members of the Club shall not exceed eight hundred and fifty; and not more than ten Resident members shall be elected during any one month.

XI, 8. Amended to read:

When the dues of any member shall remain unpaid for the space of two months, he shall thereupon be suspended from membership, and the Treasurer shall send him notice that he has been so suspended, and that unless his dues are paid within two months from the date of suspension his membership shall cease, and a notice to the same effect shall be posted in the Club; and in case such dues be not paid pursuant to such notice, his membership shall cease; but if he shall afterwards account for such default to the satisfaction of the Council it may restore him to membership upon the payment of all dues to the date of restoration.

JULY, 1887

IX, 4. Amended to read:

The number of Resident members of the Club shall not exceed one thousand, and not more than ten Resident members shall be elected in any one month in addition to the number required to fill vacancies occasioned by death or resignation.

5. New paragraph:

The number of Non-resident members of the Club shall not exceed six hundred and fifty.

XI, 1. Amended to read:

The Entrance Fee shall be Two Hundred dollars for Resident members and one hundred dollars for Non-resident members; but every Non-resident member, who shall become a Resident member, shall pay to the Treasurer an amount equal to the difference between his original entrance fee and the entrance fee for Resident members at the time of the admission as a Non-resident member; and a failure to pay said sum shall be considered a failure to pay dues, and shall subject the member in default to the penalties prescribed in section 8 of this article.

1888

X. Added to close: Such resignation shall not be accepted until all indebtedness to the Club of the member resigning shall have been discharged.

XI, 8. Amended to read:

The names of all members who shall fail to pay their semi-annual dues on or before the first days of June and December shall be then posted in a conspicuous place in the Club House, and, if such dues are not paid on the first days of July and January thereafter, such members shall cease to be members of the Club, subject, however, to the provisions of Article VI, Section 7, of the Constitution.

XVI. Amended to read:

The House Committee shall meet at least once a week. It shall be its duty, subject to the control of the Council, to manage the Club, to regulate prices, to order purchases, to audit bills, to receive complaints, to redress grievances, and to appoint and dismiss all employés.

1890

VI, 1. Amended to read:

The Council shall consist of twenty members, five of whom shall be elected by ballot at each annual meeting of the Club to replace the outgoing class and to take office at the expiration of the term of such outgoing class. They shall hold office for four years, or until the fourth annual meeting after their election.

VII, 1. For "May" read "March."

IX, 1. Add to second line: "seven of whom shall be elected by ballot at each Annual Meeting of the Club, to replace the outgoing class and to take office at the expiration of the term of such outgoing class. The term of office of the members of the Committee shall be three years, or until the third Annual Meeting after their election."

5. Amended to read:

The number of Non-resident members of the Club shall not exceed seven hundred and fifty, and not more than ten Non-resident members shall be elected in any one month in addition to the number required to fill vacancies occasioned by death or resignation.

XI, 2. For "May and November" read: "March and September."

8. For "June and December" read "April and October." For "July and January" read "May and November."

1891

VI, 2. For "May" read "March."

1892

IX, 4. For "one thousand" read "eleven hundred."

5. For "seven hundred and fifty" read "eight hundred and fifty."

XI. 3. Omit all but first sentence.

5. Any Resident member who may remove his residence and place of business to a distance of at least twenty miles from the City Hall, in the City of New York, shall, on written notice to the Treasurer of such removal, become a Non-resident member; and any Non-resident member who may remove his residence or place of business to within twenty miles from said City Hall shall become a Resident member, and shall notify the Treasurer in writing of such removal; but any Non-resident member elected prior to April 1, 1880, residing or doing business within twenty miles of said City Hall, shall continue to be a Non-resident member, unless he may remove his residence to the City of New York.

1893

IX, 4. For "eleven hundred" read "twelve hundred," and omit rest of paragraph.

XV. Amended to read:

The Council shall appoint from its own members an Auditing Committee, to consist of three members, and a House Committee, to consist of not more than five members, each Committee to be a Standing Committee for the current year.

1894

IX, 5. For "eight hundred and fifty" read "nine hundred."

1895

V. Last two sentences amended to read:

He shall furnish to the Treasurer the names of all members elected to membership, and shall advise him of all transfers or changes affecting the said membership. He shall be the Keeper of the seal of the Club.

IX, 6. New paragraph:

Any member whose name shall have been upon the roll of the Club for fifteen consecutive years, shall be entitled to become a life member on the payment of $750. The number of life members of the Club shall not exceed one hundred. Whenever a member becomes a life member, a vacancy shall be created thereby in the resident or non-resident membership, as the case may be. Life members shall have the rights and privileges, and be subject to all the penalties of the regular members, but shall forever be exempt from all annual dues.

XI, 5. For "on written notice to the Treasurer of such removal" read "on written notice to the Secretary of such removal and upon receipt of advice from him."

1897

IX, 4. For "twelve hundred" read "seventeen hundred."

5. For "nine hundred" read "thirteen hundred."

XVI. For "employés" read "employees."

1898

IX, 5. Omit:

"and not more than ten Non-resident members shall be elected in any one month in addition to the number required to fill vacancies occasioned by death or resignation."

1899

IX, 6. For "$750" read "$1000."

XI, 2. For "sixty dollars" read "seventy-five dollars" and for "twenty-five dollars" read "thirty-five dollars."

1901

VIII, 3. Amended to read:

The Council shall determine what degrees from Universities and Colleges, and from what Universities and Colleges shall qualify the holder for membership; and a list of such degrees and of such Universities and Colleges, as from time to time determined by the Council, shall be posted in the office of the Club.

IX, 4. For "seventeen hundred" read "two thousand."

5. For "thirteen hundred" read "fifteen hundred."

1903

XI, 2. After "Non-resident" add: "and Army and Navy members, except as provided in Section 7 of this article."

7. Amended to read:

Officers of the Army and Navy elected after February 9, 1884, when ordered on service outside the limits of the United States, or when stationed at a post distant more than two hundred and fifty miles from New York City for a period longer than one year, shall be exempt from the payment of dues during the period of such service.

XV. Heading changed to "Standing Committees" and amended to read:

The Council shall appoint annually a House Committee, to consist of not more than five members, an Auditing and Finance Committee to consist of three members, a Committee on Literature and Art to consist of not more than five members, a Committee on Colleges and Degrees to consist of not more than five members; such Committees to be Standing Committees for the current year. The Chairman of each of such Committees shall be designated by the Council.

XVII. Add "Finance" to heading of article.

XVIII. Amended to read:

This Committee, under direction of the Council, shall have charge of and regulate the use of the Library and Reading Rooms, and of all books, papers, and works of art belonging to the Club, and shall have power to solicit and receive donations, and to select and purchase all books, periodicals, and works of art for the Club. (XVIII was XIX in last book.)

XIX. New paragraph:

COMMITTEE ON COLLEGES AND DEGREES

The Committee on Colleges and Degrees shall report to the Council for its determination the qualifications of applicants for membership under Section 1, Article VIII.

XXII. New paragraph:

NOMINATING COMMITTEE

It shall be the duty of the Council to appoint at their stated meeting in February in each year a Nominating Committee of five whose names shall be posted immediately. Such Committees shall nominate and post a ticket of candidates for the Council and Committee on Admissions at least ten days before the Annual Meeting.

XX was XVIII in last book.

XXI was XX in last book.

XXIII was XXI in last book.

1908

IX, 6. For "fifteen" read "ten."

1909

VIII, 1. On fourth line from end of paragraph: "or the Public Service" amended to read "or for public services."

1909

XV. "Committee on Literature and Art" are now separate Committees to read: "A Committee on Literature, to consist of not more than five members, a Committee on Art, to consist of not more than five members."

XVIII. Amended to read:

This Committee, under direction of the Council, shall have charge of and regulate the use of the Library and Reading Rooms and of all books and papers belonging to the Club, and shall have power to purchase books and periodicals for the Club, subject to such limitations as the Council may impose.

XIX. New paragraph:

COMMITTEE ON ART

This Committee, under direction of the Council, shall have charge of all works of art belonging to the Club, not including such as are contained in books, and shall have power to select and purchase works of art for the Club, subject to such limitations as the Council may impose; and shall advise the Council as to works of art proposed to be given or loaned to the Club.

XIX to XXIII in last book are now XX to XXIV.

1911

XV. New paragraph:

EXECUTIVE COMMITTEE

There shall be an Executive Committee which shall consist of the President, Vice-President, Secretary, and Treasurer, and the Chairman of the several standing committees. During the recess of the Council this Committee shall be vested with all the powers of the Council so far as the same can be properly delegated, and it shall be its duty to exercise such powers whenever immediate action is required.

Five members of this Committee shall constitute a quorum.

XV to XX in last book amended to read:

STANDING COMMITTEES

XVI, 1. There shall be seven Standing Committees to be known as the House Committee, the Finance Committee, the Auditing Committee, the Library Committee, the Art Committee, the Committee on Colleges and Degrees, and the Entertainment Committee.

2. The Council, as soon as may be after each annual meeting, shall appoint the members of all Standing Committees, who shall hold office until the third Saturday of the next succeeding March and until their successors are elected. The Council shall also designate the member who shall act as Chairman of each Standing Committee, and who shall be in each case a member of the Council. All vacancies in such Committees shall be filled by the Council, or during its recess by the Executive Committee. Each Committee shall have power to fix its own quorum.

3. The House Committee shall consist of not more than five members. It shall be its duty, subject to the control of the Council, to order purchases, to audit bills, to regulate prices, to receive

complaints, to redress grievances, to appoint and dismiss employees, to manage the Club, and to perform such other similar duties as may from time to time be assigned to it by the Council.

4. The Finance Committee shall consist of not more than three members, of which the Treasurer shall be one. It shall be its duty, subject to the control of the Council, to supervise the finances and investments of the Club, and annually to make a budget setting forth the estimated receipts and expenses of the Club for the ensuing year, commencing on the first day of March, to present such budget to the Council for consideration at its regular meeting in the month of March, and to perform such other similar duties as may from time to time be assigned to it by the Council.

5. The Auditing Committee shall consist of not more than three members. It shall be its duty to audit the books of the Treasurer semi-annually, and report to the Council the accounts audited and allowed since its previous report, and to perform such other similar duties as may from time to time be assigned to it by the Council.

6. The Library Committee shall consist of not more than five members. It shall be its duty, subject to the control of the Council, to regulate the use of the Library and reading-rooms, and of all the books, periodicals, newspapers, manuscripts and unframed and unbound engravings and etchings belonging to the Club, to purchase books and periodicals, and to perform such other similar duties as may from time to time be assigned to it by the Council.

7. The Art Committee shall consist of not more than five members. It shall be its duty, subject to the control of the Council, to have the charge and care of all works of art belonging to the Club, to select and purchase works of art for the Club, to report to the Council its opinion relative to the merit of works of art proposed to be given or loaned to the Club, and to perform such other similar duties as may from time to time be assigned to it by the Council.

8. The Committee on Colleges and Degrees shall consist of not more than three members. It shall be the duty of this Committee to report to the Council for determination by it what degrees, and from what universities and colleges, shall qualify the holders for membership, under Section 1 of Article VIII.

9. The Entertainment Committee shall consist of not more than five members. It shall be its duty, subject to the control of the Council, to determine the number and character of enter-

tainments to be given by the Club, to make, or authorize to be made, all necessary engagements and arrangements to conduct the same, to take charge of all receptions and dinners given by the Club to distinguished guests, and to perform such other similar duties as may from time to time be assigned to it by the Council. (Note: The last Committee was a new one.)

Change the numbers of Articles XXI to XXIV in last book to XVII to XX, respectively.

1914

XI, 2. First two lines amended to read: "The annual dues of Resident members shall be ninety dollars, and of Non-resident members forty-five dollars."

XVI, 2. Omit: "and who shall be in each case a member of the Council."

APPENDIX III

BY-LAWS

1884–1886

ANNUAL ELECTION

Pursuant to a Resolution adopted by the Club at the Annual Meeting in May, 1884, it is the duty of the Council to appoint, at their stated meeting in April in each year, a special Committee on Nominations, whose names shall be posted as soon as appointed.

It is the duty of such Special Committee to nominate candidates for election at the Annual Meeting of the Club on the third Saturday of May, to fill vacancies in the membership of the Council and the Committee on Admissions, as ordered, Art. VII, Sec. 1, and Art. IX, Sec. 2, of the Constitution.

1890

NOMINATING COMMITTEE

Pursuant to a Resolution adopted by the Club at the Annual Meeting in May, 1890, it is the duty of the Council to appoint, at their stated meeting in February in each year, a special Nominating Committee, whose names shall be immediately posted. It is the duty of such Special Committee to nominate and post a ticket of candidates for the Council and Committee on Admissions at least ten days before the annual Meeting in March.

1893

INVESTMENTS

It shall be the duty of the Treasurer to report to the Council when there are moneys in the Treasury available for investment or reinvestment, and, if upon such report the Council shall so direct, it shall be his further duty to invest the same in such securities as may be approved by the Auditing Committee, and to report such investment at the next meeting of the Council. Such securities shall always be in the name of the University Club.

EXTRAORDINARY EXPENDITURES

It shall be the duty of the House Committee and of the Committee on Literature and Art to advise with the Council as to all extraordinary expenditures in their respective departments, and to obtain its consent thereto before incurring the same. In cases of emergency, and where the Council cannot be called together in time, the House Committee may act and report its action at the next meeting of the Council.

(The foregoing rules, in regard to investments and extraordinary expenditure, are printed by vote of the Council, passed November 7, 1892.)

1895

INVESTMENTS

Amended to read:

It shall be the duty of the Treasurer to report to the Council when there are moneys in the Treasury available for investment or re-investment. There shall be a Committee of the Council to be called the "Investment Committee," to consist of the Treasurer and three other members to be appointed by the President of the Club, and such Committee shall, when the Council shall so direct, invest such moneys as are reported by the Treasurer as available, and report their action at the next meeting of the Council. Such securities shall always be in the name of the University Club.

(The foregoing rules, in regard to investments and extraordinary expenditures, are printed by vote of the Council.)

1898

HONORARY MEMBERS

The President of the United States, the Vice-President of the United States, the Chief Justice of the Supreme Court, the Associate Justices of the Supreme Court, the General in Chief commanding the Army, the Admiral commanding the North Atlantic Squadron, the General commanding the Department of the East, and the Commandant of the Brooklyn Navy Yard, shall receive the privileges of the Club during their terms of official service.

1903

Resolution of May, 1890, creating the Nominating Committee, transferred to Constitution, XXII, being altered to read:

NOMINATING COMMITTEE

It shall be the duty of the Council to appoint at their stated meeting in February in each year a Nominating Committee of five whose names shall be posted immediately. Such Committee shall nominate and post a ticket of candidates for the Council and Committee on Admissions at least ten days before the Annual Meeting.

1911

Omitted: Paragraph on Investments.
Omitted: Paragraph on Extraordinary Expenditures.

APPENDIX IV

RULES OF THE COMMITTEE ON ADMISSIONS TO 1914 INCLUSIVE, AND THE RESOLUTION OF THE COUNCIL OF MARCH 13, 1899

JANUARY 1ST, 1880

RULES OF THE COMMITTEE ON ADMISSIONS

The attention of members is called to the following rules of the Committee on Admissions:

SECTION 10. Names of candidates shall be entered in a book to be kept in the office of the Club. In such book shall also be entered the college at which each candidate graduated, the year of his graduation, his residence, and his profession. Until such entry is made and signed by the proposer and seconder, the name of a candidate shall not be posted. The secretary of the committee may sign for members who are absent from the city, upon their written request.

The proposer of a candidate for admission to the Club is required to send to the Committee on Admissions a letter of recommendation, giving the name and place of residence of the candidate, the college at which he was a student, and the year of his graduation or of his withdrawal from college, the profession or occupation of the candidate, and such statement of his qualifications as the proposer may deem proper. A letter of recommendation shall also be required from the seconder.

SEC. 11. If the name of any candidate is called up for consideration at a meeting of the Committee, and it shall then appear that no letter of recommendation has been received from the proposer and seconder, the name shall be passed; and the secretary shall immediately notify the proposer and the seconder that the nomination cannot be acted upon without a proper letter of recommendation. In case no such letters are received before the next following stated meeting, the candidate shall be deemed withdrawn, and his name shall be dropped from the list.

SEC. 12. Letters, except those of the proposer and seconder, relating to candidates whose names have been finally acted upon shall forthwith be destroyed, unless by a vote of the Committee any particular letter be preserved.

1888

SEC. 12. Added to close: The name of no candidate for non-resident membership shall be considered by the Committee unless a letter respecting his candidacy shall have been received from a resident member of the Club, or unless such candidate shall be personally known to some member of the Committee present.

1889

Last paragraph of "Sec. 12" is now "Sec. 16."

SEC. 19. Candidates for resident membership must be personally known to at least one member of the Committee.

1890

New paragraphs:

SECTION 4. A stated meeting of the Committee shall be held on the first Wednesday evening of each month except the months of July, August and September.

SEC. 18. The names of such candidates as may be proposed before three years after their graduation have expired shall be posted by the Secretary of the Committee as soon as they shall be eligible for election; but the name of no candidate proposed before his graduation shall be posted.

SEC. 19. Add after Committee: "present."

1895

SEC. 10. On fourth line after "graduation" add: "the degree received by the candidate."

On sixth line after "stated" add: If the eligibility of the candidate depend upon an honorary degree, the fact that the degree is honorary and the year when the degree was received shall be stated.

1896

SEC. 10. Second paragraph, on fourth line after "graduation" add: "the degree received by him."

Second paragraph, on seventh line after "proper" add: "If the candidate have no profession or occupation, that fact shall be stated in the proposer's letter, and if the eligibility of the candidate depend upon an honorary degree, the fact that the degree is honorary and the year when the degree was received shall also be stated in the letter, together with the other facts which make the candidate eligible under the provisions of the Constitution relating to the holders of honorary degrees."

SEC. 18. Amended to read:

Names of candidates shall be posted as soon as subdivision 1 of Section 10 of the Rules shall have been complied with, although three years may not then have elapsed since the conferring of the degree or since graduation. But the name of a candidate shall not be entered, in the candidates' book, nor posted, before he shall have received the degree or graduated.

SEC. 20. When a candidate who is a non-resident and is proposed as such becomes a resident before the time when his name is first considered by the Committee, his name shall be transferred to the resident list under same date as that upon which he was posted as a non-resident.

When a candidate who is a resident and is proposed as such becomes a non-resident before the time when his name is first considered by the Committee, his name shall be transferred to the non-resident list under same date as that upon which he was posted as a resident.

1902

SEC. 11. Amended to read:

At every meeting, the Committee will take up the consideration of names of candidates, beginning at the top of the list.

If, when the name of any candidate shall be reached for consideration, it appear that no letter has been received from the proposer or seconder, or that the candidate is not personally known to at least one member of the Committee present, or that there is insufficient information before the Committee for final action upon the name, the name shall be passed and the proposer and seconder immediately notified. When the name of such candidate shall be again reached for consideration, if the necessary requirements under the rules of the Committee have not been complied with, or if there is still insufficient information before the Committee respecting the candidate, the name shall be dropped from the list, unless special circumstances and considerations are brought to the attention of the Committee, when by special vote, the name may be again passed or removed to the foot of the list.

1903

SEC. 22. The name of an Army and Navy candidate, who is in active service, may be considered at any meeting upon special vote of the Committee.

1905

The word "Section" at beginning of each paragraph is here changed to read "Rule."

RULE V. Closed to read: "The hour of such meeting, unless otherwise determined by the Committee, shall be half-past eight o'clock."

(This rule was Section 4 in last book.)

RULE X. On third line "the college at which each candidate graduated" amended to read: "the university or college from which the candidate was graduated."

On fourth line "by the candidate" amended to read: "by him."

Last sentence of first paragraph amended to read: "The Secretary of the Committee upon their written request may sign for members who are absent from the city."

On first line of second paragraph omit: "for admission to the Club."

On fourth line of second paragraph "the college at which he graduated" amended to read: "the college or university from which he was graduated."

On eleventh line of second paragraph "received" amended to read: "conferred."

On thirteenth line of second paragraph after "provisions" add: "of Article VIII."

Added to close: "Further letters respecting the candidate are requested from other members of the Club."

RULE XI. In second line of second paragraph "it appear" amended to read: "if it then appear."

On sixth line of second paragraph "upon the name" amended to read: "upon the candidate."

On the seventh line of second paragraph after "notified" amended to read: "that when the name shall be again reached for consideration if the necessary requirements under the rules of the Committee have not been complied with, or if the information before the Committee respecting the candidate is still insufficient, the name will be rejected, unless special considerations are brought to the attention of the Committee, when, upon vote, the name may be again passed, or removed to the foot of the list, or transferred to the special list."

Section 12 in last book, omitted here.

Rule XII. The President of any university or college, the degrees conferred by which qualify a candidate for election to membership in the University Club, shall be entitled to a preference. The names of candidates who have previously been members of the Club, and have resigned in good standing, shall be entitled to a preference and shall be specially posted as such.

The name of an Army or Navy candidate, who is in active service, may be considered at any meeting upon special vote of the Committee.

(Last paragraph was Section 22 in last book.)

Rule XIII. All Army and Navy candidates shall be placed on a special list, to which may also be transferred on vote of the Committee all candidates on whose behalf an indefinite postponement shall be requested; and names on said list, other than Army and Navy candidates, shall be only considered on motion of a member, at any time after such name would have been reached in regular order, if it has been retained on the regular list.

Section 16 in last book, omitted here.

Section 18 in last book, omitted here.

Rule XVIII. A candidate for non-resident membership shall not be considered by the Committee unless a letter respecting his candidacy has been received from a resident member of the Club. (This was part of Section 16 in last Book.)

Section 20 in last book, omitted here.

Rule XX. The name of a candidate shall not be posted unless and until the degree held by him shall have been approved by the Council.

The name of a candidate holding a degree which has been approved by the Council, and who has been duly proposed and seconded, shall be immediately posted, although three years shall not have elapsed since his graduation.

Section 22 in last book is now last paragraph of Rule XII.

1906

RULE XII. On second line of last paragraph after "service" add: "or of a candidate who is a member of the diplomatic corps or consular service of a foreign government accredited to this country, may be considered at any meeting upon special vote of the Committee."

RULE XIII. Omit on last line: "reached in regular order, if it had been."

1907

RULE XX. Amended to read:

The name of a candidate who has been duly proposed and seconded shall be immediately posted although the degree held by him shall not have been approved by the Council and although three years shall not have elapsed since his graduation.

1908

RULE XI. Amended to read:

At each meeting the Committee will take up the names of candidates beginning at the top of the list, except that by unanimous vote of the members of the Committee present, preference may be given to a candidate of special distinction, who has been duly posted, provided notice of motion for such preference shall have been given at a previous meeting. The name of a candidate to whom such preference is given shall forthwith be specially posted and may be acted on at any subsequent meeting. Preferences given under this rule shall not exceed five in number in any one calendar year.

RULE XIII. On seventh line before "been" add: "reached in regular order, if it had."

1909

RULE XI. Second paragraph amended to read:

When the name of any candidate shall be reached for consideration, if it then appear that no letter has been received from the proposer or seconder, or that the candidate is not personally known to at least one member of the Committee present, or that there is insufficient information before the Committee for final action upon the candidate, the name shall be passed and the proposer and seconder immediately notified that when the name shall be again reached for consideration if the necessary requirements under the rules of the Committee have not been complied with, or if the information before the Committee respecting the candidate is still insufficient, the name will be rejected, unless special considerations are brought to the attention of the Committee, when, upon vote, the name may be again passed, or removed to the foot of the list, or transferred to the special list.

(This paragraph was part of Rule XI in 1907 Book.)

1910

RULE XI. On second line after "candidates" add: "who have been duly posted."

On fifth line after "distinction" add: "or to a candidate who has held the degree which renders him eligible for election for at least twenty-five years."

In last sentence of first paragraph: for "five" read "ten."

On fourth line of second paragraph "to at least one member of the Committee present" amended to read: "to the number of members of the Committee present required by Rule XIX."

RULE XIX. Amended to read:

Candidates for resident membership must be personally known to at least three members, and candidates for non-resident membership must be personally known to at least one member of the Committee present.

1911

RULE XI. First paragraph amended to read:

At each meeting the Committee shall take up for election the names of candidates who have been duly posted beginning at the top of the list. Preferences, however, may be given to a candidate of special distinction, or, for special reasons, to a candidate who has held the degree which renders him eligible for election for at least twenty-five years, provided that such preference shall have been granted at a previous regular meeting of the Committee by the unanimous vote of the members present. The name of a candidate to whom such preference is granted shall forthwith be specially posted, and may be voted upon at any subsequent regular meeting. Not more than ten candidates thus preferred shall be elected during any one calendar year.

1914

RULE X. Amended to read:

Names of candidates proposed for membership in the Club shall be filed with the Secretary of the Committee on Admissions on blank forms to be supplied by the Secretary, and in such form as may be prescribed by the Committee, these forms to be signed by the proposer and seconder, and shall state the University or College from which the candidate was graduated, the date of his birth, the year of his graduation, the degree received by him, his residence, and his profession or occupation. If the candidate have no profession or occupation, that fact shall be stated.

If the eligibility of the candidate depend upon an honorary degree, the fact that the degree is honorary, and the year when the degree was conferred, shall be stated.

The Secretary of the Committee, on the receipt of such blanks in proper form shall, cause the name of the candidate to be posted.

Until such blanks are properly filled out and filed with the Secretary, the name of the candidate shall not be posted.

On receipt of these applications, if they are not properly filled out, they shall at once be returned to the proposer, indicating wherein they are not complete.

In the event of a substituted proposer or seconder the Secretary of the Committee upon the written request of either the proposer or seconder may sign these blanks, in which case a copy of the blank as signed is to be forwarded to the party for whom the Secretary is signing.

A letter of recommendation shall also be required from the proposer and seconder.

Further letters respecting the candidate are requested from other members of the Club.

Resolution of the Council

Passed March 13, 1899

No member of the Council shall hereafter propose or second a candidate for membership in the Club, nor write any letters in relation to any candidate proposed.

APPENDIX V

OFFICERS TO 1914 INCLUSIVE. COUNCILS AND COMMITTEES OF 1865 AND 1867

1865

Officers

President, Theodore W. Dwight.
Vice-President, George V. N. Baldwin.
Treasurer, Theodore B. Bronson.
Secretary, Edward Mitchell.

Trustees

Charles A. Bristed.
Joseph H. Choate.
John T. Johnston.
George T. Strong.
Henry R. Winthrop.

Council

Theodore W. Dwight, *Chairman.*

George V. N. Baldwin.
Charles A. Bristed.
Theodore B. Bronson.
Joseph H. Choate.
John T. Johnston.
Luther M. Jones.
J. P. Kimball.
W. P. Prentice.
George T. Strong.
Edmund Wetmore.
Henry R. Winthrop.

Edward Mitchell, *Secretary.*

House Committee

Henry R. Winthrop, *Chairman.*

Luther M. Jones.
George V. N. Baldwin.

Auditing Committee

Charles Astor Bristed, *Chairman.*

George T. Strong.
W. P. Prentice.

Committee on Admissions

Oliver Bronson, Jr.
Thomas Cochran, Jr.
Jonathan S. Ely.
W. A. O. Hegeman.

Abram S. Hewitt.
Burrall Hoffman.
Horace Howland.
Cortlandt Irving.
William M. Johnson.
B. F. Lee, Jr.
Emlen T. Littell.
William M. Martin.
William D. Morgan.
William B. Ross.
Alfred J. Taylor.
Charles H. Wesson.
Edmund Wetmore.
William C. Whitney.

COMMITTEE ON LITERATURE AND ART

Charles F. Chandler.
S. Whitney Phoenix.
Eugene Schuyler.
Russell Sturgis.
John C. White.

1867

OFFICERS

President, Theodore W. Dwight.
Vice-President, George V. N. Baldwin.
Treasurer, Edward Mitchell.
Secretary, Samuel Huntington.

COUNCIL

Theodore W. Dwight, *Chairman*.
George V. N. Baldwin.
William H. Fuller.
John T. Johnston.
Frank E. Kernochan.
William G. Lathrop, Jr.
Edward Mitchell.
H. E. Tallmadge.
Alfred J. Taylor.
William C. Whitney.
Frank W. Wildes.
I. V. French.
Samuel Huntington, *Secretary*.

COMMITTEE ON ADMISSIONS

B. F. Lee, Jr., *Chairman*.
W. A. Ogden Hegeman, *Secretary*.
Cortlandt Irving.
William M. Johnson.
J. Frederic Kernochan.
Charles P. Kirkland, Jr.
Emlen T. Littell.
Philip S. Van Rensselaer.
Charles H. Wesson.
Buchanan Winthrop.

From 1879 to 1914 the full list can be consulted in the file of Club Annuals in the Library. The lists of officers only are given here:

1879

President, George V. N. Baldwin.
Vice-President, Alfred J. Taylor.
Treasurer, George Hoffman.
Secretary, Buchanan Winthrop.

1879–1880

President, Henry H. Anderson.
Vice-President, George V. N. Baldwin.
Treasurer, George Hoffman.
Secretary, Woolsey Johnson.

1880–1881

President, Henry H. Anderson.
Vice-President, George V. N. Baldwin.
Treasurer, Brayton Ives.
Secretary, Woolsey Johnson.

1881–1882

President, Henry H. Anderson.
Vice-President, George V. N. Baldwin.
Treasurer, Brayton Ives.
Secretary, Woolsey Johnson.

1882–1883

President, Henry H. Anderson.
Vice-President, George V. N. Baldwin.
Treasurer, Brayton Ives.
Secretary, Woolsey Johnson.

1884–1885

President, Henry H. Anderson.
Vice-President, George V. N. Baldwin.
Treasurer, Brayton Ives.
Secretary, Woolsey Johnson.

1886

President, Henry H. Anderson.
Vice-President, George V. N. Baldwin.
Treasurer, Brayton Ives.
Secretary, Woolsey Johnson.

1887 (MARCH)

President, Henry H. Anderson.
Vice-President, George V. N. Baldwin.
Treasurer, Brayton Ives.
Secretary, Franklin Bartlett.

1887 (JULY)

President, Henry H. Anderson.
Vice-President, James W. Alexander.
Treasurer, Brayton Ives.
Secretary, Franklin Bartlett.

1888

President, George A. Peters.
Vice-President, James W. Alexander.
Treasurer, Brayton Ives.
Secretary, Allen W. Evarts.

1889–1890

President, George A. Peters.
Vice-President, James W. Alexander.
Treasurer, Brayton Ives.
Secretary, Allen W. Evarts.

1890–1891

President, George A. Peters.
Vice-President, Charles C. Beaman.
Treasurer, George C. Clark.
Secretary, Allen W. Evarts.

1891–1892

President, James W. Alexander.
Vice-President, Charles C. Beaman.
Treasurer, George Sherman.
Secretary, Stephen H. Olin.

1892–1893

President, James W. Alexander.
Vice-President, Charles C. Beaman.
Treasurer, George Sherman.
Secretary, Hugh D. Auchincloss.

1893–1894

President, James W. Alexander.
Vice-President, Charles C. Beaman.
Treasurer, George Sherman.
Secretary, Hugh D. Auchincloss.

1894–1895

President, James W. Alexander.
Vice-President, Charles C. Beaman.
Treasurer, George Sherman.
Secretary, Hugh D. Auchincloss.

1895–1896

President, James W. Alexander.
Vice-President, Charles C. Beaman.
Treasurer, George Sherman.
Secretary, Hugh D. Auchincloss.

1896–1897

President, James W. Alexander.
Vice-President, Charles C. Beaman.
Treasurer, George Sherman.
Secretary, Hugh D. Auchincloss.

1897–1898

President, James W. Alexander.
Vice-President, Charles C. Beaman.
Treasurer, George Sherman.
Secretary, Hugh D. Auchincloss.

1898–1899

President, James W. Alexander.
Vice-President, Charles C. Beaman.
Treasurer, George Sherman.
Secretary, Hugh D. Auchincloss.

1899–1900

President, Charles C. Beaman.
Vice-President, Henry E. Howland.
Treasurer, George Sherman.
Secretary, Hugh D. Auchincloss.

1900–1901

President, Charles C. Beaman.
Vice-President, Henry E. Howland.
Treasurer, George Sherman.
Secretary, Hugh D. Auchincloss.

1901–1902

President, Henry E. Howland.
Vice-President, Edmund Wetmore.
Treasurer, Walter G. Oakman.
Secretary, Otto T. Bannard.

1902–1903

President, Henry E. Howland.
Vice-President, Edmund Wetmore.
Treasurer, Walter G. Oakman.
Secretary, Otto T. Bannard.

1903–1904

President, Henry E. Howland.
Vice-President, Edmund Wetmore.
Treasurer, Walter G. Oakman.
Secretary, Otto T. Bannard.

1904–1905

President, Henry E. Howland.
Vice-President, Edmund Wetmore.
Treasurer, Walter G. Oakman.
Secretary, William Manice.

1905–1906

President, Edmund Wetmore.
Vice-President, Charles T. Barney.
Treasurer, Walter G. Oakman.
Secretary, William Manice.

1906–1907

President, Edmund Wetmore.
Vice-President, Charles T. Barney.
Treasurer, Walter G. Oakman.
Secretary, William Manice.

1907–1908

President, Edmund Wetmore.
Vice-President, Charles T. Barney.
Treasurer, Walter G. Oakman.
Secretary, William Manice.

1908–1909

President, Edmund Wetmore.
Vice-President, B. Aymar Sands.
Treasurer, Walter G. Oakman.
Secretary, William Manice.

1909–1910

President, Edmund Wetmore.
Vice-President, B. Aymar Sands.
Treasurer, Walter G. Oakman.
Secretary, William Manice.

1910–1911

President, B. Aymar Sands.
Vice-President, Thomas Thacher.
Treasurer, Walter G. Oakman.
Secretary, William Manice.

1911–1912

President, B. Aymar Sands.
Vice-President, Thomas Thacher.
Treasurer, Walter G. Oakman.
Secretary, William Manice.

1912–1913

President, B. Aymar Sands.
Vice-President, Thomas Thacher.
Treasurer, Walter G. Oakman.
Secretary, William Manice.

1913–1914

President, Thomas Thacher.
Vice-President, Henry Dodge Cooper.
Treasurer, Walter G. Oakman.
Secretary, William Manice.

1914–1915

President, Thomas Thacher.
Vice-President, Henry Dodge Cooper.
Treasurer, Walter G. Oakman.
Secretary, Samuel Sloan.

APPENDIX VI

ROLL OF MEMBERS 1865

Adams, Charles D.
Adams, Frederic.
Anderson, E. Ellery.
Andrews, James B.
Armstrong, Wm. N.

Baldwin, Geo. V. N.
Ball, Alonzo B.
Barnard, F. A. P.
Benkard, James, Jr.
Birkhead, W. H.
Bliss, Robert.
Borden, M. C. D.
Bristed, Charles A.
Bronson, Oliver, Jr.
Bronson, Theo. B.
Brown, Hubert S.
Butler, Francis R.

Carpenter, Robert J.
Chalmers, George.
Chandler, C. F.
Choate, Joseph H.
Clarke, Isaac E.
Cochran, Thomas, Jr.
Cogswell, A. K.
Cooper, Edward.
Cortelyou, A. V.

De Forest, Edward.
De Lancey, Wm. H., Jr.
Depew, Chauncey M.
Dimock, Henry F.
Dwight, T. W.

Eaton, D. Cady.
Eaton, Daniel C.
Eaton, Sherburne B.
Edwards, Alfred L.
Ely, Jonathan S.

Fiske, John S.
Fuller, Wm. H.

Gallatin, Frederic.
Gandy, William.
Gilman, Chas. M.
Greene, A. N.

Hallowell, N. P.
Harral, Fred F.
Hawley, Henry E.
Hegeman, W. A. O.
Hewitt, Abram S.
Hoffman, Burrall.
Hoffman, George.
Hopkins, L. Gardner.
Hoppin, Frederic.
Hoppin, Wm. H.
Howland, Horace.
Hunt, Thomas G.
Huntington, Samuel.
Hurlbut, Wm. H.
Hyde, E. Francis.

Irving, Cortlandt.

Johnson, Wm. M.
Johnston, John T.
Jones, Luther M.

Keese, Sidmon T.
Kennett, Thomas A.
Kernochan, Frank E.

Kernochan, John A.
Kernochan, J. Fred.
Ketcham, William.
Kimball, J. P.
Kirkland, Chas. P., Jr.

Lathrop, Wm. G., Jr.
Lee, B. F., Jr.
Lewis, Charlton T.
Littell, Emlen T.

MacVeagh, Franklin.
Manice, Edward A.
Martin, Wm. M.
Matson, Wm. L.
Mitchell, Edward.
Morgan, Wm. D.
Morris, A. Newbold.

Pennington, Wm.
Phelps, Wm. Walter.
Phoenix, Steph. W.
Pratt, W. H. B.
Prentice, Wm. P.

Roosevelt, S. Weir.
Ross, Wm. B.

Schermerhorn, H. A.
Schmidt, H. I.
Schuyler, Eugene.
Smith, Normand.
Stevens, Fred. W.
Strong, Geo. T.
Sturgis, Appleton.
Sturgis, Russell, Jr.
Sweetser, Chas. H.

Taylor, Alfred J.
Taylor, Henry A. C.

Wallis, Hamilton.
Ward, Frederic A.
Wesson, Chas. H.
Wetmore, Edmund.
White, John C.
White, Oliver S.
White, Thomas H.
Whitney, Wm. C.
Wight, P. B.
Williams, Ralph O.
Winthrop, B.
Winthrop, Henry R.

Young, Geo. B.
Young, Mason.

ROLL OF MEMBERS, JUNE 1, 1879.

Abbott, Frank.
Adee, Frederick W.
Adee, George A.
Adee, P. Henry.
Alden, R. Percy.
Alexander, Archibald.
Alexander, Charles B.
Alexander, Henry M.
Alexander, James W.
Alexander, Lawrence D.
Alexander, William.
Anderson, Henry H.
Anderson, James H.
Anderson, Nicholas L.
Andrews, Henry C.
Appleton, Daniel S.
Appleton, Francis R.
Appleton, George S.
Armstrong, William N.
Asch, Morris J.
Astor, John Jacob.
Atterbury, Chas. L.
Auchincloss, Edgar S.
Auchincloss, John W.

Babcock, Henry D.
Baker, Frederic.
Baldwin, Frederic H.

Baldwin, Geo. V. N.
Ball, Alonzo B.
Bangs, George P.
Bangs, L. Bolton.
Barlow, Francis C.
Barnes, Henry B.
Barney, Charles T.
Barry, Thomas G.
Bartlett, Franklin.
Bartlett, Willard.
Baylis, William.
Beals, Joshua G.
Beekman, James Wm.
Belknap, R. Lenox.
Belmont, Perry.
Bement, Edward.
Benson, Frank S.
Berwind, Edward J.
Betts, C. Wyllys.
Betts, Frederic H.
Bigelow, William B.
Bigelow, W. Sturgis.
Binsse, Louis E.
Bixby, Robert F.
Blagden, Thomas.
Blagden, Samuel P.
Blake, John Ellis.
Blake, Stanton.
Blanchard, Edward R.
Bliss, George T.
Bond, Henry R.
Bond, William.
Bowles, Samuel.
Briggs, James H.
Brinsmade, James B.
Bristol, Louis H.
Bristow, Benjamin H.
Bromley, Isaac H.
Bronson, Edward B.
Bronson, Theo. B.
Brooks, John E.
Brooks, Wilton.
Brown, Charles S.
Brownell, T. Frank.
Bryant, F. Eugene.
Bryce, Carroll C.
Buck, Albert H.
Bull, Charles S.
Bull, William T.
Bumstead, Freeman J.
Burden, Joseph W.
Burgess, John W.
Butler, Prescott Hall.

Caldwell, Wm. E.
Cameron, Alex.
Cammann, Donald M.
Campbell, Benjamin H.
Canfield, A. Cass.
Carmalt, William H.
Carter, Franklin.
Chandler, Chas. F.
Chase, George.
Chase, Leslie.
Chauncey, Elihu.
Chittenden, Horace H.
Clark, George C.
Clark, Louis C.
Cleveland, Clement.
Clymer, Meredith.
Coddington, Chas. E.
Coffin, Edmund, Jr.
Cole, Hamilton.
Cole, Hugh L.
Collier, M. Dwight.
Cooper, Edward.
Cornell, Robert C.
Coudert, Fred. R.
Cram, Henry A.
Crane, J. Frederick.
Crawford, Samuel W.
Crocker, Henry H., Jr.
Curtis, William E., Jr.
Cutler, Arthur H.
Cutting, W. Bayard.

Dabney, Virginius.
Dakin, Edward S.
Dalton, John C.
Dana, Paul.

Dawson, Benjamin F.
Day, Henry M.
Day, Walter De Forest.
De Forest, Henry W.
De Forest, Robert W.
Delafield, A. Floyd.
Delavan, D. Bryson.
Deming, Chas. C.
Deming, Clarence.
Deming, Henry C.
Dennis, Frederic S.
Depew, Chauncey M.
Derby, Richard H.
Dexter, Julius.
Dillaway, Geo. W.
Dimock, Henry F.
Dixon, William P.
Dodge, Arthur M.
Dodge, George E.
Douglass, George.
Drake, John.
Drayton, J. Coleman.
Duane, James May.
Dudley, Henry.
Duer, William A.
Dunning, Frank.
Dunning, Wm. F.
Dwight, Stanley.
Dwight, Theo. W.

Earle, Joseph P.
Eaton, D. Cady.
Eaton, Sherburne B.
Edgar, Jonathan.
Edmonds, Walter D.
Edsall, Thomas Henry.
Ely, Alfred.
Emmett, Bache McE.
Eno, Henry C.
Eno, John C.

Fales, Haliburton.
Farnam, Charles H.
Farnam, Geo. Bronson.
Farnam, Henry.
Farnam, Henry W.
Farnham, A. Bradford.
Farragut, Loyall.
Faulkner, Henry J.
Fellowes, Richard S.
Fitzgerald, Louis.
Flagg, William J.
Flint, Austin.
Flint, Austin, Jr.
Folsom, George W.
Foster, Fred. DeP.
Fox, Austen G.
Fuller, William H.

Gardner, H. G.
Garrettson, Francis T.
Gilbert, Frederick.
Gilbert, James H.
Gillette, Walter R.
Godwin, Bryant.
Godwin, Parke.
Goldthwaite, Henry.
Goodwin, Almon.
Goodwin, Wendell.
Gordon, F. W.
Gould, Chas. W.
Gracie, Chas. King.
Graves, Arthur B.
Green, Ashbel.
Greenleaf, Richd. C., Jr.
Greenough, John.
Grimball, John.
Gulliver, William C.

Hadden, Harold F.
Hall, Frank L.
Halsey, Frederick R.
Hamersley, William.
Hamilton, Alan McLane.
Hamilton, R. Ray.
Harper, Joseph W., Jr.
Harrison, Burton N.
Harrison, Robert L.
Hart, George.
Hawes, Granville P.

Hawley, Henry E.
Hawley, James M.
Heald, John O.
Heaton, Edward.
Henderson, Isaac, Jr.
Higgins, Anthony.
Higgins, Cecil Campbell.
Higginson, James J.
Hillhouse, James.
Hitchcock, Charles.
Hoffman, George.
Holbrook, Levi.
Holland, Arthur.
Holley, Alex. L.
Holt, Charles.
Holt, George C.
Holt, Henry.
Hornblower, Wm. B.
Horton, Chas. P.
Houston, Francis H.
Howland, Henry E.
Hoyt, Gerald L.
Hubbard, Grosvenor L.
Hudson, Edward McK.
Hunt, Thomas G.
Hunter, James B.

Imbrie, Charles F.
Ingersoll, Charles D.
Ireland, Fred. G.
Iselin, Isaac.
Iselin, William E.
Isham, Charles.
Ives, Brayton.
Ives, Robert S.

Jenkins, Francis.
Jenner, William A.
Johnes, Edw. R.
Johnson, Samuel W.
Johnson, Samuel Wm.
Johnson, Woolsey.
Johnston, Ross.
Jones, Luther M.

Kean, John, Jr.
Kean, Julian H.
Kelley, Robert.
Kent, James, Jr.
Kernochan, Frank E.
Kernochan, J. Frederic.
Keyes, Edward L.
Kidder, Camillus G.
Kingsbury, Frederic J.
Kingsford, John P.
Kinnicutt, Frank P.
Kirkland, Chas. P., Jr.
Knevals, S. W.
Knight, Charles H.
Knowlson, J. H.

Larocque, Joseph.
Lawrence, Robert.
Lawrence, Walter B.
Lawton, Francis.
Ledyard, L. Cass.
Lee, B. Franklin.
Lee, William H. L.
Lefferts, Geo. M.
Le Roy, Henry W.
Lewis, J. Ivers.
Lewis, Thomas C.
Lincoln, Arthur.
Livingston, Johnston.
Livingston, Louis.
Loomis, Alfred L.
Loring, Edward G., Jr.
Loubat, Joseph F.
Lyman, Hart.

McBride, Thomas A.
McBurney, Charles.
McCook, John J.
McKeen, James.
McKim, Charles F.
McLane, James W.
McLean, Thomas.
McMartin, Archibald.
McMartin, Malcolm.

McVeagh, Franklin.
MacDonald, James A.
MacDonough, Aug. Rodney.
Magee, George J.
Magie, David.
Mansfield, Howard.
Markoe, Thomas M.
Marsh, Charles C.
Marsh, Othniel Chas.
Mason, John J.
Matthews, Albert.
Mead, Edward S.
Mead, Frederick, Jr.
Mead, William R.
Merrill, Charles E.
Merrill, Edward B.
Merrill, Payson.
Metcalf, Jas. Betts.
Metcalfe, John T.
Miller, Charles A.
Miller, Charles P.
Miller, Philip S.
Mills, Charles A.
Mitchell, Alfred.
Mitchell, Cornelius B.
Mitchell, Edward.
Mitchell, Roland G.
Mitchell, William, Jr.
Montgomery, Wm., Jr.
Moorhead, W. E. C.
Morgan, Wm. Forbes.
Morse, G. Livingston.
Morse, Richard C.
Morse, Sidney B.
Mortimer, Henry C.
Morton, William J.
Mount, Richard E.
Murray, Augustus S., Jr.
Murray, Charles P.
Murray, David.
Murray, Russell.

Nash, John McL.
Nicoll, De Lancey.
Nicoll, Henry D.
Nicoll, Mathias.
Norton, Charles L.

Ogden, Cadwalader E.
Ogden, Charles W.
Ogden, Ludlow.
Olin, Stephen Henry.
Olmstead, Frank H.
Olney, Peter B.
Ord, Joseph P.
Osborn, Thomas W.
Osborne, Henry F.
Osgood, James R.
Otis, Fessenden N.

Palfrey, Francis W.
Pancoast, Richard.
Parker, Willard, Jr.
Parkin, William.
Parrish, Samuel L.
Paton, David.
Payne, Oliver H.
Peabody, George L.
Peaslee, Edward H.
Pell, Wm. Cruger.
Pellew, Henry E.
Pennington, William.
Perry, John G.
Perry, Robert C.
Peters, George A.
Phelps, Benjamin K.
Phelps, Wm. Walter.
Pinckney, Thomas.
Platt, Johnson T.
Polk, William M.
Purdy, John H.
Purdy, Wm. McNeven.
Pyne, M. Taylor.

Reade, Robert L.
Redmond, Roland.
Reid, Whitelaw.
Richards, Wm. W.
Richardson, W. L.

Richmond, Howard.
Robbins, George A.
Robinson, Beverley.
Robinson, Douglass, Jr.
Rogers, Archibald.
Romaine, Louis T.
Root, Elihu.
Ross, William B.
Rumrill, James A.
Russell, S. Howland.

Sampson, Edward C.
Sanford, Chas. P.
Sargent, John O.
Satterlee, F. Le Roy.
Satterthwaite, Thos. E.
Schenck, Noah Hunt.
Schmidt, Oscar E.
Scribner, Charles.
Scudder, Henry J.
Sedgwick, Henry D.
Sexton, Samuel.
Sheffield, Geo. St. John.
Sherman, Thomas P.
Silliman, Benjamin, Jr.
Simmons, J. Edward.
Simpkins, Nath'l S., Jr.
Simpson, John W.
Skidmore, Wm. B.
Sloane, Henry T.
Sloane, Thomas C.
Sloane, Wm. M.
Smith, D. Henry.
Smith, Elliot.
Smith, Harold.
Smith, James H.
Smith, John Cotton.
Smith, J. Lawrence.
Smith, Nathaniel S.
Smith, Richmond M.
Smith, Robert Hobart.
Smith, Samuel E.
Smith, Sutherland D.
Soutter, James T.
Speir, Gilbert M.
Speir, Gilbert, M., Jr.
Stead, Charles M.
Stedman, Edmund C.
Stevens, Alexander H.
Stevens, Frederic W.
Stewart, Lispenard.
Stewart, Wm. A. W.
Stimson, Daniel M.
Stimson, Lewis A.
Stoddard, Charles A.
Stone, Henry.
Stratton, Sidney V.
Sturgis, Frederic R.
Sturgis, Russell, Jr.
Sutherland, John L.
Swift, Augustus M.

Talbot, Richmond.
Taylor, Alfred J.
Terry, Roderick.
Thacher, Thomas.
Thompson, Walter.
Thornell, Henry L.
Ticknor, Benjamin H.
Tompkins, Hamilton B.
Townsend, Jas. M., Jr.
Tracy, Charles.
Tredick, T. Salter.
Tuckerman, Alfred.
Tuckermann, Walter C.
Turner, Herbert B.
Twombly, Arthur B.
Twombly, Hamilton McK.

Upham, William R.

Van Buren, William H.
Vanderpoel, A. Ernest.
Van Duzer, Henry S.
Van Nest, Alexander T.
Van Rensselaer, Alex.
Van Santvoord, Chas.
Van Sinderen, Adrian.
Van Slyck, George W.
Varnum, James M.

Wadsworth, James W.
Walker, Henry F.
Waller, Elwyn.
Ward, Edmund A.
Waters, Edward E.
Watrous, George H.
Webb, Alexander S.
Webb, G. Creighton.
Webb, H. Walter.
Weeks, Francis H.
Weld, Francis M.
Wells, Manning C.
West, Charles W.
Westervelt, Ellsworth.
Weston, Theodore.
Wetmore, Edmund.
Wetmore, William B.
Weyman, Charles S.
Wheeler, John D.
Wheeler, John V.
Wheeler, Samuel H.
Wheelock, George G.
White, John P. P.
Whitehead, G. Irvine.
Whitin, Louis F.
Whitney, Eli, Jr.
Whitney, William C.
Whitridge, Fredk. W.
Wickes, Edward A.
Wilcox, George A.
Wilkinson, Alfred.
Williams, Charles P.
Williams, Talcott.
Williamson, David B.
Wilson, William G.
Winston, Gustavus S.
Winthrop, Buchanan.
Witherbee, Frank S.
Wood, H. Duncan.
Wood, J. Hampden.
Woodruff, Morris.
Woolsey, Theodore S.
Wynkoop, Gerardus H.

Young, Mason.
Young, Thomas S., Jr.
Youngs, Graham.

Members, 502.

APPENDIX VII

LIFE MEMBERS TO JULY 31, 1914

Aitken, John W. . . . . Princeton '69
Appleton, Francis R. . . . . Harvard '75
Auchincloss, John W. . . . . Yale '73

Bannard, Otto T. . . . . Yale '76
Bement, Edward. . . . . Yale '70
Bertron, Samuel R. . . . . Yale '85
Betts, Samuel R. . . . . Yale '75
Bixby, Robert F. . . . . Trinity '70
Butler, Prescott Hall. . . . . Harvard '69

Campbell, Oliver S. . . . . Columbia '91
Clarke, Courtlandt C. . . . . Princeton '78
Clarke, R. Floyd. . . . . C. C. N. Y. '80
Cooper, Henry Dodge. . . . . C. C. N. Y. '72
Cutting, W. Bayard. . . . . Columbia '69

Davenport, William B. . . . . Yale '67
Davis, Gherardi. . . . . Univ. of France '79
Dixon, William P. . . . . Yale '68

Edmonds, Walter D. . . . . Williams '74
Evans, Hartman Kuhn. . . . . Univ. of France '79
Evarts, Allen W. . . . . Yale '69

Fish, Nicholas. . . . . Columbia '67
Foster, Fred De Peyster. . . . . Columbia '68
Fulton, Louis M. . . . . Cornell '74

Greer, Louis Morris. . . . . Harvard '91
Gurnee, Augustus Coe. . . . . Harvard '78

Hall, Frank L. . . . . Yale '72
Halsey, Frederic Robert. . . . . Harvard '68
Harkness, Edward S. . . . . Yale '97

Harriman, Oliver....Princeton '83
Heath, Frank E....Cornell '76
Hewitt, Erskine....Princeton '91
Hodges, Amory G....Harvard '74
Hopkins, A. Lawrence....Williams '63
Hyde, Henry St. John....Columbia '96
Hyde, James H....Harvard '98

Ingalls, Melville Edgar....Harvard '92
Ingraham, Phœnix....Harvard '98

Jarrett, Edwin S....Rens. Pol. Inst. '89
Jennings, Walter....Yale '80

Landon, Francis G....Princeton '81
Lincoln, Arthur....Brown '70
Loubat, Joseph F....Univ. of France '47

Markle, John....Lafayette '80
Mathews, Charles T....Yale '86
McCook, John J....Kenyon '66
Mitchell, Rowland G....C. C. N. Y. '61
Murray, Ambrose S., Jr....Trinity '71

Nott, Frederick J....Rochester '74

Parsons, Henry....Columbia '88
Peabody, George Livingston....Columbia '70
Pell, Frederick A....Princeton '71

Satterlee, Herbert L....Columbia '83
Schermerhorn, John E....C. C. N. Y. '72
Shearer, George L....Princeton '90
Sheldon, Edward W....Princeton '79
Sheppard, John S., Jr....Williams '91
Sherman, George....Columbia '75
Sherrill, Charles H....Yale '89
Sloane, William....Yale '95
Slocum, Thomas W....Harvard '90
Smith, Howard C....Harvard '93
Stout, Andrew Varick....Columbia '93

Talmage, John F....Yale '95
Tuckerman, Eliot....Harvard '94
Tuttle, George M....Yale '77

Van Nest, G. Willett.................................Harvard '74

Weld, Francis M.......................................Harvard '97
Wendell, Evert Jansen...............................Harvard '82
White, Alexander M..................................Harvard '92
White, Harold T.......................................Harvard '97

Life Members, 70

APPENDIX VIII

DEATHS

1879 TO JULY 31, 1914

ADMITTED	NAME	DIED
Nov. 1, 1893	Abbot, Philip Stanley	Aug. 5, 1896
May 10, 1879	Abbott, Frank	April 20, 1897
March 14, 1880	Adams, George H	April 8, 1900
Oct. 14, 1902	Adams, John Brown	April 3, 1907
June 2, 1886	Addison, William	Oct. 13, 1899
May 10, 1879	Adee, Frederick W	Aug. 25, 1900
May 10, 1879	Adee, Georg A	Aug. 12, 1908
May 10, 1879	Adee, Philip Henry	May 28, 1912
Oct. 4, 1882	Alexander, Henry C	June 28, 1894
May 10, 1879	Alexander, Henry M	Sept. 9, 1899
Jan. 7, 1891	Alexander, Robert C	Nov. 4, 1899
Oct. 1, 1884	Alexander, Samuel	Nov. 29, 1910
Nov. 4, 1896	Alexander, Walter	May 21, 1909
Jan. 19, 1899	Allan, George S	Jan. 15, 1911
Jan. 4, 1888	Allen, Charles Slover	Oct. 15, 1893
Dec. 1, 1886	Allen, Henry Wilder	Oct. 13, 1891
Jan. 5, 1887	Allen, John De Witt	Nov. 8, 1902
Sept. 12, 1879	Alsop, Joseph W	June 30, 1891
Jan. 5, 1898	Amen, Harlan Page	Nov. 9, 1913
Nov. 18, 1902	Ames, Sullivan D	Feb. 22, 1903
Feb. 17, 1898	Ames, William	March 8, 1914
May 10, 1879	Amory, Copley	Dec. 16, 1879
May 10, 1879	Amory, Edward Linzee	Nov. 19, 1911
Jan. 4, 1888	Amory, Robert	Aug. 27, 1910
April 4, 1888	Anable, Eliphalet Nott	Oct. 18, 1904
May 6, 1885	Anderson, E. Ellery	Feb. 24, 1903
May 10, 1879	Anderson, Henry Hill	Sept. 17, 1896
Nov. —, 1879	Anderson, Humphrey	May 13, 1880
May 10, 1879	Anderson, Nicholas L	Sept. 18, 1892
Nov. 5, 1884	Anderson, William D	March 8, 1901
Dec. 1, 1886	Andrew, John F	May 30, 1895
May 10, 1879	Andrews, Henry C	Aug. 19, 1897
Nov. 7, 1883	Andrews, William W	Dec. 23, 1897
June 16, 1898	Angell, Elgin Adelbert	July 4, 1898

ADMITTED	NAME	DIED
Nov. 2, 1887	Anthon, Edward	Sept. 15, 1903
May 10, 1879	Appleton, Daniel S.	Nov. 13, 1890
May 10, 1879	Appleton, George S.	Jan. 10, 1886
Feb. 1, 1882	Arthur, Elliott John	Jan. 26, 1886
May 10, 1879	Asch, Morris J.	Oct. 5, 1902
May 10, 1879	Astor, John Jacob	Feb. 22, 1890
Nov. 8, 1884	Atterbury, W. Wallace	Aug. 5, 1911
May 10, 1879	Auchincloss, Edgar S.	March 13, 1892
Nov. 27, 1899	Auchincloss, Edgar S.	May 4, 1910
March 5, 1884	Auchincloss, Hugh D.	April 22, 1913
Oct. 1, 1890	Babcock, William C.	March 11, 1896
Oct. 4, 1893	Baker, Alfred S.	Oct. 13, 1896
May 10, 1879	Baker, Frederic	June 15, 1913
———, 1865	Baldwin, George Van Nest	Feb. 24, 1908
Oct. 21, 1897	Baldwin, William H., Jr.	Jan. 3, 1905
May 10, 1879	Ball, Alonzo Brayton	Oct. 24, 1908
March 1, 1905	Bangs, Merwin Bolton	Dec. 25, 1909
Dec. 22, 1899	Barber, Amzi L.	April 17, 1909
Jan. 7, 1882	Barber, Thomas Henry	March 16, 1905
April 6, 1898	Barbey, Henry I.	July 9, 1906
Oct. 4, 1893	Barge, Benjamin F.	Oct. 30, 1902
Dec. 4, 1879	Barker, Fordyce	May 30, 1891
May 10, 1879	Barlow, Francis C.	Jan. 11, 1896
May 10, 1879	Barnes, Henry Burr	Jan. 12, 1911
Sept. 15, 1879	Barnes, John Sanford	Nov. 22, 1911
Dec. 3, 1883	Barnette, William G.	April 20, 1909
April 5, 1882	Barney, Albert C.	Dec. 6, 1902
May 10, 1879	Barney, Charles Tracy	Nov. 14, 1907
June 16, 1898	Barrett, Franklin R.	Jan. 5, 1912
July 6, 1899	Barrett, George C.	June 7, 1906
March 6, 1889	Barrows, William Eliot	July 30, 1901
May 6, 1903	Barstow, Donald McL.	June 9, 1906
May 10, 1897	Bartlett, Franklin	April 23, 1909
June 1, 1887	Barton, Frederick O.	Feb. 14, 1904
March 5, 1884	Batcheller, Oliver A.	Oct. 30, 1893
June 3, 1891	Bates, Alfred E.	Oct. 13, 1909
Oct. 21, 1897	Baur, William	March 22, 1913
May 10, 1879	Baylis, Abraham B.	Jan. 20, 1896
Jan. 3, 1894	Beach, Francis G.	Dec. 30, 1902
May 4, 1892	Beach, Rodmond Vernon	Sept. 29, 1898
May 10, 1879	Beadleston, William H.	Oct. 27, 1895
Feb. 4, 1891	Beale, Charles F. T.	Sept. 1, 1901
Dec. 6, 1899	Beam, John R.	July 4, 1903

ADMITTED	NAME	DIED
June 9, 1879	Beaman, Charles C	Dec. 15, 1900
May 6, 1885	Beekman, Henry Rutgers	Dec. 17, 1900
May 10, 1879	Beekman, James William	Aug. 7, 1908
May 6, 1885	Beekman, John Neilson	April 26, 1912
July 9, 1879	Belknap, Henry	Jan. 21, 1909
May 10, 1879	Belknap, Robert Lenox	March 13, 1896
Nov. 2, 1892	Belmont, Oliver H. P	June 10, 1909
May 20, 1902	Benham, Henry K	April 7, 1904
——, 1880	Benjamin, Samuel N	May 12, 1886
May 7, 1884	Benjamin, William H	Jan. 31, 1907
Oct. 3, 1888	Bennett, Charles Gibson	Sept. 8, 1910
Feb. 3, 1897	Benson, Edwin N	April 18, 1909
May 10, 1879	Benson, Frank Sherman	Feb. 28, 1907
Jan. 6, 1897	Bettens, Thomas S	July 2, 1907
May 10, 1879	Betts, C. Wyllys	April 27, 1887
May 10, 1879	Betts, Frederic H	Nov. 11, 1905
Nov. 1, 1879	Betts, George F	Jan. 19, 1898
June 5, 1882	Biddle, A. Sydney	April 11, 1891
May 2, 1888	Bigelow, Russell A	Nov. 2, 1890
Nov. 2, 1904	Bigelow, Walter P	March 7, 1907
April 6, 1898	Billings, Frederick	May 5, 1913
July 19, 1879	Bishop, William D	Feb. 4, 1904
Oct. 8, 1885	Bishop, William D	Jan. 23, 1912
Feb. 7, 1912	Bissell, Clarence H	July 7, 1912
Feb. 7, 1883	Bissell, Wilson Shannon	Oct. 6, 1903
May 10, 1879	Bixby, Robert F	Oct. 16, 1900
March 14, 1880	Blagden, George	Jan. 1, 1905
May 10, 1879	Blagden, Thomas	Nov. 5, 1892
Oct. 5, 1887	Blaine, Emmons	June 18, 1891
May 5, 1886	Blaine, Walker	Jan. 5, 1890
May 10, 1879	Blake, John Ellis	Sept. 27, 1880
May 10, 1879	Blake, Stanton	April 21, 1889
Jan. 5, 1887	Blake, Theodore A	Jan. 6, 1914
May 10, 1879	Bliss, George T	March 24, 1901
May 3, 1882	Bloodgood, Delavan	April 5, 1902
Feb. 11, 1881	Boardman, Derick Lane	Sept. 6, 1893
Oct. 6, 1879	Boardman, Edward C	Jan. 1, 1901
June 5, 1895	Boardman, Elijah G	July 21, 1900
June 5, 1884	Boies, Henry Martyn	Dec. 12, 1903
May 4, 1887	Bolton, H. Carrington	Nov. 19, 1903
May 10, 1879	Bond, Henry R	Oct. 29, 1909
April 3, 1889	Bonner, Frederic	Jan. 3, 1911
May 2, 1888	Bonney, George B	Nov. 11, 1909
May 20, 1897	Borden, Matthew C. D	May 27, 1912

ADMITTED	NAME	DIED
March 5, 1884	Bowers, Arthur F	Nov. 3, 1905
June 16, 1898	Boyd, John Y	March 10, 1914
May 4, 1887	Boyle, St. John	Jan. 7, 1906
March 14, 1904	Bradley, Arthur C	Nov. 2, 1911
May 7, 1884	Brearley, Samuel, Jr	Dec. 6, 1886
Feb. 6, 1884	Breed, Henry L	Dec. 6, 1886
Nov. 7, 1888	Brewster, Charles O	June 26, 1912
June 2, 1897	Brewster, Walter Shaw	March 29, 1913
May 3, 1883	Brewster, William Cullen	May 30, 1900
July 7, 1886	Bridgman, William R	Sept. 15, 1894
Nov. 2, 1892	Brigham, William S	May 23, 1906
Jan. 5, 1884	Bright, Osborn E	March 15, 1892
Feb. 4, 1885	Brimmer, Martin	Jan. 14, 1896
May 10, 1879	Brinsmade, James B	Jan. 4, 1884
May 10, 1879	Bristol, Louis H	July 20, 1910
Nov. 6, 1895	Bronk, John B	Jan. 22, 1904
May 10, 1879	Bronson, Theodore Bailey	Dec. 4, 1881
May 22, 1880	Brooks, Arthur	July 10, 1895
———, 1868	Brooks, John E	Feb. 21, 1913
May 6, 1885	Brown, F. Tilden	May 7, 1910
Jan. 19, 1899	Brown, Geo. Whitfield, Jr	May 25, 1903
Nov. 17, 1898	Brown, John Clifford	Jan. 16, 1901
March 2, 1887	Brown, John Crosby	June 25, 1909
May 1, 1889	Brown, John Mason	Jan. 29, 1890
June 3, 1885	Brown, Robert M. G	Dec. 14, 1906
May 10, 1879	Brownell, T. Frank	Jan. 7, 1901
July 7, 1886	Brumby, Thomas M	Dec. 17, 1899
May 1, 1895	Bryan, Joseph	Nov. 20, 1908
Dec. 2, 1891	Buckingham, Benjamin H	Jan. 15, 1906
March 1, 1893	Buckingham, Chas. L	May 31, 1909
June 2, 1886	Buell, George C	Dec. 17, 1910
Dec. 1, 1881	Buell, Henry W	Jan. 30, 1893
April 25, 1880	Buffum, Charles T	July 28, 1914
May 10, 1879	Bull, Charles Stedman	April 17, 1911
May 10, 1879	Bull, William T	Feb. 22, 1909
May 18, 1899	Bullitt, Thomas W	March 3, 1910
May 10, 1879	Bumstead, Freeman Josiah	Nov. 28, 1879
May 19, 1898	Bunce, John Lee	Oct. 1, 1907
July 13, 1881	Burden, Henry	Dec. 17, 1910
May 10, 1879	Burden, Joseph W	May 28, 1903
Dec. 2, 1891	Burden, William Fletcher	Nov. 21, 1897
Oct. 15, 1892	Burgess, Thomas	Feb. 15, 1912
Feb. 3, 1886	Burhans, Frederick O	Nov. 21, 1896
Jan. 4, 1888	Burns, Charles C	March 21, 1901

ADMITTED	NAME	DIED
Nov. 7, 1894	Burr, Charles H.	Nov. 28, 1910
Jan. 8, 1902	Butler, George P.	April 7, 1911
May 10, 1879	Butler, Prescott Hall	Dec. 16, 1901
April 15, 1902	Byers, Dallas C.	Aug. 26, 1909
Feb. 1, 1893	Byrd, Alfred H.	Dec. 5, 1897
May 19, 1898	Cabot, Arthur Tracy	Nov. 4, 1912
May 2, 1888	Cadwalader, John L.	March 11, 1914
Nov. 2, 1898	Calhoun, Frederic S.	Nov. 23, 1899
Mar. 2, 1887	Calhoun, Henry W.	March 4, 1906
Oct. 4, 1882	Campbell, William C.	Feb. 5, 1899
May 10, 1879	Canfield, A. Cass	March 24, 1904
Jan. 6, 1892	Cantine, Charles F.	July 14, 1912
March 7, 1888	Carey, William	Oct. 17, 1901
Dec. 4, 1895	Carlisle, Calderon	Sept. 16, 1901
Dec. 22, 1898	Carmalt, Churchill	Jan. 8, 1905
April 5, 1893	Carpender, John Neilson	Nov. 21, 1911
Dec. 5, 1883	Carter, James C.	Feb. 14, 1905
Oct. 11, 1881	Cary, Clarence	Aug. 27, 1911
July 2, 1884	Case, Augustus L., Jr.	Oct. 17, 1890
Nov. 6, 1879	Castle, Frederick A.	April 28, 1902
July 1, 1879	Caswell, William H.	May 3, 1908
May 5, 1897	Cauldwell, Thomas W.	April 11, 1909
April 6, 1881	Chandler, Parker C.	March 20, 1908
Feb. 17, 1898	Chapin, Frederick L.	Dec. 19, 1913
Nov. 3, 1886	Chapin, Henry Bainbridge	May 7, 1910
Oct. 7, 1891	Chapman, Henry G.	Jan. 16, 1913
May 3, 1886	Chapman, S. Hartwell	April 15, 1903
Nov. 5, 1884	Chase, William Leverett	Oct. 7, 1895
April 1, 1885	Chenery, Leonard	March 10, 1901
Nov. 18, 1897	Cheney, Knight Dexter, Jr.	Aug. 17, 1910
April 7, 1887	Chisholm, Walter S.	Dec. 4, 1890
May 10, 1879	Chittenden, Horace H.	Dec. 26, 1909
Dec. 5, 1900	Church, Theodore W.	March 27, 1914
Oct. 1, 1884	Clapp, Channing	March 13, 1904
Jan. 6, 1882	Clark, Charles P.	March 21, 1901
April 1, 1885	Clark, Charles W.	July 1, 1906
March 2, 1887	Clark, Edmund Sanford	May 28, 1907
June 5, 1884	Clark, George H., Jr.	Jan. 21, 1907
Dec. 1, 1886	Clark, William B.	Oct. 11, 1912
March 1, 1882	Clarke, Edward Smith	Aug. —, 1911
March 17, 1898	Clement, Stephen M.	March 26, 1913
May 10, 1879	Clymer, Meredith	April 20, 1902
Nov. 3, 1897	Clymer, W. B. Shubrick	May 9, 1903

ADMITTED	NAME	DIED
Nov. 15, 1904	Coffin, Edward R	Sept. 2, 1907
Nov. 8, 1880	Coffin, William H	July 31, 1912
April 5, 1883	Colby, Charles L	Feb. 26, 1896
May 10, 1879	Cole, Hamilton	Oct. 27, 1889
May 10, 1879	Cole, Hugh Laing	Nov. 5, 1898
May 7, 1902	Cole, William W	March 6, 1909
June 16, 1898	Coles, Edward	Aug. 4, 1906
May 10, 1879	Collier, Maurice Dwight	Jan. 10, 1906
Nov. 5, 1890	Collin, Roswell Park	Dec. 21, 1891
Feb. 6, 1895	Conant, Osmyn P	Oct. 8, 1910
May 4, 1887	Cooke, Augustus P	Sept. 7, 1896
———, 1865	Cooper, Edward	Feb. 25, 1905
Jan. 5, 1887	Cooper, Philip H	Dec. 29, 1912
Feb. 4, 1891	Cornwell, Charles C	Feb. 3, 1904
May 10, 1879	Coudert, Frederick R	Dec. 20, 1903
Nov. 2, 1887	Cowing, John H	Feb. 22, 1906
Oct. 4, 1899	Cowman, Edward D	Nov. 26, 1899
Oct. 5, 1904	Cox, Charles F	Jan. 24, 1912
March 2, 1892	Cox, Jennings S., Jr	Aug. 31, 1913
March 1, 1905	Cox, Sterling Browne	May 22, 1908
Feb. 2, 1887	Crane, John J	March 4, 1890
May 10, 1879	Crawford, Samuel W	Nov. 3, 1892
Dec. 5, 1900	Crocker, Adams	Feb. 8, 1910
May 10, 1879	Crocker, William B	Jan. 4, 1886
Dec. 7, 1887	Cromwell, Frederic	June 22, 1914
May 2, 1888	Cromwell, Henry B	May 1, 1896
May 1, 1901	Crowe, William M	Dec. 10, 1906
June 17, 1902	Culver, A. E	June 23, 1909
March 1, 1893	Cunningham, John M	Jan. 14, 1897
Feb. 1, 1888	Curtis, F. Randolph	June 10, 1892
Oct. 4, 1899	Curtis, John G	Sept. 20, 1913
Jan. 1, 1891	Curtiss, John W	Feb. 11, 1911
May 10, 1879	Cutting, W. Bayard	March 1, 1912
Jan. 4, 1905	Cutting, W. Bayard, Jr	March 10, 1910
Oct. 1, 1884	Cuyler, Cornelius C	July 3, 1909
May 10, 1879	Dabney, Virginius	June 2, 1894
Oct. 11, 1881	Da Costa, Charles M	June 24, 1890
Feb. 16, 1899	Dahlgren, John Vinton	Aug. 11, 1899
May 10, 1879	Dakin, Edward S	Dec. 6, 1888
May 4, 1887	Dana, George Eames	April 18, 1906
Feb. 6, 1889	Dana, William B	Oct. 10, 1910
Jan. 2, 1895	Danforth, Charles	March 13, 1896
April 1, 1885	Davenport, Russell W	Feb. 28, 1904

ADMITTED	NAME	DIED
Oct. 6, 1879	Davies, William G	July 26, 1910
Feb. 5, 1896	Davis, Charles	Dec. 21, 1913
April 5, 1883	Davis, G. Pierrepont	April 1, 1914
May 10, 1879	Dawson, Benjamin F	April 3, 1888
Dec. 7, 1887	Day, George Lord	Dec. 14, 1900
May 10, 1879	Day, Henry Mills	Oct. 12, 1901
May 20, 1897	Day, Wilbur F	May 26, 1914
Nov. 5, 1884	Dean, Richard Crane	June 9, 1910
July 6, 1898	Deans, Charles Herbert	March 6, 1909
Oct. 4, 1882	Dearborne, Frederick M	April 24, 1887
Oct. 21, 1897	De Grove, E. Ritzema	July 17, 1911
May 10, 1879	Delafield, Augustus Floyd	July 18, 1904
May 10, 1879	Deming, Clarence	May 8, 1913
Dec. 22, 1879	Denison, D. Stewart	July 1, 1898
June 1, 1892	Denny, Daniel, Jr	May 9, 1896
June 5, 1879	De Peyster, Frederick J	May 10, 1905
May 10, 1879	Derby, Richard H	July 4, 1907
June 5, 1884	DeRenne, Everard	March 8, 1894
Oct. 4, 1893	DeWitt, George G	Jan. 12, 1912
May 10, 1879	Dexter, Julius	Oct. 21, 1898
July 13, 1881	Dickins, Francis W	Sept. 15, 1910
Dec. 6, 1893	Dillon, John A	Oct. 15, 1902
Nov. 8, 1882	Dillon, John Forest	May 5, 1914
May 10, 1879	Dimock, Henry F	April 10, 1911
Nov. 2, 1892	Doane, William C	May 17, 1913
May 10, 1879	Dodge, Arthur Murray	Oct. 17, 1896
June 7, 1899	Dodge, George E	April 14, 1904
July 7, 1880	Donnelly, Edward C	Jan. 4, 1891
Oct. 1, 1884	Doolittle, Hiram L	June 15, 1903
May 10, 1879	Drake, John	March 30, 1885
Jan. 2, 1884	Draper, George	April 4, 1891
Jan. 3, 1900	Driggs, Henry Peck	July 10, 1907
May 10, 1879	Duane, James May	Dec. 2, 1912
Nov. 17, 1879	DuBois, Coert	Jan. 1, 1891
Nov. 3, 1886	DuBois, John Jay	Nov. 11, 1898
May 10, 1879	Dunning, William F	April 1, 1907
June 16, 1898	Durkee, Joseph H	July 4, 1898
Jan. 8, 1902	Duryee, Edward H	Dec. 7, 1905
June 6, 1888	Duryee, George S	Oct. 29, 1896
Dec. 5, 1883	Easton, David Augustus	March 1, 1894
May 10, 1879	Eaton, D. Cady	May 11, 1912
May 10, 1879	Edgar, Jonathan	——, 1879*

* Date uncertain.

ADMITTED	NAME	DIED
May 18, 1899	Edgerton, W. P	June 24, 1904
May 10, 1879	Edsall, Thomas Henry	Oct. 26, 1897
Feb. 1, 1899	Eggleston, Arthur F	Nov. 30, 1909
Jan. 16, 1900	Egleston, William C	March 25, 1907
July 9, 1880	Ellis, William Rogers	Jan. 31, 1903
Nov. 5, 1884	Elmer, Richard A	Oct. 1, 1888
July 13, 1881	Elwood, Frank W	June 8, 1899
Nov. 5, 1881	Emmons, Samuel Franklin	March 28, 1911
May 10, 1879	Eno, Henry C	July 16, 1914
May 4, 1887	Erben, Henry	Oct. 23, 1909
March 7, 1883	Evans, Robley D	Jan. 3, 1912
Dec. 6, 1882	Evans, Thomas Grier	March 28, 1905
Nov. 3, 1888	Evarts, Maxwell	Oct. 7, 1913
April 5, 1882	Evarts, William M	Feb. 28, 1901
Oct. 6, 1897	Ewing, David Q	Oct. 1, 1900
April 20, 1899	Faile, Thomas Hall	Jan. 26, 1902
June 6, 1906	Fair, Joseph B	Nov. 24, 1907
Feb. 1, 1899	Farnam, Charles H., Jr	May 8, 1909
May 10, 1879	Farnam, Charles Henry	Sept. 24, 1909
May 10, 1879	Farnam, Henry	Oct. 4, 1883
May 10, 1879	Fellows, Richard S	March 10, 1884
May 4, 1892	Fendall, Reginald	Feb. 22, 1898
July 13, 1881	Ferry, Charles H	May 2, 1910
Dec. 2, 1885	Fincke, Frederick Getman	Nov. 4, 1912
April 5, 1882	Fish, Nicholas	Sept. 16, 1902
Oct. 11, 1881	Fisher, Eustace W	March 5, 1894
June 2, 1897	Fiske, Robert F	Jan. 24, 1901
March 7, 1894	Fiske, Willard	Sept. 17, 1904
May 10, 1879	Fitzgerald, Louis	Oct. 6, 1908
May 10, 1879	Flagg, William J	April 15, 1898
May 3, 1893	Flick, Liddan	July 2, 1905
May 21, 1879	Flint, Austin	March 13, 1886
Feb. 5, 1902	Flower, Nathan M	Dec. 1, 1906
Dec. 17, 1901	Foote, Wallace T., Jr	Dec. 17, 1910
Dec. 29, 1879	Forbes, Francis	Feb. 18, 1904
Oct. 1, 1890	Forrest, Charles Robert	Oct. 6, 1912
April 1, 1885	Forster, H. Waldo	July 6, 1913
April 1, 1908	Fowler, Albert C	March 26, 1911
Dec. 1, 1880	Fowler, Horace W	July 20, 1888
April 5, 1883	Francke, Joaquin John	May 17, 1894
April 5, 1893	Francke, Leopold	April 16, 1902
Feb. 16, 1899	Freeman, Ernest Grey	March 6, 1900
Jan. 4, 1899	Fremont, J. C	March 8, 1911

ADMITTED	NAME	DIED
April 4, 1888	Frisby, William B	June 6, 1902
Feb. 2, 1898	Frothingham, Benjamin T	April 30, 1902
May 10, 1879	Fry, James B	July 11, 1894
———, 1865	Fuller, William H	Nov. 26, 1902
June 17, 1897	Gardiner, Thomas A	Oct. 30, 1913
Dec. 17, 1901	Garretson, Abram Q	June 3, 1907
Jan. 3, 1894	Garrison, Lloyd McKim	Oct. 4, 1900
March 2, 1892	Garth, Granville William	Dec. 25, 1903
Dec. 7, 1887	Gaul, Edward Linus	April 2, 1894
April 21, 1899	Gherardi, Bancroft	Dec. 10, 1903
May 2, 1894	Gibbs, Edward N	Oct. 20, 1900
June 2, 1886	Gibbs, John Blair	June 12, 1898
May 6, 1908	Gilbert, Charles B	Aug. 27, 1913
Nov. 2, 1892	Gilbert, Frederick	Dec. 20, 1911
Feb. 6, 1884	Gilbert, William Thurston	July 1, 1908
Dec. 2, 1908	Gill, Martin E	June —, 1911
June 1, 1892	Gillespie, John M	Feb. 20, 1908
April 4, 1900	Gillette, Daniel G	May 30, 1913
May 10, 1879	Gillette, Walter R	Nov. 7, 1908
June 6, 1883	Gilley, Franklin Wm	July 25, 1909
Feb. 3, 1897	Gillis, James H	Dec. 7, 1910
Oct. 5, 1887	Gilman, Daniel Coit	Oct. 13, 1908
May 10, 1879	Gilmore, Quincy Adams	April 7, 1888
March 6, 1889	Goddard, Norton	May 28, 1905
Jan. 2, 1895	Godey, Harry	Jan. 30, 1909
May 10, 1879	Goldthwaite, Henry	Jan. 3, 1895
May 2, 1889	Goodard, Warren Norton	July 10, 1900
July 19, 1879	Goodenow, John Holmes	July 29, 1906
May 10, 1879	Goodwin, Almon	Nov. 2, 1905
March 4, 1891	Goodwin, C. Ridgely	May 19, 1894
May 10, 1879	Goodwin, Wendell	March 1, 1898
Oct. 5, 1887	Goodwin, William H	Feb. 18, 1905
May 10, 1879	Gordon, Florian W	Oct. 26, 1885
Dec. 3, 1881	Gorringe, Henry H	July 6, 1885
June 5, 1884	Gray, Horace	Sept. 15, 1902
March 17, 1898	Gray, James	June 20, 1904
May 10, 1879	Green, Ashbel	Sept. 4, 1898
May 11, 1880	Green, Charles Ewing	Dec. 26, 1897
June 6, 1883	Green, George Walton	Dec. 13, 1903
March 1, 1899	Greene, Francis B	April 8, 1911
April 6, 1892	Greene, S. Dana	Jan. 8, 1900
May 10, 1879	Greenleaf, Richard C	Dec. 4, 1913
Sept. 15, 1879	Greenough, William	July 8, 1902

ADMITTED	NAME	DIED
May 4, 1898	Greenwood, Isaac J	Dec. 16, 1911
Oct. 8, 1885	Greenwood, Thomas	June 2, 1894
Oct. 3, 1894	Griffin, Eugene	April 10, 1907
Nov. 4, 1896	Griffith, Daniel J	July 2, 1909
May 10, 1879	Grinnell, Morton	Dec. 10, 1905
Nov. 3, 1886	Griscom, William W	Sept. 24, 1897
May 10, 1879	Gulliver, William C	May 24, 1909
May 3, 1882	Guthrie, Alexander M	Nov. 30, 1899
June 5, 1895	Hagerman, James J	Sept. 14, 1909
Jan. 6, 1904	Haight, Edward	Sept. 20, 1913
Jan. 3, 1883	Hale, Henry	Dec. 10, 1890
Oct. 4, 1905	Hale, Herbert D	Nov. 10, 1908
April 4, 1900	Hall, John Manning	Jan. 27, 1905
Oct. 7, 1891	Hall, William Cornelius	June 6, 1911
May 5, 1884	Hamersley, J. Hooker	Sept. 15, 1901
June 5, 1889	Hamill, Samuel McClintock	July 29, 1907
May 10, 1879	Hamilton, Robert Ray	Aug. 23, 1890
Feb. 7, 1893	Hamlin, Frederic H	Nov. 12, 1884
May 20, 1902	Hamlin, Teunis S	April 17, 1907
Nov. 7, 1883	Hancock, Winfield Scott	Feb. 9, 1886
June 5, 1889	Hand, Clifford A	Aug. 17, 1901
Oct. 5, 1892	Hapgood, Asa P	April 7, 1912
Nov. 5, 1884	Harding, George J	Dec. 23, 1911
June 1, 1898	Harper, Charles S	April 5, 1911
May 10, 1879	Harper, Joseph W	July 21, 1896
Dec. 5, 1900	Harper, William R	Jan. 10, 1906
June 3, 1891	Harriman, James Arden	April 20, 1909
Jan. 16, 1880	Harris, Robert Duncan	Feb. 2, 1903
May 3, 1882	Harris, William Hamilton	Nov. 6, 1895
May 10, 1879	Harrison, Burton Norvell	March 29, 1904
Dec. 5, 1906	Harrison, Charles L	Sept. 14, 1912
Feb. 7, 1906	Harrison, Edmond P	Oct. 7, 1913
May 10, 1879	Hart, George	April 2, 1883
April 6, 1887	Hartley, Frank	June 19, 1913
Jan. 3, 1883	Hartwell, Walker	July 19, 1891
Sept. 10, 1879	Harwood, Edwin	Jan. 12, 1902
Jan. 3, 1883	Hastings, George S	Jan. 1, 1909
March 18, 1902	Hathorn, Frank H	March 25, 1913
May 10, 1879	Hawes, Granville P	Dec. 29, 1893
May 10, 1879	Hawley, Henry E	Feb. 10, 1899
June 2, 1880	Hayden, Horace John	Dec. 7, 1900
Jan. 6, 1882	Hayes, Augustus A	April 17, 1892
Oct. 19, 1880	Hayes, Robert Somers	March 2, 1905

ADMITTED	NAME	DIED
Jan. 2, 1889	Haynes, David A	Dec. 8, 1890
June 16, 1898	Hazard, John M	June 7, 1900
Oct. 8, 1885	Hazard, Rowland	Aug. 16, 1898
May 10, 1879	Heald, John Oxenbridge	Oct. 10, 1911
April 6, 1898	Hegeman, John A	Sept. 22, 1908
Oct. 20, 1898	Heins, George L	Sept. 25, 1907
Nov. 7, 1888	Henry, Frank L	Oct. 25, 1899
Feb. 17, 1903	Herod, Joseph R	Aug. 13, 1908
Oct. 8, 1885	Herrick, Charles Brown	July 29, 1896
Dec. 1, 1886	Herrick, Edwin Hayden	Feb. 6, 1889
March 1, 1893	Hewitt, James	June 30, 1894
May 6, 1885	Hickox, Ralph W	March 26, 1910
May 4, 1892	Hidden, Charles Henry	May 22, 1907
May 10, 1879	Higginson, James Jackson	Jan. 5, 1911
Dec. 4, 1907	Hilton, George P	Oct. 7, 1909
Oct. 7, 1891	Hinkle, Charles M	June 7, 1913
Feb. 1, 1899	Hiscock, Albert J	March 7, 1908
May 6, 1908	Hiss, Philip H., Jr	Feb. 27, 1913
Jan. 6, 1886	Hitchcock, Henry	March 18, 1902
July 2, 1884	Hitchcock, Hiram	Dec. 30, 1900
May 4, 1892	Hoadley, Frederick Hodges	Feb. 25, 1895
April 7, 1886	Hobson, Henry Wise	Aug. 13, 1898
Sept. 30, 1879	Hodges, John H	Sept. 27, 1891
Dec. 1, 1881	Hodgson, Telfair	Sept. 11, 1893
Feb. 3, 1886	Hoffman, Burrall	Sept. 12, 1903
May 10, 1879	Hoffman, George	Sept. 1, 1885
April 4, 1894	Holden, Albert F	May 18, 1913
July 13, 1881	Holden, Daniel J	June 21, 1903
May 7, 1902	Holden, Edwin Babcock	June 8, 1906
March 3, 1909	Holden, L. E	Aug. 26, 1913
July 24, 1879	Holladay, Waller	Oct. 1, 1907
May 10, 1879	Holley, Alexander Lyman	Jan. 29, 1882
May 4, 1892	Holman, John Charles	May 18, 1898
Oct. 14, 1902	Homans, William P	May 12, 1910
Nov. 6, 1907	Hone, Joseph B	Dec. 31, 1912
Feb. 16, 1880	Hopkins, A. Lawrence	April 4, 1912
Nov. 18, 1902	Hopkins, Henry	Aug. 18, 1908
April 4, 1888	Hopkins, Henry C	Sept. 8, 1908
Jan. 3, 1894	Hopkins, William S. Bennett	Jan. 14, 1900
Feb. 1, 1899	Hoppin, Frederick S	May 29, 1907
April 6, 1892	Hoppin, J. Mason	Jan. 23, 1897
Nov. 10, 1881	Hoppin, William Warner	Jan. 3, 1913
Nov. 7, 1883	Hornblower, Joseph C	Aug. 22, 1908
May 10, 1879	Hornblower, William B	June 16, 1914

ADMITTED	NAME	DIED
Nov. 23, 1880	Horton, Henry K	Dec. 15, 1887
March 6, 1907	Hosley, H. H	Jan. 6, 1908
March 6, 1901	Houghton, Henry O	June 14, 1906
Nov. 4, 1896	Howe, John Edward	Sept. 16, 1908
May 10, 1879	Howe, Walter	Aug. 22, 1890
May 10, 1879	Howland, Henry Elias	Nov. 7, 1913
Nov. 7, 1888	Hoyt, Alfred W	Nov. 20, 1911
April 2, 1884	Hudson, E. Darwin, Jr	May 9, 1887
March 4, 1885	Huidekoper, Frederic W	April 29, 1908
June 10, 1880	Hun, Leonard G	March 11, 1891
Dec. 3, 1900	Hunsicker, Joseph L	March 30, 1900
Oct. 20, 1903	Hunt, Albert G	May 21, 1905
Jan. 16, 1880	Hunt, Richard M	July 31, 1895
May 10, 1879	Hunter, James B	June 9, 1889
May 6, 1885	Huntington, William R	July 26, 1909
Feb. 1, 1905	Hurlbut, William H	Feb. 18, 1905
May 6, 1885	Hurry, Edmund Abdy	April 8, 1912
Nov. 3, 1886	Hurtt, B. Scott	Oct. 10, 1888
Nov. 1, 1880	Husted, James W	Sept. 25, 1892
June 1, 1887	Hutchinson, Charles H	Oct. 31, 1902
June 15, 1893	Hutchinson, Morison T	Sept. 30, 1897
Feb. 7, 1900	Hutton, Laurence	June 10, 1904
Oct. 15, 1901	Hyde, Frank E	Dec. 2, 1906
June 22, 1899	Hyde, Lewis H	March 6, 1913
May 10, 1879	Imbrie, Charles F	Nov. 3, 1899
———, 1867	Ingersoll, Charles D	Jan. 8, 1905
May 3, 1905	Irvin, William	Feb. 22, 1909
Jan. 16, 1900	Irwin, Theodore D	Aug. 17, 1910
Nov. 6, 1879	Isham, Edward Swift	Feb. 16, 1902
Oct. 5, 1902	Isham, Pierrepont	May 19, 1906
April 6, 1887	Isham, Samuel	June 12, 1914
Oct. 3, 1888	Ives, Edward Bernard	Dec. 30, 1903
May 10, 1879	Ives, Robert S	June 9, 1906
July 7, 1897	Ives, Sherwood B	Feb. 16, 1907
March 3, 1897	Ivison, Henry	April 7, 1910
March 2, 1898	Jackson, Philip Nye	March 3, 1911
April 3, 1895	Jackson, William Fessenden	May 17, 1913
May 10, 1879	Jenkins, Frank	Sept. 16, 1913
Nov. 6, 1889	Jerome, John Lathrop	Nov. 22, 1903
Nov. 8, 1881	Jesup, Morris K	Jan. 22, 1908
May 10, 1879	Johnes, Edward Rodolph	March 28, 1903
Oct. 7, 1891	Johnes, Henry Pierson	Nov. 28, 1898

ADMITTED	NAME	DIED
Dec. 1, 1897	Johnson, John Mackie	Oct. 24, 1898
May 10, 1879	Johnson, Samuel Wm	Nov. 25, 1895
Feb. 17, 1901	Johnson, Walcott H	Jan. 15, 1912
May 10, 1879	Johnson, Woolsey	June 21, 1887
July 13, 1881	Johnston, Colles	Sept. 11, 1886
May 10, 1879	Johnston, Ross	March 11, 1885
June 6, 1888	Joline, Adrian H	Oct. 5, 1912
June 5, 1912	Jones, Dwight A	Dec. 7, 1913
Nov. 7, 1888	Jones, Harry Madison	Dec. 3, 1899
Nov. 7, 1884	Jones, Walter R. T	March 26, 1906
Feb. 17, 1898	Kane, Theodore F	March 14, 1908
March 1, 1893	Keener, William A	April 22, 1913
Oct. 8, 1885	Keep, William Bristol	June 17, 1906
Jan. 4, 1888	Kellogg, Wainwright	June 3, 1899
May 4, 1892	Kemp, George William	Dec. 24, 1912
June 1, 1881	Kenrick, Henry L	March 24, 1891
May 10, 1879	Kent, James	Jan. 20, 1901
Feb. 2, 1887	Kent, Linden	Oct. 4, 1892
May 20, 1897	Kernan, Leslie W	Sept. 6, 1903
May 10, 1879	Kernochan, Frank E	Sept. 26, 1884
Jan. 5, 1898	Kimball, Harold C	Feb. 1, 1911
Oct. 7, 1896	Kimball, Paul T	Nov. 3, 1910
Oct. 1, 1890	King, Charles G., Jr	July 14, 1911
May 4, 1887	King, Edward	Nov. 19, 1908
May 4, 1892	King, Hiram Udall	May 3, 1907
Nov. 12, 1880	King, John L	June 18, 1907
May 10, 1879	Kingsbury, Fred. John	Sept. 30, 1910
May 10, 1879	Kingsford, John Parish	March 7, 1891
May 10, 1879	Kinnicutt, Frank P	May 2, 1913
Dec. 6, 1893	Kip, William Fargo	July 5, 1905
Nov. 3, 1886	Knevals, Edward W	Aug. 19, 1890
May 10, 1879	Knevals, Sherman W	Dec. 4, 1908
Feb. 10, 1880	Knowlton, D. Henry	Feb. 17, 1894
Dec. 22, 1898	Lamarche, Henry J	Jan. 31, 1913
Aug. 8, 1879	Lambert, Edward W	July 18, 1904
Jan. 15, 1893	Lambert, Elliot Cowden	April 8, 1914
Oct. 4, 1899	Lamont, Daniel S	July 23, 1905
June 1, 1892	Lampson, William	Feb. 14, 1897
June 3, 1885	Lansing, Abraham	Oct. 4, 1899
May 10, 1879	Larocque, Joseph	June 9, 1908
Feb. 6, 1884	Larremore, Richard L	Sept. 13, 1893
———, 1865	Lathrop, William G., Jr	Aug. 3, 1896

ADMITTED	NAME	DIED
Jan. 6, 1886	Lawrence, Amory A.	July 6, 1912
Dec. 1, 1886	Lawrence, James	Feb. 25, 1914
Oct. 7, 1891	Lawrence, Joseph	Dec. 9, 1898
May 10, 1879	Lawrence, Walter Bowne	Jan. 12, 1912
July 19, 1879	Lawson, Leonidas M.	March 28, 1909
Dec. 3, 1884	Lawton, Alexander R.	July 2, 1896
June 1, 1904	Layng, James D. W.	Feb. 12, 1907
Feb. 3, 1904	Leatherbee, George H.	Dec. 14, 1911
——, 1865	Lee, Benjamin Franklin	March 3, 1907
Jan. 3, 1900	Lee, Franklin L.	May 18, 1911
Jan. 8, 1908	Lee, James G. K.	Sept. 18, 1909
April 5, 1882	Lemoine, Ashton	Feb. 12, 1907
Dec. 6, 1893	Lewis, Charles H.	March 31, 1911
Oct. 21, 1897	Lewis, Edwin A. S.	Sept. 5, 1906
Nov. 17, 1879	Lewis, Eugene H.	March 1, 1907
May 10, 1879	Lewis, James Ivers	April 23, 1890
May 10, 1879	Lewis, Thomas C.	Dec. 29, 1881
Dec. 3, 1890	Lillie, Abraham B. H.	Dec. 11, 1905
Feb. 3, 1897	Lincoln, Ezra	Aug. 16, 1907
Oct. 5, 1892	Lincoln, Lowell, Jr.	Sept. 19, 1906
March 2, 1881	Lincoln, Rufus P.	Nov. 27, 1900
Feb. 1, 1888	Linderman, Robt. Parker	Jan. 21, 1903
Nov. 6, 1901	Line, Arthur M.	May 29, 1904
Jan. 3, 1883	Lisle, Robert Patton	Oct. 30, 1911
Oct. 2, 1901	Livermore, John R.	May 2, 1906
Nov. —, 1881	Livingston, Beverly	June 30, 1883
Jan. 5, 1881	Loeser, Charles McK.	Feb. 24, 1896
Jan. 16, 1900	Long, Thomas J.	Nov. 20, 1905
Feb. 6, 1889	Loomis, Frank	Sept. 11, 1904
March 7, 1894	Loomis, Henry P.	Dec. 22, 1907
Dec. 1, 1880	Lord, Daniel	April 5, 1899
Jan. 5, 1881	Lord, Franklin B.	Jan. 27, 1908
Dec. 11, 1879	Lord, George De Forest	March 3, 1892
May 10, 1879	Loring, Edward G., Jr.	April 23, 1888
Jan. 5, 1898	Ludlow, William	Aug. 30, 1901
May —, 1880	Lyman, Joseph	Sept. 6, 1883
Feb. 3, 1897	Lynde, Rollin Harper	April 7, 1907
April 14, 1903	Lyon, William H. J.	May 2, 1908
April 4, 1900	McBride, Herbert	March 13, 1907
May 10, 1879	McBride, Thomas A.	Sept. 3, 1886
May 10, 1879	McBurney, Charles	Nov. 7, 1913
Nov. 3, 1897	McCammon, Joseph Kay	Jan. 2, 1907
April 14, 1903	McCandless, Harry D.	March 26, 1912

ADMITTED	NAME	DIED
Feb. 6, 1884	McClintock, Walter Lowrie	March 3, 1911
May 10, 1879	McCook, John J	Sept. 17, 1911
July 6, 1887	McCosh, Andrew J	Dec. 2, 1908
Nov. 2, 1892	McCrackin, Alexander	Jan. 3, 1911
Nov. 17, 1898	McCreery, John A	Nov. 10, 1889
Oct. 17, 1900	McGahan, C. F	Feb. 15, 1910
June 5, 1889	McIlvaine, Clarence W	Dec. 7, 1912
May 10, 1879	McKeen, James	Feb. 22, 1911
May 10, 1879	McKeever, Chauncey	Sept. 4, 1901
May 10, 1879	McKim, Charles F	Sept. 14, 1909
May 10, 1879	McMartin, Archibald	May 7, 1881
Dec. 7, 1883	McMichel, William	April 20, 1893
Oct. 5, 1892	McMillan, James Howard	May 9, 1902
Dec. 7, 1887	McMillan, William C	Feb. 21, 1907
June 6, 1894	McNair, Frederick V	Nov. 28, 1900
May 7, 1884	MacNaughton, James	Dec. 29, 1905
Oct. 5, 1887	McNeille, Robert G. S	Oct. 19, 1903
April 6, 1887	McVickar, William Bard	March 30, 1901
May 10, 1879	Magee, George Jefferson	March 11, 1897
Feb. 1, 1899	Makay-Smith, Alexander	Nov. 16, 1911
Jan. 2, 1895	Malcom, George I	Oct. 2, 1910
Jan. 6, 1882	Mallery, John Conrad	Dec. 6, 1912
May 20, 1897	Manice, William	Jan. 19, 1914
April 7, 1897	Marble, Frank	Feb. 14, 1911
April 1, 1885	Markle, George B	July 11, 1914
Aug. 4, 1881	Markoe, Francis Hartman	Sept. 13, 1907
Nov. 8, 1881	Marquand, Frederick A	Dec. 20, 1885
April 6, 1892	Marsh, Elias J	Aug. 3, 1908
July 7, 1886	Marshall, Frederic Panet	Dec. 30, 1886
Oct. 1, 1884	Martin, James Porter	Feb. 19, 1895
June 2, 1886	Martine, Randolph B	March 30, 1895
May 7, 1884	Marvin, Joseph H	Aug. 26, 1887
March 18, 1902	Marvin, Richard P	June 23, 1906
Oct. 3, 1888	Mason, Edward G	Dec. 18, 1898
Oct. 3, 1888	Mason, Theodore B. M	Oct. 16, 1899
Dec. 3, 1884	Mason, William	March 13, 1892
Oct. 3, 1883	Massey, Solon F	July 12, 1901
June 5, 1907	Mather, Robert	Oct. 24, 1911
Feb. 21, 1880	Mayo, William S	Nov. 22, 1895
May 10, 1879	Mead, Edward S	Jan. 10, 1894
Nov. 4, 1885	Medcalf, William M	Oct. 21, 1886
Feb. 7, 1900	Meigs, John	Nov. 6, 1911
May 19, 1898	Melliss, D. Ernest	March 25, 1913
June 4, 1890	Mentz, George W	Feb. 11, 1906

ADMITTED	NAME	DIED
Jan. 15, 1880	Merrick, William	May —, 1887*
June 5, 1884	Merril, George	June 24, 1888
Oct. 5, 1910	Merrill, William H.	Dec. 2, 1913
May 10, 1879	Metcalf, James Betts	Feb. 1, 1896
Oct. 1, 1884	Miley, John	Oct. 12, 1910
May 10, 1879	Miller, Charles A.	Dec. 29, 1897
June 9, 1879	Miller, Charles E.	Dec. 20, 1906
May 10, 1879	Miller, Charles P.	Aug. 24, 1887
June 2, 1897	Miller, Deane	Dec. 29, 1905
March 2, 1898	Miller, Guy B.	April 7, 1903
March 17, 1903	Miller, M. Rumsey	July 2, 1905
———, 1867	Miller, Philip S.	May 10, 1896
May 4, 1898	Miller, Theodore F.	May 20, 1913
March 7, 1894	Millet, Francis D.	April 15, 1912
Oct. 1, 1884	Mills, Arthur	Jan. 1, 1907
June 5, 1882	Mills, Samuel M.	Sept. 8, 1907
Feb. 16, 1899	Milton, David M.	Jan. 3, 1913
Oct. 6, 1886	Minor, Israel, Jr.	June 13, 1894
May 10, 1879	Minor, James Monroe	March 23, 1897
May 10, 1879	Mitchell, Alfred	April 27, 1911
April 4, 1894	Mitchell, Charles E.	March 17, 1911
———, 1867	Mitchell, Cornelius B.	May 25, 1910
May 10, 1879	Mitchell, Edward	Feb. 15, 1909
May 10, 1879	Mitchell, Rowland G.	Jan. 6, 1906
Feb. 1, 1905	Moffat, Alexander	Feb. 23, 1914
June 21, 1900	Monsarrat, Nicholas	Sept. 30, 1910
April 3, 1889	Moore, Thomas S.	April 2, 1899
May 10, 1879	Moorhead, William E. C.	Nov. 29, 1894
Nov. 4, 1908	Morgan, J. Pierpont	March 31, 1913
June 12, 1880	Morison, George S.	July 1, 1903
Nov. 26, 1879	Morison, Samuel L.	May 21, 1907
July 6, 1887	Morrison, Charles C.	May 13, 1894
May 10, 1879	Morse, G. Livingston	Jan. 13, 1894
April 21, 1898	Morse, Henry Grant	June 2, 1903
May 10, 1879	Mortimer, Henry C.	Sept. 30, 1912
May 10, 1880	Mortimer, John H.	May 15, 1883
May 7, 1884	Morton, Bowditch	July 18, 1909
April 6, 1887	Mosher, Joseph F.	April 8, 1894
Jan. 5, 1881	Mostyn, Berkeley	April 25, 1908
May 10, 1879	Mount, Richard E.	——— 1880*
March 3, 1886	Mullin, Joseph	Sept. 2, 1897
Dec. 6, 1880	Munroe, John	Dec. 1, 1904
April 21, 1898	Murphy, Archibald A.	May 19, 1905

* Date uncertain.

ADMITTED	NAME	DIED
March 16, 1899	Myers, John Ripley	Dec. 22, 1899
May 5, 1897	Mynderse, Wilhelmus	Nov. 15, 1906
Oct. 3, 1888	Nason, Daniel	March 14, 1911
May 3, 1883	Nason, Henry B	Jan. 18, 1895
Oct. 7, 1896	Nason, Henry T	April 3, 1903
Feb. 3, 1897	Nelson, Henry Loomis	Feb. 29, 1908
Feb. 6, 1889	Nevin, William W	Sept. 27, 1899
May 15, 1880	Newel, Stanford	April 6, 1907
Dec. 10, 1881	Newell, George Baldwin	April 20, 1907
Feb. 7, 1883	Nichols, Star Hoyt	May 30, 1909
Jan. 5, 1898	Noble, Alfred	April 19, 1914
April 1, 1891	Noble, John H	Dec. 3, 1904
Dec. 1, 1886	Norris, George A	June 30, 1891
May 10, 1879	Norton, Charles L	Dec. 15, 1909
July 11, 1883	Nott, Frederick J	Aug. 17, 1904
Aug. 1, 1881	Nye, Charles F	Dec. 23, 1905
May 6, 1908	O'Brien, Edward D	April 9, 1912
Oct. 2, 1901	O'Connor, Thomas D	Jan. 1, 1904
Nov. 18, 1897	Odell, Hammond	Feb. 9, 1908
May 10, 1879	Ogden, Cadwalader E	March 3, 1888
May 10, 1879	Ogden, Charles W	June 11, 1895
May 3, 1882	Ogden, Gouverneur M	Feb. 11, 1895
April 6, 1887	Ogden, Thomas Ludlow	Oct. 2, 1894
July 7, 1886	Ogden, Walter	Feb. 18, 1914
Dec. 7, 1898	Olcott, John J	April 10, 1899
June 1, 1887	Olyphant, Vernon	Dec. 14, 1893
May 10, 1879	Ord, Joseph P	Jan. 9, 1913
Nov. 5, 1900	Osborn, Arthur P	July 19, 1909
May 10, 1879	Osborn, Thomas W	Dec. 15, 1893
May 10, 1879	Osgood, James R	May 19, 1892
Nov. 7, 1894	Otis, William K	Sept. 22, 1906
Oct. 13, 1881	Owen, Henry E	Oct. 12, 1912
Dec. 2, 1885	Page, Henry D	June 15, 1904
March 4, 1903	Palmer, Lucius N	April 18, 1912
Feb. 3, 1897	Palmer, Richard S	Feb. 28, 1899
May 10, 1879	Pancoast, Richard	Sept. 8, 1909
Oct. 2, 1907	Paret, Walter P	Feb. 21, 1912
Oct. 3, 1888	Park, Roswell	Feb. 15, 1914
Jan. 8, 1902	Parker, Francis E	Feb. 8, 1905
Dec. 5, 1906	Parker, Frank J	Oct. 2, 1912

ADMITTED	NAME	DIED
Jan. 4, 1911	Parrott, Joseph R.	Oct. 13, 1913
May 7, 1884	Parsons, Charles, Jr.	Jan. 12, 1899
May 19, 1903	Parsons, Hinsdill	April 28, 1912
Sept. 15, 1879	Patterson, Albert M.	Sept. 22, 1896
Oct. 5, 1892	Patterson, Robert W.	April 1, 1910
Oct. 21, 1897	Patterson, William Henry	Nov. 18, 1901
Dec. 2, 1908	Paxton, John R., Jr.	May 20, 1912
July 24, 1879	Payne, John William	Feb. 20, 1884
April 21, 1898	Payson, Edward Payson	March 28, 1914
June 1, 1881	Peabody, Duane L.	Sept. 17, 1886
June 21, 1900	Peabody, George Lee	Feb. 9, 1911
July 2, 1884	Peabody, Richard A.	Jan. 29, 1910
May 4, 1892	Peck, George	July 26, 1906
Sept. 12, 1879	Pell, Frederick A.	Jan. 9, 1913
May 4, 1898	Pell, John H.	Feb. 5, 1902
Dec. 3, 1884	Pellew, George	Feb. 18, 1892
Nov. 2, 1892	Peltz, John DeWitt	May 7, 1904
July 1, 1879	Pennington, William	Feb. 17, 1912
April 7, 1886	Pepper, William	July 30, 1898
Oct. 7, 1891	Perkins, Samuel Welsh	Jan. 29, 1898
May 10, 1879	Perry, Alexander J.	March 26, 1913
May 10, 1879	Peters, George A.	Dec. 26, 1894
May 10, 1879	Phelps, Benjamin K.	Dec. 13, 1880
June 15, 1893	Phelps, Sheffield	Dec. 9, 1902
May 10, 1879	Phelps, William Walter	June 17, 1894
May 10, 1879	Picking, Henry F.	Sept. 8, 1899
Dec. 3, 1884	Pierce, James Mills	May 21, 1906
May 4, 1887	Pierce, Josiah, Jr.	July 30, 1902
Oct. 3, 1884	Platt, Joseph C.	July 7, 1898
Oct. 5, 1887	Plumley, Gardiner Spring	Feb. 24, 1894
Nov. 27, 1899	Polk, John Metcalf	March 29, 1904
May 10, 1879	Porter, Mortimer	July 7, 1882
Dec. 7, 1887	Post, James Clarence	Jan. 6, 1896
July 6, 1887	Postley, Clarence A.	May 28, 1908
May 7, 1884	Postlethwaite, William M.	Jan. 10, 1896
Dec. 11, 1879	Potter, Howard	March 24, 1897
Jan. 4, 1893	Potter, Jotham	Feb. 11, 1910
Oct. 4, 1882	Price, Thomas R.	May 7, 1903
Feb. 1, 1893	Proudfit, John William	Nov. 3, 1903
April 7, 1886	Pullen, Stanley Thomas	Feb. 15, 1910
March 1, 1899	Rae, Chas. Whiteside	May 14, 1908
March 7, 1888	Rafferty, Wm. Augustus	Sept. 13, 1902
Nov. 4, 1908	Rand, Laurence B.	Feb. 3, 1914

ADMITTED	NAME	DIED
Nov. 8, 1881	Randolph, John C. F	Feb. 3, 1911
May 6, 1891	Rankine, William B	Sept. 30, 1905
April 4, 1888	Ranney, Walter L	Aug. 17, 1888
Dec. 3, 1890	Ransom, Paul C	Jan. 30, 1907
April 4, 1888	Ransom, Warren A	May 19, 1903
May 16, 1904	Raymond, Charles W	May 3, 1913
Oct. 6, 1897	Raynolds, Edward V	Jan. 26, 1910
Jan. 6, 1897	Read, David F	April 30, 1914
Oct. 1, 1890	Read, N. Goodwin	Nov. 18, 1910
May 10, 1879	Reade, Robert L	Jan. 15, 1910
Feb. 17, 1898	Reamey, L. L	May 25, 1914
Dec. 1, 1909	Reed, William B., Jr	April 3, 1913
Aug. 4, 1879	Rees, Frank	Aug. 25, 1907
Jan. 4, 1899	Reid, Robert Ingersol	Nov. 9, 1905
May 10, 1879	Reid, Whitelaw	Dec. 15, 1912
July 7, 1882	Renwick, Henry Brevoort	Jan. 27, 1895
April 16, 1881	Rexford, Willie M	July 20, 1902
May 19, 1898	Reynolds, John A	Dec. 2, 1900
March 17, 1903	Rhodes, William C	Feb. 5, 1914
May 10, 1879	Richmond, Howard	Nov. 3, 1907
Jan. 7, 1880	Ricketson, John H	July 20, 1900
April 1, 1896	Ring, Frank W	July 17, 1896
March 2, 1881	Robbins, Charles A	May —, 1889*
June 2, 1879	Robbins, George Appleton	May 25, 1895
June 3, 1879	Robbins, Horace Walcott	Dec. 14, 1904
Dec. 15, 1903	Roberts, Algernon B	Jan. 8, 1909
July 13, 1881	Roberts, George F	Dec. 31, 1885
Feb. 4, 1885	Robeson, Henry B	July 16, 1914
July 2, 1901	Robinson, Herman F	June 23, 1903
Oct. 8, 1885	Rockwell, Joseph P	Nov. 22, 1885
Dec. 15, 1903	Rockwood, Chas. G., Jr	July 2, 1913
May 7, 1902	Rodman, Cary Selden	June 12, 1911
Nov. 2, 1892	Rogers, Publius V	July 3, 1895
Feb. 5, 1906	Rogers, Robert C	April 19, 1912
April 5, 1882	Rollins, Daniel G	Aug. 30, 1897
Dec. 4, 1901	Rollins, Jordan J	Feb. 25, 1912
March 7, 1887	Roosevelt, Frank	Feb. 2, 1895
May 10, 1879	Roosevelt, James	Dec. 7, 1900
May 4, 1881	Ropes, John Codman	Oct. 27, 1899
May 10, 1879	Ross, William B	Jan. 14, 1904
Dec. 5, 1894	Rotch, A. Lawrence	April 7, 1912
Oct. 6, 1882	Rotch, Arthur	Aug. 15, 1894
Dec. 5, 1900	Rowland, Eugene A	June 19, 1911

*Date uncertain.

ADMITTED	NAME	DIED
Oct. 5, 1887	Rudd, Robert S	Oct. 21, 1903
May 10, 1879	Rumrill, James A	Jan. 20, 1909
June 2, 1897	Rumsey, William	Jan. 16, 1903
May 10, 1879	Rush, Richard	Feb. 12, 1912
Oct. 6, 1886	Russell, Edward B	June 22, 1900
Sept. 10, 1879	Russell, Horace	June 14, 1913
Dec. 19, 1899	Russell, Philip G	July 22, 1900
Jan. 5, 1881	Russell, Robert Shaw	Sept. 21, 1887
May 10, 1879	Russell, S. Howland	April 18, 1892
April 6, 1892	Russell, William Eustis	July 16, 1896
May 1, 1889	Russell, William Hamilton	July 23, 1907
Oct. 10, 1880	Ruth, Melanchthon L	Dec. 14, 1891
March 31, 1880	Ryerson, Arthur	April 15, 1912
May 4, 1881	Sackett, Frederick M	Oct. 9, 1913
Nov. 17, 1879	Sage, Dean	June 23, 1902
Oct. 21, 1897	St. Gaudens, Augustus	Aug. 4, 1907
April 20, 1899	Salisbury, Frederick S	June 14, 1908
Oct. 3, 1894	Sampson, Robert DeWolfe	July 9, 1895
Nov. 5, 1890	Sandford, Eliot	Oct. 27, 1897
Dec. 11, 1879	Sands, Philip J	Oct. 18, 1900
Oct. 5, 1887	Sanford, George P	July 13, 1908
May 10, 1879	Sargent, John Osborne	Dec. 28, 1891
April 1, 1885	Sargent, Joseph	March 11, 1910
March 3, 1886	Sargent, Lucius Manlius	Nov. 14, 1893
Oct. 7, 1881	Sargent, Nathan	Dec. 5, 1907
March 6, 1889	Savin, John W	April 11, 1899
Oct. 3, 1883	Sawtelle, Charles J	Jan. 4, 1913
May 10, 1879	Schenck, Noah Hunt	Jan. 5, 1885
Sept. 15, 1897	Schermerhorn, George J	Nov. 3, 1904
Feb. 7, 1883	Schermerhorn, John E	June 21, 1906
Feb. 17, 1898	Schofield, Charles B	Feb. 1, 1901
Jan. 6, 1892	Schuetze, Wm. Henry	April 4, 1902
June 16, 1903	Scott, James L	Jan. 9, 1912
April 6, 1881	Scribner, John M	June 16, 1908
May 10, 1879	Scudder, Henry Joel	Feb. 10, 1886
June 2, 1880	Sears, Clinton B	Feb. 17, 1912
Nov. 3, 1897	Sears, Joshua M	June 2, 1905
Nov. —, 1880	Sedgwick, Charles B	Feb. 7, 1883
May 10, 1879	Sedgwick, Henry D	Dec. 26, 1903
Oct. 2, 1895	Seward, Clarence A	July 24, 1897
Dec. 4, 1895	Sewell, Wynn Reeves	Dec. 9, 1899
Nov. 5, 1890	Seymour, Charles	April 25, 1913
May 10, 1879	Sexton, Samuel	July 11, 1896

ADMITTED	NAME	DIED
Dec. 3, 1890	Sharp, George M	July 7, 1911
July 7, 1897	Sheffield, J. Earl	Oct. 16, 1903
Oct. 5, 1887	Sheldon, George P	Dec. 25, 1909
July 19, 1880	Sheldon, Richard	May 16, 1906
June 23, 1879	Shepard, Edward M	July 28, 1911
Aug. 14, 1879	Shields, Charles W	Aug. 26, 1904
May 7, 1880	Shipman, William D	Sept. 24, 1898
June 1, 1881	Short, Edward Lyman	July 30, 1905
Dec. 11, 1879	Silliman, Benjamin	Jan. 7, 1885
May 10, 1879	Simmons, J. Edward	Aug. 5, 1910
Oct. 3, 1888	Simpkins, John	March 26, 1898
May 10, 1879	Simpkins, Nathaniel S., Jr.	Oct. 20, 1883
Nov. 18, 1902	Skaife, Wilfred	April 9, 1913
May 10, 1879	Skidmore, William B	March 1, 1905
May 20, 1902	Slack, John R	Aug. 1, 1904
Oct. 4, 1882	Slack, William H	Oct. 1, 1895
Oct. 5, 1892	Sloan, George B., Jr	July 10, 1914
Feb. 6, 1895	Sloan, William S	May 11, 1896
May 10, 1879	Sloane, Thomas C	June 17, 1890
May 10, 1879	Smith, Daniel Henry	June 4, 1908
Oct. 21, 1897	Smith, Edwin B	Jan. 5, 1914
April 6, 1881	Smith, Henry St. John	Oct. 3, 1896
May 10, 1879	Smith, James H	March 26, 1907
May 10, 1879	Smith, John Cotton	Jan. 9, 1882
May 10, 1879	Smith, John Lawrence	March 17, 1889
Nov. 3, 1886	Smith, John Sabine	Nov. 6, 1900
May 10, 1879	Smith, Nathaniel Stevens	March 23, 1912
June 5, 1895	Smith, William Allen	March 24, 1899
March 7, 1894	Soley, James Russell	Sept. 11, 1911
Nov. 20, 1879	Southworth, Edward W	April 30, 1902
May 10, 1879	Soutter, James T	April 17, 1883
May 10, 1879	Speir, Gilbert M	Oct. 26, 1910
May 2, 1888	Spencer, Samuel	Nov. 29, 1906
Jan. 4, 1893	Sperry, Charles S	Feb. 1, 1911
Feb. 6, 1889	Squires, James Duane	Sept. 12, 1893
Jan. 6, 1882	Stanfurth, F	Sept. 15, 1913
April 2, 1884	Stanton, Louis Lee	May 11, 1911
Nov. 5, 1884	Stapler, Henry B. B	Dec. 1, 1906
Nov. 3, 1886	Starey, Alfred B	Aug. 7, 1893
Feb. 2, 1887	Sterling, George L	Aug. 8, 1913
Jan. 19, 1899	Stetson, Joseph A	Oct. 29, 1909
Nov. 6, 1889	Stevens, Frank Jerome	April 4, 1905
May 10, 1879	Stewart, William A. W	March 12, 1888
July 2, 1884	Stickney, Albert	May 4, 1908

ADMITTED	NAME	DIED
July 6, 1899	Stickney, Joseph L	May 25, 1907
Oct. 5, 1904	Stillman, George S	March 15, 1907
March 1, 1893	Stillman, Thomas E	Sept. 4, 1906
Oct. 8, 1885	Stockton, Henry T	May —, 1886*
May 5, 1882	Stockton-Hough, John	May 6, 1900
March 7, 1888	Stockwell, William H	May 20, 1902
Dec. 3, 1890	Stoddard, Enoch V	June 6, 1908
April 7, 1909	Stone, Charles F	April 27, 1910
May 10, 1879	Stone, Henry	Jan. 18, 1896
April 1, 1891	Stone, Henry B	July 4, 1897
Oct. 15, 1880	Storer, William B	Oct. 6, 1884
Nov. 18, 1902	Strang, Clifford H	Aug. 30, 1903
Jan. 2, 1889	Sturges, Jonathan	June 9, 1911
Dec. 16, 1902	Sturges, Walter K	May 9, 1913
May 20, 1897	Sturgis, Danford N. B	Aug. 19, 1911
May 7, 1890	Sturgis, Robert	May 3, 1900
May 10, 1879	Sutherland, John L	Sept. 18, 1901
Oct. 2, 1907	Swann, John V	Aug. 8, 1910
Jan. 4, 1893	Sweet, Elnathan	Jan. 26, 1903
May 10, 1879	Swift, Augustus M	March 27, 1884
May 6, 1891	Swift, Franklin	Nov. 10, 1906
Feb. 1, 1882	Swift, Thomas M	March 3, 1888
Oct. 1, 1890	Swift, William N	Oct. 27, 1911
April 5, 1893	Switzer, Charles M	June 26, 1906
May 10, 1879	Talbot, Richmond	July 3, 1887
June 6, 1894	Tallmadge, Albert M	Feb. 13, 1905
Dec. 6, 1905	Talmadge, Arthur W	Jan. 10, 1910
——, 1865	Taylor, Alfred J	July 12, 1901
Oct. 1, 1884	Taylor, Daniel Morgan	March 26, 1907
June 1, 1881	Taylor, Henry C	July 26, 1904
June 15, 1893	Taylor, John H	Feb. 25, 1911
Nov. 17, 1879	Taylor, Robert E	May 6, 1896
June 6, 1900	Taylor, William H	Feb. 7, 1914
May 7, 1902	Tenney, George Sanborn	March 3, 1909
Nov. 2, 1898	Terrell, Herbert L	Nov. 9, 1909
Jan. 5, 1887	Terry, Stephen	April 23, 1889
Dec. 2, 1885	Teschemacher, Hubert E	Jan. 25, 1907
May 3, 1882	Thacher, John Boyd	Feb. 25, 1909
Feb. 3, 1883	Thacher, Ralph W	Feb. 27, 1903
June 7, 1899	Thomas, Joseph B	Aug. 4, 1909
May 4, 1881	Thompson, Albert H	Dec. 7, 1891
Feb. 5, 1902	Thompson, David	Sept. 24, 1912

*Date uncertain.

ADMITTED	NAME	DIED
May 3, 1882	Thompson, E. Ray	Aug. 14, 1899
March 4, 1908	Thompson, James MacN	Dec. 26, 1908
July 7, 1886	Thompson, Thomas D	Jan. 11, 1893
Nov. 11, 1881	Thomson, Mason	July 6, 1911
Dec. —, 1883	Thurston, Benjamin F	March 13, 1890
May 6, 1885	Thurston, William W	May 13, 1890
May 19, 1903	Tiffany, Charles C	Aug. 20, 1907
Feb. 6, 1884	Tiffany, Otis C	Oct. 31, 1897
Dec. 7, 1898	Tilley, Benjamin F	March 18, 1907
April 4, 1888	Tillinghast, Henry A	March 18, 1907
June 12, 1879	Tobey, Salathiel H	July 9, 1906
May 4, 1881	Totten, George M	May 29, 1888
Jan. 3, 1900	Toucey, Donald Butler	July 24, 1905
March 4, 1885	Tourtelotte, John E	July 23, 1891
March 16, 1899	Tower, A. Clifford	Dec. 28, 1903
April 6, 1898	Townsend, Charles J	July 2, 1908
May 10, 1879	Townsend, James M	Oct. 31, 1913
Jan. 5, 1882	Townsend, S. Van R	Jan. 15, 1901
July 15, 1880	Townsend, William K	June 1, 1907
May 10, 1889	Tracy, Charles	March 17, 1885
Dec. 7, 1887	Train, Abner L	Feb. 10, 1891
Nov. 2, 1887	Train, Charles J	Aug. 4, 1906
July 1, 1879	Tredick, T. Salter	Jan. 27, 1900
April 3, 1889	Trenholm, William Lee	Jan. 11, 1901
Oct. 4, 1893	Trowbridge, George	Sept. 10, 1898
May 2, 1900	Trudeau, Edward L., Jr	May 3, 1904
May 3, 1882	Tryon, J. Rufus	March 20, 1912
May 6, 1891	Tuck, Henry	Sept. 2, 1904
Dec. 7, 1887	Tucker, Gilman H	Nov. 14, 1913
May 10, 1879	Tuckerman, Walter C	April 18, 1894
May 2, 1900	Tullock, Alonzo J	July 21, 1904
May 10, 1879	Turner, Herbert B	July 8, 1903
Feb. 3, 1892	Turner, Samuel B	Aug. 19, 1906
July 5, 1882	Tuttle, George M	Oct. 29, 1912
May 10, 1879	Twombly, Hamilton McK	Jan. 11, 1910
Nov. 7, 1888	Twombly, Horatio N	Oct. 17, 1896
Feb. 6, 1884	Tyler, Augustus C	Nov. 27, 1908
Oct. 7, 1896	Tyng, Sewell Tappan	April 3, 1913
May 19, 1903	Tytus, Robb deP	Aug. 14, 1913
Oct. 20, 1898	Ulshoeffer, Wm. G	Oct. 3, 1904
Jan. 5, 1887	Upham, George P., Jr	Sept. 26, 1891
May 10, 1879	Upham, William S	May 24, 1882
June 5, 1889	Upton, George B	Feb. 7, 1904

ADMITTED	NAME	DIED
Oct. 6, 1897	Vail, Davis R.	Dec. 20, 1906
July 7, 1882	Van der Poel, Herman W.	March 16, 1906
May 10, 1879	Vander Poel, A. Ernest	Sept. 26, 1898
Feb. 6, 1884	Vander Poel, Samuel Oakley	April 22, 1912
April 6, 1898	Vanderpool, Eugene	July 12, 1903
May 6, 1896	Van Ingen, Edward	Oct. 27, 1905
May 10, 1879	Van Nest, Alexander T.	Aug. 10, 1896
June 2, 1886	Van Rensselaer, W. B.	Sept. 25, 1909
May 10, 1879	Van Santvoord, Charles T.	July 5, 1895
May 8, 1880	Van Vechten, Ab. Van Wyck	Aug. 28, 1906
July 7, 1886	Van Wickle, August S.	June 8, 1898
March 16, 1899	Varnum, James M.	March 26, 1907
Oct. 4, 1893	Vernon, F. Joseph	Feb. 16, 1914
Jan. 2, 1889	Voorhees, Philip Randall	April 15, 1896
May 7, 1884	Walcott, Edward O.	March 1, 1905
Dec. 2, 1891	Walker, John G.	Sept. 16, 1907
Dec. 12, 1879	Walker, Stephen A.	Feb. 6, 1893
Dec. 9, 1880	Walker, Willis E.	May 3, 1886
June 2, 1897	Wallace, John	Sept. 17, 1909
Oct. 6, 1886	Wallace, William C.	Sept. 3, 1901
Aug. 1, 1879	Walton, Luis P.	Sept. 8, 1903
Jan. 31, 1880	Ward, Charles S.	July 31, 1898
May 10, 1879	Ward, Edmund A.	June 16, 1906
Feb. 3, 1897	Ward, Jacob E.	July 30, 1913
Oct. 1, 1913	Ward, Stanley	June 27, 1914
June 1, 1881	Wardwell, Edward H.	April 22, 1911
Jan. 2, 1884	Warner, Charles Dudley	Oct. 20, 1900
June 21, 1900	Warren, B. H.	Oct. 15, 1906
Oct. 1, 1890	Warren, Frederick	Sept. 3, 1901
Nov. 4, 1896	Warren, G. Thornton	Jan. 1, 1909
April 7, 1886	Warren, Samuel D.	Feb. 19, 1910
March 7, 1883	Waterman, Joshua W.	June —, 1892*
May —, 1883	Watkins, Hezekiah	Feb. 12, 1884
April 6, 1892	Watrous, Charles Ansel	Jan. 20, 1899
Feb. 3, 1886	Watson, William Henry	Jan. 1, 1913
Mar. 7, 1888	Weatherbee, Edwin H.	Feb. 11, 1912
May 10, 1879	Webb, Henry Walter	June 18, 1900
May 10, 1879	Weld, Francis Minot	Dec. 31, 1893
Nov. 5, 1884	Weld, George W.	Feb. 14, 1905
May 10, 1879	Wells, Manning C.	Oct. 19, 1897
Oct. 1, 1890	Wendell, Frank Thaxter	July 12, 1906
Jan. 6, 1897	Wendell, Jacob, Jr.	April 22, 1911

*Date uncertain.

ADMITTED	NAME	DIED
May 5, 1880	Wentworth, Thomas F	Nov. 11, 1907
May 7, 1884	Wesson, Frank B	Sept. 11, 1903
Dec. 17, 1879	Wesson, Frederick	Nov. 30, 1904
May 10, 1879	Weyman, Charles S	April 13, 1893
June 1, 1892	Wheeler, George M	May 3, 1905
May 10, 1879	Wheeler, John Visscher	Jan. 20, 1902
May 10, 1879	Wheelock, George G	March 22, 1907
Oct. 3, 1883	Whipple, William D	April 1, 1902
April 5, 1893	White, Arthur	April 19, 1901
April 4, 1894	White, Arthur E	Feb. 21, 1901
April 6, 1892	White, Charles A	June 19, 1909
Jan. 8, 1897	White, Edwin	Dec. 23, 1903
Jan. 4, 1893	White, George Edward	Dec. 19, 1908
Oct. 7, 1891	White, John Allison	June 10, 1904
May 10, 1879	White, John P. P	Dec. 4, 1882
July 6, 1898	White, Raymond S	Dec. 21, 1903
Nov. 8, 1881	White, Stanford	June 25, 1906
May 10, 1879	Whitehead, Gerard Irvine	May 11, 1898
April 6, 1892	Whitehead, William	Jan. 8, 1893
Oct. 6, 1880	Whitehouse, Edward N	Oct. 20, 1904
Jan. 5, 1881	Whitehouse, Wm. Fitzhugh	April 9, 1909
June 1, 1887	Whiting, John B	Feb. 7, 1895
Dec. 16, 1897	Whitney, Edward B	Jan. 5, 1911
——, 1865	Whitney, William C	Feb. 2, 1904
Feb. 1, 1899	Wildes, Frank	Feb. 7, 1903
March 7, 1888	Wilkinson, Robert F	June 30, 1903
Oct. 4, 1882	Wilks, Matthew	June 20, 1899
Oct. 4, 1882	Willcox, David	Apiil 24, 1907
May 5, 1896	Williams, Coleman G	May 28, 1900
Jan. 3, 1884	Williams, Norman	June 19, 1899
Oct. 17, 1900	Williams, Norman A	Nov. 4, 1910
May 26, 1879	Williamson, David B	July 12, 1886
March 2, 1904	Williamson, Edwin B	March 24, 1906
March 16, 1899	Williamson, George N	April 27, 1905
March 16, 1899	Williamson, Samuel E	Feb. 21, 1903
May 3, 1883	Wilson, William Penn	July 30, 1891
May 10, 1879	Winston, Gustavus Storrs	Dec. 29, 1899
——, 1865	Winthrop, Buchanan	Dec. 25, 1900
Oct. 5, 1892	Winthrop, Robert D	April 16, 1912
March 7, 1900	Wood, H. Holden	May 11, 1912
March 14, 1904	Wood, Stuart	March 2, 1914
Nov. 2, 1887	Woodbury, Charles H	Sept. 13, 1893
July 7, 1886	Woodford, Stewart L	Feb. 14, 1913
May 10, 1879	Woodruff, Morris	March 3, 1894

ADMITTED	NAME	DIED
June 15, 1893	Woodruff, Timothy L.	Oct. 12, 1913
Oct. 1, 1890	Woodward, Joseph J.	July 6, 1906
Feb. 17, 1903	Woodworth, William McM.	May 28, 1912
June 2, 1887	Worcester, Franklin E.	March 3, 1894
June 16, 1898	Wordin, Thomas Cooke	April 6, 1905
June 6, 1894	Wright, Frank	June 16, 1903
Feb. 6, 1884	Wright, M. Fisher	Maıch 4, 1890
May 10, 1879	Wynkoop, Gerardus H.	May 16, 1909
June 1, 1892	York, Samuel A.	Nov. 5, 1898
May 10, 1879	Young, Mason	March 29, 1906
May 10, 1879	Young, Thomas S.	May 21, 1909

APPENDIX IX

REPORT ON THE LIBRARY, MAY 1, 1882

The following were the subscribers to the original Library Fund:

Aitkin, John W.
Alexander, Archibald.
Alexander, Charles B.
Alexander, James W.
Alexander, William.
Anderson, Henry H.
Asch, Morris J.
Astor, John J.
Auchincloss, John W.

Baldwin, G. Van Nest.
Bangs, L. Bolton.
Bartlett, Franklin.
Beadleston, William H.
Beaman, Jr., Charles C.
Bigelow, W. Sturgis.
Blake, John Ellis.
Brooks, Arthur.
Bull, William T.
Butler, Prescott H.
Butterworth, Wm. H.

Chandler, Charles F.
Chapin, Edward R.
Chauncey, Elihu.
Cutting, W. Bayard.

Dodge, Arthur M.
Donnelly, Edward C.
DuBois, Coert.
DuBois, Mathew B.

Earle, Joseph P.
Eaton, Sherburne B.

Fairchild, Charles.
Farnam, Henry.
Farragut, Loyall.
Fox, Austen G.

Garrettson, Francis J.
Godwin, Parke.
Gorringe, Henry H.
Gouley, John W. S.
Green, Ashbel.
Gulliver, Wm. C.

Hawley, Henry E.
Higginson, James J.
Holt, Geo. C.
Hornblower, William B.
Howe, Walter.
Hunter, James B.

Imbrie, Charles F.
Ives, Brayton.

Kernochan, J. Frederic.

Larocque, Joseph.
Lewis, Francis D.
Lewis, Thomas C.
Loubat, Joseph F.
Lusk, Wm. T.

Mansfield, Howard.
McBride, Thomas A.
McBurney, Chas.
McKim, Chas. F.

Morton, Alex. L.
Murray, Chas. P.

Osborn, Thomas W.
Otis, Fessenden N.

Palfrey, Francis W.
Parker, R. Wayne.
Peabody, Geo. L.
Pellew, Henry E.
Perry, Alexander J.
Peters, Geo. A.
Phelps, B. K.
Porter, Mortimer.

Robbins, Horace W.
Rodiigues, José C.

Sloane, Henry T.
Stedman, Edmund C.
Stevens, Frederic W.

Thacher, Thomas.
Tompkins, Hamilton B.
Tuckerman, Walter C.

Unknown donors.

Vanderpoel, A. Ernest.

Waller, Elwyn.
Weld, Francis M.
Wetmore, G. Peabody.
Wheelock, Wm. E.
Whitney, Wm. C.
Wickes, Edward A.
Witherbee, Frank S.
Work, J. Henry.

Young, Mason.

Total amount given, $3,936.

APPENDIX X

(A) MEMBERS OF DISTINCTION

It would, of course, be impracticable within the reasonable limits of a book like this history, to catalogue the names and services of all the distinguished dead who have passed out of our membership. In selecting a few it must not be suspected that invidious distinctions have intentionally been made. The compiler recognizes the fact that among those not mentioned are not only many whose loss is greatly deplored by admiring friends, but whose character and eminence have placed them in the foremost rank. The references are, therefore, to be regarded simply as specimens, indicating the high class of those who have adorned the University Club by their presence, and left behind them honored names.

Appropriate tribute has already been paid to the memory of Henry H. Anderson (Williams '48), the first President of the Club, who piloted it through the early years of its successful voyage.

John Jacob Astor (Columbia '39), who was a member of the first council, and warmly interested in the affairs of the Club, was a citizen of such prominence and a man of such character that the mere mention of his name will recall the influential place filled by him in the city of New York.

Richard M. Hunt (École des Beaux Arts '55) was acknowledged to be the leading architect of his day in the United States. His work still lives not only in New York but throughout the country, and is held to be artistically great.

General Alexander R. Lawton (U. S. M. A. '39) was a South Carolinian, and a general in the Confederate Army. After the war (1885) he was appointed Minister to Russia by President Cleveland, and later Minister to Austria.

George DeForest Lord (Yale '54) was the son of the elder Daniel Lord, who was regarded by many as the leader of the New York bar in his day. His son inherited his father's qualities, and occupied a prominent position both at the bar and in the social life of New York.

The Reverend Noah Hunt Schenck, D.D. (Princeton '44), was a celebrated clergyman of the Protestant Episcopal Church.

Clarence A. Seward (Hobart '48) was the gifted son of the great William A. Seward, Secretary of State in the Cabinet of Abraham Lincoln at the time of the latter's assassination, and an object of the assaults made by the Booth conspiracy. Mr. Clarence A. Seward was a leading member of the New York bar.

Benjamin Silliman (Yale '37) was the son of the eminent scientist of the same name, and himself a distinguished chemist, the pioneer in the formation of a School of Applied Science at Yale College, which resulted later in the Sheffield School at that institution, and the author of many works on scientific subjects.

Charles Tracy (Yale '32) was the partner of William M. Evarts, and himself a leading member of the New York bar. He was president of the Yale Alumni, 1879–1882, and prominent in the councils of the Protestant Episcopal Church.

Charles C. Beaman (Harvard '61), who was President of the Club at the time of his death in 1900, has been mentioned, and his brilliant qualities referred to in the earlier pages of this book.

The Honorable William M. Evarts (Yale '37) was one of the most distinguished men enrolled in our membership. He was easily the chief among the lawyers of his time, an eloquent orator and a great statesman. He was an active Republican, was the leading counsel for Andrew Johnson in his impeachment trial, the leading counsel for Henry Ward Beecher in his celebrated trial, Attorney-General of the United States in 1868 and later, Secretary of State under President Hayes, United States Senator (1885–1891), and conspicuously the great man of his day.

James Roosevelt (Union '47), a member of a distinguished family, was himself a prominent citizen of New York.

Charles Dudley Warner (Hamilton '51) was celebrated as an essayist, author, editor, lecturer, and litterateur.

Frederick R. Coudert (Columbia '50), the head of the well-known law firm of Coudert Brothers, was recognized as one of the most learned and brilliant men of his day. He was a fine public speaker and lecturer. Among other offices held by him were president of the United States Catholic Historical Society, president of the Manhattan Club, president of the Bar Association of the City of New York, and president of the Columbia College Alumni Association. He was decorated with the cross of the Legion of Honor of France.

Admiral Bancroft Gherardi (U. S. N. A. '52) has already been mentioned in this book. He was conspicuously renowned as one of our successful naval officers.

Stanford White (Univ. of N. Y. '81), of the firm of McKim, Mead & White, was almost without a peer as a skilful architect of unusual taste. The city of New York is full of his remarkable work, and his reputation has been too high and too generally known to need further reference.

Daniel S. Lamont (Union '72) was United States Secretary of War 1893–1897, and a prominent citizen of New York.

Frederick H. Betts (Yale '64) was a leading member of the New York bar.

Frederick J. DePeyster (C. C. N. Y. '60), of the well-known family of that name, was a man of high position in social and other circles of New York City.

Edward Cooper (Columbia '46), the son of Peter Cooper, although engaged in business in New York, gave much attention to public schools and Columbia College. He was an active Democrat, one of the leaders in the overthrow of the Tweed Ring, and Mayor of New York City, 1879–1881.

General Burton N. Harrison (Yale '59) was famous as the private secretary of President Jefferson Davis of the Confederate States. After the war he lived in New York, and was respected as a prominent citizen. His son, Francis Burton Harrison, is now Governor-General of the Philippines.

Doctor Edward W. Lambert (Yale '54) was a distinguished physician in New York. He was the chief medical director of the Equitable Life Assurance Society of the United States. For a long term of years he was the Chairman of the Committee on Admissions of the University Club. His three sons have all become physicians of eminence in New York City.

The Reverend Charles W. Shields, D.D. (Princeton '44), was a distinguished professor in Princeton University.

George V. N. Baldwin (Rutgers '56) and Charles T. Barney (Williams '70) have both been officers of our Club and have received proper recognition in previous pages of this book.

Morris K. Jesup (Hon. Williams '81) was a banker, but devoted much of his time and money to educational and philanthropic objects. He was president of the New York City Mission, of the Five Points House of Industry, of the Y. M. C. A.; trustee of the Union Theological Seminary; and president of the Museum of

Natural History. His gifts to the latter and other institutions were munificent.

Doctor Francis H. Markoe (Princeton '76) stood in the very front rank of surgeons in the city of New York at the time of his death in 1907.

Augustus Saint-Gaudens (Hon. Princeton '96) had the reputation of being the most distinguished sculptor in the United States.

The Reverend Charles C. Tiffany (Dickinson '50) was the rector of Zion Episcopal Church in New York until he became the archdeacon of the diocese, which office he held at the time of his death in 1907.

George A. Adee (Yale '67) was a prominent Yale graduate and has already been mentioned in this book.

Doctor William T. Bull (Harvard '69) held a position in the first rank of New York surgeons.

General Louis Fitzgerald (Hon. Princeton '75) was distinguished in the New York National Guard and has received notice in these pages.

Daniel C. Gilman (Yale '52) was one of the foremost educators of America. He organized and was president of the Johns Hopkins University; received honorary degrees from numerous universities; at one time president of the University of California; president of the Carnegie Institution at Washington; member of learned societies; president of the Slater Fund; vice-president of the Peabody Fund; trustee of various educational bodies; author and editor-in-chief of the New International Encyclopædia.

Edward King (Harvard '53), one of New York's most prominent bankers and a member of a distinguished family. Concerned in many philanthropies and public institutions.

Doctor Andrew J. McCosh (Princeton '77) was at the time of his death, in 1908, one of a very small group of surgeons in New York who were acknowledged to be the foremost in the profession.

John Crosby Brown (Columbia '59) was the head of the banking house of Brown Brothers, and a leader in philanthropic enterprises.

Cornelius C. Cuyler (Princeton '79), one of the most popular and useful graduates of Princeton has already been made the subject of remark.

Admiral Henry Erben (U. S. N. A. '49), a renowned naval officer, has been mentioned and his qualities described in an earlier part of this book.

Charles F. McKim (Harvard '70), the architect of the University Club House, has received appropriate notice in this volume.

Hamilton McK. Twombly (Harvard '71) was a citizen universally recognized as capable and useful. He was engaged in many large financial enterprises, and greatly esteemed in social circles.

J. Edward Simmons (Williams '62) was one of the best-known citizens of New York. Besides many connections of honor and active usefulness, he was president of the Fourth National Bank, president of the Chamber of Commerce, and president of the New York Clearing House.

Captain John Sanford Barnes (U. S. N. A. '54), after brilliant service in the navy, became successful in railroad enterprises, and was a prominent citizen of New York.

George G. DeWitt (Columbia '67) was one of the best-known citizens of New York. Although not engaged in public life, his position in social circles, at the bar, of which he was a leading member, and in civic and private enterprises for the benefit of the community, was in the front rank.

Admiral Robley D. Evans (U. S. N. A. '63), a famous officer in the navy, has already been mentioned in this book.

The Right Reverend Alexander Mackay Smith (Trinity '72) was an eminent prelate of the Protestant Episcopal Church.

Francis D. Millet (Harvard '69) was a most versatile and popular man. Not only an artist of fame, he was a literary man of talent. He was decorated with the Legion of Honor in France, and by numerous foreign countries, and the recipient of distinctions from societies of painters in different lands. He lost his life on the steamer *Titanic* in 1912.

Edward M. Shepard (C. C. N. Y. '69) was a distinguished lawyer of New York. He was candidate for mayor and governor, as well as for other public offices. He was active in the public service and a writer of recognized force and merit.

Hugh D. Auchincloss (Yale '79), the former Secretary of the University Club, has already been mentioned in these pages.

William Warner Hoppin (Brown '61) was a leading citizen and member of the New York bar. He served for some years on the Council of the University Club.

J. Pierpont Morgan (Göttingen; Hon. Yale 1908), banker, philanthropist, patron of arts, was so universally known as to need no further description.

Whitelaw Reid (Miami '59), editor, ambassador to France and Great Britain, has been already made the subject of remark.

General Stewart L. Woodford (Columbia '54), lawyer, soldier, and holder of civic offices, has been referred to in the earlier part of this book.

The temptation is great to pay a tribute to the memory of a host of other honored members who have passed away, but these will suffice to indicate the character and standing of those who have adorned the Club by their membership.

The selection of living members worthy of special reference would be a matter even more delicate. No attempt, therefore, will be made to present such a list.

(B) ARMY MEMBERS OF THE UNIVERSITY CLUB, NEW YORK

The following details have been kindly furnished by General George S. Anderson, U. S. M. A., '71:

Prior to 1879 the Club books show no army members, but the book of June 1, that year, shows seven names of army officers, or those who had been in the regular service. Among the latter class were Major-General Webb, Major Morris J. Asch, Loyall Farragut, and W. B. Wetmore.

In the books for January 1, 1880, and June 1, 1880, there are found ten names additional, all bearing the date of May 10th, 1879, the same date as borne by those on the 1879 list. This makes a total of seventeen as entering at the new start of the Club. Of these, fourteen were admitted on their U. S. M. A. diploma and three were from other institutions.

Doctor John T. Metcalfe and General Horace Porter were not then in service, but were elected on their U. S. M. A. diplomas. In this list were men of such distinction as Generals Webb, Crawford, Porter, Perry, Fry, Gilmore, McKeever, and Doctor Metcalfe. The list for December, 1881, shows thirteen new names, among which are Professors Kendrick and Tillman. All were admitted from the U. S. M. A. and nearly all were at the time in the army. On the December, 1882, list there were added eleven new names, the most distinguished being Generals James H. Wilson and Wager Swayne. All but the last were from U. S. M. A.

I find no list for 1883, but the one for June, 1884, contains fourteen new names, the most distinguished of which are Generals Hancock, Whipple, and Sawtelle. All but two were from U. S. M. A.

The next list found is of 1886, with no month given.

On this I find nine new names, all from U. S. M. A. The most distinguished were General Alexander R. Lawton and the present U. S. Senator, H. A. DuPont.

The list for March, 1887, contains but three new names, all U. S. M. A., and the most distinguished is General F. V. Greene.

In July, 1887, are four new names, with General H. L. Abbott distinguished and all from U. S. M. A.

July, 1888, has six additions, four from U. S. M. A., but one of the other two graduated from U. S. M. A. after his other degree. General H. C. Hasbrouck was the most distinguished of this year's elect.

July, 1889, shows two new names, July, 1890, three, and July, 1891, three more—none of any particular distinction at the time of their election.

There are seven new names on the August, 1892, list, six of which are from U. S. M. A.

August, 1893, shows six additions; all but one were U. S. M. A.

There are no new names on July 25, 1894, list, and only two on July 1, 1895; none on April 1, 1896, and two on April 1, 1897. These four all U. S. M. A.

The list for April 1, 1898, has five new names, four U. S. M. A., with General Wm. Ludlow as the most distinguished.

On March 1, 1899, there are nine names added, all U. S. M. A., General Caleb H. Carlton and Colonel George W. Goethals being the most prominent.

March 1, 1900, has five additions, all U. S. M. A., including Professor W. P. Edgerton.

March 1, 1901, shows only four new names, the most famous being General Leonard Wood, who has an honorary degree.

Only one joined to March 1, 1902, and he not U. S. M. A.; but six, all U. S. M. A. but one, were elected prior to the list of March 1, 1903.

On March 1, 1904, we find five new names, all U. S. M. A. and including General T. H. Barry.

March 1, 1905, has four; March 1, 1906, has four, all U. S. M. A.; and March 1, 1907, only two, one of whom is not U. S. M. A.

On April 30, 1908, we find only two names and one is a re-election of a former member. Both are U. S. M. A.

The April 12, 1909, list has only one new name; the April 11, 1910, only two; and the April 10, 1911, but one, and of these, one is not U. S. M. A.

The list of May 31, 1912, has six additions, all U. S. M. A.

The April 30, 1913, list shows three additions, all U. S. M. A.

The latest list, April 13, 1914, has three new names; two are U. S. M. A. Gen. Peter D. Vroom, late Inspector-General of the Army, is not U. S. M. A.

The total number of army men admitted to the Club is 164. All of these but fifteen are U. S. M. A. Only one is honorary.

A few had army antecedents, but were not in the army when elected. Others were in the army at election and subsequently left the service.

The following account of distinguished men in the army who are, or have been members of the University Club, compiled by General George S. Anderson (U. S. M. A. '71), is too interesting to be curtailed:

Brief mention of the distinguished services of some of the Army members of the Club would include Drs. John T. Metcalfe, Morris Asch, and E. J. Marsh, all well known as distinguished in their profession. Maj.-Gen. Samuel W. Crawford was present at the firing on Ft. Sumter in 1861 as a Surgeon U. S. A. Later he joined the line of the Army, and was finally retired as a Maj.-Gen. and died in Nov., 1892.

Gen. Alex. S. Webb, well known to all of the older members, became a Maj.-Gen. by brevet for gallantry at Gettysburg and other hot battles of the war, and was several times wounded. After quitting the Army in Dec., 1870, he became president of the College of the City of N. Y. and retained the position for 33½ years. He resigned from the Club in 1897, and died Feb. 12, 1911.

Loyall Farragut (1868), son of the distinguished Admiral, is still a member and well known to all. Charles P. Miller was rather known as a lawyer, but he was a retired officer of the Army. He was famed as a raconteur and genial companion. He died in Aug., 1887.

Col. Edward McK. Hudson (1849) was noted for his gallantry in the Utah, Seminole, and Northwest Indian Wars, as well as in the Rebellion. As his name only appears on the lists for 1879 and 1880, it is probable that he soon resigned. In 1887 he was living in Washington, D. C., and was paralyzed. He died July 20, 1892.

Gen. A. J. Perry (1851). After service in the Indian war in Minnesota he was assigned to the Quartermaster Dept., in which he served most efficiently during the entire war, receiving the brevet of Brig.-Gen. He was retired in 1892, and died Mar. 26, 1913.

Gen. Horace Porter (1860), as is well known, is living in this city. He saw conspicuous service during the Rebellion, becoming A. D. C.

From a photograph, copyright by Underwood & Underwood.

From a photograph, copyright by Harris & Ewing.

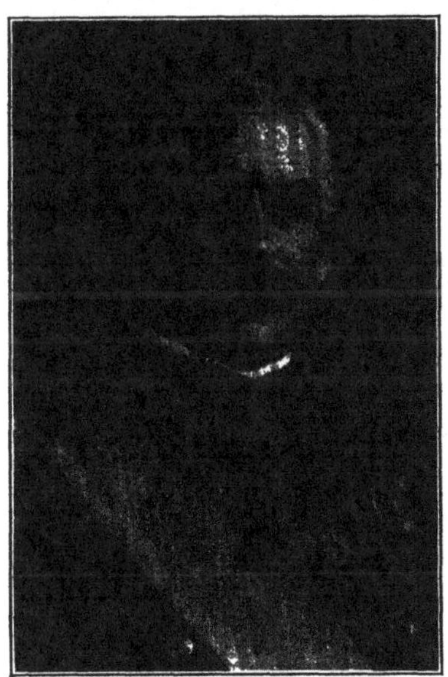

From a photograph, copyright by Harris & Ewing.

From a photograph, copyright by Harris & Ewing.

Brigadier-General Horace Porter.
Major-General Thomas H. Barry.

Major-General Leonard Wood.
Colonel George W. Goethals.

AN ARMY GROUP.

to Gen. Grant, and later his secretary when he was Pres. Grant. He received the brevet of Brig.-Gen. for gallantry in the field and resigned from the Army in Dec., 1873. Since this time he has been vice-pres. of the Pullman Car Co., chairman of the executive com. of the Met. El. Ry., and pres. of the West Shore Ry. He is engaged in the operation of numerous railroads and manufacturing and financial institutions, and was our Ambassador to France 1897-1905.

Gen. Walter S. Schuyler (1870) was for a long period A. D. C. to Gen. Crook, and was in many engagements with the Indians. He is now a Brig.-Gen. U. S. A. and was retired in April, 1913.

Gen. James B. Fry (1847) served on the frontier and at West Point until the outbreak of the Rebellion, when he was assigned to the Adjt.-Gen.'s Dept. and became the Provost-Marshal-Gen. of the Army, which position he held until it was abolished in Aug., 1866. He received the brevet of Maj.-Gen.; was retired in July, 1881, and died July, 1894.

Gen. Quincy A. Gilmore (1849) prior to the Rebellion was engaged in engineering work. He attained the rank of Maj.-Gen., commanded the Tenth Army Corps, and was in charge of the operations against Charleston and had large commands until the close of the war, when he returned to his engineering work and was engaged on many works of coast defence and river and harbor improvement. He was the author of works on Limes and Cements, and other Structural Material. He died 7 April, 1888.

Gen. Chauncey McKeever (1849). After service in Indian campaigns against the Seminoles and on Puget Sound, and in the Utah expedition, he was, at the beginning of the Civil War, made an Asst. Adjt.-Gen. and served on the staffs of Gens. Heintzelman and McDowell. He received the brevet of Brig.-Gen. for meritorious services, was retired in Aug., 1893, and died 4 Sept., 1901.

Gen. Edward J. McClernand (1870). He has had distinguished service on the frontier among the Indians; he is now a Brig.-Gen. U. S. A. He was retired in Dec., 1912.

Col. Samuel N. Benjamin (1861) was engaged in most of the battles of the Army of the Potomac and was severely wounded at Spottsylvania. He became a Maj. and Asst. Adjt.-Gen. in 1875, and died May, 1886.

Prof. Henry L. Kendrick (1835) was brevetted Maj. for gallantry in the Mexican War, was made Prof. at the U. S. M. A. in 1857, and retired in Dec., 1880. He died 24 May, 1891. Prof. Samuel E. Tillman (1869) succeeded to Prof. Kendrick's chair in 1880 and continued to hold it until his retirement in Oct., 1911.

Maj. William J. Twining (1863) received several brevets for gallantry in the Civil War. He was an Engineer Officer and made Commissioner to run the line between U. S. and Canada, and also was Engineer Com. of the Dist. Columbia. He died 5 May, 1882.

Gen. Clinton B. Sears (1887) was an Engineer of distinction. He retired as a Brig.-Gen. and died in Feb., 1912.

Col. Charles McK. Leoser (1861) had gallant service in the Cavalry during the Rebellion, was severely wounded and captured. He resigned in Oct., 1865, and became a merchant and publisher in N. Y. He died 23 Feb., 1896.

Col. Joseph H. Willard (1868) is a distinguished officer of Engineers, recently retired.

Col. Wm. H. Coffin (1873) was one of our best-equipped Coast Artillery officers. He died July 31, 1912.

Henry B. Ledyard (1865) resigned in Oct., 1870, and devoted his energies to railroading. He became president of the Michigan Central Ry. in May, 1883.

Leonard G. Hun (1869) resigned Aug., 1870, and became a distinguished lawyer in Albany, where he died in Mar., 1891.

Harry H. Landon (1872) resigned 1880. He is now in business in this city.

Brig.-Gen. Geo. S. Anderson (1871) is an officer on the retired list. (See p. 87.)

Gen. Wager Swayne, a distinguished veteran of the Civil War, where he was seriously wounded in one of the last battles, was well known here as a lawyer of large practice. He died 18 Dec., 1902.

Gen. Thomas H. Barber (1867) resigned in July, 1885, and died 10 Mar., 1905.

Gen. Samuel M. Mills (1865) was one of the best-known Arty. officers and became Brig.-Gen. Chief of Arty. in June, 1905, was retired Sept., 1906, and died 8 Sept., 1907.

Gen. Charles Shaler (1867), one of the ablest Ordnance officers of the Army, retired as a Brig.-Gen. in Jan., 1905.

Gen. John McClellan (1867) of the Arty. was retired a Brig.-Gen. June, 1906.

Col. William T. Rossell was an Engineer officer of great ability and was retired Oct., 1913.

Gen. James H. Wilson (1860) took a gallant and conspicuous part in the Civil War, reaching the rank of Maj.-Gen. and the comd. of a Cavalry Corps. Resigned in Dec., 1870, and engaged in engineering and railroad enterprises with great success. Re-entered the Vol. Army during the Spanish War and served as Brig. and Maj.-Gen. in Cuba, Porto Rico, and China. Afterward retired as Brig.-Gen. U. S. A. Is the author of numerous books and published articles.

John P. Story (1865), an Arty. officer of distinction, was made Brig.-Gen. Chief of Arty. Jan., 1904, and was retired as Maj.-Gen. June, 1905.

Gen. Winfield Scott Hancock (1844), the distinguished commander of the 2nd Corps during the Civil War. He had gallant service in Mexico and against the Indians. His services are too well known to require further notice. He was a candidate for the presidency in 1880, and died 9 Feb., 1886.

Gen. Wm. Crozier (1876) is a very able Ordnance officer, and has been Chief of Ordnance since Nov., 1901.

William H. Bixby (1873) was Chief of Engineers, with an able career in that branch. Was retired Aug. 13, 1913.

Alexander Piper (1851) was a most gallant officer of Arty. during the Civil War, reached the rank of Col., and died 22 Feb., 1902.

Gen. Charles F. Roe (1868), after long and severe service against Indians in the Northwest, resigned and until lately was the Maj.-Gen. in comd. of the N. Y. National Guard.

Gen. Charles G. Sawtelle (1854) after service on the plains became a quartermaster in 1861, reaching the rank of Col. and Bvt. Brig.-Gen. during the war. He was made Q. M. Gen. in Aug., 1896, and retired in Feb., 1897. He died Jan. 4, 1913.

Gen. Wm. D. Whipple (1851) had long and severe service on the plains prior to the Civil War. He became a Brig.-Gen. of Vol. in the war and was brevetted Maj.-Gen. for gallantry. He was retired in Aug., 1890.

Col. John E. Tourtelotte was for years the efficient and scholarly A. D. C. to Gen. Sherman. For particular gallantry he was given brevet of Brig.-Gen. He was retired in 1885, and died July, 1891.

Col. John P. Wisser (1874) is an able and efficient officer of Arty., at present in comd. of the defences of San Francisco Harbor.

Col. George P. Scriven (1878) is a prominent officer of the Signal Corps, and next in rank to its Chief.

Col. Augustus C. Tyler (1873) left the service in 1878, and re-entered it as Col. of a Vol. Regt. in July, 1898. He died 27 Nov., 1908.

U. S. Senator Henry A. DuPont (1861), after especially gallant service during the Rebellion, resigned in 1875 and became a manufacturer. Was elected to the U. S. Senate in 1906.

Alexander R. Lawton (1839) resigned from the Army in Dec., 1840. Became a lawyer and was prest. of a R.R. Was Minister to Austria 1887–89, and died 2 July, 1896.

Col. James P. Martin (1860) was one of the ablest of the Adjt.-Gens. with brevets for gallantry during the Rebellion. He died 19 Feb., 1895.

John Millis (1881), Col. Corps of Engineers and one of its able and distinguished officers.

Brig. Henry G. Sharpe (1880) resigned June, 1882. Appointed Capt. and Comy. Sept., 1883, and was made Commg. Gen. in Oct., 1905.

Daniel Morgan Taylor (1869) was an officer of Ordnance and was highly regarded for his ability. He became a Col. in Nov., 1906, and died 27 Mar., 1907.

Col. John R. Williams (1876), an able officer of Arty., reached the grade of Col. in Jan., 1908, and was retired in June, 1910.

Gen. Francis V. Greene (1870), distinguished both as a civil and a Military Engineer and as an author, resigned Dec., 1886, and re-entered the service in 1898, becoming a Maj.-Gen. of Vol.

George A. Garretson (1867) resigned Jan., 1870, and became a merchant and banker in Cleveland, O. Again entered the service as Brig.-Gen. Vol. in May, 1898, and was discharged in Nov. Is an officer in many corporations in Cleveland.

Col. John Pitcher (1876) became a Lt.-Col. of Cavalry in April, 1908, and was retired in May of the same year. He was for several years the efficient Supt. of the Yellowstone Park.

Gen. Henry L. Abbott (1854) was very distinguished as an Engineer officer during the Rebellion, earning the brevet of Maj.-Gen. for gallantry. After the war he resumed his work on the coast defences and the improvement of rivers and harbors. Is a member of many learned societies and has written many scientific papers. He was retired in 1895.

Gen. C. E. L. B. Davis (1866) is an Engineer officer of distinction. He was promoted to Brig.-Gen. in Jan., 1908, and retired in Feb., 1908.

Gen. H. C. Hasbroucke (1861) served in the Arty. during the Rebellion and was twice brevetted for gallantry, was a Brig.-Gen. of Vol. during the Spanish War, became Col. of Arty. in Feb., 1899; he was made a Brig.-Gen. in Dec., 1902, and retired in Jan., 1903. Died 17 Dec., 1910.

Gen. George G. Greenough (1865) was a polished and scholarly officer of Arty. He was retired as a Brig.-Gen. in Dec., 1890, and died in 1912.

James Clarence Post (1865) was a Maj. of Engineers and for a time our attaché at London. He died in Jan., 1896.

William A. Rafferty was graduated from Princeton in 1861 and from the M. A. in 1865. After much service on the plains, against the Indians, he died in the Philippines while Col. 5th Cav., on 13 Sept., 1902.

Col. George B. Sanford (Yale 1863) entered the Army at the beginning of the Civil War, reached the grade of Col. of Cavalry, and was retired. He died 13 July, 1908.

John B. Bellinger (1884) was first in the Cavalry, became an Asst. Q. M. in Aug., 1894, and is now Col. and Chief Q. M. of the Eastern Div. at Governors Island.

Montgomery M. Macomb (1874) is an Arty. officer of especial distinction. He became Col. in April, 1908, and Brig.-Gen. in Nov., 1910. He now comds. in Honolulu.

Gen. A. E. Bates (1865) served in the Cavalry on the plains and at the U. S. M. A., was made Paymaster in Mar., 1875, Paymr.-Gen. in July, 1899, and retired as Maj.-Gen. in Jan., 1904. He was for a time in 1898 and 1899 our attaché in London and Paris. He died 13 Oct., 1909.

Alexander Rodgers (1875) is a Cavalry officer of distinction, became Col. in 1906, and was retired in Jan., 1911.

T. Lincoln Casey (1879) is an Engineer officer of much ability, was promoted Col. in Sept., 1909, and retired in 1912.

George M. Wheeler (1866). Retired June, 1888, and died 3 May, 1905. He was the distinguished head of the "Wheeler Surveys" of the country west of the 100th meridian.

Walter L. Fisk (1877), an able and active Engineer officer, became Col. in 1908, and was retired 1911.

William W. Gibson (1879) is a most capable Ordnance officer, now in comd. of the Arsenal at West Troy, N. Y. At one time he was our attaché at Saint Petersburg.

Henry D. Borup (1876), one of our most able Ordnance officers and for a long time our attaché at Paris, was retired in 1904.

Henry P. Kingsbury (1871) has had long and able service against the Indians and is now Col. and Inspector-Gen. of the Central Div. at Chicago. He was retired April, 1914.

Henry L. Ripley (Mass. Inst. of Tech., 1873) was retired as a Lieut.-Col. in 1912.

Stanhope E. Blunt (1872) has had some of the most important comds. in the Ord. Dept., including the Rock Island and the Springfield Arsenals, and was retired a Col. in 1912.

Eugene Griffin (1875) became a Brig.-Gen. of Vol. in May, 1899. Was a very distinguished electrical engineer, president of the Thompson-Houston Co. Died 11 April, 1907.

Francis J. Crilly (1859) served with gallantry during the Civil War in the Inf. and the Q. M. Dept. and resigned in Feb., 1869. He became a merchant and banker in Philadelphia and later a banker in N. Y., and died 25 Jan., 1908.

Royal T. Frank (1858) was an officer of Infantry during the Rebellion and served with distinction, receiving two brevets for gallantry. He was transferred to the Arty. in 1870, and was retired as a Brig.-Gen. Oct., 1899. Died 14 Mar., 1908.

Gen. William Ludlow (1864) had gallant service during the Civil War and was three times brevetted. Was Chief Engineer of the Philadelphia Water Dept. and Engineer Commissioner of D. C. Was Brig. and Maj. Gen. of Vol. May, 1898, to Jan., 1900, and Brig.-Gen. U. S. A. 21 Jan., 1900. Died 30 Aug., 1901.

Gen. Caleb H. Carlton (1859) served with gallantry during the Civil War, receiving two brevets. He was assigned to the Cavalry in Dec., 1870, became a Brig.-Gen., and was retired in June, 1897.

Granger Adams (1876) has always been an officer of Arty. and is now the able Col. of the 5th Regt. L. Arty.

George W. Goethals (1880) is a Col. of Engineers and famous as the Engineer of the Panama Canal.

Wright P. Edgerton (1874) became Professor M. A. in 1898 and died 24 June, 1904.

Gen. Leonard Wood (Hon. Harvard 1899) entered the Army as Asst. Surg. in 1886, and has risen by distinguished service and conduct to be the senior officer in the Army and the very able Chief of the General Staff.

Gen. Thomas H. Barry (1877), after service for years in the Cav. and Inf., was made an Adjt.-Gen. in Jan., 1897, a Brig.-Gen. in 1903, and a Maj.-Gen. in 1908. He is now in command of the Philippine Islands.

Walter A. Bethel (1889) served in the Arty. until July, 1903, when he was appointed Maj. and J. A., and he is now, by detail, Prof. of Law at the U. S. M. A.

Oscar T. Crosby (1882), assigned to the Engineers, resigned Oct., 1887. Is distinguished as an electrical engineer, and famed as a traveller in all parts of the earth.

Gen. Charles W. Raymond (1865) was an Engineer Officer of note, and was retired as a Brig.-Gen. in June, 1904. He held many positions of prominence as a consulting engineer on important works. Died May, 1913.

Gen. John B. Kerr (1870) served in the Cavalry until April, 1908, when he was promoted to Brig.-Gen. He was retired in May, 1909.

Beverly W. Dunn (1883) was an officer of Ordnance, and became noted for his knowledge of explosives, and is employed by transportation companies to supervise the shipment of them. He retired from the Army in 1911.

Major W. S. Guignard (1896), distinguished military attaché at Paris for several years.

Col. W. A. Simpson (1875) is Adjt.-Gen. for the Eastern Dept.

Gen. Tasker H. Bliss (1875) was our Collector of Customs in Havana during our occupation, and is one of the most cultivated men of our Army.

(C) NAVY MEMBERS OF THE UNIVERSITY CLUB, NEW YORK

The officers of the United States Navy, all graduates of Annapolis, have formed such a conspicuous group in the membership of the Club, that the compiler considered it fitting that special reference should be made to them, and called on Commodore Jacob W. Miller to contribute a chapter with that object.

In selecting Commodore Miller for this purpose, his familiarity with the subject and his capacity were the determining factors.

Miller is the son of Honorable J. W. Miller, U. S. Senator from New Jersey. After graduation at Annapolis in 1867, he served in the navy in various capacities and with distinction. He afterward became connected with the merchant marine, and took an active part in the development of the Naval Militia of New York, and was its commodore. He re-entered the navy in 1898 and had command of the Third District Auxiliary Naval force in the Spanish-American War. After filling various important offices he accepted the vice-presidency of the Cape Cod Canal Construction Company, which position he now occupies.

This important work was completed under Commodore Miller's direction. Had not the public attention been riveted upon the stupendous enterprise of the Panama Canal, the Cape Cod Canal would have been recognized more conspicuously than has been the case as a signal advance movement for the facilitating and cheapening of our coastwise commerce. It is thirty feet deep at high water, with a minimum of one hundred feet width at the bottom, and only eight miles long, but is greater in its dimensions than the original Suez or the present Manchester Canal. It cuts Cape Cod in two, and saves to all vessels as far south as Charleston seventy miles to and from Boston. It was officially opened on July 29, 1914.

Commodore Miller was for some years a most useful member of the Club Council, and, busy man as he is, has taken the trouble to write the ensuing story of the naval members of the Club, which is given entire.

AN OFFICIAL REPORT UPON THE NAVY MEMBERS TO ONE WHO HAS EVER BEEN THEIR CONSTANT FRIEND

By Commander Jacob W. Miller (U. S. N. A. '67)

New York, October 20, 1913.

My dear Alexander:

The habits of a life time, coupled with the respect of a subaltern towards his superior almost led me to write "My dear Admiral"; remembering, as I do, with what executive force and diplomatic tact (two traits essential to naval rank) you commanded the talented but undisciplined crew, known as the Council, when I had the honor of serving on that august body, as a "plebe" member thereof.

Nor shall I ever forget the night when Bob Thompson with his usual appreciation of the right man in the right place, and in the same room where the Council ate its usual forecastle feed, asked you to speak to our Alumni for Princeton, and you did for Annapolis, giving a tribute to the navy which both in matter, diction and wit together with a knowledge of marine affairs confirmed my opinion that you were entitled to at least a brevet naval title, as you were to the heartfelt thanks of all who attended that Naval Academy feast; Therefore I begin again.

SIR,—

In obedience to your orders, but with full knowledge of my lack of ability, I have the honor to make the following report upon THE NAVY IN THE CLUB.

I have assumed that good fellowship is the standard of desirable membership and that genial characteristics are more valued among us than rank or the tabulation of an official list: This end I have tried to reach, and also to follow your instructions that no names should appear in the following pages except those who are or who have been in the navy list.

My contemporaries may question the accuracy of the personal application of certain of the following reminiscences; while on the other hand, those who are not mentioned will consign me to "double irons."

As for the "Youngsters," they are writing their own history, making their own popularity, while I, an "Oldster," am one of the doddering crowd harking back to the past.

I am credibly informed that you, Sir, in conformity with your known religious principles, gave your sanction to that dignified body known as the "Sunday School." It has of course been impossible for the Ancient Mariners, who manned the decks of both the old and the new clubs, to emulate the lofty moral tone of that orthodox association: for sailor yarns, tinged now and again with salty expletive, can never be ranked in the same class with the solemn momentous questions of law and current events so dear to judges and journalists when they are keeping the Sabbath Day holy unto the Lord.

Yet why not a record of the sayings of sailors? For mingled with their stories is an undercurrent of patriotic spirit—often dulled in the rest of us as we forget, in the turmoil of life, the broader aims of our college days.

The modesty of the Annapolis graduate, his tendency to belittle courageous acts, as if they were all in the day's work, has lost us many a story of daring adventure, yet here are a few of the tales of

THE UNIVERSITY'S WARD ROOM MESS

One day way back in the "90's" J. H. Upshur still a youth at eighty, George Dewey, the disciplinarian, Bancroft Gherardi the typical sailor of former days, Leonard Chenery—who gave his few well days to creating the Naval Order—and Babcock who died at the Club in 1896, were discussing old times. The conversation turned upon the

From a photograph, copyright by Clinedinst, Washington, D. C.

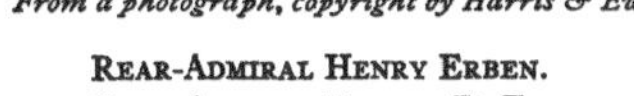

From a photograph, copyright by Harris & Ewing.

Rear-Admiral Henry Erben.
Rear-Admiral Robley D. Evans.

Admiral George Dewey.
Rear-Admiral Alfred T. Mahan.

A NAVY GROUP.

work of the navy on the west coast and in Central America. How little the country knew of the minor engagements in the tropics.

Seventy years ago the Gulf of California was the special scene of historic interest, according to Upshur, as he told the story of the burning of the *Condor* in 1846, and of a thrilling trip of two daring young officers to help *Los Gringos,* during the Mexican war: both had future distinguished careers. Each has descendants in the Club: one a Columbia '78 man with a Persian reputation, the other a Harvard '97 graduate with sufficient pluck to serve as a very "ordinary seaman" the year after he graduated.

Speaking of *Los Gringos*, one is naturally reminded of the YANKEE's crew and its respect and love towards her distinguished Commander during the Spanish-American War. He is often with us though the last to tell of his baptism of fire when he and Dick Rush destroyed the *Pirate Forward* off St. Blas in 1870. Brownson's Boswell was Tom Perry, each today as gallant admirals as ever flew a flag, ploughed a Maryland farm, or perfected target practice against inimical ducks in North Carolina.

On another evening McNair, Cooke and Belknap were telling how climatic diseases took the heart out of men, how yellow jack decimated ship's companies, and how the *Jamestown* nearly came to grief from smallpox when another of our associates was on board.

"Tehuantepec, Nicaragua, Panama and Darien had been the 'sick bay' where many of our members had toiled at risk of life to solve the 'secret of the strait.' There they had surveyed and made perfected reports, and died."

The wonder was if civilians would ever appreciate that to the navy it owed the solution of the Interoceanic Canal problem. As I write today, with full appreciation of the magnificent work of our greatest army member, record must be made of the original labor so quietly done by the sister Service, so simply told in government documents, read by none. Perhaps, at some not far distant time the world will ask why the recommendations of men who were to sail ships through the canal were not followed.

In an old pamphlet long out of print, I find a tribute to a most promising young officer, one of several who perished upon the Isthmus, an extract from it may keep in mind the former death-dealing work at Panama.

I

"He stood it seems but yesterday,
Upon an Isthmian hill whence lay,
On either side the waters of two seas,
Around him tropic jungle thick, disease.
He gives the word, nor thought he'd fail,

"Onward to Pacific cut the trail."
Down, down, through rank and poisoned dell
At duty's call e'en to the gate of Hell,
If ordered, this strong soul would go,
Ne'er asking why or wherefore it were so.
Self-sacrifice in truth he counted naught
If western tide to eastern stream be brought,
And ships sailed through fabled strait that men
Dreamed of long years ago at Darien.

2

Upon the barrier of life's mystic sea,
Parting the past from all eternity,
Again he stood prepared, and ever brave,
To meet the order that the Father gave.
Before him looms the "great divide"
Parting death's isthmus from the farther side,
Then slowly, surely life's tide ebbs away,
And comes the flood of the eternal day.
His glory's won, his sorrows all are o'er,
With rest at last on God's Pacific shore.

What an example was John S. Barnes of diversified culture and occupation, as he let loose his flood of information concerning life in and out of the service. When he related his experience, as a lawyer in the north and a railroad builder in the south, told us of the incidents contained in his navy manuscripts, and Paul Jones's log books—he was at once surrounded by men keen to absorb his narrative. Ward listened as he collected data for the Navy League; Jackson, of New Jersey (today representing the government in other foreign lands) talked of ancient Greece; its marine power of old and renaissance of today. Gillis may have been of the party one night recalling his rescue at Montevideo in 1859 of the crew of a stranded vessel. The while, R. M. G. Brown, Reamey, or Wilson was describing in graphic style the loss of the *Trenton* and *Vandalia* at Apia during the March hurricane of 1889; and Tilley telling of how he governed that port and Samoa in general.

Many a time tribute was paid by Staunton, Lillie, Whitehouse or Long to the unchronicled but equally important work during the period of stagnation after the Civil War, when officers serving on board outclassed, archaic ships, still preserved their traditions and prepared themselves for a fleet which was yet to come. When that fleet was born in 1886 they were ready for modern commands, and through studies at home and abroad, proved experts fitted to master all the details of steel, ordnance and mechanical appliances essential for the battleship of today.

In August, 1891, the Club gave a dinner to Admiral Walker, and the officers of the *White Squadron*. The Army and Militia joined us in doing honor to the first Flag Officer who ever commanded a composite crew of regulars and volunteers. The symposium began with solemnity when the oysters were opened with prayer; and ended—but—it is well perhaps to omit the closing hilarious scene as we "piped down" and sent the steerage members of the mess to their hammocks during the morning watch.

Many of the more sober after-dinner talks about that period were of timely interest, others showed the awakening trend towards marine matters. Discussions ranged from those on steam engineering by Rae, on construction by Woodward and Powelson, and on the contrast between the old era and the new by Amory, White, Dayton, Little, Wildes and Cooper. There were many of us who also recall the shortened hours when the lamented Buckingham told his tale of a trip through Siberia, while the story of fights in Formosa, China and Corea, of the earlier "Cubian" wars and of happenings in both hemispheres came either at first or second hand from such men as Casey, Veeder, Wright, Colwell, Very, Jewell, Lemly, Sargent or Marble.

Four bells of the first "dog watch" often struck before we were tired of listening to seamanship from Dickens; tactics from Smith; frigate lore from Mead, or to the modest recountal of how a New York City boy, Theodore Mason, while serving on board the *Guerrière* saved two men from drowning, and put out a fire on an Italian merchant ship in 1874.

None of us will ever forget that dear old sea dog "Bully" Erben, as keen in recollection of the days of "wooden walls" as he was apt in tribute to the men "behind the gun" on board his ship of the new navy at London in 1894. And then his yarns. Here is one.

"On my last cruise, when in command of the European station, I returned the Admiral's call at Cowes, as I went over the flagship's side there was no music to give the official air. Whereupon the officer of the deck apologized with the statement 'Unfortunately grandma's got the band.' Grandma was Queen Victoria, and the officer of the deck is now the King of England."

Higginson used to revel in Harry Lyon's story of Admiral ———. "A certain ship was going into Alexandria. The admiral sent for his flag lieutenant. 'Lyon,' he said, 'Egypt is a dependency of Turkey, but we must play the local national air, as we drop anchor: What is it?' Lyon had a crass ignorance, but would interview the band leader. All that they jointly could rake up was 'Moses in Egypt' and 'Aida.' These classical compositions did not suit the admiral.

There happened to be a popular song about that time called 'Not for Joseph,' and Lyon had it played as the salute was fired. Now the spouse of our worthy commander-in-chief (a most rigid Presbyterian) was on board, and the Admiral rushed out of the cabin, and with quarterdeck wrath attacked Harry with 'My wife wants to know why in hell you are raking up that old Potiphar scandal at this late date.'"

The oriental yarn reminded another navy member of when he "was with Grant" in the *Vandalia* at Smyrna in 1878. One of the ship's quartermasters was an old shellback whom the General liked to quiz. They met one afternoon ashore and Grant asked him what he thought of the East.

"Well sir, no Koran country where the women wear baggy trousers and hides their ugly mugs, which no one wants to see, with Yasmiks—no haremed household in a land where churches is moskees and steeples is mignonettes—can (begging your pardon sir) have, in my humble opinion, any virtuosity of a permanent nature.

"However, Sir I seen the real western spirit a while ago, and longed to drink it in. There's a camel across the street loading with Medford rum from Massachusetts."

The cosey corners were merry down on Madison Square; but there were also serious discussions as to the future of the navy, especially when the various centennials brought the fleet to New York and the "White Squadron" in 1891 became an object lesson to the people.

That was the time when Vanderpoel, Kent, Wetmore and Dr. Thomas were organizing the naval militia, and Jack Miller was a nuisance with his hobby of the necessity of an "Intermediary between the Service and the people." All the same, the Naval Militia became an accomplished fact; and with them a patriotic lot of club youngsters proud to serve side by side with the blue jackets, and preparing themselves later under the guidance of Scheutze, Marsh and others for their fine record seven years later.

Of all the men who made the "Reserves" a success none deserves more credit than Herbert Satterlee. His services to that body and to the nation, during the Spanish-American War, were partially rewarded when in 1908 he was made Assistant Secretary of the Navy.

The great Columbian Parade of 1893 helped towards the revival of naval sentiment when we entertained distinguished foreign officers. Commander Davis was then as courteous to Princess Eulalia as he and his brother officers were harmful to her country five years later.

Speaking of the war with Spain, reminds one of those pessimistic growlers who divided their criticism between the lack of preparation of the country and the want of homelike features in the new club.

Both the club and the country remain today, broadened in scope and on firmer foundations through the experiences of 1898.

I like to hark back to those days when, with rapt attention we listened to military experts. To Mahan, with his scholarly diction, predicting, from the past, our future pre-eminence at sea; while Taylor and Evans were confident that the navy would live up to its traditions.

What distinctively different types those brothers-in-law were. Harry Taylor—the student of naval tactics and strategy, as President of the War College, the staunch advocate of an Isthmian canal. "Fighting Bob" Evans, the man of action; against every abuse in time of peace, never sparing in his words (even when a court martial threatened) and living up to his nickname in time of war, at Santiago. The mementoes of that fight deposited in the club house are not needed to recall to our minds these two genial companions. Dead though they be, the memory of them ever lives. Chadwick the historian—the Commander of the NEW YORK during the memorable action of July 3d, 1898, sinks his own distinguished deeds in praise of the commanding officers of the INDIANA and IOWA.

This was about the time when Park Benjamin, Hunt and Miller were thrashing out the design for the Naval Academy Seal to be placed on the exterior of our new building.

"Park" as clever with pencil as he is magnetic in argument, and electric of tongue, evolved a seal which was subsequently adopted by the Navy Department; its motto being "Ex Scientia Tridens," which being liberally translated means "From the University Sea Power."

The autographs of the subscribers to the seal were framed—signatures of men who have had much to do with the shaping of American history. I wonder if any one remembers the proposed sale of Dewey's letter, written from the OLYMPIA sending his subscription—but that is another story.

Those last days at Madison Square just about the close of the war were memorable. Officers came and went with tales from the blockade and Cuba.

One night there was a group of navy men—Tremaine, Hunker, Carter, Johnston, Newton and Morrell discussing the want of preparation by the army, and the lack of hospital facilities at Montauk Point when the rough riders landed sick and worn from Santiago. Criticism ran higher and higher, when a man from across the room loitered up to the crowd saying "Gentlemen, I am an army officer—as such I resent your attitude: if club rules permitted, I'll be damned if I would not do much more. I want you to distinctly understand, that the U. S. Army is the best military organization in the world."

Then, his expression changing from wrath to smiles, came this postscript "The only trouble is, along came the war, *and broke the organization all up*." The drinks were on the crowd—gin and joy replacing possible pistols.

It sticks in my mind that the famous "European Squadron Quartette" Wells Field, Bob Berry, Tom Stevens and Sebree were also present that night, and that Tom was elected to satisfy the honor of the army which he failed to do, having sworn off, since the time when as Poet Laureate of the Navy, he had evolved two sea doggerels entitled "Nothing for Me" and "The farther the bar the safer you are." Field's recent virtue had also reached immaculate heights since he had commanded the *St. Marys*, and lived up to the name of that sanctified craft. So the checks must have had the valuable autographs of the big-limbed and big-hearted gentlemen from Missouri and Kentucky.

We classmates—Hagenman, Colby, Clover, Boyd—used to often foregather and forgetting age, dignity and rank sing the temperance "chanteys" of the midshipmen who followed us. The first stanza of one of them running as follows:

"The schooner, it is empty,
Its wreck is on the floor,
Its foam is lingering lightly,
There's beer for us no more."

This must have been the product of auburn-haired Poundstone, or of Toppan or of those pretty poets Blow or Bricker. It is difficult to keep track of the varied talents of marine authors.

Briggs used to run down from Providence sometimes insisting that the first flag officer in the navy came from the head of Narragansett bay, and commanded the first frigate launched from there. That the *Gaspee* was the original craft to chuck tea overboard.

To which Bristol replied that, by the same geographic token, he was a Rhode Island man notwithstanding his associations with New Jersey and Texas.

The Rodgers family, with its six members, presents rare examples of men who perpetuate the sterling qualities of a long line of naval forebears. Admiral Fred heads the list. The dinner table of the "Northwest corner" sadly misses his laconic, bluff manner as he lies ill in his Long Island home.

High in the role of heredity was Dana Greene; truly Christian in his life, in his death he set an example of romantic devotion to the wife he vainly strove to save from drowning on January 8, 1900. To the gentle traits of his Quaker ancestry were added the military qualities of Nathaniel Greene; the scientific attainment of his grandfather; and the bravery of his father, who fought the *Monitor* after Worden was wounded. Graduating at the head of his class at the Naval Academy and at the Newport Torpedo School, he resigned in 1887, and, at the age of 35, attained high position in his adopted profession. This he gave up at a moment's notice for junior rank in the Navy when called to serve in the Spanish-American War.

Somehow I always connect the name of Sloan with that of Greene, as they both served with me in 1898, but panegyric of the living is out of place. After navigating all oceans he "Bobs" up serenely with a fund of Munchausen tales from Jerusalem to Madagascar or equally remote spots, and with reminiscences of the time when he, Gibbons (today the awe-inspiring Superintendent of the Naval Academy) and Harlow wrote bad poetry, poor stories, and worse editorials to relieve the monotony of a 112 days at sea as the *Jamestown* rounded Cape Horn in 1882. The date was that of the birth of the modern battleship—many of the nineteen junior officers who rounded the stormy Cape, reefing topsails as they went, are today commanding dreadnought fleets. Marlin-spike seamanship and lofty canvas fitted them for all emergencies during the rapid transition from canvas to floating citadels, witnessed during the last thirty-two years. Among them a bright soul I remember well on that *Jamestown* cruise—poor Brumby, who lived only a year after he obtained his medal and five numbers for conspicuous bravery on board the *Olympia* at Manila.

Why a man whose first name is William should have been nicknamed "Ben" it is difficult to comprehend, especially as Franklin is comparatively free from Quaker attributes, except that he occasionally proves that a glass insulates shocks from Jersey lightning. When that passing thunder-storm clouded the summer horizon of "98," his meteoric change from peaceful banking to patriotic duty for state and nation showed his distinguished military and naval ancestry.

You who have not listened to Tom Wood tell of his blockading experience off Cuba should take the first opportunity to do so, and urge him to put in print his modest, but thrilling description of the *Gloucester* fight. Hazeltine's yarn of the voyage of an "auxiliary" is also worth listening to, while John Hubbard's experiences with millionaire sailors are both amusing and fair to the embryo seamen.

The men in the card room need no reminder of Morris Mackenzie, as expert in the game there as he is with "bridge" tactics on board ship. He, with his cousin Raymond Rodgers, we hope will soon return to their old haunts. Another cousin was Belmont, named after his great-uncle who a hundred years ago won the battle of Lake Erie.

March 19, 1902, was a cold day outside the club, but warm within with international cheer, as we dined Prince Henry of Prussia. The menu ranged from the sadness of set speeches to the final felicity of unofficial freedom mingled with darkey songs. There were many web-feet at that German love-feast: Perhaps Cornwall, Kellogg, Barnette and Lisle, all were "AB" in fight or frolic. Now "DD," stricken from the muster roll of the navy and club forever.

I especially call to mind three men who were much at the club then and later; all rose to the highest attainable medical rank in the navy —Tryon, Bloodgood and Peck. Tryon a Beau Brummell and Ruth also a magnificent specimen of manhood; both gone to the land where surgeons are no more needed, but where genial good souls must be as welcome as they were in 54th Street. Pity it is that they had not lived to command their own hospital ships. Perchance Van Reypen, their distinguished colleague, may yet see a "chiropodist as Captain of an army transport containing infantry—commonly known as 'foot soldiers.'"

In any event Dr. Lung deserves executive position after his "courageous reconnaissance" in Samoa in 1899.

Those two classmates Cowles and Logan never sat on the weather side of the gun deck, or in easy chairs ashore without the latter spinning some yarn full of mimicry.

On one occasion the talk turned on the necessity of dignity in high rank. John said: "You remember old Admiral ——— with his pompous Chesterfieldian manner. Well, a young chaplain just caught from a theological seminary was ordered to the ship; he reported on board in full uniform, including a sword. The skipper looked him all over and sarcastically remarked 'Sir, I have been given to understand that ecclesiastical regulations require that those who take the sword shall perish by the sword. Therefore, you can confine your church militancy to affairs of the spirit, and I will take care of the flesh and its propensity for fighting' ——— The sword was unbuckled. 'Now Sir, far be it from me to interfere with your religious work, nor do I presume to imagine what my future status may be in the heavenly realm, but here I am supreme, and maintain that the Service has various ranks and positions. Therefore, Sir, when Church Call sounds and the officers and crew take their places according to their several grades, you will not say the Lord is in his holy temple until you see *me* in my seat.'"

"Speaking of dignity," said Perkins, Hodges or Key who joined the circle, "was it not the same officer who, as Superintendent of the Naval Academy, asked the midshipmen after a hard drill on a hot day, whether they wished lemonade or tea after the next sham fight and a cheeky youngster replied, 'Admiral, of the two we prefer beer.'"

Train and Delehanty were criticising the Department one evening for its senseless nomenclature of ships; one had command of the *Prairie* and the other the *Suwanee* during 1898; there was again the old joke that the former should have been schooner rigged with four wheels, while Delehanty said that the closest association he had with his craft, was that he was "far, far away"; whereupon Train, who was a mighty hunter, remarked, "I had a friend named Quail, and always asked him to stay with me when I had to break in a new pointer. You should have seen the dog's tail when Quail came inside the kennels!"

To those who care to follow the development of the modern fleet, no better education could have been afforded than through listening to Folger the ordnance expert, to Swift the brains of department organization, to Fiske the inventor; to Capps and Bowles the constructors of war and commercial ships; to Stockton—who as President of the War College and Naval Attaché in London gained high reputation—to Schouler with his acquaintance of international usage; and to Sperry who supplemented theoretic studies at Newport with practical ability while circumnavigating the world on board the battleships of the twentieth century.

In the triumph of steam, the qualities incident to the days of sail have been preserved and emphasized, especially in the school of the torpedo boat, fitting such men as Winslow for quick decision at high speeds when maneuvering the dreadnoughts; and the gallant Fremont when on outpost duty off Cuba at 20 knots an hour. His life was as full of incident and romantic adventure as that of his father the *Pathfinder*.

The reader who has navigated thus far through this stream of memories would now do well to come to anchor and have Nicoll Ludlow tell of the *Florida* episode; of how she was taken out of Rio Harbor; how the man who commanded the *Wachussett* was dismissed to satisfy the honor of Brazil, only to be immediately reinstated in our navy; how the *Florida* was *accidently* sunk at Fortress Monroe and a court martial convened which never adjourned, and consequently still exists, leaving a great international question affecting the amicable relations of two American governments still unsettled. The gravity of the situation was only surpassed by the humor of its details.

The crowd which have left the Service have in the best sense done it for their country's good. Sprague, the builder of the first trolley road. Louis Duncan, the electrical expert. Semple, as good a lawyer as his friend Soley, who died two years ago. Dan Case, enlarging his agricultural knowledge in Rhode Island by studies of grape juice in Italy. Van Schrader, he of the play-writing clan. Deering, who dared to leave the hustle of Chicago for the quiet of New York. Emmet, the bright incandescent light of the Edison octopus, and Derby, once the matinee idol of private theatricals of Annapolis today living in the peace of dull Newport. Phoenix, who left the easy navy life only for the hard work of continually keeping the sea in the most shipshape yacht that ever won a cup.

There is a man whom we will call "Colonel" so as to be certain he is not a skipper, or "Bob" if you please, who has always been the angel of Navy Athletics, spending his "nickels" freely for the good of the Naval Academy. I wish he would let me use his name and tell how he helped poor Ned Berwind to obtain a sinecure in the Service at $1,800 a year during the Spanish war. It is well, however, not to bring the animosity of the indigent upon one's head.

It is close towards "eight bells" and time to call the watch: to turn over the deck to that right good crew of landlubbers shipped from other colleges and universities. Hayseeds though they may be, and unable to distinguish at this late hour between starboard and port, they have ever been *right* in their love for us beggars of the sea and seen to it that we never got *left* when the boatswain piped to skylark. May the next fifty-year cruise be as merry and smooth for you as you have made it pleasant and jolly for us of the "Seven Seas!"

To you, sir, my thanks for permitting me to recall many happy hours.

We, of the Navy, feel that our sea horizon has become extended through association with the men of clear vision ashore—our observations, as we sail life's waters, rendered more exact through the help of those who are steering a true course on land.

Together we—officers and civilians—have perhaps accomplished some little for the future safe navigation of the Ship of State.

Respectfully,

Your obedient servant,

J. W. MILLER.

APPENDIX XI*

OLD ITALY IN NEW YORK

THE PINTORICCHIO LIBRARY AT THE UNIVERSITY CLUB

WHEN the building of the University Club, at Fifth Avenue and 54th Street, was completed several years ago, the Library on the second floor excited admiration just as it stood, a long and stately chamber, lined with dark woodwork, above which the vaulted ceiling showed no touch of color. Recently this ceiling and the walls between it and the shelves have been decorated by Mr. H. Siddons Mowbray, who has based his work on Pintoricchio's paintings in the Borgia apartments at the Vatican, and the beauty of the Library has thereby been enormously increased. It is now, in fact, a masterpiece of architectural and decorative design, in which one can read the intention of the architect, Mr. Charles F. McKim, to produce a monumental scheme of flawless unity. To the dignity of fine proportions he has added the charm of just the webs of form and color which the room was waiting to receive at a painter's hands. Other expedients may very naturally have suggested themselves. A modern building seems to call on most occasions for the ministrations of a modern decorator. But in this instance nothing, we believe, could have been so felicitous as Mr. Mowbray's acclimatization of the spirit of an old master in the heart of New York. He has played his part in the solution of Mr. McKim's problem from the inside, and his paintings are fused with the constructive elements in the room into an organic whole. It is doubtful if this could have been done through the adaptation of any early Italian ideas save those of Pintoricchio.

This Umbrian master occupies a clearly defined place in the history of his school. In the backgrounds of his paintings the influence of the landscape of his native province is at once perceptible, an influence making for revery and a kind of sweet simplicity. No sensitive artist could dwell within sight of the soft lights and

* From the *New York Tribune*, October 13, 1904.

shadows which turn the Umbrian plain into a land of dreams as you gaze out upon it from the heights of Perugia or Assisi, without being stirred to delicate emotions; and from Pintoricchio's work the note of tenderness so characteristic of his early surroundings is rarely missing. His madonnas show, too, that he had his share of the religious inspiration so bountifully bestowed upon the painters of his time. But there was in him a peculiarly mundane strain of feeling. He could be devotional, but something kept him from going to the lengths of Perugino, for example, whose swooning ecstasies were little, we fancy, to his taste. For Pintoricchio's religious emotion was none the worse for a tinge of earthly happiness and pride. He painted with a blithe spirit, and tended more and more, as time went on, to express the ideas of the Church that were within the range of the artist in terms of gorgeous pageantry. He saw everything, for that matter, in a genial human light. Whether he dealt with history or the Scriptures, with allegorical or familiar Italian figures, he seems to have reserved a candid, almost naive frame of mind. The sophistication which seems to lie on the surface of much of his work has nothing philosophical about it, it is rather an affair of craftsmanship, of a painter loving rich costumes and trappings, noble colors and all the pomp of a luxurious society, and painting these things with a shrewd eye for their decorative effect. He is one of the most splendid of fifteenth-century Italian artists and one of the least esoteric. Though he developed many a high erected theme in the course of his busy life, he leaves, when all is said, the impression of an artist whose gift was, above all, for the building up of charming fabrics of designs; he was a disinterested manipulator of form and color.

That is why he gave Mr. Mowbray so much to go upon at the University Club. If Pintoricchio had been saturated in spiritual and imaginative qualities, his designs would have defied reproduction, and especially the kind of reproduction which is to be noted on this occasion. Mr. Mowbray has not baldly transferred to New York compositions existing in Rome. On the contrary, he has been a copyist in only part of his work. In four of the alcoves at the Club he has given us as many of his master's designs, following with close fidelity, practically throughout, the details of certain panels, symbolizing Geometry, Arithmetic, Music, and Rhetoric in the Borgia rooms. In addition to these lunettes, there are panels in the ceiling illustrating mythological types and episodes, wherein Pintoricchio again occupies, as it were, the centre of the stage. But over the door at one end of the room the American artist has enthroned a figure of his own symbolizing History; at the other end he has an original interpretation of Romance, and in the ceiling there are portraits, and figures standing for Science, Philosophy, Literature, the Fine Arts, and other interests, which are likewise the fruit of his own invention. In the execution of all this original work, and of the formal decoration, the rich arabesques, in which the figure paintings are everywhere enveloped, Mr. Mowbray has reverently followed the broad lines of his model. He has sought to make his own compositions as Pintoricchio might have made them; he has adopted the Italian's style, using particularly, whenever opportunity has offered, that device of exhibiting an architectural detail or an item of costume in high relief, gilded, which is so effective in the Borgia rooms, in the Siena Library and in other schemes of Pintoricchio's. It is no discourtesy to Mr. Mowbray to say that his success in these endeavors is positively astonishing. To have copied the master as he has copied him in the lunettes aforesaid is in itself to have achieved much. To have gone infinitely further, to have blended his own work with the old Italian's in perfect harmony, and to have done this while adjusting the entire assemblage of pictorial and decorative motives to a room different in many respects from the scene of Pintoricchio's labors, is to have put to his credit a *tour de force* which is quite without precedent.

There is not a factor in this work that fails to fall naturally into the right place. This is due not alone to Mr. Mowbray's careful distribution of his figures, and to the placing of his panels with wise reference to the construction of the room, but to the homogeneity of the color scheme. This is filled with Pintoricchio's dusky blues and grays, his dull, tawny yellows, his delicate greens, and still more delicate rose tints. Constantly, too, the rich gold of which he was so fond makes its appearance. The result you would call sumptuous if it were not so subdued in its brilliance, so steadfastly kept within the limits of a refined scale, that the eye, while filled with delight, finds only repose. Here, indeed, is an ideal key of color for a decoration brought within the atmosphere of a library. The room is bound to remain an object of high curiosity. No one could enter it without immediately falling into study of what is, in truth, a very elaborate and imposing piece of work. But its great virtue lies in the fact that, for all its importance, it never violently seizes the attention; like the well filled bookcases, it simply envelops one in a sense of something stimulating and fine. Mr. McKim and Mr. Mowbray, between them, have here created one of those works of art which bear the mark of permanence upon them.

APPENDIX XII

PAINTINGS, PRINTS, AND ENGRAVINGS IN THE UNIVERSITY CLUB

Paintings

President Woolsey. By Eastman Johnson. Gift of Yale members, 1884.
President McCosh. By M. Munkacsy. Gift of Princeton members, 1886.
President Nott. By John F. Weir. Gift of Union members, 1888.
President Eliot. By R. C. Hardie. Gift of Harvard members, 1890.
President Hopkins. (Unsigned.) Gift of Williams members, 1885.
President Barnard. By Eastman Johnson. Gift of Mrs. Barnard, 1890.
President Woods, of Bowdoin. Gift of (?).
President Porter. Copy of portrait at Yale. Gift of Miss Bannister, 1902.
President Wayland, of Brown. (Unsigned.)
General Grant. By William Curtis. Gift of E. C. Hurry, 1887.
Chief Justice Marshall. By John Trumbull. Purchased by subscription, 1888.
George Washington. By Gilbert Stuart. Purchased by subscription, 1888.
Admiral Farragut. By John F. Weir. Gift of Navy members, 1889.
Daniel Webster. By Lawson. Gift of Edward King, 1889.
H. H. Anderson. By George B. Butler. 1890.
George A. Peters. By Eastman Johnson. 1891.
James W. Alexander. By John W. Alexander. 1899.
Charles C. Beaman. By J. N. Marble. 1903.
Henry E. Howland. By F. P. Vinton. 1905.
Edmund Wetmore. By Irving Wiles. 1911.
B. Aymar Sands. By William T. Smedley. 1914.

The marble busts of Æschylus, Sophocles, Euripides, Socrates, and Plato by M. Ezekiel. Presented by John W. Simpson (Amherst '71) in 1905.

The bronze bust of Voltaire was the gift of Doctor Haight. The remaining busts are bronzed plaster.

Prints and Engravings

General Winfield Scott. Designed and engraved by T. B. Welch. Open letter proof.

James K. Polk. Engraved by J. Sartain, after the painting by T. Sully, Jr. Open letter proof.

John Tyler. Engraved by J. Sartain, after the painting by J. R. Lambdin. With autograph of John Tyler. Open letter proof.

William Henry Harrison. Engraved by Sartain and Tucker, after the painting by T. Sully, Jr. Open letter proof.

Thomas Jefferson. Engraved by C. Tiebout, after the painting by R. Peale. Letter proof.

Samuel Seabury, D.D. Engraved by W. Sharp, after the painting by T. S. Duche. Presented by F. R. Halsey.

David Rittenhouse, LL.D., F.R.S. Engraved by E. Savage, after the painting by C. W. Peale. Letter proof. Presented by F. R. Halsey.

Theodore Roosevelt. Etched by Albert Rosenthal, after the painting by J. S. Sargent. Signed artist's proof. Presented by F. R. Appleton.

William Howard Taft. Etched by Albert Rosenthal, after the painting by Anders Zorn. Signed artist's proof. Presented by F. R. Appleton.

John Quincy Adams. Engraved by A. B. Durand, after the painting by T. Sully, Jr. Letter proof.

James Madison. Engraved by D. Edwin, after the painting by T. Sully, Jr. Letter proof. Presented by Adrian H. Larkin.

John Adams. Drawn and engraved by H. Houston. Letter proof.

N. P. Willis. Engraved by C. Meadows. Open letter proof.

Worcester College, 1741. Engraved by G. Vertue.

Baliol, 1742. Engraved by G. Vertue.

Saint Mary's Hall, 1746. Engraved by G. Vertue.

All Souls College, 1720. Engraved by G. Vertue.

Lincoln College, 1743. Engraved by G. Vertue.

Chapel of Lincoln College (from the ante chapel). Engraved by G. Lewis, after drawing by F. Mackenzie. Presented by B. Aymar Sands.

View of Oxford from the Gallery in the Observatory. Engraved by J. Black, after drawing by W. Turner. Presented by B. Aymar Sands.

Gate of Christ Church from Pembroke College. Engraved by J. Reeves, after drawing by F. Mackenzie. Presented by B. Aymar Sands.

High Street Looking West. Engraved by J. Black, after drawing by A. Pugin. Presented by B. Aymar Sands.

MAGDALENE COLLEGE. Engraved by S. Sparrow, after drawing by J. Burford. Proof before letters.

CAIUS COLLEGE. Engraver (?).

TRINITY COLLEGE, CAMBRIDGE. Engraved by S. Sparrow, after drawing by R. Burford.

CATHERINE HALL. Engraved by S. Sparrow, after drawing by J. Burford.

SENATE HOUSE AND UNIVERSITY LIBRARY, CAMBRIDGE. Engraved by S. Sparrow, after drawing by R. Burford.

TRINITY COLLEGE LIBRARY. Engraver (?).

JESUS COLLEGE, CAMBRIDGE. Engraved by S. Sparrow, after drawing by J. K. Baldrey.

THE NEW BUILDINGS OF TRINITY HALL. Engraved by E. Challis, after drawing by B. Budge.

VIEW OF ONE OF CAMBRIDGE COLLEGES. Engraver (?).

QUEENS COLLEGE, CAMBRIDGE. Engraved by S. Sparrow, after drawing by J. K. Baldrey.

TRINITY HALL. Engraved by S. Sparrow, after drawing by J. K. Baldrey.

VIEW OF EXETER COLLEGE AND ALL SAINTS CHURCH FROM THE TURL. Engraved by James Basire, after drawing by I. M. Turner, R.A.

VIEW OF NEW COLLEGE CHAPEL, OXFORD, 1773. Engraved and drawn by E. and M. Rooker. Letter proof.

THE LIBRARIES AND SCHOOLS FROM EXETER COLLEGE. Engraved and drawn by M. A. Rooker. Letter proof.

THE NEW BUILDINGS, MAGDALENE COLLEGE FROM THE GROVE. Engraved and drawn by M. A. Rooker. Letter proof.

THE LIBRARIES AND SCHOOLS FROM EXETER COLLEGE GARDENS. Engraved and drawn by M. A. Rooker. Letter proof.

THE NEW LIBRARY AT ORIEL COLLEGE. Engraved by Isaac Taylor, after drawing by D. Harris.

QUEENS COLLEGE. Engraver (?). Proof before letters.

A WESTERN VIEW OF ALL SOULS COLLEGE. Engraved by Isaac Taylor, after drawing by D. Harris. Letter proof.

A PERSPECTIVE VIEW OF THE NEW GATE AT CHRIST CHURCH. Engraved and drawn by M. A. Rooker. Letter proof.

COLLEGE PROSPECT. Engraver (?). Proof before letters.

KINGS COLLEGE CHAPEL, THE PUBLIC LIBRARY AND EAST END OF SENATE HOUSE IN THE UNIVERSITY OF CAMBRIDGE. Engraved and drawn by Thomas Malton. Letter proof.

SOUTH VIEW OF THE SEVERAL HALLS OF HARVARD COLLEGE. Engraved by Annin and Smith, after the painting by Fisher.

PLAN OF THE BUILDINGS AT BRISTOL COLLEGE ON THE DELAWARE. Drawing. Artist (?).

View of Nassau Hall, Princeton, N. J. Lithographed in color, after a drawing by F. Childs. Letter proof.

Dartmouth College. Engraved by C. Meadows. Open letter proof.

Girard College for Orphans, Philadelphia, Pa. Engraved by A. W. Graham. Letter proof.

Perspective View of St. Luke's Hospital. (Site of the present University Club.) Lithographed by Sarony & Co., New York, after architect's drawing by J. W. Rich.

West Point. Engraved by J. Hill, after drawing by G. Catlin. Letter proof.

Hamilton College. (Two views.) Engraved by I. N. Gimbrede, after drawing by Louis Bradley.

Amherst College. Engraved by J. Archer, after drawing by A. J. Davis. Letter proof.

A Front View of Dartmouth College with Chapel and Hall. Engraved by S. Hill, after drawing by J. Dunham.

View of Dartmouth College. Engraver (?).

Andover Theological Seminary. Engraver (?).

Columbia College. Drawn by A. J. Davis.

Yale College, 1845.

Prospect of Yale College. Engraved by T. Johnston, after drawing by J. Greenwood. Letter proof.

Yale College and State House, New Haven, Conn. Engraved by J. Archer, after drawing by J. A. Davis. Open letter proof.

Old Princeton College. Drawn by Richardson, N. A. Letter proof.

A Northwest Prospect of Nassau Hall. Engraved by S. L. Smith, after Drawing by W. Tennant. Letter proof.

Harvard University, Cambridge, Mass. Open letter proof.

View of the Colleges at Cambridge, Mass. Engraved and drawn by F. Hull. Letter proof.

Universita di Cambridge. Water-color drawing.

Printed Examination Sheet, Harvard, July 21st, 1784.

Printed Examination Sheet, Harvard, July 19th, 1786.

Catalogue of Alumni of Brown College from 1768 to 1789.

APPENDIX XIII

COLLEGES AND DEGREES, 1914

List of degrees of universities and colleges qualifying the holders for membership, as determined by the Council. This list is subject to amendment by the withdrawal of the names of any of the universities or colleges or degrees contained in it, or by the addition of others, as the Council may from time to time determine. (Article VIII, Section 3, of the Constitution.)

Members desiring to propose a candidate who is the holder of a degree not included in this list are requested to submit the name of the university or college of which the proposed candidate is a graduate, and his degree, to the Council, with full and detailed information as to the requirements of study and residence for such degree, and particularly as to such requirements at the time the candidate received his degree.

Amherst—A.B., B.S.
Bates—B.A., B.S.
Beloit—B.A., B.S.
Bowdoin—A.B.
Brown—A.B., B.P., Ph.B.
Bucknell—B.A., B.S., Ph.B.
Case School of Applied Science—B.S.
Colby—A.B.
Colgate—A.B.
College of the City of New York—A.B., B.S.
Columbia—A.B., M.E., C.E., E.E., E.M., Ph.B., B.S.
Columbian—A.B. (Name changed, December 1, 1904, to George Washington University.)
Cornell—A.B., B.C.E. (up to and including 1885), M.E., C.E. (after 1885), B.S., B.L., Ph.B., B.Arch.
Dartmouth—A.B., B.L., B.S.
Dickinson—B.A. (up to and including 1850).
Georgetown—A.B.
Hamilton—A.B., Ph.B., B.S.
Harvard—A.B., B.S., C.E. (up to and including 1888).
Haverford—A.B., B.E. (up to and including 1890), B.S.
Hobart—A.B., B.S. (1876 to 1891), B.L.
Johns Hopkins—A.B.
Kenyon—A.B.
Knox—B.A., B.S.
Lafayette—A.B., C.E., Ph.B., B.S., E.M., E.E.
Lehigh—B.A., E.M., M.E., C.E., B.S. in Mining and Metallurgy (up to and including 1900), and Met.E. subsequent.
Leland Stanford, Jr.—B.A.
Massachusetts Institute of Tech-

nology—S.B., in thirteen following courses: I. Civil Engineering. II. Mechanical Engineering. III. Mining Engineering and Metallurgy. IV. Architecture. V. Chemistry. VI. Electrical Engineering. VII. Biology. VIII. Physics. IX. General Studies. X. Chemical Engineering. XI. Sanitary Engineering. XII. Geology. XIII. Naval Architecture.

Middlebury—A.B.

New York—A.B., B.S., Ph.B.

Northwestern—A.B.

Oberlin—A.B.

Ohio State—A.B., conferred by the College of Arts, Philosophy, and Science in the course in Arts; B.Sc. conferred by the College of Arts, Philosophy, and Science in the course in General Science; B.S., conferred by School of Science (up to and including 1892); M.E., conferred by School of Engineering in 1890 (up to and including 1892).

Ohio Wesleyan—A.B.

Princeton—A.B., B.S., Litt.B., C.E., E.E. (up to and including 1895).

Purdue—B.S.

Racine—A.B.

Rensselaer Polytechnic Institute—C.E., M.E., B.S.

Rutgers—A.B., Degree of B. S., in Courses of Agriculture, Civil Engineering, and Mechanics, Chemistry, Electricity, Biology, Clay-working, and Ceramics.

Stevens Institute—M.E., B.S.

Syracuse—A.B., Ph.B., B.S.

Swarthmore—A.B., B.S.

Trinity—A.B., B.S.

Tufts—A.B., B.M.A.

Tulane—A.B.

Union—A.B., B.E.

University of California—A.B., B.L., Ph.B.

University of Chicago—A.B., B.S., Ph.B.

University of Georgia—A.B.

University of Illinois—A.B.

University of Michigan—A.B., C.E. (prior to 1882); B.S., conferred in the Department of Literature, Science, and Arts, and in the Department of Engineering, Ph.B. (prior to 1901).

University of Minnesota—A.B., C.E., M.E., E.E., B.C.E. (prior to 1897), B.S., in Engineering.

University of Missouri—C.E., of School of Engineering (up to and including 1896), B.S., in Civil Engineering of School in Engineering (after 1896).

University of Nebraska—A.B.

University of North Carolina—A.B., Ph.B., B.S.

University of Pennsylvania—A.B., B.S.

University of Rochester—A.B., B.S.

University of the South—B.A.

University of Vermont—A.B., Ph.B., B.S. in E.E. and in Commerce and Economics.

University of Virginia—A.B., B.L., Degree of M.A. (down to and including 1891), C.E., Min. Eng., Mech. Eng., Elec. Eng., Chem. Eng.

University of Wisconsin—A.B., B.L., in Modern Classical, Civic, Historical and English Courses.

Vanderbilt—A.B., B.E., B.S.
Washington—A.B., B.S., Ph.B. (1876 to 1892), C.E. (1889 to 1895), M.E. (1889 to 1895), E.M. (1889 to 1895), B.E. (1871 to 1888 inclusive).
Washington and Jefferson—B.A., B.S.
Washington and Lee—B.A., B.S., C.E., M.E.
Wesleyan—A.B., Ph.B., B.S.
Western Reserve—A.B.
Western University of Pennsylvania—A.B.
Williams—A.B.
Worcester Polytechnic Institute—B.S.
Yale—A.B., B.S., Ph.B.

Foreign Universities

Great Britain and Ireland:
Oxford University—B.A.
Cambridge University—B.A.
London University—B.A.
Edinburgh University—B.A., M.A.
Dublin University (Trinity College)—B.A.
Glasgow University—A.M., B.A., B.S.
Germany:
Freiberg in Saxony, Royal School of Mines—Min. Eng., Met. Eng., Iron Met. Eng., and Mine Surveying Eng.
France:
École des Beaux Arts—Diploma or Grand Prix de Rome.
University of France— }
University of Paris— } Any degree from the Paris Faculty of Letters or Faculty of Science.
Canada:
McGill College—B.A., B.Ap. Sc. (prior to 1899) and B.S. (after 1898).
University of Toronto—B.A., B.A. Sc.

APPENDIX XIV

LIST OF COLLEGES AND UNIVERSITIES REPRESENTED IN MEMBERSHIP OF CLUB

AMERICAN

Adrian.
Albany.
Amherst.

Bates.
Beloit.
Bethany.
Bowdoin.
Brown.
Bucknell.
Burlington.

Case School of Applied Science.
Centre.
Colby.
Colgate.
College of Charleston.
College City of New York.
College of Physicians and Surgeons.
Colorado.
Columbia.
Columbian.
Cornell.

Dalhousie.
Dartmouth.
Davidson.
Delaware.
Dickinson.

Emory.

Georgetown.
George Washington.
Hamilton.
Harvard.
Haverford.
Hiram.
Hobart.

Johns Hopkins.

Kenyon.
Knox.

Lafayette.
Lehigh.
Leland Stanford, Jr.

Manhattan.
Marietta.
Massachusetts Institute of Technology.
Miami.
Middlebury.
New York.
New York Free Academy.
Northwestern.
Norwich.

Oberlin.
Ohio State.
Ohio Wesleyan.
Pennsylvania State.
Princeton.
Purdue.

Racine.
Randolph-Macon.
Rensselaer Polytechnic Institute.

Richmond.
Rutgers.

St. Francis Xavier.
St. John's.
Seton Hall.
South Carolina.
Stevens Institute.
Swarthmore.
Syracuse.

Trinity.
Tufts.
Tulane.

Union.
U. S. Military Academy.
U. S. Naval Academy.
University of California.
University of Chicago.
University of Georgia.
University of Illinois.
University of Iowa.
University of Kentucky.
University of Maryland.
University of Michigan.
University of Minnesota.
University of Missouri.
University of Nebraska.
University of North Carolina.
University of Pennsylvania.
University of Rochester.
University of the South.
University of Vermont.
University of Virginia.
University of Wisconsin.

Vanderbilt.

Washburn.
Washington.
Washington and Jefferson.
Washington and Lee.
Wesleyan.
Western Reserve.
Western University of Pennsylvania.
Williams.
Worcester Polytechnic Institute.

Yale.

Foreign

Great Britain:
- Oxford.
- Cambridge.
- London.
- Edinburgh.
- Dublin.
- Glasgow.

Germany:
- Berlin.
- Dresden Polytechnic.
- Freiberg in Saxony.
- Göttingen.
- Heidelberg.
- Königsberg.
- Leipzig.

France:
- École des Beaux Arts.
- University of France.
- University of Paris.

Belgium:
- University of Ghent.
- University of Liège.

Canada:
- McGill.
- University of Toronto.

APPENDIX XV

OTHER UNIVERSITY CLUBS

List of University Clubs Organized Since the Reorganization of the University Club of the City of New York, in 1879

Name	Date of Organization
Albany, N. Y.	1901
American Universities Club, London, England	March, 1910
American University Club, Shanghai, China	1901
Atlanta, Ga.	1911
Austin, Tex.	December, 1904
Baltimore, Md.	October, 1887
Bethlehem, Pa.	——
Boston, Mass.	January, 1892
Bridgeport, Conn.	1905
British Schools and Universities, New York	November, 1895
Brooklyn, N. Y.	June, 1901
Buffalo, N. Y.	December, 1894
Chicago, Ill.	February, 1887
Cincinnati, Ohio	1881
Cleveland, Ohio	June, 1898
Decatur, Ill.	1902
Denver, Col.	January, 1891
Detroit, Mich.	June, 1899
Dublin, Ireland	——
Edinburgh, Scotland	June, 1864
Erie (in process of formation, 1913)	——
Evanston, Ill.	February, 1904
Geneva, N. Y.	1909
Graduates Club of New Haven, Conn.	1891
Hawaii	——
Hudson Co., N. J.	December, 1897
Indianapolis, Ind.	1899
Kansas City, Mo.	March, 1901
Lawrence, Kan.	——
Litchfield Co., Conn.	June, 1897
Los Angeles	March, 1903

Name	Date of Organization
Madison, Wis	1907
Manila, Philippines	1900
Milwaukee, Wis	November, 1898
Montreal, Canada	March, 1907
Nashville, Tenn	——
Nassau Club, Princeton, N. J	1889
Niagara Falls, N. Y	September, 1895
Omaha, Neb	1911
Panama, C. A.	1905
Philadelphia, Pa	March, 1881
Pittsburg, Pa	1890
Portland, Oregon	1898
Princeton, N. J	1898
Providence, R. I.	1899
Rochester, N. Y	June, 1909
Rogue River Valley, Oregon	October, 1910
St. Louis, Mo	March, 1872
Sacramento, Cal	August, 1909
Salt Lake City, Utah	June, 1886
San Antonio, Tex	——
San Francisco, Cal	August, 1890
Seattle, Wash	January, 1901
Spokane, Wash	1905
Sydney, Australia	1905
Syracuse, N. Y	September, 1899
Toledo, Ohio	December, 1897
Toronto, Canada	1906
Washington, D. C	February, 1904
Women's University Club, N. Y	October, 1891

It would perhaps be considered presumptuous for the University Club of the city of New York, on the doctrine of *post hoc propter hoc*, to claim parentage to the forty-eight university clubs which have been organized in other towns and cities of the United States, since the reorganization of our Club in 1879. Nevertheless, it does not seem too much to regard the remarkable multiplication of such clubs as influenced in a large degree by the example of the University Club of New York City.

Pains have therefore been taken to correspond with the officers of all existing clubs of college men, and from the replies received, the following information has been compiled which cannot fail to be of value to those interested enough in the subject to observe the development of organizations composed of college graduates, and the spirit of university enthusiasm which swept through the country, after the successful establishment of our own Club in its new birth.

There cannot be a question but that this emphasis put upon the advantage of a college education has had its effect in stimulating a desire to belong to the guild of educated men. There are those—and not a few by any means—who bitterly regret the carelessness of youth which has lost them the "degree" which would have made them eligible to membership in the University Club, and even if the motive be a lower one than the genuine thirst for knowledge, it is not without its importance and significance.

The University Club of St. Louis is the first club organized after the birth of our own original Club in New York, and inasmuch as it came into existence before the reorganization of the New York Club in 1879, its initiative was clearly not due to that active revival, but was an independent movement. Professor Marshall S. Snow, one of the founders of the St. Louis club, has been good enough to furnish a history of its life, from which the following extracts are taken:

On the afternoon of the thirtieth of December, 1871, 22 college graduates met in the office of Garland and Greene, 203 No. Third St., to take the preliminary steps towards the formation of a University Club. The institutions represented were the following: Harvard, Yale, Dartmouth, Princeton, Amherst, Williams, Brown, Hamilton, Oberlin, Kenyon, and Aberdeen, Scotland. The meeting was an enthusiastic one, although no one seemed to have any very definite idea as to matters of detail. Whether the proposed organization should be called a *club* was one of the subjects of a lively debate, although the call for the meeting had indicated its object to be "the formation of a University Club." Some of those present had very hazy notions of what a club was. To some the word conveyed the idea of a place where idle men met after dark, drank strong liquor, played dangerous games of cards, and exchanged doubtful stories and all the scandal of the day. This class was represented by a kindly old gentleman who begged in really piteous tones that this organization should not be called by that opprobrious name, *club*. "Why, gentlemen, I tell you frankly that if we call this union of college men a *club*, my wife will never let me darken its doors." It was decided, however, at that very meeting to call ourselves *The University Club*, and I am happy to say that our protesting friend succeeded in running the blockade, and was for several years an active and useful member.

To Charles C. Soule must be given the credit of founding the University Club.

The committees appointed at the first meeting went to work at once. Articles of Association and By-Laws were drawn up. The question of permanent quarters was diligently considered. College graduates were hunted up, button-holed anywhere they could be caught, and pledged to the new enterprise. Weeks were spent in the work of organization, accompanied by hot debate, and at times, great weariness of spirit. A number of burning questions soon arose. Should the membership be limited to those who had received a degree from a college or university? Should any one be admitted who had left college before the completion of the course, either from unfortunate circumstances, or by his own wish, or for the good of the college? Should graduates of West Point and Annapolis be given equal privileges with college graduates? Should anybody be admitted who had never entered college (unless it might be on a tour of observation just to see what the thing was like) but whose attainments were such as to make him amply worthy the distinction of an election to the University Club? About the usual Articles of Association and By-Laws there was little discussion, but on the above questions great differences of opinion were discovered, and debates were long and spirited. Graduates of West Point and the Naval Academy were admitted with little or no opposition. Discussion upon the other questions, however, was continued from time to time during nearly three months. Some of us recall those long evenings spent in debate sometimes verging on the acrimonious. There was no lack of interest on the part of the members, and almost every one had something to say, and said it. It was not always pertinent; it was sometimes impertinent; but it was said. It was finally agreed that non-graduates might be elected to membership, not to exceed in number one-fifth of the graduate members. The door, which some had wished to keep locked against non-graduates, was thus left ajar, until at the quarterly meeting in October, 1874, it was thrown wide open. It would doubtless have been wiser to take this step at first. Those in our club who understood something of club life and club needs doubted from the very outset the ability of the comparatively few college men in the St. Louis of that day to maintain such an institution as we had in mind. This was one of the reasons for allowing a certain number of non-graduates to become members. Two years' experience made it very clear that for that reason, if for no other, the doors should be thrown open, as they were in 1874. In the meantime a formal charter was obtained under which the first regular meeting of the club was held, March fourth, 1872. Not until June of that year was the question of a location for the home of the club settled, when after much discussion the club leased for three years the Tilden House, so called, an old-fashioned mansion on Olive St. near Ninth St., then almost on the outskirts of the city, the site of which is now covered by a portion of a large department store. On the evening of June sixth the Club met for the inauguration of its first president, the Hon. Thomas Allen, Union College 1832. The life of the University Club had now really begun.

The life at the Tilden House was delightful. It flowed on easily and quietly and peacefully. No questions arose which could make factions or ill feeling. We had, of course, a club kicker; indeed there were two or three of them; but they only made life merrier and were not vicious enough to make the members weary. Before the expiration of the Tilden House period we had made some progress in the ways of club living.

The initiation fees and annual dues required in those days show how modest were our aims. At first the initiation fee was only five dollars but was soon raised to ten, while the annual dues were only ten dollars. Before we left the Tilden House, however, the initiation fee had been raised to twenty-five dollars and the dues to fifteen and then to twenty dollars. In 1876 the initiation fee was raised to fifty dollars, and in 1858 the Board was given authority to assess fifty dollars as the annual dues. These dues were finally fixed at seventy-five dollars, as at present.

The second period in the history of the club began in July, 1875, in another hired house, the Harrison House, 1125 Washington avenue, on land now covered by a large wholesale warehouse. This was the home of the club for seven years, and the years spent here were in some respects the best in the early history of the club. Its affairs were in a prosperous condition. The membership was large enough for comfort. That feeling so hard to define or to explain, which we sometimes call "college spirit," was strong; and although we had let down the bars before we left Olive St., and no longer required a diploma as a passport to admission, we were more of a University Club than ever. We growled and grumbled at the restaurant; we heard it said more than once that the Directors knew nothing about running a first-class club; that there was an economy of brains in the management; that everything was going to the dogs; we had members who talked shop, apparently for no other reason than to hear the sound of their own voices. We had all these drawbacks, and yet we were happy.

In 1880, Hon. Thomas Allen, who had been chosen President of the club year after year eleven times, died on the eighth of April. One of the most prominent citizens of the city, his life is a part of the history of St. Louis. As our President he had commanded the respect and affection of every member of the club. At the next annual meeting the club unanimously elected Judge Samuel Breckinridge to fill the vacancy, who also served until his death in 1891.

Early in 1879 began the agitation for a change in the location of the club house, an agitation that continued for three years before a final settlement was had. Three parties developed after a while upon this question: the down-town party, the up-town party, and the stay-where-we-are party. The two first-named parties said that the club should be either down-town or up-town, not in that "middle place 'twixt heaven and earth," 1125 Washington avenue. The third party deprecated a change which would cost a large sum of money and displease a large number of members. They said we were doing very well as we were and could not afford to move. But the down-town party prevailed and a lease of the Jaccard Building, Fifth and Olive streets, was authorized by the club, and now begins the third period in the history of the club. It was at first a period of inflation. We soon reached a membership of nearly four hundred, and resignations came pouring in the very next day. We spent money right and left. In our enthusiasm we did not take pains enough to get our money's worth. The amount of our indebtedness swelled at every investigation of our financial situation. Members began to desert the club. The general feeling was one of despondency, but many were true to the club and determined to cling to its fortunes. The earnestness and influence of President Breckinridge, aided by the generous cooperation of the officers and directors, kept in solid ranks those who otherwise would have given up the fight. It is not saying too much to ascribe to Judge Breckinridge the honor of saving the life of the club at this vital crisis in its history.

At length, after great and unselfish efforts on the part of the friends of the club, all its debts were paid and a lease was taken of the Walsh Mansion, No. 2721 Pine street. The club entered upon this fourth period in its history with fear and trembling, but at the annual meeting in January 1887, the Treasurer reported that every bill was paid and no member owed a dollar for dues.

Life went on for ten years in that pleasant house on Pine St. in the main smoothly and pleasantly and prosperously. For a city club our situation was unsurpassed. The old-fashioned house with its generous grounds, its sunny and airy exposure, was cosey and homelike. The porch in the rear of the house, the garden, the summer-house and the tennis-courts, these were features rarely to be found in a club situated in the heart of a great city. Club life in the Walsh Mansion was a reminder of that in the Harrison House. There was a return of that good feeling, that fraternity of interests that marked the former home, and which had been so sadly lacking in the down-town house, and we succeeded in making the club seem like a genuine University Club, although the graduation test had so long been abandoned.

On the twenty-eighth of May, 1891, Judge Breckinridge, our second President, was suddenly taken from us by death. The sorrow that followed the announcement of this event was deep and universal. He had joined the club at its second meeting, was an officer almost from the beginning, and was chosen President for ten successive years. In critical times in our history he had been of the greatest service. He had all the qualities of person and character to make him loved and respected by our members, and his name will always be given a high place in our annals. The vacancy thus created was filled at the annual meeting in January, 1892, by the election of Mr. Marshall S. Snow, who served the club to the best of his ability until January 1896, when he declined to become a candidate for re-election. Mr. Benjamin B. Graham, for many years the efficient chairman of the Board of Directors, was his successor, and was re-elected in 1897. From that time to the present, by a sort of unwritten law, the office of President has been held only two or three years by any incumbent.

With the year 1896 may be said to end what may be termed the early history of the club. The rapid extension of the residence district toward the west side of the city and the increasing difficulty of maintaining the club in its location, then down-town, called for radical action, and in March, 1896, arrangements were made for the purchase of the Allen House, on the northwest corner of Grand and Washington avenues, and the club removed from the Walsh Mansion into their own house in August of that year. Since then the life of the University Club has been one of continued prosperity. It is once again, however, in a down-town location, and the time is not far distant when the question of a change is likely once more to arise.

The most important event in its later history is the action at the annual meeting, January 26, 1909, when an amendment to the By-Laws was adopted, so changing the eligibility rule of membership as to restore the club to its original character contemplated by its founders. Graduation from an approved college or university, or at least two years of college or university residence, is now required of all candidates for admission. The University Club of St. Louis in a sound financial condition, with a large and loyal membership, is now one of the most important factors in the social, intellectual, college and university life of the growing city of St. Louis.

To the University Club of Philadelphia, however, must be conceded the distinction of being the first club organized after the University Club of the City of New York, which has had a continuous and successful existence to the present time.

William D. Neilson, Esq., of the Philadelphia bar, one of the oldest members of the club, gives the following interesting account of its career:

The incorporators were distinguished men—the then Bishop of Pennsylvania, William Bacon Stevens, who was the First President of the Club and served for two years; Dr. William Pepper, then Provost of the University; Samuel C. Perkins, a distinguished lawyer and a high official of the Masonic Order; Benjamin Harris Brewster, afterwards Attorney General of the United States; James T. Mitchell, afterwards Chief Justice of Pennsylvania, who enjoys the distinction of being the single honorary member of the Club, having been elected thereto shortly after his retirement from his office as Chief Justice; G. Colesberry Purves, at the present time head of one of the most important of Philadelphia's financial institutions; and John Neill, to whom perhaps more than to any other man do we owe the inauguration and fostering the Club to maturity. He unfortunately did not live to see the Club reach its present prosperity, but those members who were identified with the early days of the Club are one and all ready to yield to him the palm as the leader of the movement. Others there were, too, who were imbued with earnestness of effort almost as great as that of Mr. Neill, among whom were Henry Charles Olmsted, now deceased; E. Coppee Mitchell, Esq., a distinguished lawyer and professor in the Law Department of the University of Pennsylvania; Alfred G. Baker, the late Dr. Persifor Frazer, Mr. S. Davis Page, whose interest in the Club has ever been of the most active kind. He is a son of Yale, was actively connected with the founding of the Club, and has served in the government of the same with unflagging interest and without intermission, from the beginning to the present time. There are many others to whom all praise is due for their interest and attention: Dr. William W. Keen, Dr. Joseph G. Rosengarten, Mr. Walter Wood, and Mr. John Cadwalader, the fourth President of the Club, who has retained office from 1893, having been re-elected for the eighteenth time at the Annual Meeting in December last.

For the first few months of the Club's existence, it occupied quarters in Walnut Street now numbered 1321 but on January 21, 1882, it was moved into No. 1316 Walnut Street; six years later this same house was rebuilt—the Club in the meantime having found temporary quarters in 15th Street below Walnut Street—and again the Club occupied 1316 Walnut Street, and ten years and six months later, that is to say on October 17th, 1898, it took possession of the present home of the Club.

The present home of the Club is 1510 Walnut Street, which is a large brown building—six stories in height with roof garden. Extensive alterations were made to the premises in 1904 and the property is now assessed for taxation at over $250,000. The membership in March 1912 was divided as follows:—One honorary member and fifty life members; eight hundred and twenty-five (825) resident members and Two hundred and ninety-one (291) Non-resident Members; and Two hundred and twenty-one (221) Army & Navy members. The dues of the Club are but $50. a year for Resident members and one-half that sum for Non-resident members, giving advantages presented by no other Club in Philadelphia; thus obtaining on its roster many men of great learning and ability whose incomes might not permit their participation in a more expensive organization. A degree in course or Honorary Degree is required as an initial step for eligibility and this only from those Colleges approved by the Board of Governors. The applicant must further be known personally to at least two members of the Admission Committee, besides the requirement of letters from his Proposer and Seconder and at least three members of the Club. Further, his name is posted for the consideration of the entire Club upon his desirability, which results in the selection of a class of cultivated and congenial gentlemen. The financial condition of the Club is very strong and the property rights, participated in by each member, are most valuable.

The roll of active members has increased from 332 in 1881 to 1382 members in 1912.

The Hon. Samuel Clarke Perkins succeeded Bishop Stevens as President from 1884 to 1890; he was followed by the late Samuel S. Hollingsworth, who served two years only when death claimed him; and Mr. Cadwalader was elected his successor in office.

The first club making itself known after the reorganization of the University Club of the city of New York in 1879, was the University Club of Cincinnati, which opened its doors in November of that year, but it was not actually incorporated until 1881. The University Club of Philadelphia was organized on the 23d of March, 1881, and incorporated on the 22d of September, 1881.

These two clubs were therefore neck and neck in inaugurating the system of clubs outside of New York City.

The University Club of Cincinnati passed through an experience analogous to that of the early days of our own Club. Its first club house was 122 West 7th Street, and later 165 West 7th Street, which was occupied for five years. Then, for ten or fifteen years, its domicile was at the corner of 4th Street and Broadway. In 1897 it liquidated and went out of business.

In 1879 it had no kitchen, but William Fawcett, a colored caterer, set a *table d'hôte* lunch there, every day but Sunday, for which he made the modest charge of 25 cents. At 4th and Broadway, Bruno Balz, the club steward, gave the membership the best service in Cincinnati. But the club dwindled and practically passed out of existence, although the charter may have been kept alive. Charles P. Taft, brother of the President, was the last president of that organization, Governor Hoadley having been the first.

In 1905, a triangular meeting of Yale, Harvard, and Princeton men was held, which after delays and consultations resulted in the organization of the present club, with comfortable quarters at the corner of 4th Street and Broadway, in April, 1907.

This club has made a successful start, having in 1912 about 250 resident members and 40 non-resident, and promises to be prosperous.

The compiler is indebted to Mr. Murray M. Shoemaker for the foregoing information.

The next club to be formed was the University Club of Salt Lake, which was organized in a primitive way in 1886. The project was started by Robert J. Jessup (Rochester '73 and Yale '76), to whom the compiler is indebted for these particulars; George Gage, a graduate of Amherst; and Edward Elliott, a Harvard alumnus.

Mr. Jessup is a classmate of John Kean, Otto T. Bannard, and Henry W. DeForest, of the University Club.

It was some years before the club was sufficiently opulent to engage rooms, but the movement was upward and onward, until in 1900 the club took up its permanent abode in the present fine quarters on East Michigan Street, a handsome building elegantly equipped. The value of the club's real estate is probably $135,000, and the membership a little under 300. Hopes are entertained of paying off the debt which, as is usual with such enterprises, has been incurred to launch the club on a proper scale. This club maintains a library and has banquets, lectures, dances and social gatherings. The transient character of local residents is a difficulty which confronts the club. There is, however, a wide range of college representation, with Columbia in the ascendency for undergraduate degrees, and Michigan overshadowing all in law degrees. Harvard, Princeton, and Pennsylvania are well represented, but there are few Yale men in the club, although there were thirty-four in the State of Utah in 1912.

The University Club, Chicago, was the next to be organized. Edward S. Rogers, Esq., the secretary of the club, has supplied the following account of its prosperous career:

On behalf of the University Club of Chicago, permit me to felicitate the University Club of New York on the completion of a half century of existence. The University Club of Chicago is the merest infant in comparison. It was organized in February, 1887, and on May 9, 1887, obtained a few small rooms at 125 Dearborn St., which were occupied by the Club until April 25, 1890. The Club facilities were pretty meager and the rooms were used by the members as a place to take luncheon and read the magazines. A nucleus of a library was got together. On April 25, 1890, the Club moved into its quarters at 116 Dearborn St. Here we had a much more complete Club, the whole building was occupied by the Club and while the accommodations were modest they were fairly complete. This building was occupied until April 3, 1909, when we moved into our present building at Michigan Avenue and Monroe Street. It is of thirteen stories, the architecture is Gothic and it is occupied entirely by the Club. The facilities and arrangement are complete and we are very proud of the building and of the men who use it. Our resident membership is limited by the constitution and by-laws to 1800. The University Club was organized in the beginning to enable men who had tastes and traditions in common to meet and renew old acquaintances and make new ones. This spirit has continued to the present time. I do not know of a club anywhere, certainly not in Chicago, where the men know each other so well as they do at the University Club. I once had occasion to take a much travelled Englishman to the Club and on leaving he said to me, "I never saw such a first name crowd as you seem to have here." This is the spirit of the Club, a spirit of friendliness and sociability. For example, in one of the dining-rooms, College Hall, there are long tables where luncheon is served to men who may happen to be in a hurry or may not want to go to the regular Club dining-room. It is the etiquette of this room for every man to talk to every other man whether he has ever been introduced to him or not or whether he has ever seen him before or not. Our present building, which cost $1,100,000, was put up without a bond issue and the Club has no bonded debt. We have been in the new building since 1909 and while it took a good deal of work to get things readjusted the Club is in excellent shape financially, owes nobody a cent and has a very respectable bank balance.

Through the courtesy of Albert H. Buck, the secretary, the following particulars of the University Club of Baltimore City have been obtained:

This club was organized October 11, 1887, and chartered October 24, 1887. Its club house at 1005 North Charles Street was opened November 25, 1887; its house at 801 North Charles Street, October

14, 1892; and its house 801 and 803 North Charles Street, June 1, 1901.

Professor Basil L. Gildersleeve, the distinguished Greek scholar, was its first president. Among other eminent members, President Daniel C. Gilman and Professor Ira Remsen have been governors of the club.

The objects of the club are stated to be "the advancement of its members in literature, science and art; the promotion of social intercourse among them; the acquisition and maintenance of a library; and the collection and care of materials and appliances relating to the above objects."

"University and College graduates, provided they are twenty-one years of age; and others interested in literature, science or art, provided they are twenty-five years of age, shall be eligible for membership." The number of resident members is limited to four hundred. At the time of the publication of the latest club book (1907) there were 375 resident, 51 non-resident, and 3 temporary members. The entrance fee for residents is $50, and annual dues $50. The dues of non-residents are $25 (1907).

The University Club of Indiana was organized in 1889, Benjamin Harrison, ex-President of the United States, being one of its founders and its first president. The club house is at No. 450 North Meridian Street, Indianapolis. The president, at the time of this writing, 1911, was Frederick M. Ayres, Esq. The object of the club is "the establishment and maintenance of an association for social, literary and scientific purposes." This organization has a capital stock of $65,000 divided into 650 equal shares; and until May 1, 1904, the possession of one share was a condition of eligibility to membership. In that year this condition was annulled, and an initiation fee of $125 was imposed on new resident members, and provision made for a gradual retirement of the stock by purchase. Non-resident's initiation fee is $25.

The annual dues are $60 for resident and $15 for non-resident members.

Women of the families of members are admitted to the club during specified hours and with restrictions as to the use of certain rooms at certain times.

There are in all 381 members.

On November 11, in each year, the club celebrates at a banquet the battle of Tippecanoe, and the victory won there, on that date, by the grandfather of the club's first president.

The compiler is indebted to J. D. Strachan, Esq., assistant secretary, for the foregoing particulars.

The Nassau Club, of Princeton, N. J., although not exclusively a graduates' club, is to all intents and purposes a university club, inasmuch as by far the preponderance of the membership is of university men. These, like the Graduates Club of New Haven, are in a great measure alumni of the university situated in the town where the club is domiciled, but the roll includes graduates of other institutions, and a moderate sprinkling of townspeople who are interested in university affairs.

This club was organized in November, 1889, and was incorporated June 15, 1903. The club for some years occupied rooms in "University Hall," a college building, and maintained no kitchen.

In the year 1903 a commodious house at No. 6 Mercer Street was bought and altered appropriately.

In 1912, an addition was built doubling the accommodations, and providing bedrooms with baths, etc., for visiting members. The club has a commodious dining-room with a complete cuisine.

The Resident and "Associate" Membership is.........	183
The Non-Resident Membership.....................	631
Total in 1913................................	814

Residents pay $20 initiation fee, non-residents, $10. The annual dues of residents are $20; of non-residents, $10.

"Associate Members" are those only temporarily residing in Princeton. Their annual dues are $20, without initiation fee.

"No graduate or former student of Princeton University shall be eligible to membership until the college class of which he was a member has been out of the university one year."

This club is in a most flourishing condition, and furnishes, in addition to its regular clientèle, a rendezvous for graduates returning to Princeton to attend university exercises, class reunions, and intercollegiate contests on land and water.

The University Club of Pittsburgh, Pa., organized in 1890, passed through similar vicissitudes to those which decimated our own club in the sixties.

Edward B. Vaill, Esq., its secretary, furnishes the following data regarding the club's history:

During the first two years of its existence, it occupied a small room in the downtown section of the city. As it grew, it leased a house in the business section of the city, where it continued quite prosperous until about 1904. At that time, for various reasons, the Club declined and almost lost its organization. Several of the members reorganized the Club and built in the neighborhood of the Carnegie Libraries a modern club house, costing about Two hundred thousand dollars. During the last six years the Club has been extremely prosperous. Its personnel is admittedly as good, if not better, than any club in this community. Its membership is about seven hundred, and at present steps are being taken to expend about One hundred and twenty-five thousand dollars more, for the purchase of land and the enlargement of the Club.

The Club has always looked to the University Club of New York in many things. It has always considered the degrees accepted by the New York University Club as its standard. The organization is primarily a social one, although of late an attempt is being successfully made to have during the winter months addresses or talks from prominent men throughout the country.

There is no club in this city with a better standing than the University Club of Pittsburg.

Mr. E. E. Brownell, the secretary of the University Club of San Francisco, has kindly supplied the following information:

The University Club of San Francisco was incorporated in 1890, its first meeting being held July 24 of that year.

The first board of directors consisted of:

Frank J. Carolan.
Elliott Mc Alister.
Sydney V. Smith.
Charles J. Swift.
G. F. E. Harrison.
Francis Michael.
Frank Soulè.
William Thomas.
Harold Wheeler.

Mr. William Thomas was the club's first president. There were 50 members at the time of the club's organization.

Rooms were engaged on Pine Street between Montgomery and Kearny, and at first luncheon only was served. This, however, satisfied the members but a very short time.

Mr. William T. Coleman, one of the club's members, was persuaded to buy the property at 722 Sutter Street, and the club occupied this location and enjoyed a very prosperous period until the great fire of April 18, 1906, when the club's home was entirely destroyed. However, on May 17, 1906, scarcely a month having elapsed, the board of directors leased the private dwellings at 1815 and 1817 California Street, where the club remained until the new club building was ready for occupancy, namely, October 4, 1909. The present location is the southeast corner of California and Powell Streets.

The club now owns its own building and the land on which it stands. It has recently purchased some adjoining property on which it is proposed to erect a building accommodating handball courts, swimming pool, garage for the use of the members, etc.

The club is in good financial condition. The membership is as follows:

Regular	363
Academic	33
Non-resident	83
Clergymen	3
Army, Navy and Scientific Corps	100
Consular	2
Honorary	5
Life	3

making a total of 592 members.

The club functions are entirely social.

The gallantry of the members of the University Club will make them eager to learn the workings of the "Women's University Club," of the city of New York, which was the next one to be formed, October 10, 1891, being the date of its incorporation. This prosperous club formerly occupied the building at 99 Madison Avenue, corner of 29th Street. On March 6, 1914, it opened its spacious new club house in 52nd St. east of Park Avenue. The organization raised $100,000 for this new club house, a feat of which it may well be proud. It has approximately 1,000 members. The members consider its function to be purely social, and have carefully abstained from taking part in any of the questions of the day which agitate so many other women's clubs. This is mentioned because the attitude of the women's club is sometimes misjudged.

Miss Helen M. Kelsey (Wellesley '95), the corresponding secretary of the club, has kindly supplied the following information:

The Women's University Club of New York was founded in 1889 by Mrs. James P. Kimball, then Miss Marian P. Brace. It was the first Women's University Club in the country. Similar clubs have since been founded in other cities, and I think have usually taken the name "College Club"; but, with the Men's University Club of New York in mind, it was our desire to make a club that should be to women what that meant to men. We felt that the name Women's University Club was exact, and left nothing vague as to our aims.

The Club was soon afterwards incorporated, with Miss Brace as its first president. It began with forty members. Women were eligible who were eligible to the Associations of Collegiate Alumnæ. Barnard College began in 1889, at 343 Madison Avenue, and as there was a pleasant sort of kinship between the two undertakings, we rented a large room in their building. This was fitted up as a club room, and there were monthly meetings. The Club continued as a purely social organization, without attempting to provide a club house for members for about ten years. It occupied rooms in the studio building at 96 Fifth Avenue and afterwards rented rooms at 23 West 44th Street from the League for Political Education. The membership then numbered about one hundred. This first period of the Club's history was experimental. What it accomplished was the working out of the conviction that college women did want to come together, but that they wanted a different kind of club from this tentative social organization—one that should include that, and offer its members a home besides.

Miss Brace's was the first effort for such a thing, and *she studied the constitution of the Men's University Club, talked with its members, and tried to start this as the feminine counterpart of that.* To her belonged the initiative in all the enterprises of this nature. The "College Club" of New York is never to be confounded with our Club. That has non-graduates and "associate members," if I am not mistaken.

Mrs. Edward Perry Townsend (Vassar '02) is the president (1914). The vice-presidents are Mrs. William Reynolds Brown (Vassar '69) and Mrs. Charles L. Tiffany (Bryn Mawr '97).

The house committee consists of nine members, and men may well envy the housekeeping presided over by nine expert ladies, and compare the disadvantages of our own establishment in which five males must wrestle with problems generally regarded as not within their province.

The initiation fee is $20. The annual dues are $20 for resident members and $15 for non-resident.

The year book of the women's club kindly furnished by the secretary is a model, both in its letter-press and the completeness of its contents.

The compiler is indebted to Mrs. George B. Ford (Smith '99), corresponding secretary (1913), for supplementary information.

The University Club of Denver, Col., was incorporated January 31, 1891, with Henry S. Rogers, Esq., as president. Its first club house, 1422 Curtis Street, was opened April 18, 1891, and its present club house, December 31, 1895. It has 234 resident members, 91 non-resident, and 17 army and navy members, 342 in all.

One half of the membership comes from Yale, Harvard, Michigan, Columbia, Princeton, Dartmouth, and Denver. The preponderance being in the order named.

The qualification for membership seems to follow the rule of the University Club of the City of New York, except that the term of probation after graduation is two years instead of three. The resident membership is limited to 250. The admission fee is $100 for residents and $50 for non-residents. The annual dues are $60 for residents and $30 for non-residents. Bedrooms and a dining-room for ladies are among the conveniences of the club.

The University Club, Seattle, Wash., was organized in 1891, "for mutual acquaintance and social companionship among men who have been matriculated students or attendants at such Colleges or Universities" "as shall be named" "in the By-Laws." Those eligible to membership must have been regularly connected as students for the period of at least two years with a university or college of a recognized standing or with the United States Military or Naval Academies, or who shall have received an honorary degree from such university or college.

The resident membership is limited to 200; non-resident to 100. The club in 1912 had 156 resident and 49 non-resident members. The admission fee for resident members is $50; for non-residents, $15. Dues for residents are $6 *per month;* for non-residents $15 *per annum.*

This club maintains a club house, with cuisine, and living-rooms for members.

The compiler is indebted to S. L. Russell, Esq., the secretary of the club, for the above information.

The Graduates Club of New Haven is virtually a University Club.

David Daggett, Esq. (Yale '79), the president, has courteously furnished the following information:

The Graduates Club of New Haven originated in bi-weekly meetings of graduate students, who during 1891 and 1892 met in their rooms. Near the close of 1892 the Club found its first fixed home in the old Anketell house on Elm Street, New Haven, where it remained until the rental of the Club House at No. 954 Chapel Street. At this time the Club was incorporated and occupied the Chapel Street premises until October 1902, when the present building on Elm Street was bought and the alterations completed.

The membership of our Club is limited to graduates of approved colleges and universities and every name has to come before a Committee on Admissions—the same as in the University Club of New York. We have four hundred resident members and about one thousand non-resident members and the organization has been financially prosperous since its start.

Ours is distinctly a social club and we maintain a restaurant, have illustrated talks about every two weeks during the winter season and for the last two years have maintained a summer club also at Double Beach, Connecticut. This last has now passed from the control of our Club to a new corporation who will hereafter run it independently and with whom we have no connection, save as to the privilege of membership.

I think you are quite right in assuming that we may in a certain sense be considered the offspring of the University Club, as our house rules and regulations are in a large measure copied from theirs.

The following account of the University Club of Boston was supplied by the courtesy of W. V. Kellen, Esq.:

The University Club of Boston was organized on January 18, 1892, under a special act of the Massachusetts Legislature. This organization was the result of combined efforts on the part of Amherst, Brown, Dartmouth, Harvard, Williams and Yale men, who represented groups of graduates of their respective colleges. The incorporators were as follows: Walbridge A. Field, Dartmouth '55; John Lowell, Harvard '43; William Gaston, Brown '40; Phillips Brooks, Harvard '55; James M. Barker, Williams '60; Henry L. Higginson, A.M., Harvard '82; Winslow Warren, Harvard '58; John Fiske, Harvard '63; Moses Williams, Harvard '68; Stephen M. Crosby, Dartmouth '49; George M. Towle, Yale '61; Alfred Hemenay, Yale '61; Maurice H. Richardson, Harvard '73; Arthur C. Walworth, Yale '66; Arthur Little, Dartmouth '60; Richard H. Dana, Harvard '74. The first president was the Hon. William Endicott, a graduate of Harvard, and the first secretary was William Vail Kellen, a graduate of Brown. The Club was started with 443 resident members.

The club house is charmingly situated on the water side of Beacon Street, looking over the Charles River Basin. This renders the club house an especially pleasant resort during the summer. The club is equipped with a good working library and a satisfactory ladies' restaurant. No club in Boston could live for a moment without a ladies' restaurant.

In addition to the customary resident, non-resident and Army and Navy membership, the club has from the beginning had an "Honorary Membership." This consists of the presidents of all the New England institutions of learning whose graduates are eligible for membership in the club, and they have all the privileges of non-resident members without the payment of either entrance fees or yearly fees. By a recent change in the by-laws, a "Faculty Membership" has been created, under which the members of all the academic Faculties of the same institutions may enjoy the same privileges without the payment of any entrance fees, by paying virtually half dues,—$30 yearly within 30 miles of Boston, and $15 without that limit.

The present membership of the club consists of 469 resident members, 130 non-resident members, 10 Army and Navy members and 23 honorary members. The club has flourished from the beginning and now occupies a satisfactory financial position. Each year, during the winter, the club gives a series of Smoke Talks, as well as a series of concerts, for the benefit of the members. The club is now considering seriously the making of very substantial additions to its club house, which will very materially increase the comfort of its members and probably tend to increase very largely its membership.

The University Athletic Club was organized in 1892, and has been fully mentioned in another place. It is now extinct.

The University Club of Buffalo, N. Y., was organized December 18, 1894. The "Club Historian," Frederick J. Shepard, has furnished the following complete account:

The need of a university club in Buffalo was a hobby of the Rev. Dr. Walter Clarke, Yale '37, pastor of the First Presbyterian Church of that city, from 1861 to 1871, and his son, the Rev. Samuel T. Clarke, Hamilton '62, was known during the eighties as an ardent advocate of such an institution. Nothing, however, came of his agitation until the autumn of 1894, when the project was taken up actively by Sherman S. Jewett, Yale '91, Lewis Stockton, Lehigh '81, and William B. Wright, Jr., Yale '92. Jewett's father, Josiah Jewett, Yale '63, was a member of the New York University Club, and the son had heard much of that institution and had seen something of it while studying law at Columbia, while Wright was fresh from New Haven, full of college enthusiasm, and desirous of seeing a club established in Buffalo on more modest and circumspect lines than any then existing. Stockton was especially inspired by a wish to offset what he regarded as a radical dinner club, then recently formed, by a club of conservative college men. On Dec. 18, 1894, an organization was effected.

A house at 884 Main street, between Virginia and Allen streets, was hired. This building was used until Oct. 16, 1897, when the Club moved to more commodious quarters at 295 Delaware avenue, the former home of Postmaster-General Wilson S. Bissell. The present clubhouse, at the corner of Delaware avenue and Allen street, was dedicated October 24, 1904, Judge Henry E. Howland, president of the New York University Club, delivering the address of the occasion. The Club's possession of a house of its own was largely due to the liberality and public spirit of John J. Albright, Rens. Pol. Inst. '68, and to the zeal of William H. Glenny, Yale S. S. '65, who was president of the Club at the time and devoted himself to the supervision of the undertaking. It is a handsome four-story brick structure in strict colonial style. The official seals of Harvard, Yale, Williams, Cornell, and Rensselaer, copied from the New York University Club building, adorn the mantelpieces of different rooms, and there are Princeton and Amherst clocks, while the walls are hung with pictures of many other institutions of learning. Among the paintings owned by the Club are a full length of Bishop Coxe by Anderson and a portrait of Mark Hopkins.

From the first the practice has been followed of having addresses on Saturday evenings by distinguished speakers, among whom have figured most of the leading college presidents. Receptions have been given in honor of President Taft, Governors Hughes and Dix, the Akademischer Gesangverein of Vienna, etc., and such learned and philanthropic societies as have chanced to meet in Buffalo. Minstrel entertainments, burlesque presidential inaugurations, athletic exhibitions, and similar frolics have taken place, the most important having been the elaborate presentation by the Club of Booth Tarkington's "Honorable Julius Caesar" in April, 1901. Every winter a musicale and ball has been given, and this has become one of the most important social events of Buffalo. A feature of club life much enjoyed by the participants are the dinner clubs of choice spirits which meet monthly during the winter. There are three of these at present: the Pioneers, the Sedate Sixteen and the Uncommon Council, the first two having been in existence since the Club's origin. Discussions of municipal affairs have been held before the Club, and the clubhouse has served the public, as well as its members, in many useful ways.

The Club's organization is based upon that of the New York University Club, the governing body being a council of twenty members, five of whom go out of office annually, while there is a separate committee on membership, consisting of twenty-one, the terms of seven expiring each year. The eligibility requirement is a degree standing for at least three years of residence and study at a college recognized by the Regents of New York University, exclusive of theological, law, and medical schools. Besides Messrs. Viele and Glenny, the following gentlemen have served as presidents of the Club: Henry H. Seymour, Cornell '71; John J. Albright, Rens. Pol. Inst. '68; Loran L. Lewis, jr., Williams '87; Henry R. Howland, Col. City of N. Y. '63; Stephen M. Clement, Yale '82; Dr. Charles S. Jones, Cornell '84; and the Rev. Dr. Andrew V. V. Raymond, Union '75. At present, November, 1911, Mr. Lewis is again presiding over the club.

The British Schools and Universities Club of New York was organized November 19, 1895, the Reverend D. Parker Morgan, D.D. (Oxford), being the first president. The object of the club is "social and intellectual intercourse among men of British education." The club holds at least two dinners in each year: the annual dinner on November 9, the anniversary of the birth of King Edward VII, and the semi-annual dinner on Empire Day, May 24, the anniversary of the birth of Queen Victoria.

The annual dues are $5 and the initiation fee $5. The club does not maintain a club house. The president in 1912 was the Right Reverend Frederick Courtney, D.D., D.C.L. (Christ's Hospital and King's College, London). Among the Honorary members are: Field-Marshal Earl Roberts, V.C., K.G.; Honorable Joseph H. Choate (D.C.L., Oxon., LL.D., Edinburgh); The Right Honorable James Bryce (O.M.); and Doctor Wu Ting Fang. The membership numbers 284.

The Litchfield County University Club, Connecticut, was organized June 16, 1897. Its objects are "the promotion of social intercourse and good fellowship among its members, and the advancement of the interests of the higher education." Its membership includes gentlemen residing in thirty-three different towns of Litchfield County, and numbers in all 196.

The compiler is indebted to the courtesy of Howard W. Carter, Esq., secretary of the club, for the following account of it:

This University Club is quite unlike other University Clubs in that it exists in a country district in which there is no city, has no building or club rooms, and meets but twice a year; once always with the founders as their guests, and the other meeting is held in a different town each year.

The Club owes its origin and its continued success to the generosity of one member and his wife who are constantly adding some new feature. In recent years the Club has published several volumes by members of the Club and other volumes are in preparation.

Four volumes of the "Litchfield Literature Series" have been published: "Litchfield County Sketches," by the Rev. Newell M. Calhoun; "The Sport of Bird Study," by the Rev. Herbert K. Job; "The County Regiment," by Dudley Landon Vaill; and "The Clergy of Litchfield County," by the Rev. Arthur Goodenough.

The Litchfield County University Club has also acted in conjunction with The Litchfield County Choral Union, in bringing out original musical compositions, which have been rendered at the annual concerts of the latter society. Honoraria of $1,000 are given to the composer who is selected by a committee. Composers have been:—Prof. Horatio Parker of New Haven, G. W. Chadwick of Boston, Henry Hadley of Seattle and Coleridge-Taylor of London. The composer conducts the first performance in the so-called "Music Shed," a structure built by Mr. Stoeckel for the purpose and seating about 2,000 people, and with an orchestra of 75 of the best musicians in the world, i. e. selected from the Metropolitan Orchestra and the New York Philharmonic.

The University Club of Hudson County, N. J., is situated in Jersey City, and was organized December 28, 1897, and incorporated October 17, 1900.

W. P. Atkinson, the secretary, states that "its inception was due very largely to the influence and talk of Mr. Horace C. Wait (Yale '76), who for a number of years was connected with a private school in Jersey City. His words bore fruit in a gathering of former pupils after they had graduated from college."

Its first president was Flavel McGee, LL.D. (Princeton '65). Charles D. Ridgway (Princeton '69) was the president in 1912.

The objects of the club are "to afford opportunities for College graduates to renew and continue early friendships, to preserve and perpetuate the traditions of their Alma Maters, and to unite in any suitable undertaking of public utility."

The annual dues are $10.

The club does not maintain a club house. It provides a club scholarship, the incumbent of which receives the benefits of the same in a university. There are one hundred and four members, representing thirty colleges.

The University Club of Cleveland, O., was organized June 20, 1898, with C. W. Bingham (Yale '68) as its first president. The secretary, Charles S. Brooks (Yale, 1900), states that its membership at that time was 200; since then increased to approximately 400. In 1911 the club was occupying the residence formerly belonging to Governor Todd, of Ohio.

Mr. George A. Welch, the secretary of this club, writes on April 17, 1913, that the club expected to move into a new building at the close of the year.

Among the original incorporators was Honorable James R. Garfield.

The purpose for which the club was formed is stated in its charter to be "for the promotion of literature and art and for social and other kindred purposes."

This club, unlike most university clubs, has a stock capital of four hundred shares of the par value of $50 each, and "no person may become a resident member until he has become a stockholder." The club has a first lien on the stock to secure indebtedness of members.

The annual dues are $40 for resident and $12 for non-resident members. The latter pay an initiation fee of $25. The purchase of stock appears to take the place of the customary initiation fee for residents. By the last published book, there were seventy-eight colleges represented in the membership.

The University Club of Milwaukee, Wis., was organized November 7, 1898, with August H. Vogel, Esq., as president. Mr. Vogel is still an active member of the club, and has kindly supplied a history of the club, from which the following extracts are made, with regret that the limits of this publication preclude the printing of the whole interesting account:

> The Charter was obtained November 7, 1898. The Constitution and By-Laws were adopted by the same body of men, (the organizers) numbering about twenty-five college graduates, and the Club was launched. The purpose of the Club was expressed in the Charter as follows: "The purpose and object of this corporation shall be to secure a closer union and co-operation of college and university men in maintaining a Club for the purpose of cultivating interest in the sciences and liberal arts, and for social enjoyment; also for the purpose of acquiring, owning and holding real estate for a Club house, and acquiring all other property which may be desirable in order to carry into effect the purposes of this association."

In August (1899) the Club found itself located in a building specially furnished and equipped for its use, including restaurant, buffet, billiard-room and reception and reading rooms.

At that time the membership did not exceed one hundred members. There was a steady increase in the membership, however, as the months passed, which made the necessity of a larger and better appointed building apparent, so that steps were taken in April, 1903, authorizing the Board of Directors to solicit funds and issue bonds for the purchase of a site and for the erection of a new building for the exclusive use of the Club.

One year from the date when the Club ratified the purchase of property, and endorsed the plans recommended by the Board of Directors, the new building was occupied and dedicated to use. It is a four-story building facing east on the Court House park, central enough in location to be freely used by Club members at lunch time, being near the heart of the business district.

The Club from time to time has had lectures upon historical, scientific, literary, or sociological topics for the benefit of its members and their guests, thus carrying out one of the aims of the founders.

The membership is limited to five hundred. By the annual report May 1, 1913, it had reached almost four hundred.

The desire of the founders that the University Club should provide a home for young college men, and become a center for meetings of any kind in which college men have an interest, has been attained. It has also, in some measure, fulfilled the hope that it would be for college men something more than a social center, such as characterizes the usual commercial clubs. They believed that college men, when organized, should cultivate and represent in their communities a strong influence for social and political betterment.

The following account of the University Club of Portland, Ore., was courteously furnished by James B. Kerr, Esq.:

The University Club of Portland, Oregon, was organized in the year 1898 with a small but enthusiastic membership. For about 7 years it maintained quarters in various office buildings but in 1905 purchased property in the business district of the City upon which it caused to be moved an old dwelling house. These quarters sufficed until two years ago the Club purchased a new site and has now just completed a new home. Its new Club home has been erected and furnished at a cost of $140,000.

The Club has a resident membership of 230 and a non-resident membership of 100. Its qualifications for membership have been consistently maintained and require either a bachelor's or a doctor's degree or attendance at some recognized institution of learning and pursuit for at least three years of a course leading to a bachelor's degree.

The Club is in excellent condition and with its new quarters looks forward to an era of prosperity.

Harry C. Bulkley, Esq., the historian of the University Club of Detroit, Mich., has furnished the following account of its history and status:

The University Club, of Detroit, was founded January 24, 1899, with 34 charter members.

The Club learned a lesson from a previous unsuccessful attempt to organize a University Club in Detroit, which was started on too elaborate a plan and was not a financial success.

The present University Club started out most simply and economically, and we still adhere to that policy as far as possible. The membership of the Club has been increasing slowly and conservatively from a long waiting list. The Club has about 350 resident and 150 non-resident members, representing all of the American and several European universities and colleges. Our list of eligible universities and colleges is substantially the same as that of the University Club of New York.

The Club occupies an attractive old house in the centre of the business district, which was remodelled and enlarged to meet its requirements. Its appointments and furnishings are exceedingly simple, but afford the members all of the comforts of a city club. All the departments of the Club are conducted upon a cash basis, which has worked out most satisfactorily. The Club employs Japanese servants. The luncheon attendance averages about 100. During the winter, the Entertainment Committee arranges a play, given entirely by Club members, which has always been most successful.

The Club Library consists of 1500 volumes. Books are acquired through contributions made by the members to the Library Committee and also by gifts from members.

The initiation fee for resident members is $75.00 and for non-resident members $25.00, of which amounts $37.00 and $5.00, respectively, go into the Club's Permanent Building Fund, which now amounts to about $35,000.00. The present annual dues are $50.00 for resident and $15.00 for non-resident members; and of these amounts $10.00 and $5.00, respectively, go into the Permanent Building Fund.

The University Club of Syracuse, N. Y., was organized on September 28, 1899. Since 1905 the annual dues for resident members have been $15, and for non-residents $5. The initiation fee is $10 and $5, respectively.

The following particulars are from a statement kindly furnished by Forbes Heermans, Esq., one of the charter members:

The Constitution of the Club is based in form upon that of the University Club of New York, with such modifications as have been found necessary to meet the conditions existing in Syracuse.

The Club first secured rooms on the fifth floor of the Larned Building, located near the business centre of the City, but these were soon found too small, and then nearly the entire fourth floor of the same building was leased.

The membership of the Club has steadily increased since its organization and now numbers upwards of 250. On Saturday nights light refreshments are set forth and there is usually some other form of entertainment; a short address by a member or guest, or music. Members are permitted to bring their men friends who are non-members on these evenings. Four or five times each year special entertainments are given, usually lectures upon literary or scientific themes of current interest, delivered by men distinguished in these lines of thought, and to these lectures both men and women are admitted by card. Audiences frequently number 300, which is all the assembly room will hold.

The Club has an excellent library and receives all of the best university and college publications. The walls of the various rooms are hung with framed photographs showing views of all the universities and colleges represented in our membership; besides portraits of many men who are distinguished in educational affairs.

The Club is highly prosperous financially and is accumulating a fund out of income to purchase a house.

The following résumé of the history of the University Club of Providence, R. I., was prepared by F. Webster Cook, Esq., secretary of the club:

In the spring of 1899 two Professors of Brown University became convinced that a University Club in Providence had every chance for success. Their idea of such a Club was doubtless modelled on that of the New York and Boston Clubs, the nearest University Clubs in the East. These two Professors attended to the practical details, discovered that such a Club was practicable and by personal solicitation, assisted by a number of their friends, secured two hundred and seventy-five members, at the time the Charter was issued. To show the general interest taken in this Club I might mention that among those gentlemen to whom the Charter was issued were three of the greatest Cotton manufacturers of the State, one University Professor, the Episcopal Bishop of the diocese, Governor of the State, two of the State's best known physicians, and two of the oldest members of the Rhode Island Bar. The possession of a degree from some institution of recognized standing was early insisted upon and a clause in the original By-Laws which allowed men prominent in the community to be elected as associate members without such a degree was never used but once, fifteen members only being elected under that provision.

The Club secured one of the oldest homesteads in the city, located within five minutes' walk of the centre of the office district, and by remodelling and adding to it, secured very comfortable and homelike, though not impressive, quarters. If the present growth of the Club keeps up, however, it will be necessary in the near future to make either very extensive changes in the house or to entirely rebuild.

The Club apparently filled a want in the community, for it at once became popular and is now one of the two strong clubs of the State, its only rival being the old and conservative Hope Club of Providence.

Its function at present is to provide a congenial meeting-place for the University-bred men of the State without regard to age or occupation and in this it is succeeding admirably. The membership is made up of men holding degrees from almost every well-known institution in the world, from the Imperial School of Technology of Moscow, to our own Harvard and Yale. It is especially popular with the younger business and professional men of the city, as it gives them an attractive opportunity for Club life without an undue financial burden.

The Club has so far consistently kept to its ideal of the democracy of all University men and its success has proved the saneness of that ideal. It is the custom every two weeks throughout the winter to have some gentleman prominent in the outside world address the Club on some subject of general interest. The Club has been especially fortunate, being able to number among the men who have spoken there within the past few years, the British and German Ambassadors, Professors Hugo Munsterberg of Harvard, George W. Prothero of Cambridge, Inazo Nitobe of Tokio, Dr. Hamilton Wright Mabie, the Honorable Elihu Root and very many others.

From a material point of view as well the Club is very prosperous. It had four hundred and twenty-five resident members and about seventy-five non-resident members in 1912, with a long waiting list from which to fill any vacancies. It does a large business in its several departments and I think is one of the few of the smaller University Clubs to make its restaurant practically self-supporting.

The University Club of Manila was organized November, 1900. E. G. Shields has kindly furnished the following information:

The first page of the records shows as follows:

"In the Beginning.

"In Manila there was no organization where University graduates could meet for goodfellowship and social intercourse. Mr. Lucius

Cary Tuckerman conceived the idea of forming a Club of University Alumni. The University men with whom he discussed the subject entertained the idea enthusiastically. After several preliminary meetings the following declaration was signed:

"'We, the undersigned, organize ourselves in an association to be called The University Club of Manila, P. I.'

"Signed Wm. H. Taft, (the first President of the Club) and nineteen others.

"Article I of the Constitution

"The objects of the Club shall be goodfellowship and social intercourse among its members."

This was the time when the Government of the Philippine Islands was about to change from military to civil.

Manila was not devoid of Club facilities. There were the Spanish Club, the Manila Club (English) and the newly formed Army and Navy Club, but there was nothing approximating the distinctive features of the University Club. There was a comparatively small American population here at that time and the desire of the few University men to have a common place of meeting for promoting social intercourse among men of University education and those interested in literature, science and art led to the final organization.

The first election was held in the ante-room of Mr. William H. Taft's office, in the north wing of the Ayuntamiento. Upon the inauguration of Mr. Taft as the Civil Governor of the Philippines, the Club gave its first reception in honor of its first President, at which over six hundred people were present.

The Club grew steadily, but the enthusiasm soon cooled, and though there was a goodly membership, there was very little attendance.

In 1904–5 a reorganization was effected, a new lease on a desirable site was acquired with permission to make suitable additions to the premises and ten thousand dollars was borrowed for the purpose of making improvements. Since then there has been a steady and rapid growth and the Club is upon a firm financial basis.

The membership of the Club in 1912 was 544, divided as follows:

Collegiate and University	328
Non-Collegiate	32
Military	132
Eligibles	52
	544

By the courtesy of H. C. Knapp, Esq., secretary of the University Club of Brooklyn, the following particulars are given respecting that Club which was founded in the spring of 1901 and has its house at No. 109 Lafayette Avenue, Brooklyn, N. Y. There are 334 members in it. The president is Henry J. Davenport, Harvard 1900.

Among its prominent members are:

Hon. William B. Hurd, jr.
Hon. Harrington Putnam, Supreme Court, Kings Co.
Hon. Frederick E. Crane, " " " "
Hon. Abel E. Blackmar, " " " " presiding justice.
Hon. Almet F. Jenks, Appellate Division.
Hon. Franklin W. Hooper, Brooklyn Institute of Arts and Sciences.
Hon. Charles N. Chadwick of the Aqueduct Commission of the City of New York.
Hon. George Foster Peabody.
Messrs. C. M. Pratt, G. B. Pratt, F. B. Pratt and H. I. Pratt, all of whom are interested in the Pratt Institute of Brooklyn.
Chief Justice Isaac Franklin Russell of the Court of Special Sessions of the City of New York.

The chief objects of the club are to bring college and university graduates together and afford them the opportunity to keep up the spirit of the university.

The first officers of the club were:

Hon. William B. Hurd, jr., President.
Herbert L. Bridgman, Vice-President.
William F. Atkinson, Treasurer.
Henry E. Hutchinson, Secretary.

The council was composed of the above-named officers and:

Hon. Joseph A. Burr.
Hon. Abel E. Blackmar.
Edward H. Holmes.
Dr. Walter B. Gunnison.
John A. Thompson.
Seymour K. Fuller, and
Dr. Arthur R. Paine.

The present house was the old Oxford Club, which is the fourth house the University Club has occupied. Each of the previous houses was outgrown by the growth of the club.

J. E. McPherson, Esq., secretary of the University Club of Kansas City, Mo., has kindly supplied the following information:

The present Club was organized on the 7th day of March, 1901, for the purpose as stated in the Articles of Association, of owning, leasing, establishing or maintaining a club house for social purposes, and obtaining and enjoying a place of common and friendly intercourse, and of advancing by rational amusement the mental and bodily welfare of ourselves and our associates, and promoting acquaintance among university men.

On April 15th, 1906, the second floor of a new building at the southwest corner of Eleventh Street and Baltimore Avenue was leased for a Club-House. This has proven a very desirable location, being close to the theaters and principal hotels and convenient to office buildings.

The membership is now limited to 300. The membership list has been filled for more than a year and the Club has a small waiting list and 62 non-resident members. The present initiation fee is $75.00 and the dues $60.00 per year.

A permanent Building Committee has considered plans for more commodious quarters, preferably a home of our own.

It is the aim to make the Club the center of all college activities, social, charitable and educational, and the scene of college dinners and reunions.

To establish most cordial and close relations among all the members and to promote good fellowship the Club holds an annual dinner following the annual election, keeps open house on New Year's and holds during the year several distinctive dinners with appropriate ceremonies such as Old English, George Washington, Old Virginia, Mexican, Japanese, etc. Other entertainments are offered from time to time along social and educational lines, at times as an accompaniment of the dinners, and at other times as special features.

The compiler is indebted to Robert E. Whalen, Esq., for the following particulars regarding the University Club of Albany, N. Y.:

The primary purpose of the Club, which was incorporated May 9, 1901, was to afford a place where Albany boys, recently out of college, and thus for four years out of touch with their home city, might readily get in contact with one another, as well as with older college men who had become established in the city. Albany then had four prominent clubs, each with a long waiting list, which required an applicant for membership therein to wait three or four years for admission; yet it was felt that the city did not have a place for another club, unless that club should have a distinctive feature of its own.

The club opened its quarters in a leased house, July 1, 1901, and there remained for nearly six years, struggling to keep its limit of 175 resident members nearly filled, but never quite realizing that end, members feeling free to resign when the whim moved them, because they knew that, with no waiting list, it was easy to obtain re-admission.

In the spring of 1907, the club purchased its own club house into which it moved, and which it ever since has occupied. The acquisition of its own house marked a sudden increase in membership, the constitutional limit was rapidly filled, and from time to time since the limit has been increased by ten or fifteen, so that it now stands at 250, with a long list of applicants upon the board.

The club is now established upon a firm footing, ranks second to none in the city, is rapidly paying its floating debt, and has sustained the judgment of those who, at its inception, felt that Albany had a place for a club composed of university men.

The total membership of the Albany Club (1913) is 335. The purpose of the club is stated to be "to establish and maintain a library and reading and assembly rooms, to promote social intercourse among the members thereof, and to cultivate and maintain university spirit."

The qualification for membership is a degree from a college or university of recognized standing to obtain which, in regular course, at least two years of residence and study shall have been required, including the United States Military and Naval Academies. The board of directors may by unanimous vote admit persons without limitation as to duration of residence. The entrance fee is $25 for residents and $15 for non-residents. The annual dues are $30 for residents and $15 for non-residents. This club makes a feature of its annual dinners. At these entertainments many distinguished men have been guests, as, for example, Governor Charles E. Hughes, now of the U. S. Supreme Court; William Howard Taft; Earl Grey, Governor-General of Canada; James Bryce, British ambassador; and the presidents of numerous universities.

The University Club of Decatur, Ill., was organized in 1902. The object is stated to be "investigating and discussing current sociological and economic problems, and for mutual improvement and social enjoyment." None but graduates of approved colleges or universities, authorized to confer degrees in the arts and sciences, and the holders of a Ph.D. are eligible. Each member is required to pay an initiation fee of one dollar, and such fees thereafter as the club may order.

The following description of the Club has been furnished by its president, Doctor Herbert C. Jones (1913), one of the original members:

The founding of "James Milliken Univer." by a wealthy citizen at this place—the organization of the College—the coming of a few chosen members of the faculty was the probable inspiration of the Club. Dr. Taylor called on a few professional and business men, some Ministers and the Supt. of Schools and we first met in the office of a physician (oculist) who is now Pres. of the Bd. of Trustees of the Univ.

The original membership was limited to 35 regular and 10 associate members. The number of both has been doubled and is usually nearly or quite full.

For the last six or seven years we have had a room (furnished by ourselves) in the Y. M. C. A. Bdg. for our fortnightly meetings. At the end of the year we have a banquet to which ladies and guests are invited and at which some distinguished educator or sociologist is invited to deliver an address. We also have two other meetings at which ladies are present during the year. One of these is simply called "Ladies Night" and has a slightly modified regular program—the other, a gradual development, is known as the "Midwinter Frolic," which is a somewhat modest imitation of the "Grid Iron Club" with a light banquet. It has come to be the most popular of our entertainments.

The earliest list of members I have been able to find is inclosed. The original membership probably embraces two thirds or more of this list.

Our Club is still thriving and much enjoyed by all. The College and High School faculties furnish the bulk of the membership tho' we still have lawyers, doctors, ministers, and men of business. Our papers are sociological, educational, legal, medical, commercial, and economic, and the discussions in which all take part bring out many points of view. Occasionally, failing a paper, we discuss "Current Events," &c.

The University Club of Washington, D. C., was organized February 15, 1904. Its present membership (1913) is 1,169. The club has recently completed its new club house at the corner of 15th and I Streets, at a cost approximately of $340,000, including furnishings. The club is in very good condition; the membership is growing and it is well patronized by university men in the national capital.

Its first president was William Howard Taft, at the time Secretary of War. Other presidents have been George B. Cortelyou, Charles D. Walcott, Stephen B. Elkins, and Gardner F. Williams.

The compiler has not been furnished with the constitution and by-laws, but it may be taken for granted that the club has been formed substantially on the basis of the University Club of New York.

The compiler is indebted for the information here given to the courtesy of Ralph P. Barnard, Esq., the secretary of the club.

The University Club of Evanston, Ill., was organized February 13, 1904, and incorporated April 24, 1905. At first it was a Northwestern University Faculty Club. Later resident alumni of the Northwestern were included, and finally the existing conditions made all college graduates eligible to "active" membership, as well as non-graduates in number not to exceed twenty-five per cent of the limit of active membership. A class of "associate members" includes instructors in Northwestern University, Garrett Biblical Institute, Evanston Academy, and Evanston Township High School. The club has a large waiting-list of non-graduates.

"The objects of the organization are the promotion of social life and good fellowship among college graduates and the maintenance of a reading-room and library for the membership."

Omera Floyd Long, Esq., vice-president of the club, to whom the compiler is indebted for these particulars, states that about sixty colleges are represented in the membership. The lists of "active," "associate," and "non-resident" members are not quite full.

In the new building some eighteen rooms are occupied by members. A cafe is maintained without loss by letting the housekeeper, an ex-trained nurse, run it as a concession.

Lectures or informal talks are given, usually by invited guests, every Saturday evening.

The Club lot cost $19,000.00, the building, furnished by Hoggson of New York, about $55,000. The money was raised by stock subscriptions and a loan of $25,000.00. The directors have paid a 3% dividend on stock, have retired three $1000.00 bonds (anticipating one of these by a year) and have purchased a $7500.00 lot adjacent for tennis courts.

We consider our record a pretty good one with small dues; and the Club could not be spared in the town.

The University Club of Texas, at Austin, was organized December 14, 1904, with W. J. Battle, Esq., as president. The club was "instituted for the association of members of the faculty of the University of Texas, and other persons interested in literature, science, or art."

There does not appear to be any condition of college graduation for the eligibility of candidates for admission. The club had 139 members in 1912, of whom 92 are connected with the University of Texas, either as members of the instructing staff or administrative officers. The others are professional and business men of Austin, a few being alumni of the University of Texas.

The annual dues of resident members are $20, and of non-resident, $5. An initiation fee of $5 is paid by residents only. The resident membership is limited to 150.

The club house is at 2304 San Antonio Street, and the constitution prohibits the use of liquors in the same.

The University Club of Sydney, New South Wales, although not in the United States, was only founded in 1905, and may fairly be included with the American clubs which have followed the example set by our own organization. The president in 1911 was the Honorable Sir Normand MacLaurin, Kt., M.L.C. The membership at foundation was 188. It is now 800.

The sixth annual report (September 19, 1911) states: "The progress of the club has made it evident that in the very near future increased accommodation for its members must be provided. Quite a year ago your Directors submitted plans for new premises, adjoining those now in the occupation of the Club, but at the present time there is nothing definite to report in regard thereto." No further information has been received on this subject.

The objects of this club are stated more voluminously than in other cases, but comprise the usual purposes of literary, artistic, and scientific culture and research, and special interest in the well-being of the University of Sydney.

Graduates of the University of Sydney are eligible to membership, as well as graduates of universities recognized by the University of Sydney.

The determination as to dues and initiation fees is lodged with a board of directors.

The compiler is indebted, for documents from which the foregoing particulars have been extracted, to N. Heath, Esq., secretary of the club.

The University Club of Spokane, State of Washington, was organized October 2, 1905, and reorganized March 18, 1908.

The club occupied rooms in the "Rookery Building" from May 1, 1908, to February 28, 1911, and its club house, at the corner of Wall Street and Second Avenue, since February 28, 1911.

The object of the club is "the encouragement of literature, science, and the social enjoyment and securing of a closer union and co-operation of college and university men."

There are resident, non-resident, temporary, and honorary members. The total membership is 245 (1913) and is limited, as to residents, to 250.

To be eligible, one must have received a bachelor's, engineer's, master's, or doctor's degree in the arts, science, philosophy, law, medicine, or divinity from a college or university of recognized standing (including United States Military and Naval Academies), or must have been for two years a student in good standing at such institutions.

The entrance fee for residents is $25; for non-residents, $10.

The *monthly* dues of residents are $3, and of non-residents, $1.

The University Club of Bridgeport, Conn., was formed in 1905 with a charter membership of ninety. Bridgeport being very near New Haven, the club has a great many Yale members. Indeed, it was originally intended to be a Yale club, but after deliberation the promoters called a meeting for *all* college men interested in the formation of a university club. The response was enthusiastic, and the Bridgeport University Club was the result.

The club started in a modest way, having one-half of a two-story building for a club house. In 1908 it was moved to the present site, a commodious house at the corner of Golden Hill and Broad Streets.

W. A. Kinsman, Esq., the secretary, to whom the compiler is indebted for the information here given, states (under date March 15, 1913) that the membership is 233.

The object of the club is "to promote social intercourse among University men in the City of Bridgeport and its vicinity."

Graduates of colleges and universities and the military and naval academies of the United States as well as those who have spent one year of resident study in any of these are eligible for resident membership. There is also a non-resident class. The entrance fee for both classes is $10. The annual dues for residents $25, and for non-residents, $10.

The University Club of Panama was organized in 1905, mainly through the efforts of Mr. T. W. Osterheld, of the Department of Engineering of the Isthmian Canal Commission; and Mr. John K. Baxter, who has courteously supplied the data for this reference, was active in its organization and on its governing board until the spring of 1912. The charter membership included most of the young engineers and a small number of college men in other branches of the canal service, and some Panamanians who had taken professional or technical courses in the United States or Europe. Charles E. Magoon, then Governor of the Canal Zone, and American Minister to Panama, was the first president.

Although organized as a university club, the exigencies of the case led to relaxation as to eligibility, and it became primarily an American club, to include all classes, and thus avoid caste feeling or antagonism.

Among the presidents who succeeded Governor Magoon have been Colonel Gorgas, renowned for his successful eradication of disease on the Isthmus; and Joseph Bucklin Bishop, secretary of the Canal Commission, and our fellow member well known as a former habitué of the University Club in New York.

This club has had among its members many men of distinction, among whom may be named Colonel George W. Goethals, whose administration as the chief engineer of the Canal has made him justly famous throughout the world, and the four successive Presidents of the Republic of Panama, Doctors Amador, Obaldia, Arosemena, and Porras.

In the early years the club mess was one of the few places where good food was to be had, and on Saturday nights and Sundays there has always been a gathering from Culebra, from Empire, from Balboa, and elsewhere, of engineers, business men, lawyers, tourists, magazine writers, promoters, concession hunters, cocoanut planters, bridge-playing skippers, revolutionists, visiting Congressmen, and other strange creatures. Mr. Baxter expresses the doubt that any club has issued visitors' cards to so varied and interesting a procession of strangers as were entertained at Panama.

The club has a building of its own overlooking a corner of Panama Bay, and is apparently in a flourishing condition. The terms have not been furnished.

G. F. McFarland, Esq., the president of the University Club of Toronto, Canada, has courteously supplied the following particulars regarding that club:

Our organization has been in existence such a short time that its history is simply that of the development of a frequently tested idea along the lines suitable to local conditions. The club was founded in September, 1906, by three men, graduates of the University of Toronto, who had been out of college only about three or four years. These three, H. L. Hoyles, A. C. Snively, and the writer, gathered together a group of a dozen congenial spirits and this group lunched together once a week, having no club rooms or anything of that sort. This group gradually added to its numbers until, when it numbered 25, two rooms were leased and furnished and daily lunches were served. On the 1st of November, 1909, when the membership had reached fifty-three, the top flat of an office building was leased, and for the first time the club established a complete house service. In June 1911 a building was purchased on King Street, which is now the Wall Street of Toronto, and was remodeled and renovated, and this is the present home of the club.

At the present time we are adding additional Billiard accommodation and Squash Racquet Courts to the building, and the whole when completed will represent a value of approximately $60,000.00. This has been financed entirely by the members of the club. At present the membership is as follows:—

Resident	299
Non-resident	188

Three hundred has been set as the limit of the resident membership. In order to be eligible for membership the candidate must be a holder of a degree from the University or College, recognized by the Directors of the Club as being of sufficient standing. Dues are $100.00 entrance, and $35.00 per year for resident membership, non-resident membership being $15.00 per year with no entrance fee.

The University Club of Rochester, N. Y., was organized in June, 1909; incorporated in November, 1909; and its club house, No. 50 Gibbs Street, opened January 10, 1910.

"The particular objects for which said corporation is formed are to promote social intercourse among its members, to cultivate and maintain university spirit, and to establish and maintain club, reading, and assembly rooms."

Mr. Kingman Nott Robins, the secretary of the club, has kindly given the compiler the following information:

The University Club of Rochester was organized in the belief that no matter how many clubs there might be in the city devoted to social purposes in general, there should be a place for the gathering of University men because of their bonds of common interest, and to crystallize the favorable feeling in the community towards university education, work and ideals.

We have believed it more consistent with the ideals of the Club to restrict membership to holders of degrees and have modelled our requirements on very much the same basis as that adopted by the parent Club in New York.

The entrance fee of resident members is $25; of non-resident members, $15.

The dues of residents are $30; of non-residents, $15.

Women of the immediate family of a member, and their guests, may be admitted to the café on Thursdays from three o'clock.

The club had 214 members in 1911.

The University Club of Geneva, N. Y., was organized in 1909. The purposes of the club are "to promote social intercourse and exchange of ideas among its members, and to further the interests of Colleges and Universities and the public welfare in any non-partisan manner that may seem expedient to its members."

The constitution provides that "any man shall be eligible to membership" "who has received from a reputable College or University, an Academic, Scientific, Engineering, Medical, or Legal degree; or shall have graduated at a professional school of good standing; or who shall have received an honorary degree from such college or university, or who shall have graduated at the United States Military Academy or at the United States Naval Academy."

The entrance fee is $1 for resident members, and the annual dues, $3.

The club in 1913 had 106 members and meets from October to May, every two weeks, at the Hotel Seneca, in the evening, to listen to a paper or address by some member or invited speaker from outside and partake of light refreshments.

The foregoing information has been kindly furnished by W. P. Woodman, Esq., the secretary of the club.

The compiler is indebted to Charles Lumbard, Esq., the secretary of the University Club of Sacramento, Cal., for the following information about that club:

RISE OF THE U. C. OF SACRAMENTO.

Shortly after the holidays in 1909 quite a crowd of Greek letter men met at a banquet in one of the restaurants of Sacramento City. The idea was suggested to form a club composed of Greek letter members—but this was abandoned and the suggestion gave place to a desire to form a University Club. This idea was adopted and upon August 9, 1909, the first meeting of college—university—men residing in Sacramento was held in one of the Superior Court Rooms in the Court House and the club was organized, by about thirty-two members, representing ten or twelve different universities who signed the Charter Roll and calling themselves the University Club of Sacramento.

Like the formation of nearly every University Club, this one sprang out of a desire to bring university, and college grads, and eligible men together for social, educational and fraternal reasons.

The club is now in good condition, rents a good spacious house, just off the business center, consists of about one hundred and sixty members—resident and non-resident—ranks as one of the best clubs in the city, and its function is to establish a meeting place for its members to keep alive the memories of past college days,—furnish rooms for its bachelors, and a table under which university legs may be extended—and where the body may be supplied with food that nourishes, and the good things of college conversation may be indulged in as in days of yore.

The American Universities Club of London, England, was founded in March, 1910, "to provide a *pied-à-terre* abroad for the American University Graduate, where, meeting in the Mecca of foreign travel, old friendships could perhaps be renewed, and a deeper insight gained of his fellow Anglo-Saxon Collegians from those ancient universities—Oxford and Cambridge."

George G. Knowles, Esq. (Yale '92), the chairman of the general committee, through whose courtesy these particulars have been obtained, states as an important feature that this club was not established for Americans *living* in London so much as for those *visiting* London.

The membership has reached 300. The annual dues for residents are £10 10*s.;* for non-residents, £5 5*s.* The entrance fee for residents is £10 10*s.;* for non-residents, £5 5*s.*

North American university graduates who are active members

of university or other clubs of standing, and senior or junior undergraduates being members of recognized fraternities, are eligible for election, in conformity with the universities and degrees obtaining in the rules of the University Club of New York.

The University Club of Atlanta, Ga., was chartered July 5, 1910. Thomas Whipple Connally, Esq., the secretary of the club, who has kindly furnished the information here given, in a newspaper article signed by him, acknowledges the influence of our own Club, by stating that "the pioneer University Club after which practically all others were modeled, is located in New York."

The object of the club is "the bringing together of University and College men, the cultivation of social relations among those interested in every line of broader culture and the advancement of the interests of liberal education."

"The membership is confined to those who hold degrees or diplomas from Colleges approved by the Council and those who by special achievement or interest in intellectual pursuits are deemed eligible. The membership without College degrees can never exceed ten per cent of the entire membership."

The membership, which numbered 368 on January 1, 1913, includes an unusual proportion of eminent men, not only of Georgia, but elsewhere.

The club's quarters are on Peachtree Street, where many distinguished persons have been entertained.

Papers have been read at the club on numerous scientific, intellectual, and economic subjects. Many scientific societies have met at the club.

The club expects to maintain the best reading-room in the State, and a first-class library is being accumulated.

The entrance fee for residents is $25; for non-residents, $5. The annual dues are $30 and $10 respectively.

A unique and altogether interesting association is the Rogue River Valley University Club, of Medford, Ore., organized October 28, 1910, with club rooms in the Mail-Tribune Building, Medford, which were opened on January 7, 1911.

The unusual feature of this club is the fact that it is composed mostly of farmers and fruit-growers.

Stanton Griffis, Esq. (Cornell '10), the secretary, who has kindly supplied this information, remarks, as a reason for a slight delay, that "Spring Correspondence may sometimes be delayed by the Spring ploughing." Certainly, the existence of a university club with a membership of 108 among the farmers of a small area in Oregon, may be regarded as not only remarkable but as a most encouraging sign, indicating the trend of university education.

The financial condition of this club is flourishing and its functions are solely social. "Any resident or property owner of the Rogue River Valley who has been a sometime attendant at some recognized college or university shall be eligible to membership." The entrance fee for residents is $25, and the annual dues, $25. Non-residents, one-half of these figures. The club has rooms and maintains a "grill," a billiard-room, reading-rooms, etc. Yale University furnishes 12 members; Harvard, 8; and 41 institutions scattered over the country, East and West, those remaining.

The University Club of Omaha, Neb., was started February 21, 1911, on which date a large gathering of representative alumni of various colleges was held and a temporary organization effected. It is characteristic of the Western push that in addition to an executive committee, a "hustling committee" was appointed, and the result of the activity of these ardent graduates was the formal incorporation of the club on June 15, 1911. On this date the club purchased the furniture and equipment of the Railroad Club, and leased its quarters on the second floor of the "Barker" Block, (southwest corner of 15th and Farnam Streets). These quarters were occupied in social gathering September 15, 1911.

In the fall of 1912, the club made a lease of the quarters in the Board of Trade Building, which were vacated by the Commercial Club. These were opened January 2, 1913, with a reception and dance.

The club has been active in entertaining various organizations from colleges who visited Omaha, especially Glee Clubs and athletic teams. It has also given moral and financial assistance to games and meetings of other kinds.

The club adopted Lincoln's Birthday as the date of its annual dinner. Amos Thomas, Esq., the secretary, through whose kindness these particulars have been obtained, states (under date of March 15, 1913) that the club is in a most flourishing condition, having at that time 350 members, with very bright prospects. The club was expecting in the week following to entertain at dinner the Honorable William Jennings Bryan and his wife.

The constitution provides that the object of the club is "to promote education, literature, the arts and sciences, athletics and social intercourse among university men in Omaha and vicinity."

The club has a stock capital of $20,000, divided into four hundred shares of $50 each. In addition to stockholding members, there are "associate members," consisting of those who have been out of college less than five years. Also a class of "non-residents." Voting and managing the club affairs are confined exclusively to stockholding members. The admission fee is $50 for stockholders, $25 for associates, and $20 for non-residents. Annual dues, $36, $20 and $10, respectively. Clergymen and army and navy men are put on the basis of non-residents.

The restrictions as to eligibility are those usual in university clubs, persons having spent two years of residence study in a college being qualified for election.

The by-laws provide that the capital stock shall be $15,000 instead of $20,000, as provided in the articles of incorporation.

C. Arthur Blass, Esq., of Erie, Pa., states under date March 13, 1913, that he and others are endeavoring to form a university club of Erie, and has asked for and received one of our own Club books, so that our constitution and by-laws may be used as a pattern for their organization.

The University Club of Toledo, O., was, some years ago, merged into the Commerce Club, and so no longer exists as a University Club.

A. M. Hamann, Esq., Secretary of the University Club of Niagara Falls, N. Y., has given interesting details as to that organization. It was organized September 19, 1895, has over sixty members, and occupies a stately house. The active portion live at the club house, the intention, unlike that of most university organizations, having been to provide a pleasant home for its members rather than the usual limited facilities of club life.

The University Club of Los Angeles, Cal., according to an account kindly furnished by Russ Avery, Esq., was incorporated

March 12, 1903, and occupies the two upper floors of a building ideally located and overlooking Central Park. It is out of debt and contemplates having a building of its own. The club is flourishing and has a constantly increasing membership. Its characteristic feature is a monthly dinner, and the original idea of its founders was to foster intellectual as well as social fellowship.

Information about the University Club of Lawrence, Kan., has not been received.

It will have been observed that there is a decided disproportion in the length and completeness of the foregoing accounts. This is due to the fact that the gentlemen who have supplied the information have in some cases given more data than in others, and in the two cases last mentioned the matter was received after the type had been made into pages. In all instances it has been intended to make the statements as complete as possible, as to important and interesting particulars.

Members of the University Club of New York surely have the right, without undue vanity, to take some pride in the extension of the university-club idea throughout the country, and for the most part, if not altogether, due to the example set by our own Club. It would be difficult to estimate, and perhaps impossible to overestimate, the silent influence in favor of university education exercised by these associations of college men, all engaged in upholding the dignity and importance of learning, and publishing to all intelligent communities the value of a college training. Many are the instances of men who bitterly regret the neglect of advantages offered them in college days which has denied them the degrees requisite for admission to university clubs which, like our own, adhere strictly to the exclusive rule. And many are the instances of men who since the organization of our Club have been led to give more earnest attention to the studies of their college course in order at some time to become eligible for membership. This motive may be regarded by some as a low one in comparison with a genuine thirst for learning, and undoubtedly there would be reason in such a view, but taking human nature as we find it, sensible people will not condemn a motive which, while not the highest, at all events works for what is good.

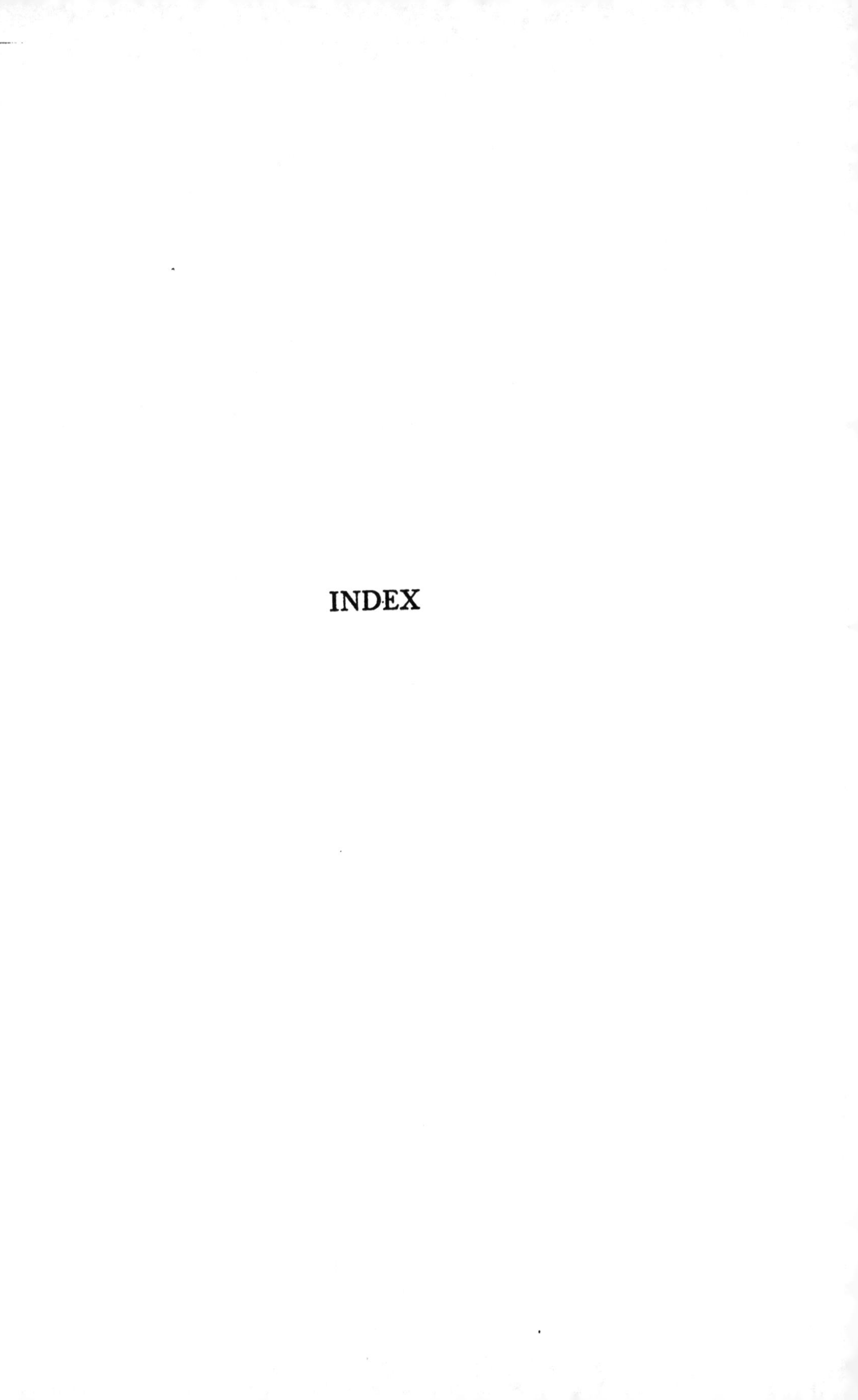

INDEX

INDEX

www.ingramcontent.com/pod-product-compliance
Lightning Source LLC
LaVergne TN
LVHW010829120826
845149LV00016B/41

* 9 7 8 1 4 1 8 1 8 9 1 6 7 *